BEHIND THE FENCE

BEHIND THE FENCE
LIFE AS A POW IN JAPAN 1942–1945

The Diaries of Les Chater

Transcribed and Edited by Elizabeth Hamid

Vanwell Publishing Limited
St. Catharines, Ontario

Vanwell Publishing acknowledges the financial support of the Government of Canada through the Book Publishing Industry Development Program for our publishing activities.

Design: Linda Moroz-Irvine
Cover: Linda Moroz-Irvine

Vanwell Publishing Limited
1 Northrup Crescent
P.O. Box 2131
St. Catharines, Ontario L2R 7S2

Printed in Canada

Canadian Cataloguing in Publication Data

Chater, Les, 1909-
    Behind the fence : life as a POW in Japan, 1942-1945 : the diaries of Les Chater

ISBN soft cover edition:1-55125-086-1

1ST ed.
Includes bibliographical references.
ISBN 1-55125-064-0

1. Chater, Les, 1909- –Diaries. 2. Prisoners of war–Canada–Diaries. 3. Prisoners of war–Japan–Diaries. 4. Canada. Royal Canadian Air Force–Officers–Diaries.
5. World War, 1939-1945–Prisoners and prisons, Japanese. 6. World War, 1939-1945–Personal narratives, Canadian. I. Hamid, Elizabeth II. Title.

D805.J3C45 2001   940.54'7252'092   C2001-900781-7

CONTENTS

To my family

Editor's Foreword

LES CHATER'S DIARIES consist of four small, tattered booklets. The first, a 9 cm by 14 cm journal, records the events from his capture on April 23 1942, to July 7 1943. The second, even smaller, 7½ cm by 11½ by ½ cm, carries on, without missing a day, and relates the events from July 8 1943 to January 14 1944. Third and last is the largest journal, written between January 15 1944 to February 4 1946. It measures 9 cm by 14 cm by 1 cm.

Mr. Chater was an officer, and a conscientious one. The front pages of the first diary are filled with a long list of the names of fellow POWs, in minuscule printing, followed by addresses. The back cover, somewhat broken off from the text, is also covered densely, with script writing which can best be described as ultra minuscule. In truth it is largely unreadable. One cannot emphasize too much the minute size of Mr. Chater's handwriting in these little booklets. It borders on being indecipherable, and it is only by wearing strong reading glasses and with the help of a hand-held magnifying glass that I was able to comprehend the text. Obviously, not only were Mr. Chater's eyes incredibly healthy, but he expected to be recording his prison experience for some time and realized further booklets might be difficult to find. One cannot help but be in awe of the consistent effort it took to keep the diaries, in good health and bad, spirits up or down.

There are a number of racist terms used in the text. At least, they would be considered racist by today's standards. It is probably not necessary to remind the reader that these journals were written at a different time in our history, at a different stage in our development as a world society. Yes, the Japanese are referred to as Nips, the indigenous people of Java as Wogs, etc. But I hasten to point out that Americans were also called Yanks, the Australians, Aussies, the British, Brits and so on. In defence of Mr. Chater, I might explain that, in the time I have come to know him, I would suggest he sees all people as equal, and I suspect he always did. Sad to say, such racist usage was not only common at that time, but widely accepted, even by those bearing the labels!

We have come a long way since then toward understanding the importance of showing respect to different groups.

Mr. Chater holds no grudge against the Japanese people for his captivity. In his time as a POW he found the Japanese civilians and at times even some of the guards to be likeable people. They were political enemies, and of this they were always fully aware, but hating each other often simply required more energy than they could muster. War is essentially an unnatural state and one that requires constant work, to maintain the high level of vilification required to induce people to kill each other. During World War II, propagandists on both sides did an amazing job. But when isolated from such indoctrination, both the POWs and the Japanese found themselves in the peculiar position of constantly having to remind themselves of the antagonism that was supposed to exist between them.

Clearly, the unnecessary pain and death that was suffered by so many cannot be minimized. Life as a POW in Japan was nothing short of horrendous. In reading the diaries you will come to your own conclusion about issues pertaining to the war with Japan. One thing is certain. The Japanese had not expected to find themselves with thousands of Canadian, American, New Zealand, Australian, Indian, South African, Chinese, Korean and British prisoners who required housing, feeding and clothing at a time when their own economy was thrown into a turmoil.

Remember, too, the Japanese soldier lived by the fierce, prideful Bushido code. Bushido warriors are trained to fear nothing, not even to behave with brutality and cruelty. They go into battle to win, by whatever means necessary, and they fight, as you will often read "until the last man." No act is more loathsome than surrender.

Today, as we begin the twenty-first century, it is fascinating to look back over more than fifty years to one of the most difficult and dramatic times of recent history. I am thankful to Mr. Chater for sharing his experience with us, and hope you will agree these diaries are a rare and amazing voice from the past. Les Chater had the foresight to recognize the importance of the historical time and experience he was living through and the endurance to write down his impressions of what he saw around him.

You will be transfixed by what you read, taken out of your everyday existence, to look behind the fence in Semplak, Mitsushima, and Kanose. You will suffer with Mr. Chater the horror of the boat voyage from Java to Japan, and may be moved to tears, as I was, by the terrible toll of unnecessary deaths. A diet of seaweed stew, rice, barley and daikon tops will make you more conscious of the abundance on our own tables. You will feel the cruel cold of an unheated barracks in the middle of winter in the mountains of Japan. You will laugh at the sardonic humour that was necessary to the survival of Chater and his fellow POWs. And the triumph at the end of it all, when through what has since been debated as questionable means, freedom once more is gained.

The Japanese encouraged the writing of diaries shortly before the end of the war. The reason given for this was that if the prisoner died there would be something to send home to relatives. The only catch was that these diaries were regularly checked to ensure that only *good* things were written. Certainly a challenge to the authors!

Les's diaries, written mainly at night, were carefully hidden at all times. But even if they had been discovered, Japanese Interpreters would have had difficulty deciphering the multitude of short forms that were used: wx for weather, gg for going, Int. for Interpreter, to name the least puzzling. In editing the diaries, I have taken the liberty, with Mr. Chater's permission, to alter this. The long form of the word is generally used, rather than the abbreviation. What I attempted to do was be true to the text in every way I could. Mr. Chater's underlining of words has been retained. All entries were printed in capital letters, but I have followed the form more commonly used. When it is clear what word is meant, I have corrected the rare spelling error. The handwriting was mostly understandable, except when the pencil needed sharpening!

As his term of captivity lengthened, Mr. Chater began to use more and more Japanese words in his diaries. During the fifty-two years of freedom that followed, the diaries were stored in a cardboard box, along with pictures, photos and letters from that time. Many of those Japanese words were forgotten. During our transcription work, in 1998, Mr. Chater did his best to recall their meaning. When he could not, we consulted with a Japanese translator, Mrs. Nabuko McNie of Hamilton, Ontario. But, because Mr. Chater had written the words down as they sounded, using the English alphabet, the job was very difficult. We have done our best, and a glossary accompanies the diaries to help with this, but, unfortunately, some words remain unknown. Should readers be able to solve some of these "mystery words," we would be happy to hear from them.

Mr. Chater wrote an entry for each day of his capture. We are grateful to Vanwell for publishing *Behind the Fence*, but for practical purposes it was necessary to omit a number of entries—or risk issuing a publication as thick as a telephone book! Students and scholars interested in reading the complete diaries will find them in a bound manual at the National Archives in Ottawa, along with the actual pictures and artifacts.

My friendship with Les Chater began because of my research work for my war novel. I wanted to fully understand what it was like to be a POW in Japan during the Second World War. A mutual friend had worked with Les and suggested I talk to him. At first he was reluctant to stir up so many old memories, but then he graciously agreed to speak with me. In our second discussion he brought the diaries, pictures and memorabilia up from his basement, in a cardboard box. He hadn't looked at them since he'd packed them away in 1946. "Would you like to read these diaries?" he asked. "They might help you."

They certainly did.

I hope they will do the same for you.

Elizabeth Hamid
Burlington, Ontario
2001

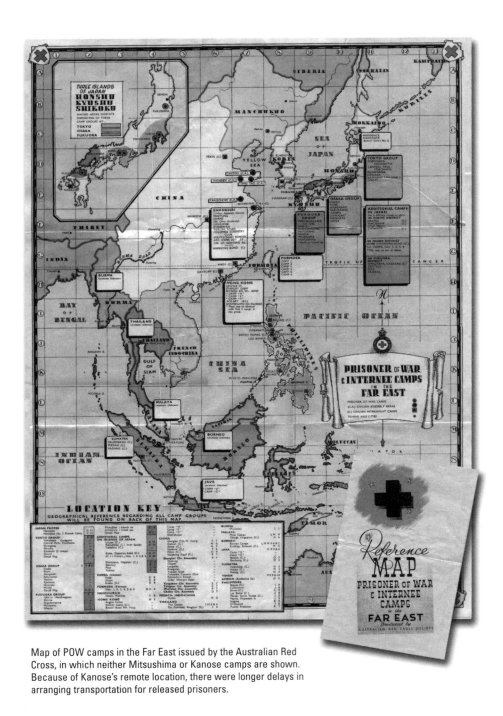

Map of POW camps in the Far East issued by the Australian Red Cross, in which neither Mitsushima or Kanose camps are shown. Because of Kanose's remote location, there were longer delays in arranging transportation for released prisoners.

To my fellow Prisoners of War—to those who made it home,
and especially to those who didn't

Introduction

1998: Looking Back

I GREW UP IN SASKATOON, the youngest of five children, my father a bookkeeper, my mother a homemaker. In those days, when money was scarce, I learned to fix anything and everything in our home that needed repairing. If the washing machine was broken, I'd figure out what was wrong and get it going again. If there were electrical problems, or plumbing problems, I'd tackle those as well. Like most Canadian families at the time, it was the only way we could manage. I joined the YMCA in 1920, and have been a member, except for wartime, ever since. It's my belief that my fitness and leadership training at the Y can be directly linked to my survival as a POW.

I graduated in civil engineering from the University of Saskatchewan in 1932. We were deep into the great depression and no real engineering jobs existed in the area. So, like thousands of young men, I rode the rails to find work anywhere I could. One of my more bizarre jobs was in Hamilton, where I learned the technique of examining day old chicks to determine what sex they were! I worked at this until the season ended before moving on to Montreal and eventually worked my way to England on an old freighter in August 1935.

Also, in my early twenties I had been commissioned as an officer in the Canadian reserve army. It was necessary to get a leave of absence before leaving the country. In the same year, 1935, with the rank of Captain, I left for England, where engineering work was plentiful. I got various jobs with contractors and consulting engineers. It was while working in Wales that I met and married my wife Muriel.

In July of 1939 I applied for a job with the British Air Ministry. The work I was hired to do was to supervise the building, maintenance and changes to RAF airstrips and aerodromes in the Far East. I was to work out of Air Headquarters, Far East, in Singapore. So my wife, my infant son and I made our way there.

Because I was working for the British Air Ministry I held relative rank as an officer in the regular RAF, although we did not wear uniforms at this time. In 1940 I was sent to Hong Kong to look into additions and changes to Kai Tak airport. When it became obvious the job, which was originally supposed to last six weeks, would instead stretch to six months, I sent for Muriel and Michael to come from Singapore.

In the Days Before Capture

In the autumn of 1940 the first warnings were issued regarding possible impending difficulties with the Japanese. Women and children were evacuated to Manila and from there Muriel and Michael made their way back to Singapore and I followed shortly after. We were in Singapore on December 7, 1941. On the "day of infamy," when so many places in the Pacific were targets for attack by the Japanese, we were awakened by bombs rattling our steel trellis. From the first, it was obvious that Singapore was ill-prepared to defend itself. It had completely underestimated the strength of the Japanese Air Force and seasoned troops. Within no time the island was being invaded. British military bureaucracy hindered definite action and of course we had no planes that were effective against the Japanese Navy Os. My wife and son got out on the US troop ship *West Point*, although the ship was bombed and hit a couple of times before they embarked.

When the Japanese entered the war I was put into uniform and became a Flight Lieutenant in the Royal Air Force. On February 11th, all RAF personnel were ordered off the island. We were part of a convoy of six ships. I was named Embarkation Officer for the *Empire Star*. Boarding went quite well until six bedraggled Australian soldiers appeared and informed me they would be boarding my ship. I told them this was impossible, since there was barely room for the number already required to go on. They were tough looking and bleary-eyed, armed with guns, as I was. My refusal to allow them to board was not what they wanted to hear. They had fought their way down the peninsula and their determination to board the *Empire Star* was equal to my own to refuse them. Though it took some persuading, I convinced them that other ships would be able to take them aboard, and, with time fast disappearing, they should start searching for one. It was with my great sense of relief that they left. I have worried about them since then, although I'm confident they were able to find a way off the island.

At daybreak, February 12, 1942, we sailed from Singapore. Within an hour, about 57 Japanese bombers appeared overhead. At first they dive-bombed us, hitting us about four times. We defended ourselves with small arms fire and they began high level bombing. How we did it, I'll never know, but somehow we managed to get through and the next day, February 13, 1942, we landed in Batavia, Java, which is now part of Indonesia. Already in dock was our escort, a heavily damaged Australian cruiser, which had to have taken a lot of casualties. I felt instantly even more grateful for our survival when I saw an example of what could have been our own fate.

We disembarked on February 14th and unloaded the ship. We had been carrying a shipment of spare plane parts. Considering there were no planes, I had to shake my head at such a cargo. We were billeted out to various places to sleep, and set up headquarters in Batavia. There was nothing to do but set up the old bureaucracy again and shuffle paper.

In the days before capture, I began taking notes to keep my own mind clear as to the sequence of events. What happened to those early notes I have no idea. All that remains are the four entries that follow.

At station at Parbolinggo: Chief Engineer phoned and said there was still a chance of going. I told him I would go to Powerkerto to H.Q. and he could get me there after 1 p.m. I told S/L Harrison who was in charge of our group and he sent me on with F/L Dorney to Powerkerto. In the afternoon I went to H.Q. just as the order came through that all works personnel were to go to Tjilatjap that night for embarkation. You can imagine my relief after I had given up hope of getting out. I phoned the station at Parbolinggo and told the works man there he had to get everybody in the train by 6 o'clock.

In the meantime another order had come cancelling this. I did not phone again because there seemed to be some doubt. After an hour we were again told to move and I went on ahead with 2 other works officers with the ration lorry. We arrived at Tjilatjap about 6 p.m. and spent another hour trying to find the RAF embarkation officer. When we did find him he said that there was nothing definite yet about ships but to keep in touch with him every half hour in case we had to get the rations aboard. This we did but the train from Parbolinggo did not arrive until 12:30 a.m. We went to meet it having made arrangements for the works people for sleeping accommodation. This consisted of an open verandah. There seemed no accommodation in the town and everything was closed up. When we got to the train there were no works personnel on it and we learned that they had all been taken off at the last minute and told they would be the last to go. I decided anyway that if I got the chance I would go because I sensed no useful purpose staying behind having done nothing since arriving in Java. In fact there was obviously no reason at all why the works people should have come to Java but should have gone straight on.

March 5, 1942

Reported to embarkation officer Tjilatjap and there was still no news of any ship to take us off. Stayed with Welfare crowd parked on side of the road and at 9:45 a.m. raid started. This lasted over an hour and was very nerve-wracking. I thought every minute would be my last. The Japs were dive-bombing. After the raid Welfare moved into an old school. Refugees came pouring out of Tjilatjap. I drove around in search of petrol and saw the damage that had been done. It became obvious to me that we would not get away from that port and if we did we would not last long anyway. Still, I would have taken my chances. I kept in touch with the embarkation officer all day but no further orders on embarkation were issued. In the morning I had phoned the Chief Engineer and told him that all Works people had been taken off the train to Tjilatjap by order and asked him why. He did not know they had and promised to look into it and phone me back. He said works people who were already at Tjilatjap could go if they got the chance. The bombing prevented him from phoning me back.

March 6, 1942

With Welfare crowd in Tjilatjap. RAF started to move out and walked back to Powerkerto in morning. We loaded all rations and I went to try and get petrol. All petrol stores were locked and there was a Dutch guard on them. I went back to the cottage and found the rest had already left so I loaded the remaining rations on the lorry and set out for Powerkerto finally catching up with the rest of Welfare. Arrived in Powerkerto and had to send 2 lorries back with rations for marching troops. It was obvious we were not going to get out of Java and could only await orders. We had lunch at the Tram Hotel and in the afternoon an order came that all RAF were to move that day to Tjamis. The motor convoy started and I drove with Padre Giles. The troops were awaiting trains when I left. Saw a few of Works crowd but more were in our convoy. Left Powerkerto at 6 p.m. and did not arrive near Tjamis until 1 a.m. Then we were told by the RAF we would not be allowed in Tjamis so the convoy parked on a side of the road all night and I slept in the car, or tried to.

March 7, 1942

[text missing] for them which we did and found them in a cottage. Padre Giles proceeded to Tjamis to try and get some information. Came back and said all arms had to be collected and sent in to Tjamis. The idea was for all to proceed to one place unarmed and the Dutch would inform the Japs that we were there to be surrendered as Prisoners of War. Admittedly there seemed to be no alternative but it seemed to be giving in rather easily. However, it would save a lot of useless bloodshed. Padre again made contact with S.H.Q. and the order was given for the whole convoy to proceed to Garost in the a.m. We slept that night in the cottage. Learned that trains carrying RAF troops had been attacked by Japs and abandoned and that a bridge they were walking across had been blown up by Dutch thinking they were Japs.

In the preceding notes, the confusion that prevailed during that time is clear. In fact, we found ourselves trapped in Java with no way to get out after the Japanese invaded. On March 8th, myself and two other Works Department officers decided to go up into the hills and fight. Transportation was not a problem as we had a stationwagon loaded with arms. However, we were stopped at an armed Dutch checkpoint at Garoet. "Stop the car and get out, please," was the order given.

Everything but our luggage was confiscated by the Dutch and we were left to wander around. The situation was such that the Dutch had surrendered to the Japanese and declared Batavia an "open" city, to prevent bombing of civilians.

Eventually we met up with some armed Japanese soldiers who were somewhat confused themselves, not knowing really what to tell us to do. Eventually we ended up at Tasik Malai Aerodrome along with most of the rest of RAF personnel.

We went up to Pameggatan tea plantation and stayed there for a few days. Of course, this was not acceptable to the Japanese and after a short stop at Wanerasa, we were

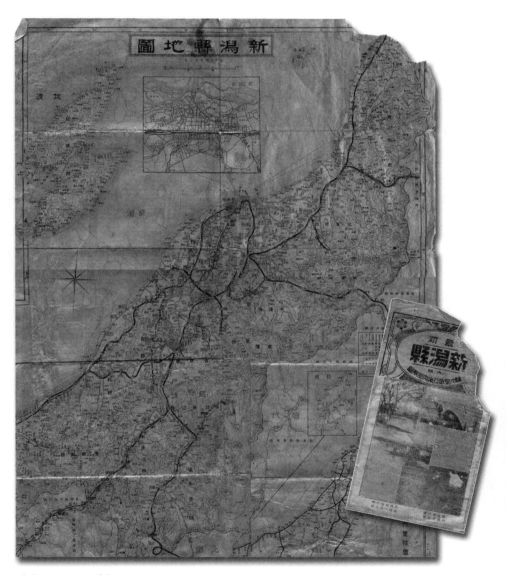

A Japanese map of Japan.

marched to Semplak Aerodrome near Buitenzorg where, if I recall accurately, there were perhaps a thousand or more POWs and it is here, some time later, that I began my diaries.

What's Not in the Diaries

I left a lot of information out of the diaries for obvious reasons. First of all, I always had to keep in mind the dangerous possibility that the diaries might be discovered. I kept them hidden in various places—some I don't remember very well. I know at Kanose I tucked them into a panel in the wall behind where I slept. Had they been found, and read, I was well aware that the punishment might be severe. I have no idea, now, why I kept the diaries. Perhaps I kept them just to try to make sense of what was happening. The pencil I used was sharpened with sandpaper or with a nail file. I certainly had no dark motivation for keeping the diaries. I didn't want to use them against the Japanese after the war, although it turned out they were used in the War Trials in Tokyo.

But as to what I didn't put in the diaries, I'd like to tell you that the scenery around the Japanese camp was beautiful. We think the colours here in Canada are beautiful in the fall, but in my memory the Japanese countryside was equally, if not more, out-standing. The civilian people were very respectful to us whenever we were outside the camp. There was no taunting or ridicule, not even any anger in their faces. Sometimes the adults would bow. Civilians were, on the whole, very kind. One time we were on a work detail with a civilian guard. One of our boys pinched some daikons from a garden and the guard saw him take them. We had just gone down the road a little when the owner of the garden came running after us, brandishing a sword or scythe, shouting that we had stolen from his garden. The guard defended the prisoners and denied the charge, saying "Not my boys."

The guards were usually army men wounded in battle, or men with some physical disability. They were often very severe in dealing with us. Once something our POW doctor said was misinterpreted and taken as an insult. He was made to hold a block of ice with his bare hands for a good length of time. Toward the end of the war the Japanese were calling up every available man to fight, and civilian guards took their places. They were less harsh.

We sometimes saw children as we marched along to work details. They would often be exercising and carrying small wooden guns. They, too, were polite and respectful.

Of course we all got discouraged. At times it seemed the war would never come to an end. In Kanose I often had to go up into the woods and gather firewood and I thought of a way to build a raft so that I could perhaps escape. A river ran through the camp and I hid away some good long pieces of wood and some rope. We had often been told that the most dangerous time for us would be at the end of the war, if Japan lost. I thought I might be able to build a raft and travel along this river. I had no idea where I'd end up but it was better than sitting around waiting to be shot.

We did put together a radio, and I touched on this very briefly in the diaries. In fact, this was the most secret thing we did. If we'd been found out, we would have been dealt with most severely. The radio was put together by RAF Sgt. Whitley. He had a radio tube and a set of earphones and he made a coil of wire and rigged up a shortwave receiver. He had won prizes for making a radio out of scrap material at minimum cost in England. When he finished, late one night, we strung an aerial along one barrack and he started operating the radio. Guards had been posted. He got KFI Los Angeles short-wave station. (At least I think those were the call numbers. It certainly was Los Angeles.) We heard that the Allies had recaptured Paris, so we were overjoyed. The memory of this stays with me even after fifty-three years. But we were very afraid to use the radio and we didn't very often. Not much later, during an inspection our ear-phones were discovered by the Japanese. We had a difficult time explaining where they came from. In order to work the radio after that, we pinched an old telephone receiver from the office and that worked quite well.

At the end the CC asked me if I knew why Japan had capitulated. I guessed it was because Russia had entered the war. No, he told me, it was because of a new bomb that had been developed by the Americans, called the atom bomb. I knew nothing about this of course. Later I was also told that if the Japanese had not surrendered after the bomb-ing of Nagasaki the Americans planned to bomb Niigata next. This city was located only a relatively short distance from us, where many Canadian POWs captured in Hong Kong were working as well.

In reading through Elizabeth's transcription of these diaries, a lot of old memories were stirred up. I had never taken the time to read the diaries through before this. It has caused some nightmares where, to my horror, I'm back at the camp reliving those days.

I sincerely hope that my diaries will be found useful to students and all people in general interested in knowing exactly what it was like to be a POW in Japan during the Second World War.

It is my sincerest hope that as you read these diaries you will develop a greater aware-ness of the terrible waste of humanity and the earth's resources as a consequence of war. I hope, too, that you will be moved to promote the benefits of good health and fitness and the elimination of Hate, especially in our children and youth.

Les Chater
Hamilton, Ontario
October 1998

Top left: Les Chater, working on an anti-malarial project in Malaya, 1941. He worked tirelessly as a POW to maintain sanitary conditions and prevent disease in the camps.

Right: One year later, now POW No. 86, Les appears grim-faced and tight-lipped. Worse conditions were yet to come.

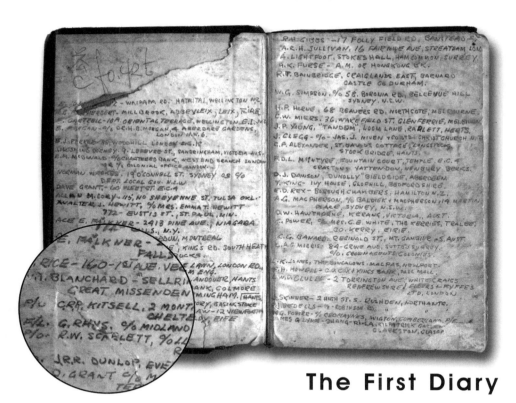

The First Diary

Monday April 27, 1942

Extended exercises a little—leg okay. Mended socks. In a.m. went with Doc Morgan south of aerodrome on anti-malarial (a/m) expedition. Found a lot of mosquitos breeding. Took measurement for garage trailer.

All troops on aerodrome.

Early times as a prisoner: The first camp was Semplak Aerodrome. There were a great number (perhaps a thousand) of POWs. Life was not too difficult, as the following entries will show.

Tuesday April 28, 1942

No exercise. Slept in. With Doc south of quarters and found many mosquitos breeding. Drained these places.

In p.m. CC came and told us must repair shovels and give them to him. Went and got handles and fixed seven.

Put in tap for CC's kitchen. Played chess with Dorney at night. Exercise and to bed. Let moustache start to grow again.

Wednesday April 29, 1942

Emperor of Japan's birthday. No work on aerodrome.

CC inspected kit at 10:30. All cameras had to be handed in. CC took my small knife during inspection. Also took all flying equipment, tin helmets, etc. Also took something someone wanted to keep as souvenir and said if he didn't the Police would <u>when we get to Japan</u>.

Played chess with Howell in afternoon. Studied Malay at night.

Semplak. Thursday April 30, 1942

In morning helped dig garbage pit. Went around camp. Found in filthy state. Told Adjutant and asked him to chase batmen to keep their sections clean.

In afternoon went with Doc around Jap quarters on a/m work. CC was interested and gave us oil for very bad hole outside kitchen where thousands were breeding. Also found drain needed cleaning.

Watched football match after parade but did not play for fear leg would give out which was bad again yesterday. Studied Malay after.

Rumour, Germans had bombed York as reprisal raid. US had raided Tokyo and lost nine planes. Rumour that we are going to Japan persists.

Saturday May 2, 1942

My Birthday but I didn't realize it until night parade at 7:00.

Only 200 boys required on aerodrome tomorrow because clearing of hangars complete.

In a.m. gathered pipes with plumbers. In afternoon oiled bad mosquito breeding places.

Lights bad at night so could not study. Exercise 4 times today and taught new chap at night. No celebrations this birthday. Will make up for it next year.

Rumour that Japs have broadcast that if bombing of Tokyo doesn't stop they will take prisoners to Japan and publicly execute them. Strikes me that this is very improbable because the British do not do this when Germans do indiscriminate bombings and Japs have so far treated us more or less in accordance with rules of war.

Rumour Russians are still advancing and have broken through German lines.

**The Battle of the Coral Sea took place in the Pacific from
May 4th to May 8th, 1942**

Tuesday May 5, 1942

Put new battery in Thornycroft and collected wood in a.m.

New Buitenzorg commander here today and CC away all day. New commander seems very decent according to reports. Said we would not be leaving island.

Hauled wood by pushcart in afternoon. Watched football match at night. Studied Malay and exercised.

Rumours, Yanks have recaptured N. Guinea and Timor. Yank Navy in Indian Ocean. British have raided Heinkel works and Germans have raided 3 cathedral towns as reprisal. News bad from Burma. Germans have started counter-offensive in Russia but are stuck in mud.

Wednesday May 6, 1942

Jap officer who was here yesterday was officer in charge of prison camp guards. He took note of complaints and said he would see what he could do.

Took day off because foot sore. Played football at night and had infected finger dressed. No exercises.

Rumour: Hitler in his speech blamed the weather for German defeat in Russia but said after all Napoleon was beaten by same thing.

Sunday May 10, 1942

Exercise. Turned off water so drain could be fixed. In a.m. went on drome for nails. In afternoon fixing garage for CC.

Watched football at night. 5th Malay lesson, exercised and to bed. Troops on drome had tea again today, exercised and to bed. Fruit ran out today and cannot buy more.

Was talking to Jap soldiers on drome today. They are a jolly lot and asked innumerable questions, usually your nationality, rank, married and have children, where from. They gave me cigs. On the whole the Jap private is a very decent chap and very jolly. Not at all aggressive.

Rumours of naval battles off New Guinea vary from 1 battleship, 2 A. carriers—cruiser sunk by Japs for loss of 1 carrier, to 8 Japs sunk for aircraft loss only by Yanks.

Tuesday May 12, 1942

Exercise. Worked on garage for CC all day. Football rained out. Studied.

Jap General was here today in inspection.

Later CC said we are going to be paid—25 cents a day! But what is the use if we are not allowed to buy anything.

Friday May 15, 1942

Exercised. Fixed a/m grease gun and cleaned drain under officer's lavatory. Work west quarters in afternoon. Watched football match at night. Have neglected Malay lately since it is so hard to learn it by yourself.

Still 200 men on aerodrome every day. Remainder rest the one day in three and it is practically impossible to get men to do any jobs around the camp.

Everybody in fairly good spirits lately. Rumoured vegetable and meat ration are to be increased again.

No blackout after all.

Monday May 18, 1942

Exercised. Nobody worked on drome. Rain nearly all aft. Working on basketball standards in a.m. In afternoon making pair shoes.

Guard changed again today. New guard surly and antagonistic. They are stopping all card games it appears because they assume we gamble. They also stopped some of boys smoking—ordered all fires out at 9 a.m.

Rumour: that the new guards are direct from Tokyo.

Rumour: Yanks raided Tokyo and machine gunned streets but do not believe this.

Tuesday May 19, 1942

Exercised. Nobody on drome again today.

Guard changed today again. CO told CC re guards stopping card playing etc. and CC went and told guards off about it. So CC as I have always said, is not such a bad sort after all. He has been giving us Japanese words of command on parade the last few days.

Working on baseball pitch today. Went to welfare committee meeting at night and 6th Malay lesson. It appears that something is happening in change of attitude of guards, etc.

Rumour: Yanks have raided Batavia and M.G. it [machine-gunned].

Thursday May 21, 1942

Exercised. Fixing basketball standards when CC came along and made me start work on path from bridge to guard house. Working on this path all day. Played football at night for officers. Did bar work. Football secured today.

CC in bad mood today—much face slapping for battle over Batavia. 3 Japs rammed 3 Yanks.

Sunday May 24, 1942

Exercise. Nobody worked on drome. Worked on path in a.m. In afternoon did a/m work for one and a half hours to north west quarters.

Stew for tiffin now that vegetable rations have been increased.

Concert at night which was very good. It was announced that one would be held every Sun. night.

Rumour: 500 Japs down with malaria in Batavia.

Monday May 25, 1942

Exercised. Woke with stiff neck which was bad all day. Nearly finished path today. In afternoon went to get chain block but couldn't. Will get tomorrow.

22 passenger Douglas plane landed here today and took off after short stay.

We have been here now 2 months. Doesn't seem quite that long. On the whole we haven't been treated too badly for POW and the food has been plentiful although very much of a sameness. Rice predominating at every meal as to be expected. My big worry is that Muriel will be worrying herself sick about me. I sincerely hope the POW lists have been forwarded through the Red Cross to the British and that she knows I am a POW. But even then she will worry over the kind of treatment she will visualize me to be getting. If only I could get a letter through.

Wednesday May 27, 1942

Exercised. Finished path. Watched football at night and did bar work.

Guard changed today as usual. Has been changed every day lately. Buitenzorg No.1 here twice today.

Some of present guard speak good English. All Japs you speak to want war to finish so they can go home. All say they have no quarrel with English but they hate Yanks. Recent guards say they have come direct from Tokyo. Today's guards confirm Tokyo been bombed.

The famous "miracle of Dunkirk"—the evacuation of
350,000 British soldiers from France, across the English Channel
to England, took place from May 27 to June 4.

Sunday, May 31, 1942

Exercised. In a.m. started to do high bar but found pipe unsuitable. In afternoon went on drome and brought back scales and pipes and started to mend scales. Had to work till 9 p.m. on chocks for CC for planes which are due to arrive tomorrow. 10 made for 5 planes.

Lots of Jap officials here today. Two separate officers inspected our quarters and war correspondents are looking around and talking to our chaps. All this activity is for Japanese General who is supposed to be coming tomorrow on opening of aerodrome to planes.

Concert tonight but I couldn't go. Some of chaps talking to war correspondents and the latter said they expect to be in touch with Britain through Lisbon re prisoners of war in about one month's time. This is cheery news and I hope it is news so my wife and people will at least know that I am alive and well. There may be a chance of getting letters through too.

Another month gone. Food is still good. Conditions in the camp in relation with Japs are good. I can go out of camp and wander around any time during the day. This is due to my a/m (anti-malarial) work mostly but even then, nearly anyone can do it. Pushcarts have been going out consistently to bring in material. The Japs are still not using the aerodrome though signs point to an early occupation.

The troops are quite cheerful but still as lazy as ever. If you get a fatigue party they disappear in no time. There is definitely lack of proper control over them from our own officers. In my opinion the quarters are kept in a disgraceful sanitary condition through lack of supervision and rubbish disposal. God knows what it would be like if we did not have water laid on and quite decent sewage disposal.

Drawing of guard in Semplak, Java, by a POW cartoonist. (actual size)

Things on the eastern war front seem quiet and it looks as though we will be here about 6 months more although the optimism of the troops is tremendous. You'd think they were on a holiday. Still, the majority of them have no faith in their officers anymore and I can understand it.

Tuesday, June 2, 1942

Exercise. No work on drome today.

CC gave order that after 10 a.m. tomorrow no carts would be allowed out without his permission. He was in conference this afternoon. Officers were here all day. Plane arrived at 5 o'clock but don't know if it was Jap general or not.

Finished scale today and worked on high bar. Watched football at night and did bar work.

Rice and vegetable ration cut today by half. Reason not given. But I think it is just local shortage. Flour is offered in lieu which seems strange since this comes from Australia. No rice for supper.

Rumour: we raided Germany with 1,000 bombers. Germans have recaptured Karkov but Russians holding them on. Roosevelt and Churchill reputed to have said they will not make compromise peace with Germans or Japs.

The Battle of Midway took place from June 4–7, 1942

Friday, June 5, 1942

Exercised. Went to Buitenzorg in a.m. Saw few people and few cars. Town is very quiet. In afternoon made hand guards for high bar work and did bar work. Played football for officers at night. Boys on aerodrome today and cart out.

There is a rice shortage in Buitenzorg and for the last three days we have only had rice once or twice per day. However flour ration has been increased although dumplings and jam rolls are all we can make with it.

Guard changed today and there are 3 English-speaking Nips on it who have been to Yank universities. Nip paymaster and ration officer here from Batavia but just had cursory glance around quarters.

Rumour: big battle in Lybia and we have captured German H.Q. there. Nips have raided Rabaul.

Saturday, June 6, 1942

Exercised. Out on aerodrome in a.m. collecting pipe. In afternoon repaired pipe for CC and he gave me 3 packages cigs for it. Boys on drome today. Did some bar work.

Water pressure on station dropped a lot today so only 4 out of men's showers work. Wogs came and took out meter and he says pipe from Buitenzorg is broken and being repaired and pressure will be o.k. tomorrow.

Concert at night and very good—boys are in good spirits and concert well attended.

Following is some confusion in dates, which is straightened out a few days later. Certainly, one can understand the difficulty of keeping days and dates in prison camp. No doubt one of the main functions of these diaries was to keep track of time's passing. Tuesday should have been dated June 9th. This mistake is rectified on Thursday, June 11th.

Exercised. Played chess with Dorney. In afternoon went on aerodrome and did a/m work with Dorney. No football at night — rain. Read and to bed.

In a.m. officer was to come at 9:30 to inspect camp. He came about 10:30 but did not inspect our quarters.

All the officers are making separate beds now. Up to now we have slept on long bamboo beds which means the centre people have not much room and cannot get to the side of their beds. Our room has not started this yet. I am lucky in having a mattress which I brought with me from Pamegettan.

Tuesday, June 8, 1942

Exercise in a.m. Did a/m work inside camp. Found breedings in small ovens that have sprung up all over and since been abandoned. Also inspected disposal pits which are terrible but this is not a Works responsibility. Try and get anybody else to do anything about them though!

Cleared drain outside of camp. In afternoon went on aerodrome with Dorney and brought back material for bed and also large tyre to make shoes with. Watched football at night and then walked and talked. Mostly discussed what a mess England would be in if it wasn't for her colonies and what thanks do we get! How superior the Englishman thinks he is!!!

Thursday, June 11, 1942

Guard changed early this a.m.

Exercise in a.m. Worked on my bed and also in afternoon. Got permission for wagon to go out in afternoon.

Attended complaints meeting in afternoon. Main complaints about food but some other very petty grievances were brought up. It seems each airman is scared his pal will get one more grain of rice than him or that he will get out of more work than he manages to do himself. It is really pathetic. They don't realize how well off they are as POWs.

Rumour: Nips lost 21 ships in battle at Midway Island. Also lost two aircraft near Alaska. Yanks are going to use Vladivostok in few weeks.

Monday June 15, 1942

Exercised in a.m. Hauled wood for workshop. In afternoon ditto and got wardrobe for MacDonald's mess. Bar work twice today. Rain at night stopped football so played chess with Dorney.

Nip officer came at 10 p.m. and looked around quarters. CC had ordered all timber to be brought in off drome and put in compound. This is a good idea since the Wogs are gradually getting away with it and the Erks are doing the same from the workshops. When all the timber is finished there won't be much to do around here.

Tuesday June 16, 1942

Exercised in a.m. Went out and got concrete blocks for timber piling and sorted out timber. In afternoon went out and got firewood and then moved single bed into mess. All in our officers' mess now have separate beds.

Watched football at night and did bar work with some new pupils from next door mess.

CC looking around quarters this afternoon and seemed in good mood.

100 days are up today which, according to Javanese legend is the time the invaders would be in possession of Java. So another legend goes by the boards. The troops had set great store by this and the disappointment is great although they will soon forget. All along they have been confident that they would not be here long. But I am beginning to have differ-

ent ideas. I can't see us getting out for a long time, as long as it will take for the US to get started.

Rumour: British and Yank troops coming in.

Wednesday June 17, 1942

Exercise in a.m. Clearing up timber yard. In afternoon did up my bed. Bar work twice today.

Guard changed today. Same type of cheerful Nip again.

In evening watched England and Scotland football match which was very good.

Nip's first question is "Are you married?" and then "How many children?", their ages and then everybody's ages. "Where from?" They all want to go back to Japan. They delight in showing and being shown photos of relations. They are good hearted giving away cigs and occasionally food. They will always pass the time of day with you.

Rumour: British, US and Russia have come to agreement re course to be followed in future: e.g. to knock out Germany first.

Thursday June 18, 1942

Didn't get up for exercises. In a.m. brought in 2 loads of concrete blocks for timber racks. The Second In Charge came and got me and took me to garage where he wanted another ramp added. Gathered timber for this and in afternoon worked on it. Watched football at night, walked and then exercised.

Food still as good as ever. We have been having jam dumplings every 3rd day, the jam being donated by an officer but now since no jam left we are just having the roly-poly and it is just as good.

Rumour: Germans attacking Sevastopol and Leningrad. Also Japs have landed in Canada!! Wait till they hear that at home.

Friday June 19, 1942

Exercise. Finished garage job in a.m. In afternoon started putting up basketball standards but only 2 (Canadians) offered any help. The rest (500) just sat around and watched—as usual, with any work, but they will all want to play.

Rumour: Yank and British Air Forces operating with Russia in strength.

Rumour: Tobruk is threatened.

Saturday June 20, 1942

Exercise in a.m. Put up basketball standards in afternoon. Cut grass on baseball pitch. I asked for volunteers to help on the pitch and got one out of 500! Then we started to throw the ball around and soon they began to drift out and join in the fun but none of them had been willing to help. (They lie around all day and sleep, read or play monopoly, totopoly, bridge, cribbage, etc. or make things out of perspex.)

Concert at night with beard competition.

Sunday June 21, 1942

Exercise. No work on aerodrome today. In a.m. fixed my bed so it's not so wobbly. In afternoon practised uke with Dorney and read. Also did bar work. Baseball pitch was in use by a few this afternoon I don't know if it will take because the class that will be played will be low for a while. Still with the shoe position so serious (we have had to buy our own leather etc. to date and do our own repairing with nails) football will have to be curtailed. Originally the Nips promised in lieu of paying us for work done, etc. that they would supply all necessities e.g. toothpaste, razor blades, clothing, etc. But so far we have had to buy all these ourselves. (See end of month.) Watched football at night.

Monday June 22, 1942

Exercised. Ask CC if I could go out for wood but he refused.

Marked out baseball pitch and removed stones from it. Chaps aren't much interested in baseball as long as football is going and they think it's a girl's game. I was going to fix up a game in afternoon but rain stopped it so read and slept for awhile and then did bar work. More people are becoming interested in exercising especially among officers and they certainly need it most of them being unable to chin themselves more than once or raise their feet to the bar.

Local Nip-controlled paper published today. Ship losses on both sides since start: America 7 battleships, 7 aircraft carriers, 8 cruisers, 1300 planes. British 3, 1, 7 and 1200 planes. Plus Dutch losses. Merchant shipping 900,000 tons. Nip 0, 2, 1, 283 planes. Although greatly exaggerated the propaganda value is admittedly large among native population and even among our own bunch. A map was also given showing Nip attacks, landings, bombings and sinkings.

The following was written at the back of the diary, on the last page:

On 22nd June, Dorney and I talked to guards on main gate. In fact they made the first advances. Their opening was to make indications of throwing their rifles away and then saying, "English-Nippon friends" and shaking hands with themselves. They had obviously not been brought up on a basis of hatred for the English and they were definitely fed up with the war and wanted to go home. They showed us pictures of their families and between the four of us there were 7 children who were suffering to the extent of being brought up in an atmosphere of war, and without the influence of their fathers, to say nothing of the mental suffering of their wives and relations. One insisted on shaking hands with me. All the guards have been cheery and very friendly and they don't interfere with us at all. None of our possessions or money have been taken from us.

Tuesday June 23, 1942

Exercise. Asked CC if I could go out and get wood but he said no again.

CC slapped Sgt. who tried to go out with barrel this a.m. Also slapped W/C Alexander.

Bombs were brought in from Buitenzorg today so it looks as though the drome will be put into use soon. If so, will they move us? The Nip cook today told us the aerodrome guards are going to Australia soon!! There seems to be something afoot as the CC has been doing a lot of paperwork lately and checking over the petrol. Nip officer also here today.

Picked stones off baseball pitch today and had practice in afternoon but only 5 turned out.

Rumour: Nip Second In Charge has been promoted to W.O. Class 1. The same as the CC. This Second in Charge is a very likeable chap and has treated us very decently. He is a person who above all, I would like to call friend and he would be a true and faithful friend. He is sensible, possesses an honest sense of humour and has a magnetic personality which draws you to him. I would like nothing better than to visit him in Japan or have him visit me after this war. Later this rumour unfounded.

Rumour: Tobruk fallen and Bardia threatened.

Wednesday June 24, 1942

Exercise in a.m. Worked on baseball pitch and did exercises. CO came out and did some this a.m. Told plumbers to make plan of quarters showing water mains and drains so we can put in enough points to flush down all quarters. Also intend to whitewash all quarters by rooms.

Complaints meeting today. Decided to form football committee to draw up future program of football now that league is complete.

Complaint that No. 1 mess was drawing flour separately resulted in decision that nobody could draw flour from Cook House: i.e. all flour to be made up into dumplings and rolys in Cook House.

It looks as though work on the aerodrome probably is finished because all the rammers were removed today.

The duty squad has been clearing drains all last week and has not been on drome. Also Nips today were buying cameras which were taken from us during the search mentioned a while back. So something must be happening. Anyway, I don't think anybody expected to see them again and the purchase of them is a surprise. The Nips are certainly being decent. Although they aren't giving what they are worth, they are respecting our property and they haven't taken any money from us. They buy any watches, lighters etc. from the troops if they fancy them. Not take them.

Played football in afternoon and watched football at night.

At meeting reps said nobody interested in sports meeting—what a bunch. Had sing song playing uke in Aussie's mess.

Rumour: Huns still advancing in Libya and Sevastopol about to fall. Our Air Force doing good work at latter.

Thursday June 25, 1942

Exercise. Played football for officers at 9:30. Got kicks on foot which more or less laid me up for day. Planned layout of pipe for quarters in afternoon, had sun bath and arranged baseball game but rain stopped it. Did bar work and played bridge at night.

Well it's 3 months today since we came to Semplak. I admit the time has not seemed longer. I think because I kept myself busy and also concentrated on exercises. I am wonderfully fit and brown. I wish there was some way of letting Mu know I'm all right and then I would have nothing to worry about. If only she doesn't undermine her health worrying, it's going to be a good life when this is over.

Rumours during the month do not show much progress on either side except for the Nips in Burma and Philippines. Everywhere else there seems to be deadlock, although one of Japs here said they were going to Australia next month. The Huns seem to be making some problems in Russia and Libya but with allies increasing it looks as though Russia can hold out and I think Libya will become a deadlock again. It looks as though the Allies intend to try and finish Germany first but in the meantime, can they hold Japan?

Friday June 26, 1942

Exercised. Went out and got pipes in a.m. In afternoon had sun bath and baseball game. Game was rough and scrappy but the enthusiasm was there. I think a good league can be arranged. Watched football at night.

CO took P/O McDonald off ration lorry this a.m. There will soon be open revolt if this keeps up. More about the whole chain of events leading to this later.

Only 1 flight on drome today. Moving barrels, etc. Tools were cleaned up and it looks like the end of work on drome. The question rises will we be left here now? CC was testing surface with Nip officer in car.

Food is quite good these days consisting of rice for breakfast, sweetened every 3rd or 4th day. Rice for tiffen with 2 onions, a piece of cucumber. Vegetable stew at night with minute meat ration added. Not very variable or profuse in different vitamins but enough to subsist on comfortably. It suits some more than others. I seem to thrive on it but a lot of the airmen are getting septic sores from small scratches.

Rumours: fighting in Timor. Nips have at last captured Philippines. Russians still holding o.k.

Saturday June 27, 1942

Exercises. Practised for concert tonight with W.O. Loveday, dressed as women, at various times during day. No work on drome today. Evidently work is finished.

Voluntary P.T. was started today at 9:30. It went over very well—it's just what the troops need. A Sgt. who has been a P.T. instructor and in the guards took it and he certainly knew his stuff. It is to be held every day now.

Concert at night was best yet. Our turn was success. There's some very good artists in camp now and everybody is now learning the uke.

Tuesday June 30, 1942

Slept in and didn't do exercises but did them twice during day.

Went on drome in a.m. and got firewood. CC seemed in preoccupied mood when I asked him, but in good mood. Also went out in afternoon and got pipes started fixing base of men's showers today with tiles and also started extending water main around building.

Got up baseball game for evening, officers vs. Erks. Refereed game which was of poor calibre but interest seems to be increasing. The sergeants had a game after. There has been no activity on the drome for over a week. The Japs evidently only intend to keep it in working order to use it in emergency.

The end of another month and we seem to be as far from relief as ever. In fact, the news the last month appears to be worse.

Work on the drome now appears to be finished. In some ways this is a good thing because it goes against the grain to help your enemy's war effort and it's against international law for us to do work but we must remember that the Nip did not sign the Hague Convention, although they told the A.V.M. they would abide by it when we first made contact with them. On the other hand, the lads have nothing to keep them occupied during the day now and that is very bad for their moral and physical condition. Daily voluntary P.T. which has been started will help take the place of drome work but I have noticed that the numbers taking P.T. has dropped to about 20% of those on this camp. This is disgraceful that they would sooner lie around and sleep and read, play cards etc. It's certainly not going to help them when they get out. None of them will want to or be fit to work again.

A few words about our prison guards. They number about 16 and work in shifts of 3, changing every hour. The guard is now changed every 3 days from troops in the barracks two miles up the road to Buitenzorg. The Nip soldiers are a very cheery sort and generous. They hold no ill feeling towards us, in fact there is more comradeship between them and our boys. You often see a group consisting of Nip guards, off duty, and RAF laughing and talking together.

Rumour: we are doing well in Russia but not so well in Libya. The situation in Libya, according to Nip sources, looks serious. The German offensive in Russia seems to be making some headway, but not a lot, thank goodness, although the Nip report of the fall of Sevastopol is serious. Evidently the Allies are now giving considerable help to the Russians.

Thursday July 2, 1942

Exercised in a.m. Fixed two holes in baseball pitch. Also set two Erks on whitewashing first shower telling them to report to me when they finished. Naturally they didn't and left the shower half done. The floors of the shower, which were tiled and cemented have turned out well. In afternoon had sun bath and then did exercises on bar.

Rain at night washed out 2 basketball games so played chess with Dorney.

Marked out baseball pitch in afternoon with lime but rain washed it out.

Nip paper claims Huns have captured Mersa Mahru, the railhead on the Mediterranean from Alexandria. It looks like a long time before we get out of here at this rate.

Friday July 3, 1942

Exercised. In a.m. we took everything out of our quarters and whitewashed it and washed the floor. It certainly made a difference besides clearing a lot of dirt out. We are lucky in having lime in the station which was left by the contractor who was building at the time of evacuation.

In afternoon rest because of sore foot which I cut yesterday. Cuts etc. fester up very quickly here and you have to watch them like a hawk. It's probably the hot climate which is suitable for bacteria and also the diet.

Did bar work with Howell before dinner. We have not had Cook House roly-poly now for 3 days for some reason. The Erks are getting it but officers not. However our mess is lucky since we have built an oven and cook our own, by drawing dough in lieu of night's dumplings.

Played basketball and bridge at night and then talked to Jap guard until 12. Talk was very interesting. He said they didn't expect to take Singapore so easy and his convoy was going there but while still on way it fell, so they came to Java. I've always wondered how they reorganized so quickly after Singapore but this is the answer. He also said Turkey had entered war but he didn't know on whose side. I think he didn't really understand us and it was other news of Turkey he read for us from Nip paper.

Rumour in Nip paper that Huns are 75 miles from Alexandria and have captured Sevastapol. This is certainly bad news but it may be only propaganda.

Saturday, July 4, 1942

In a.m. got working party and cleaned out drain. Went to CO and told him quarters were in disgraceful state and nobody seemed to be looking after sanitary arrangements and suggested a Duty Officer be detailed each day to see that camp cleaned up. He agreed and is making out roster. Flies are getting bad and one garbage tin near our quarters had not been emptied for 3 days and was overflowing. Sun bath in afternoon and concert at night. Concert not as good as usual. The same artists keep the thing going and hardly any new people come forward.

Sunday July 5, 1942

Exercise. Read in a.m. *Design* by Anthony Bertram. Pelican book and very good. Guards changed today.

Some of the sergeants and officers are now starting gardens. The chief vegetables seem to be sweet potatoes and tomatoes. I asked the Nip Second In Charge if he could get me some seeds such as radishes, lettuce, spinach, carrots, etc. but he tried and said he couldn't get them in Buitenzorg or Batavia. I don't think the Wogs market seeds. They just use them for their own use. The soil is marvellous in Java but the vegetables are mostly grown in the mountains and I don't know if they'll be successful in this lower region. Time will tell but worms and grubs will be the biggest enemies.

Read in the a.m. and exercised on bars twice today. In afternoon went out and got wardrobe for F/L Julian's mess.

While out killed hooded cobra. Skinned it and salted it when I got back.

Rain spoiled baseball at night so played chess with Dorney.

CC agreed 2 weeks ago that one man a day could go to Buitenzorg on ration lorry to have his teeth fixed by qualified Wog dentist. This is first chance we've had to have teeth fixed. He only charges $1.50 an hour. Originally Nips said they would do our teeth but that was later rescinded. Actually I went in one day and had a temporary filling put in one of my teeth. That filling had fallen out 2 days previously but that was by Wog tooth merchant who didn't even clean cavity.

Rumour: Chinese attacking Nips from South China. (Nip paper.)

Monday July 6, 1942

Exercised. In a.m. started Loveday repairing stairs of quarters. Also started Erks lime-washing their quarters. Fixed tap in officer's quarters and started fixing set of Erks's show-ers. 2 Erks rooms finished limewashing today. In afternoon went out with lorry and got wood and stands for limewashing. Also fixed Erks showers.

As a result of my talk with CO on Saturday, duty roster came out for officers today. P/O and F/O only are included. Why, I don't know. And the moans that went up! Officers com-plaining because they have to do one day's work every 16 days! And that work for their own health and good as well as the cleanliness of the camp! I'm afraid the camp wasn't cleaned up even with a D.O. It's beyond comprehension that people are too lazy to keep a place clean in which 500 men are crowded when there is every facility for keeping the place clean!

At night there were 3 games of baseball. The brand is improving and competition is keen.

Rumour: Russians are doing well on Moscow front. Rumour: Nips are now recognizing International Red Cross again. It's seems they repudiated the Red Cross some time ago say-ing we had bombed one of their hospital ships. We may now be able to get a letter home soon. That would be a big day.

Tuesday July 7, 1942

Got lorry and went out and got tin sheeting from W/T station to repair roof with. Got another Erks room limewashed today. Also got some good timber from drome but CC wouldn't let me go out to old contractor's yard south of camp for wood.

CC was around this morning, saw 2 Erks with hair shaved off and went up to adjutant and said all boys have to have hair shaved off. When asked by Erks "Officers too?" he grinned and said "Yes." Still there is no official order out yet although 40 Erks were shorn yester-day! Wouldn't mind having my hair shaved however, as it would do it good but a lot of the officers are <u>horrified</u> at the thought. We'll have to wait and see.

Rumour: 20 Yank planes over Batavia but did not drop bombs.

At night had pick up baseball game and thoroughly enjoyed it. Brand of baseball improv-ing a lot.

Wednesday July 8, 1942

Exercise. Started another Erk's room limewashing. Ration lorry got 3 brushes for this today paid for by F/L Young at 15 cents each 'cause CO would not allow them to be paid out of Imprest. Started fixing hole in roof of main verandah in a.m. Went round with Doc in afternoon to look at men's quarters re crowding and ventilation. A great many of the door-ways are boarded up and this stops air circulation. Erks didn't want hole in roof repaired 'cause it would cut out light from their rooms. I told them they shouldn't be in their stuffy, dark rooms reading and sleeping during the day when they could get outside in the shade.

Dorney and I marked out garden today. Very good game of baseball tonight for one hour. Every sport, social, games, gardening, etc., has now an officer in charge. I am in charge of basketball and baseball. This is a good scheme if the officers get busy and put a little work and energy into it.

The whole area south of quarters has been staked for allotments. Some seeds, tomatoes, sweet potatoes, cucumber, beans (string), corn, onions, have been planted already. I must say this is one thing the Erks work really hard at—their own gardens.

Have one cig today. Hair cut today.

Rumour: we are holding Huns in Egypt. Big naval battle off Midway Isle and Russians doing well.

Four months today since Dutch capitulation of Java and things very quiet on island. No sign of counter-attack.

Saturday July 11, 1942

Worked on roof in a.m. Had sun bath and refereed basketball match in afternoon. There was to be a basketball flight meeting at 2 but only two showed up so asked W/O Vickers to get hold of sergeants from each squad and try and get a rep here tomorrow at 2.

Bar work twice today. Concert tonight. Mostly singing but very good. Welfare complaints meeting skit exceptional.

Finished reading H.G. Wells *Rights of Man*. He mentions his books, *The Fate of Homo Sapiens* and *The New World Order* and Clarence K. Streits *Union Now*. Wells's book is very good but unfortunately a very small percentage of the world's population can read it, and a large percentage that do will put it down and say "very good," and then leave it to the other fellow.

Rumour: all Dutchmen between 16 and 69 being interned.

Sunday July 12, 1942

Asked CC if I could go out in a.m. and was in a good mood, I think, because of my short haircut. Anyway, he grinned all over when he saw it.

Went out and got barrel, tar and sand. Barrels are for tomato plants. P/O Kitsel in our mess had done a lot of gardening in Malaya and he says must grow tomatoes in separate containers and look after them like babies.

Had basketball meeting in afternoon with rep from each flight. Decided to have a flight league and play at 4:30 in afternoon. It really is too hot then but after dinner would interfere with football.

Repaired towel in afternoon. My clothes are gradually going to pieces. But I still have plenty. After all I've had my shorts three years and I never wear a shirt now.

Refereed basketball match. W/C Alexander was allowed over here in afternoon today. Played bridge at night.

Monday July 13, 1942

Fixed roof in a.m. Heated tar in afternoon for roofs and then gave basketball instruction to A squad and refereed basketball match.

CC called parade at 1:45 and inspected haircuts, and then what I expected, happened. The CC picked out all those who had not cut their hair really short. No 1 Mess officers had not done anything to their hair. CC then got scissors and made to cut CO's hair but CO dodged and CC slapped him. After CO had dodged two slaps and asked him why he had not carried out his orders (which had been given twice to the Adjutant). "All boys must have hair cut." CO tried to explain didn't think it meant officers but when CC says "All boys on aerodrome," he includes officers. So why not in this instance? Anyway, CC said everybody's hair must be very short—$1/4$ inch by night parade, and it was when he inspected it.

Did bar work at night and played chess with Dorney. All officers are now having hair clipped and they "Wouldn't have their hair clipped!!"

Kit planted sweet potatoes.

Rumour: Aussies have recaptured New Guinea, Guam, Timor, and Flores. All Dutch between 13 and upwards, males, being sent to Christmas Island.

Tuesday July 14, 1942

Repairing roof in a.m. Trying tar on it which I melted yesterday. Guard changed today. Had hair clipped again today and shaved very front where it has receded. Dorney and I are massaging each other's hair now for at least $1/2$ hour a day starting Sunday.

Read in afternoon and refereed basketball match. Also refereed after supper. Food is still fair. We are still drawing dumpling dough and making roly-poly and biscuits every day. Breakfast: 1 egg, rice with milk, (very weak, tinned, and sugar.) Small spot with tea (no milk or sugar if on rice.) Tiffen: 2 spring onions, piece cucumber, $1^{1}/_{2}''$ long and rice etc. As before we now have roly-poly which we make. Yesterday had bread pudding. Every second or 3rd tiffin we have a savoury of tinned fish, or beans mixed with rice and then we don't have roly-poly. For dinner vegetable stew from Cook House with dumplings for the troops (which we have drawn) and roly-poly every second night. We now have about 3 small biscuits made from dough and at 9 we have tea and toast and 2 more biscuits. We have 3 pieces bread and butter a day and tea is issued for 3 meals. So far we have managed to keep in salt. The only meat we get is a little buffalo in the stew.

Did bar work twice. Weight 168 lbs today.

Nip paper says Huns have captured Rostov. Persistent rumours of landing on island which I disbelieve because there is certainly no indication here.

Thursday July 16, 1942

Fixed roof in a.m. Quarters still being limewashed at one room a day. 2 panels taken out of ceiling of main room for more light.

Bar work twice. Read in afternoon and at night.

Basketball games washed out by rain in evening. Rain in late afternoon or early evening is becoming more frequent and the weather is cooler and has been cooler for the last month to six weeks.

Second In Charge left today along with some of drome guards. Too bad because he was a wonderful fellow.

Rumour from Jap guard that war is over and that we will be free in four days.

Rumour: Yanks have landed in South New Guinea. This is peculiar 'cause all previous rumours indicate that they have been in possession of this territory for a considerable time. Nip paper says Russians in bad way on all fronts, but this may be only propaganda.

Friday July 17, 1942

Rested today, reading and having last Malay lesson. Refereed 2 basketball matches.

Rumours thick and fast today. One from an English-speaking Jap guard which has just come today is that Japan has made peace overtures to America and Great Britain and that America prepared terms which were too harsh and unacceptable, but that Great Britain's terms were acceptable and Prince Kanoye is on his way to Great Britain. This appears very unlikely since Great Britain and Yanks would hardly render different terms and none of this has appeared in the local papers.

Following the rumour that the war is over, the Erks are convinced that they will be out of here in a week. They take every favourable rumour to heart. Also rumoured all Dutch men are being interned, Yank planes have machine gunned Sourabaya and Bandoeng, and that there are very few Nip soldiers about, that the Russians are hard pressed, that we have pushed Hun back to Egyptian border and things going well in Far East. Rumours re peace may be spread by Nips to keep Java quiet so they can take away troops for attack elsewhere.

Sunday July 19, 1942

Weight today 171 lbs—a gain of 17 lbs since arrival!

Read and worked on Malay lessons today.

Nobody turned up for basketball meeting at 11:30 today so am having announcement on parade and holding tomorrow.

Doc Dawson painted my portrait. Very good. I'm going to get him to do one for myself.

Bar work twice.

Rumour: Yanks are attacking Bali. This is likely with Nips holding sports meeting at Kalijati!

Monday July 20, 1942

Guard changed.

W/C Alexander today received a letter from W/C Frow, O.C., RAF prisoners Kalijati. This letter was brought by our CC who had been there to attend a sports meeting and asked Frow if he would like to send a letter. This is very decent of the CC. Frow said they are being treated well, although clothes and shoes are falling apart and they have not the recreation facilities we have. They had a bad attack of dysentery 2 months ago which is now cleared.

C squadron were working clearing ditches around Nip quarters today. We had rooting out of people who had been dodging parade this a.m.

Fixed showers in a.m. and did Malay all afternoon. Started basketball league off with two games in evening. Very keen and good start. Had basketball meeting in a.m. and decided to have games at night until football started. Still doing hair massaging every night.

Rumour: Rommel's in retreat and over border. Big battle in Russia. Yanks and British have landed large force in France from Dieppe to Bordeaux. Yanks have captured Koepong in Timor. Yanks have captured Macassar. Nips lost lot of ships in battle Midway and Aleutian Isles.

Tuesday July 21, 1942

In a.m. started Loveday fixing tiles on back verandah. Still limewashing one room per day. In afternoon went out and got more lime. Did Malay in afternoon. Bar work twice.

Nip officer flew in today, inspected the drome but not our quarters. He left 2:00. Fifty men again working, cleaning around Nip quarters obviously for officers' visit.

Two games basketball at night and interest has certainly grown. Last game was very good.

Workshop putting on concert on Saturday night and I am to put on first turn.

About five new drome guards came today.

Rumour: confirming Yanks attacking Timor.

Friday July 24, 1942

Bought new basketball from town and paid for it—$4.50. Got it pumped up and margarine put on the strings and used it at night for two games which were very good and the Erk spectators really enjoyed them. In afternoon rehearsed sketch which went off well.

Guards which are old drome guards are very carefree and easy. They are not a bit taken with their new job. They joke and laugh about it all the time. CC now has some sort of duty which takes him into Buitenzorg every day and we have to ask him if we can go out before he leaves.

A3 threatened to withdraw from league today. It seems they had practice arranged and S.L. Julian had the new ball and the custodian said I wanted to see the ball after." When I went down later the custodian was throwing into the basket himself and A3 said if they couldn't have it, why should he. He said he was watching Julian's mess playing and that they finished and threw the ball to him, and he had just thrown a couple at the basket. They had a grouse, I suppose, but then these Erks grouse at anything and of all the childish attitudes to adopt to withdraw from league. As far as I was concerned they could if they were going to make that much fuss.

Rumour: Yanks are in Celebes.

Saturday July 25, 1942

In a.m. finished "Thunder Box" sketch and had 2 rehearsals. Sketch went off very well but concert was held up during night by an order of Nips for a parade. Rumour has it that Erks were talking to 2 Dutch boys at the fence and were hauled in and that a Wog said he had seen a European going down the road. The Nips got the wind up and held a parade to count us. After the second count, they okayed us and the concert went on. But everybody was upset and only half the concert was run off. The next half will be tomorrow night. It was held out the back where a new stage (15 x 15) has been built complete with footlights, curtains, etc. I offered to do another turn tomorrow to extend the show.

Rumour: we are holding Port Moresby. In a sea battle two weeks ago a few hundred miles from here, the Nips had 14 ships damaged and lost 50 planes and the Yanks had 2 ships damaged. There are very big battles going on in Russia. In one, 1,000,000 men on each side. Rommel is in retreat in Libya. The Chinese have recaptured Hangkow.

Four months today since arrival at Semplak.

Sunday July 26, 1942

Made up verses and learned song for "Anyone Seen the Colonel" and "Bessie Couldn't Help It" and sang them at the concert night. The workshop concert, second half, was held tonight and it was very good but there was an interruption again. The CC came and then made a fuss about nobody standing up. We stopped the concert but when it was explained to him that nobody saw him he told everybody to carry on and sat down and listened for a while and then wandered around the quarters. I think it would be a good idea if the order was given on parade that anyone, or the first person to see the CC no matter who he is, is to give the Nip command for attention (kioske), not wait for the senior person present to give it. I have sewn the seed for this.

About 2 a.m. tonight a plane went over with no lights. The lights here were turned out as soon as the plane was heard. Later I heard it passing in the distance, but no lights were dimmed. This time I'm not attaching much to it however.

Monday July 27, 1942

Fixed tap in Young's lavatory. Looking for pipes for new parallels. Slept in afternoon and refereed basketball game at 4:30. Watched renewal of football at night.

Had hair clipped again. A lot of air activity today. Five bombers flew over and three army 96s practiced in drome.

Rumour: in naval battle near Aleutians, Nips lost 14 warships and 10 transports and Yanks lost 4 ships. Still very heavy fighting in Russia. Nips paper yesterday says Roscov threatened and Stalingrad, so still don't know who is in possession. British and Yank troops consolidate in position in France. Rumour: we're going to Batavia but I think phony.

Friday July 31, 1942

Read in a.m. We were going to fix drain around our quarters today but nobody seemed anxious. Had sun bath in afternoon and read. Still doing bar work twice daily.

Have had bread for last 2 days again. A sort of rice bread, very good, although too moist for toasting. Vegetables seem a bit low these days. We are getting a lot of extra dishes from our oven these days—savouries every second day of sweet potato, rice cakes of coconut and peanut, banana fritters using Cook House dough, chocolate cake using cocoa, Cook House dough and chocolate rolys. We are doing well as long as the money holds out.

Tomorrow I'm due at the dentist's. Watched football at night. Had a few golf swings.

Saturday, August 1, 1942

Went to Buitenzorg this a.m. and had teeth checked by qualified Wog. He told me there was nothing wrong. That was funny because dentist in Singapore told me I had one to fill and I have never had it done. In afternoon read and in evening concert of request artists. Very good.

Rumours: Russians are holding their own and again position in Russia bad. Germans 30 miles south Rostov. We're sending 500 planes a day over Germany. Chinese have captured big town and several dromes in China. Nips in retreat there. They and Yanks have attained air supremacy in this sector. We're bombing Timor and Nips bombing Australian ports. Nips in North Guam expected to capitulate. No action in New Guinea. Six hits on Nip convoy 100 miles near New Guinea.

Tuesday, August 4, 1942

Went out and got lime in a.m. Had two long sessions with golf swings today and by relaxing legs got better swing. Did not do bar work. Played 31 at basketball today in afternoon and won. Some of the boys and two officers took two lorries to civil airport in Batavia today. They are moving all the petrol from here. Boys said sirens went while they were there but since there are A.R.P. exercises on, it was undoubtedly a trial. They say Batavia very dead and only saw 6 white women, no men. Saw 3 lorry loads of British troops who looked very fit, evidently coming from work on the docks. Only petrol at airport they could see had come from here. Only four army 96s and couple of transport planes on drome. Only saw one private car driven by Nip officer. Some strings of private cars (US) being towed to Batavia. Most shops closed. Wogs seem happy. There is certainly very little air activity this end of the island.

Had hair cut today. Finished reading *The New World Order* by H.G. Wells. In afternoon did some cooking. Weight today 166½ pounds.

Two lads who were taking P.T. classes before asked me today if I could restart classes. They are coming out tomorrow in Air Raid Practice. Twenty-second siren means brown out and thirty seconds, blackout.

Wednesday, August 5, 1942

Two lads turned out for P.T. in morning.

Making slippers and rice flour grinder in morning. In afternoon learning Malay. Watched football at night.

Chaps taking petrol to Batavia again today. Say more there than came from here.

Saw five Navy Os and 4 Army 96s. Saw some 95 British troops, hair not cut. (Evidently our hair-shave, whim of local CC) Saw big Attap camp, like coolie lines, being erected five miles out of Batavia. This may be to house POWs but I hope not. If Nips recognize Hague convention they will have to move us from this drome, if they intend using it.

Other observations same as yesterday. European women look glum.

Rumour: Nips in N. Guinea have capitulated. Item in Nip paper says there has been an exchange of wounded Nip and Yank POWs between Madagascar and Durban. This and the item that appeared the other day that a Red Cross representative was in Hong Kong points to the fact that the Nips are recognizing Red Cross. I hope so because then the POW lists are probably getting through and we should get letters through soon.

Friday, August 7, 1942

Working on rice flour machine and tried it in afternoon but too slow. Will have to get other method. Also trying to figure out fan driven by water power for organ bellows. (An organ is being made from bamboo.) Had basketball pick-up game at night. Finished Gibb's toothpaste today.

Nip is supposed to have said all boys go Batavia in ten days and by Christmas all boys go home—Peace. Of course the last is wishful thinking 'cause the Nips are as fed up with the war as us.

Rumour: Russians holding Huns who are thirty miles east of Rostov. We gave Hun convoy in Mediterranean Hell. Yanks claim to have badly shaken Jap sea power since start. Churchill going to Moscow. Chinese claim to have advanced 60 miles on all fronts.

Saturday, August 8, 1942

Working on rice flour machine. Decided to make hand blower for organ so put pump together.

CC over this morning and slapped a few people. Protest? But what's the use?

Found that if rice left wet overnight very easy to grind. But would have to dry it out otherwise it would go sour.

Guard slapped a couple of Erks today. I don't know what for.

Lorries brought in three loads of flour and rice today. Balance of stock of Nip ration office which is moving to Batavia. It doesn't look as though we are moving for awhile anyway. Our ration lorry beginning Monday has to go to Batavia every day for vegetables, etc. This seems screwy when most vegetables go to Batavia from Buitenzorg. It may put a crimp in buying for awhile.

I was asked in afternoon to have a turn at concert tonight. Did "Who Killed Cock Robin" to my own words. Concert very good, especially our symphony orchestra skit. Five months today since capitulation. In very good health and had no trouble with my stomach at all. Boys still in very good spirits and slightly optimistic. Rumours set them off. Rumour: Russians doing better.

Sunday, August 9, 1942

Take Sundays off from exercise. Hair cut today. Noticed gums sore since using cheap Chinese toothpaste but can't get any other.

Tried grinding rice that had been steeped today but still very slow. In afternoon got grinder from Cook House and ground a lot of rice which made cakes. Did cooking in afternoon. Watched football. Think I can make water wheel with siren spinner.

Adjutant asked at night if any lorry drivers would drive bombs down to Batavia. There are a lot of Dutch bombs on drome without fuses, etc. which Nips are taking away. I don't know what for. Perhaps scrap. Perhaps they have succeeded in making fuses.

Workshops have fixed up cure for Singapore foot [similar to Athlete's foot] which is proving very successful. They use a 4 volt battery which passes about $1/2$ amp through a $CuSo4$ solution, from the Cu plate on which the foot rests to a Cu plate around ankle, leaving Cu deposits on bad parts of foot.

New order by Nips that all fires to be out by 8:30 which means we have our night tea earlier. All officers had group photo this morning taken with CC by Nip photographer. I think for his own use.

Tuesday, August 11, 1942

Fixing taps in morning. In afternoon sun bathed and studied Malay. Played pick up baseball game in evening.

CC is supposed to be going away on 14th, another CC coming up from Batavia. He has been severe at times, though never with me. If his orders were carried out there was never any trouble but he would not tolerate any disobedience. Never mixed with our chaps like the rest of the guards and at times he was inclined to be arrogant. I think the thing that infuriated him most was his lack of English and if he could not express himself or understand an explanation of why a thing was not done he would lose his temper and slap people. But he never slapped anyone for nothing.

Lights were turned out at 8:15 for blackout practice. There is to be another blackout tomorrow.

Rumour: Huns through Caucasus. Russians counter attacking in centre.

Wednesday, August 12, 1942

Fixing taps. In afternoon working out anticipated horsepower from running siren as water wheel, then sun bathed and bar work once. Practice golf at night and read.

Rumours: Russians 300 miles south of Rostov. Yanks successfully attacking Aleutians and Solomons. British Parliament summoned to discuss landing on continent. We are raiding Germany with 2000 planes a day and dropping 2 ton bombs. Yank Red Cross ship with 3000 parcels for us awaiting permission to come here.

Thursday, August 13, 1942

Took morning off and read and practiced golf swing. Do latter at least two days now. In afternoon read, studied Malay and ground rice.

New order today that we are to salute every Nip soldier with gun. Boys took another load of bombs to Batavia again — 9 Navy Os and 18 large twin engine craft.

Good stew tonight with two days' meat ration.

CC talking with some officers today and it still seems as though we are going to Batavia. An attap camp 5 miles outside is nearing completion. Present guard far stricter than usual and given to face slapping.

Rumour: Chinese doing well with Yanks' help. Huns still advancing in Caucasus. Moscow threatened Nips massing on Russian borders. Huns say if we invade continent Belgium officers will be shot and women and children put in front of troops. Sounds screwy to me. Nips told boys in Batavia that we had landed in three places on continent and were pushing Huns back.

**The next stage came in mid-summer, when the prisoners were moved to Batavia.
Notice how things got a little more difficult.**

Friday, August 14, 1942

Reading in morning and practiced golf swing with Herd at noon.

CC came over and asked Doc how many boys could not march because sick. Doc said 30 but of course that does not include all those who have no shoes or shoes unfit to march in. He sized up Mack's luggage and sick quarters equipment. From all this it certainly looks as though we are at last going to move, whether to march to Batavia or to Buit and then train, I don't know. I'll be very sorry to leave this place with all its amenities because I don't think the next place will be so good.

Boys started loading bombs from dumps of aerodrome. There's enough to keep them busy for four days there.

In afternoon fixed rubber shoes and studied Malay at night.

Rumour: Russians retreating on all fronts. Nips persist in saying we have landed at three points in France and are pushing Huns back. Turks massing on Caucasus front and on Bulgarian borders and Bulgaria and Rumanians also massing. Still fighting in Solomons.

Saturday, August 15, 1942

Fixed shoes in morning.

Nips had kit inspection at 10:30, what for I don't know. It didn't look as if it was to assess how much we have. Otherwise they would have had us pack it. They took a couple of small drugs.

We had foot inspection today. It seems about 25–33% are sick or mostly without shoes.

At 7:30 the CC called all officers out and said we had to go to Batavia and be ready to move off at 7:30 in the morning. He would give us transport for heavy luggage, mattresses, etc. No tools or cooking utensils, no showers were to be taken as everything was ready for us. We would have to walk to Buit and there get train. But he would not say where in Batavia we were going. There was feverish activity until 11:00 when lights out. I put high bars in and parallel bars with Lorry pile in hope they would go. Starting time was later put on to 8 in morning.

I decided to carry my kit bag bum fashion.

Sunday, August 16, 1942

We didn't get away from Semplak until 9:00 what with counting the men and a little speech by CC saying he hoped we'd be better treated and said he regretted having to be harsh with us at times and wished us luck. We marched to Buit with one fifteen minute rest and got there at 10:30. My feet stood up quite well for the five miles although I developed one blister on my heel. We loaded on train at 12:00 and started at 12:15 . We stopped at Meester Cornelius station at 1:30 and unloaded. The ten trucks which had brought our luggage were there. Then we had to stand in the sun for about $1\frac{1}{2}$ hours while the Nips took our number again. It took them about six efforts before they were satisfied. Then we started to march again in the heat of the day, back along the road to Buit but my feet didn't trouble me unduly. (I had changed socks.)

We stopped early on and Dutch people gave us cigs and ice water and later tinned food. They were very good and plucky too as the Nip guards were none too friendly.

After an hour we had a short rest and then people began to lag. I dropped back with Doc Dawson to help the stragglers with two guards. Finally we were allowed to lead them into two horse carts and then a lorry picked them up. We resumed and came on another gang. We now had four guards and we rested and I bought popsicles for the bunch. Finally the Nips stopped a lorry and we all piled in and rode the last half mile. It was the barbed wire camp mentioned on the thirteenth.

We arrived about 5:05 having marched about six miles. (We had been handed over to our new CC, a second lieutenant, at the station.) We were lined up and read out orders that we were to obey all Nip orders, fire orders, to conserve water. Then we moved in. 511 of us were pushed into two huts—one for 336 men, and the other 316. A double bed space or 2.6 feet by 6.5 feet equals 17 sq feet per man with a 5 ft. passage in the middle. Height to eaves 7 feet with 5 ft rise to crown. Beds continuous bamboo slats 2 ft off the ground, no floor. One light per 50 ft. There were no cooking utensils but luckily we had brought some, but not nearly enough. And so we had a frugal meal of rice, our second meal of the day. Received orders for schedule:

Morning roll call: 7:30

Breakfast: 8:30 rice.

Dinner:1:00 rice, one onion.

Supper: 7:00 vegetable stew, with little meat. Tea every meal.

Fixed up net and went to bed early. Evening roll call 8:00 p.m. Lights out 10:00. At 10:30 140 of STC arrived from Tasikmayala Drome under Chinese Sgt. They had been on their own since May 10th. Other ranks and officers left on that date for Sourabaya. They'd had about the same treatment as we had. W/C Alexander has resumed CO of our lot.

Monday, August 17, 1942

Rigged up shelf above bed. In afternoon CO came to me re lavatories. I went to look at them and found each to consist of reservoir to collect wash water: septic tank, 10 x 12 x 6 ft. deep and overflow to 4 ft. diameter well—30 to 35 ft. deep as soak away.

When I looked I found 2 pipes on full bore and soak pit could not take water away soon enough. Consequently everything backing up. Also Erks had put onion, cucumber peelings and rice in all pits and none of the pits covered. No septic action. I sent men on to clean out tanks with shovels from Nips. I could not get timber—they said it was all numbered and they could not let us use it without Batavia Headquarters authority. (Sounds like RAF.) I arranged to have first night picket turn it on for a few seconds every half hour. I had usual trouble getting fatigue and they forget that operation of sanitary arrangements is not Air Ministry Works Department but they are so helpless. By night I had water level down, one tank cleaned out. Asked Nips for cement etc. to cover tanks, and drain channels for wash water from Cook House. Also if we could go to Semplak to get taps, cooking utensils, etc. They said they would ask their headquarters. Asked CO to arrange for guards to prevent Erks washing rice, etc., out in ablutions. Gave lecture on septic tanks to all troops.

Tuesday August 18, 1942

Water level nicely down in tanks this morning. Asked CO to put man on each lavatory from now on to turn on flushes for 5 seconds every 5 minutes. Water level still high in soak-away. Some of STC found relieving themselves in wash house. Cleaned out other wash tank this a.m. and fixed broken pipe. After tiffin Max said CC had told him he didn't want any concrete work done because they didn't think we'd be here that long and they weren't planning for more than a year anyway. Cheerful! Said to use bamboo, matting and earth to cover tanks. So got gang in afternoon and lugged in this mat and got workshop gang and finished one tank. Other tank covered by old wood and is starting to react.

W.C. Frow and 400 others moved in from Kalijati this afternoon They had been treated similar to us but had to work harder and in one or two cases had more than face slapping. They had not had amenities we had but looked quite fit. Ask Nips again today if we could go to Semplak to get taps, etc. but they had no reply from headquarters.

Rations have been meagre last two days because we are cooking for whole camp and we have not enough utensils for our own.

In Dieppe, France, a disastrous raid took place on August 19, 1942. The majority of the force was Canadian, although British and American military, in smaller numbers, were involved as well. Death toll was high as was the number of soldiers taken POW.

Wednesday August 19, 1942

Big air activity today. Formation 23 bombers went over and 11 Navy Os. The latter returning later. They all were going north.

CC moved all his stuff out today. He is being replaced.

Spent day in bed as my feet were starting to turn septic from blisters which had not healed. Played two games of chess with S/L Grant.

Finished covering one tank today. Had big argument in afternoon re bamboo reserved for other tanks.

Thursday August 20, 1942

In morning got second septic tank covered and wash water tank with bamboo and existing tops. Covered valve chambers with bamboo. Nips gave one half-inch bolt as Tommy bar for valve keys but valves rusted and won't move. Nips then gave us thick oil and petrol to put on valves to loosen.

Nips gave us cigar ration of 23 for 14 days but still have no soap issue. Boys have no soap and it hasn't been mentioned to Nips yet.

Nobody on ablutions today seeing that boys don't dump rice, etc. New Nip CC came today and talked to CO—seemed okay—and said Yanks were coming. 500 here captured in Solomons. This seems queer to me, but we'll see.

Showed Nips leak in main pipe and asked for more taps and washers. Two taps already out of action. Notice everybody acting very childishly over small bits of wire and bamboo. The workshops and the Air Ministry Works officers brought wire, etc., from Semplak and now every other officer wants it and is very offended when they don't get it. They didn't think of bringing things and sat round for first two days while we worked and got material. Now they come round helplessly begging for things and saying they didn't have the chance to get things. What a spoon fed bunch.

Third tank, new one, finished today. More food today (quantity). Officers are now grabbing bamboo instead of letting us finish important work of covering tanks, etc. I gathered several pieces of wire just walking around camp.

Wrote up diary since leaving Semplak. Had hair cut yesterday. First time since Semplak. Also started massaging. Rice drier and better today.

Friday, August 21, 1942

Got permission to remove ablution doors and w.c. pedestals. Set aside 4 taps for officers. Pedestals came off far better than I expected. We have to make garbage compounds with them.

Nips said officers could move into one hut but not long as 1000 Yanks were moving in. That would certainly crowd the place out.

Finished covering tanks today. Colin and Lavery volunteered to one bathroom each. No batmen today. They all left last night when we fired one. Still, they aren't necessary. A lot of air activity today.

Seven suspected cases of diphtheria in the camp today. The Nips were told but they didn't indicate alarm or interest and refused to remove them to hospital saying there was no medicine there. An epidemic would spread through this camp like lightning due to overcrowding etc.and I can't understand Nip attitude.

Started bridging drains between huts today and it was a Nip doctor who saw suspected diphtheria cases.

We haven't had rain for over a week and things are pretty dusty. Nips told Mac today that we could occupy another hut which gives us far more room. Five huts between 1040 men or two square meters per person which is a little better. They gave us new plan showing space for shop, sick bay and isolation bay. They say sailors moving into other two huts now but mention no nationality.

Saturday, August 22, 1942

Nip officers had our officers over this afternoon and told them this is only a temporary camp and one is being prepared for us in Batavia and they hope it will be ready by rainy season, November, as this camp will be dangerous in rainy season. They said in battle at Solomons we lost 35 ships and 50 aircraft for 1 Nip damaged and 29 planes lost. Also we lost 15 ships including a carrier in Mediterranean battle.

There is a terrific movement of stuff moving into Batavia. Lorry after lorry load and today about 16 big 6 ft. guns with tractors. They are moving old lorries also. Looks as if they are moving everything useful out of the island.

Nip CC is going to see about soap and toothpaste issue, and also possibility of having shop. We all (officers) required to sign paper saying written oath: "The undersigned has solemnly sworn henceforth the absolute obedience to all orders of Dai Nippon gun." I don't know what they are driving at but when our CO pointed out that they could order us to fire on our own troops CC expressed horror and said "Oh nothing like that."

Finished taking pedestals out today. Nips said we could have ten bags cement but we have no aggregate. I was making bamboo chair all day and afternoon gave lecture on who is going to look after our lavatory re flushing. Other lavatory working okay but water level still too high for my liking.

Boys moved into new hut this morning giving a lot more room. Got rid of batman today. Asked CO if he mentioned letters home to CC at meeting but he said he didn't think of it.

Rumour: Yanks bombing Timor, and Celebes. Nips lost 6 transports off Indo-China. Chinese attacking toward Shanghai and have inflicted 80,000 casualties on Nips. We lost 120 planes against 200 in raid on Germany and destroyed 3 aerodromes.

Sunday, August 23, 1942

Played chess in morning with Grant. Have started exercising in morning and night again.

Mixing butter with sugar and putting it on our rice which makes it quite palatable. But this won't last long, I'm afraid. No onion or cucumber for tiffin now.

Nobody else seems to have got diphtheria so maybe it's just a scare. We were allowed to buy serum ourselves to give to people who were in close contact with suspects.

It rained a little tonight which stopped concert and made the place very muddy. There are no paths and least bit of rain makes quagmire. Mud is tracked into latrines and wash places and washed into septic tanks.

I gave a turn at concert tonight before it was rained out. 2 new batmen today.

Our new CC is a full Lieutenant.

Rumour: Yanks have recaptured south Philippine Islands. Heavy fighting in Celebes.

Turkey has declared war on Germany. Nips say Yanks have captured all but one of the Solomons but have been repulsed at Celebes.

20 heavy tanks and innumerable lorries raced down road to Batavia.

Monday, August 24, 1942

Meeting of CO and CC this afternoon. We have to fill out another form giving rank, etc., if we drive cars, hobbies, etc. Goodness knows what this is for. There is much speculation re this. In morning we all signed obedience form.

Shop is now a fact and tomorrow first instalment comes in of fruit, eggs, cocoa, sauces, cigs. Nips have set prices which are all high. All day getting in bricks for latrine floors and Cook House. Idea is to brick and render floors of latrines which are now earth and smell badly. Make washing place for Cook House and fix fireplaces which are now falling apart—all with 7 bags of cement.

Asked CO when he came back if he'd asked about writing letters home but he said he'd forgotten again. This is the second time in three days this has happened.

Rumour: Sourabaya being besieged (Duff!).

Wednesday, August 26, 1942

Got permission to take lorry and get sand. Eventually found some on road to Batavia. On way back found place where there are reinforcing rods and also oil drums but too big a load to put on. Asked Nip if I could go back with lorry but he said not now.

CO said today he had asked CC re letters home but Nips said nothing doing.

Boys out today and yesterday extending fence about 400 yds. to North camp. Just 4 feet, 3 strand. I don't know what for. Also Nips measuring our buildings. They have asked for 50 carpenters and list of tools we have so it looks as though they intend building something. Rations well down from Semplak . No onions or cukes for tiffen and stew thinner.

Thursday, August 27, 1942

In morning made level and adjusted it. Workshop crowd started to lay bricks on Cook House floor saying Nips had said that was to be concreted first. Didn't bond the bricks or anything so I stopped them. Took levels at Cook House for floor. Checked up and found latrines to be done first as originally decided, which will use up all cement. Wash place for Cook House abandoned by workshop crowd because rice on it. Asked Dorney to take on the job, also floor. Boys filling in new form today.

Bottom lavatory got flooded in afternoon so had to shut it down until water seeped away in well.

Stew very poor these days—hardly any meat and few vegetables. Found out Cook House staff were cooking fried spuds and getting lots of meat and vegetables for themselves. They were told off by the CO.

Three diphtheria cases taken by lorry to POW hospital. Had to sleep on floor and not treated too kindly. Dutch doctor with Nip orderlies.

Air Vice Marshall and Major General seen in cottage near hospital. Took CC on camp for drainage scheme. Rain at night stopped concert. Played game of chess and game of draughts with Grant.

Rumour: Yanks bombing Timor and Celebes. Stalemate in Libya near railhead. Yanks occupy all Solomons and had beaten off Nip counter-attack with 2 Battleships and 2 Aircraft Carriers and smaller ships lost by Japs. Heavy fighting in New Guinea for aerodrome.

Friday, August 28, 1942

Got 4 cocks from wash sump closed this morning. Pipes must be plugged because flow very small. However this should help keep water level down as we can use water in tank to flush instead of fresh water. Showed Nip again leak in pipe. Got Nip lorry and made two trips out this morning. Got drums and half inch reinforcing rods and concrete blocks for Cook House floor. Also found cement store with about 20 tons of cement. However most cement has got wet and was set. Brought 10 bags to try however.

In afternoon, told latrine squad how to operate new valves.

Shop came in again today. Today Nips asked CO if we had any government money. No, of course. Then said we were spending too much money at the shop—$390.00. But CO pointed out this was only 30 cents a man. He should also have pointed out that we have to buy our own soap, toothpaste, etc. and that we had to buy food because food supply was not variable enough.

Did turn at concert at night. "Anyone seen the W/C." Concert given by STC and very good on instruments. Nips came and watched it. Nips said camp very dirty and untidy and would have to be fixed tomorrow. Nets to be folded back. Nothing to be hung near front of bed. Nothing to be left in aisles. Huts surrounds to be kept clean. I admit they are very dirty now and it's an impossible job to try and get the Erks to keep it clean. Or I should say our administration is not effective enough. They even urinate in the earth drain around the huts at night because they are too lazy to walk to latrines. Dorney left our mess today. When he suggested dropping out months ago because he had not much money they would not hear of it and said we would all stay in until nobody had any left. Others paying extra as some run out of money. When he ran out they would not lend him money and would not carry him. He has joined 252 mess.

Saturday, August 29, 1942

Nips say two tried to escape from Tanjong Priok and are now in jail having tough time and that they think it reflects adversely on camp.

In morning took levels for cut-off drain near playing field and started laying concrete blocks on floor of Cook House. Also did more latrines and in afternoon did job of concrete for Nips in their Cook House.

Cleaned up my billet and started overflow weir from wash water tank. Found original scheme of weir no good because water would build up in wash house so have to lower weir. Intention is to let wash water run down open drain during rush hour. To stop well being flooded, Nips say must dig drain from Cook House east through fence and put soak-away pit on Recreation Grounds.

Monday, August 31, 1942

Shut off E. latrine until it's finished. Gang working on it morning and afternoon. Got permission from Nips to get their lorry and made 2 trips with it collecting a load of concrete blocks, 10 bags cement, 40 metre of channels, some bricks and steel rods. Nip in charge party very decent and bought papaya for lads.

Got top knocked off steel drum and now using two for refuse bin. Before dumped rice etc, and carted it to pits once day which was very unsanitary. Had a look at refuse pit in afternoon with Adjutant and found they are never sprinkled with earth and hence flies breed profusely. Nobody is interested and we have five cases of dysentery in camp. Our boys very dirty and useless when any work is to be done, grumbling all the time.

Cricket has started on recreation grounds. My shoulder's sore so not doing much exercise. Think I strained it exercising.

Joined 232 mess this morning.

Have to start pit on recreation grounds tomorrow. Nips wouldn't agree to ditch along recreation fence. Say fall is two metre, not two feet as I levelled it.

Eleven Navy Os went over this morning.

Tuesday, September 1, 1942

Deepened ditch for overflow from #1 Wash Reservoir. Dorney started wash place at Cook House. Finished concrete on #1 latrine today. Knocked top off another drum.

Nips got out 40 men in morning as punishment fatigue for being so long in coming out yesterday morning and I don't blame them. This morning I had to wait until 10 for my men then I didn't get all I ordered.

Nips brought in free soap issue this afternoon 500 bars to last 1,150 men one month—about 2" x 1½" x ½ per man. Not much for dhobying and washing soap. Shop in again today but prices terrible. Soap 17 cents which was 10 cents, paper 6 cents which was 3 cents, tobacco 40 cents—17 cents and so on. Somebody's on to a good thing. Asked Malay mess for my egg and banana ration but they weren't inclined to give to me. Found out the next day that I had paid for it so got money back in lieu.

Nips say must keep hair cut less than a ¼".

Rumour: Shanghai fallen to China.

Wednesday, September 2, 1942

Nips brought in towels (golf size at 1 per man) and 100 sheets toilet paper per man a month for free issue. Opened six of newly concreted latrines today—very satisfactory. Set the bamboo overflow pipe in concrete from wash water tank.

Chaps at docks have not had their hair cut.

Mac says vegetable ration increased.

There doesn't seem to be nearly as much stuff moving to Batavia these days. Perhaps they have removed nearly everything they want or the rush may have been for a convoy going to New Guinea as reinforcement.

Nip General supposed to be coming today so all boys have to cut grass around huts.

Rumour: Churchill says war will be over by Xmas.

Thursday, September 3, 1942

Started soak-away pit on recreation ground this morning. Couldn't get lorry since taking more chaps to hospital. Started bricking #2 latrines. Tried overflow on #1 lats. Okay. Open all #1 latrines.

Got 5 pictures which were taken at Semplak. Quite good. Don't know if we can all get one yet.

Had bit of run in with MVAF mess. They wouldn't let Julian use table of asbestos sheeting for washing. When I told him to go ahead Dane got peeved and handed them over.

Nips counted men on parade this evening and found 9 missing from that shown on slips which we hand them. It took about an hour to get things straight. Evidently the squadrons had given in wrong figures (9 short) of people sick, on duty, etc., which when subtracted from known squad strength gave 9 shown on parade which weren't there. Nips didn't get peeved but rather jeered and said it wouldn't happen in Nip army. Altogether bad show and typical of this bunch.

Rumour: Chinese advancing very fast; fighting in Timor and Celebes and Yank's ship-building far ahead of schedule.

Friday, September 4, 1942   (Note on side—letter sent)

Couldn't get lorry again. Probably because of last night. Aussie bringing firewood in lorries yesterday and today but Nips wouldn't let us talk to them. Notice they haven't had hair cut.

Had to ask CO about 6 times today about emptying garbage from middle camp. Usual arguments about which squadron were responsible and in the meantime they haven't been tipped for three days. We still play at soldier and all divided into squadron and flights, etc. to "facilitate operation" but from what I see it just produces squabbles about which is to do the work. Finally I asked CO what would happen if a high Nip officer happened to inspect camp and saw garbage. If he was told they hadn't been tipped for three days it would give the Nips a fine opinion of our cleanliness. They would probably treat us like pigs because we obviously act like them. On the other hand if he said it had been tipped that morning, the Nip would say our rations must be cut if we could waste 2 60 gallon drums of rice per meal. Besides there's our own health to consider since they are a breeding place for flies and we already have 8 cases of dysentery in the camp. Incidentally these cases have been allotted the two latrines nearest the Cook House and food stands round the Cook House covered with flies. I have recommended to one of three docs that a man stands permanently on duty on this lat and washes it down immediately after it is used.

Word came at tiffin that a Nip officer was coming to inspect camp in afternoon. That at last woke them up and they got the bins dumped but only after another squabble about whose duty it was. The Nip officer made quite a thorough inspection for a change. He wanted to know why the latrines and wash houses were not concrete. Our Nip CC told him we didn't have any cement and the major retaliated by saying you never asked for any. So obviously our requests for things like wood, cement taps, etc. which we were told had been turned down by Nip H.Q. had never reached that source. He also said the officers must keep themselves in good condition so they can go home that way after the war. I don't quite get the idea. He wanted to know where our cameras were and when we told them they were at

Semplak he asked how much money we had and was told "very little." Said sick quarters must be removed away from latrines and put in empty hut.

CC told Mac at night that Major General who is to take over prison camps has not yet arrived from Tokyo but that he is bringing directly from Nip government details of pay we are to receive, etc. and he is reputed to be easy going and decent. Nip inspecting officer was not asked about letters home, variation in diet, have our relatives been informed, etc. Our CO seems to be afraid to ask about these things instead of hammering at them to every Nip officer that comes. A big stink should also be made about the prices we have to pay the Wog who brings the shop. Things have doubled and salt 6 times in one week but we meekly pay every time.

Rumour: Nip leave on isle cancelled. Rumour: Tojo cabinet resigned.

Saturday, September 5, 1942

No lorry this morning. Both overflows on wash water tank in operation today but even then #1 latrine still too high so hardly flushed all day and didn't at night. Dorney doing grease trap with Cook House out of concrete blocks. Wash place at Cook House complete except for curing. Waited 1 hour for my fatigue this morning. Took Doc around camp this p.m. to show him disgraceful conditions. Garbage pits (he didn't know where they were even) were full and hadn't been covered with earth. There were no new pits started. The Nip pit was not covered and was full of bluebottles. Garbage bins had no top. Food at Cook House was not covered and flies were enjoying it. Suggested that fly-proof bucket latrine be made for dysentery cases and bins be dumped twice daily. He saw Nips about all this at night and Nip sick orderly was told to go round with him tomorrow.

Got lorry in afternoon and CC drove it. Brought in old lorry packing case for making garbage tops, etc. and bricks and sand. Officer was quite decent and told me I could go back for more tomorrow.

All officers are now posted to squadrons probably because of balls-up the other night. We have to take names of all chaps doing fatigues for Nips, ostensibly for payment but this was also suggested for CC at Semplak and didn't come off.

Thursday, September 10, 1942

Finished reading *Science and Everyday Life*, J.E.S. Haldane, Pelican Book A-88 — very good, must get.

Deepening drain from #1 wash reservoir and concreted #2 latrines today.

Starting reading *Army Manual of Hygiene and Sanitation* today. In afternoon Sgt. reported maggots in #1 latrines. Got Doc Dawson and had look. They looked like bluebottle maggots and seemed to be coming from the septic tank. This is possible because there is no trap between latrine channel and tank and flies could get in. Water level is high and found has been flushing 2 minutes every 20 minutes which is more than soak-away can take, after I've told them a dozen times. Ten seconds every 10 minutes. Mac went to see Nips about maggots. They say they phoned waterworks people yesterday and will phone them again tonight. That's all you ever get out of them. Anyway, have closed latrines down.

Stew very thin these days. Meat is all fat and there is hardly any vegetables. I understand the Nips have been approached and it is suggested that they again be asked tonight why we are being cut. According to ration officer the total vegetables now for 1050 men is less than we were getting for 500 at Semplak. If we had strong leaders they would hammer at Nips every day until something was done. I don't think our complaints get any farther than the Nip CC.

Friday, September 11, 1942

W/C Mathews said Nips had said we would only be here another 30 days (in this camp). This was said two days ago. Also told him Yank Red Cross ship was meeting Nip one between Japan and Australia with letters.

Meat didn't come in today until 6:30 which means 8:30 before we get dinner—12:45–8:30 is a long time between meals. I understand also that we are practically out of flour having only 2 bags left for tonight instead of usual 3 so it looks like a frugal meal. Also no vegetables came in today for tomorrow. Tea has been cut down now for two weeks. Why tea I don't know 'cause it is grown in this country. We now have 2½ pounds of tea to do 1050 men for 1 day. It's time a very big fuss was made to the Nips but I doubt if our leaders will do anything—they are very obsequious with the Nips.

Two cases of malaria in our hut now on either side of me one bay away (1 metre)—not a bright prospect on the whole.

Evidently the Nips have the same system for getting supplies as we had so there is some hope for the Yanks!! They must indent to their H.Q. We asked for brushes to clean the lats 3 weeks ago and so far none have arrived and also the buckets we asked for and which the Nips phoned for on Monday.

Rather an amusing incident happened tonight. Our orchestra, Sgt. Williams, S.T.C etc. on guitar and homemade cello were playing outside our quarters (after 8, of course)—they are extremely good and the Nips came and stood by the fence and eventually two of them climbed over the fence to get in. So is the fence to keep us in or keep the Nips out!!??

Mac saw G/C Bishop, A/C Staton, W/C Franklin today and others in barracks in Batavia.

Cleaned out channels on #1 latrines. Boards, concrete, etc. came out—40 gal drum full—this will help the flushing but pit still high and that is deciding factor. Will open it tomorrow. #2 latrines finished concrete. Asked Mac to ask Nips for 30′ pole to scrape side pit with.

Nips complained again today that we aren't saluting and bowing when we pass them. At camp where Mac was today were Yanks. Also men had hair cut but officers no.

Store in but only ¼ cigarettes ordered arrived. There is shortage.

Rumour: fighting in Bali.

Saturday, September 12, 1942

Language of Erks is terrible. Worst I've heard. Every second word and every adjective is obscene. It's the lowest class I've ever heard. What's going to happen when they go back? They're not educated and hardly any have a trade!!

Nips have been buying things from Erks lately and they are going for heavy warm things. This may be an indication of some move. Some Nips in Cook House said we are moving to Batavia.

#1 lats open today although water level down only 9″ below channel.

Big excitement in afternoon—23 new arrivals. They were British troops (anti-aircraft gunners) who had been captured in Timor about same time as Java fell. They are all sick cases and had just come from Timor with 100 others. They say 1800 captured by 20,000 Nips. But Aussies took to hills and are still fighting—getting supplies dropped to them by air. Yanks have raided Timor (they were at Kopeng) first with Hudsons, then with F.F.S. But last raid was month ago although reconnaissance over frequently. They have had lot of sickness, malaria and septic sores and lot of casualties and they give this as a reason they were moved. Nip troopships going out of Batavia when they came in. They were treated well by Nips, complaining to officer if struck. He would tick Nips off.

Food has been bad however. Nips bombed 3 of their own lorry loads after capitulation.

Rather disappointing actually. I thought we would get more news. They look pretty sick and worn out but their spirits are good and they certainly showed our blokes up for discipline and smartness.

Wing Commanders decided we wouldn't eat till 7:30 now (from 12:30) because it was too long from 7:00 p.m. till 7:45 morning. But you always have that long between evening meal and breakfast and you're asleep. It's in the afternoon you get hungry and they should put it earlier not later!! Also decided to have one pint (?) of stew per man instead of 1½ and have it thicker. This is quite a good idea.

Sunday, September 13, 1942

Cleared channels #2 latrines. All latrines working ok now though #1 very high and seepage slow. No lorry today so can't start shower floor concrete. Asked Mac to ask Nips again re brushes for lats, 40' pole. Got word at 12 that Nip Major General who is to be Officer Commanding Prison Camps, had landed and would be here in ½ hour. An awful rush and tiffen postponed. He arrived at 2 and the Nips sat around drinking etc. until 4 before they came over to inspect and we were supposed to eat at 12:30! He didn't go into any of the huts and pushed off after the inspection. None of our people spoke to him so no complaints were made re poor food, letters home, etc. The people in charge didn't open their mouths. W/C Mathew said he was going to speak to him re haircuts but didn't. The Nip Major who accompanied him seemed the most interested in things. Anyway we have had no further orders re hair cutting. Mac was called over after General gone and they told him that they now have a book of "Treatment of POWs" which he is to translate to English. They also said that now nobody was to be allowed out of camp (on ration lorry etc). Two days ago we had to give particulars to Nips on new form giving father and mother's names, place of birth, age, occupation, address and name of person to be informed that you are a POW. Mac says Nips now want this info put on cards in triplicate — one to go to England, one to Tokyo and one to stay here. So it looks as though family still not informed that we are POWs etc and it will probably take a few months yet since the English copy must go through Geneva. Also Nips are providing printed cards which can send home once a month. Printed matter will be such as "I am well. I am content. Are you all well?" etc and you strike out what you don't want. Nothing about receiving letters. I gave Father as address to send to.

No concert because of rain.

Monday, September 14, 1942

Got lorry and brought in sand and packing cases. In afternoon found #3 lat pits full and flies breeding on faeces in well. Mac and Doc went to see Nips re this and ask for petrol to burn on top and saw to make new fly proof tops. Nip doctor would not come over to see and got anti. They say they have no petrol. Got doc to put disinfectant in well although bad policy because kill bacteria in septic tank.

Started carpenters making tops. Had tops shut down and also gave order ablutions to be closed down at 12 midnight to allow to dry so can concrete tomorrow. But even then some Erks and 1 officer sneaked in and used in early morning. These lats are ones used by dysentery cases in camp so quite alarmed. Also closest latrine to Cook House. Got carpenters to make fly-proof latrine in evening. When Doc over with Mac he said extra pit at each lat would help, although this is exactly opposite to what I told Mac. Obviously ground is saturated and horizontal flow away from existing wells is negligible. Nips said get out scheme for this and they will supply bamboo for shuttering.

Had meeting of Works Committee and Docs at night and decided to build extra septic tank, and use old tank to well, to new tank and any overflow into open drain through camp at each lat. Also asked for 20 petrol drums to make fly-proof lats. Drew out scheme to show Nips in morning. Felt pretty lousy and fed up as seemed Nips were just sticking us behind barbed wire and weren't going to help us combat disease or anything and I had hoped when the General came we may get things.

Tuesday, September 15, 1942

Got conc. #1 ablution floor started and finished today. Got gang on emptying wells #3 lats. But trouble finding tins and rope to empty with as Nips will not give us petrol tins. Also started emptying #1 wash tank and cleaning and scraping of #1 latrine well which is in bad condition. Both well and tank very offensive.

Treatment of prisoners' rules not yet in force.

Went with Mac to Nips and discussed plan we had agreed on for disposal works. They said okay they would supply bamboo for shuttering, pipes from place we get cement from and use coconut trunks for struts. Found later bamboo they promised was from old shed now standing in North camp and not much good. Later Nips called us over again and said officer had been to Headquarters and got following info—all officers are to be paid the equivalent of corresponding ranks of the Nip army. He couldn't say when this would become operative and we have been told before that officers that work would be paid but so far nothing has come of it. If it is true it will be a godsend 'cause we can buy things to supplement our diet. Erks will not be paid but that is usual for POWs unless they are working. He also produced a vaccine (602) which is supposed to be for cholera, typhoid, and dysentery combined. The Nip medical orderly didn't seem sure of the dose but finally wrote down 0.5, 1.0 and 1.5—we assumed it meant c.c.s and he said week between each shot. I understand Nips and Dutch use this triple vaccine but British no. He is giving us enough to do all men and supplying extra needles etc. so they are obviously afraid of an epidemic breaking out.

Officer also said we were to prepare complete scheme to deal with sewage from camp, give material required and ready to go to Headquarters tomorrow afternoon. I asked him if we could pipe sewage outside of camp and put disposal works there and he said O.K. Got Dorney and Weekes and we got out scheme after much squabbling—piping sewage other side sports ground and disposing in 20 x 40 x 6 ft. septic tank and 40 x 60 x 4 ft. filter. Wash water to be in separate pipe and bypass system. Also decided to convert 24 #3 lats to showers.

Nip officer also said 700 more men coming into this camp but I'm sure I don't see how they are going to crowd them in. Also said give them list attap required to repair hut roofs.

Wednesday, September 16, 1942

#1 ablutions closed all day. Finished bailing out wells #3 latrines and cleaning out #1 wash water tank. Worked all morning on quantities for sewage system and finishing Cook House. Got them typed and handed to Nips just after 1 but they said it was too late to go to Headquarters today. Later in day Nips called me over again and said it would take too long to supply all the materials because it would have to go through so many departments before finally vetted and also they were short of petrol. (Sounds like our own H.Q.) Said they could supply cement, wood, and perhaps bricks but pipes and tools, etc. would have to go to high authority and big delay. Asked us could we not modify scheme or put up alternative using these materials we could supply immediately. But also put up main scheme as well. After haggling decided to have another works meeting.

At meeting 4 schemes were discussed, bucket latrines to be used when soak pits too full. Extra tanks at each latrine and discharge effluent into wash water drain, run effluent from pit overflow to big road drain and erect latrines on sports field and build original septic tank to be used during day, using existing at night. Put to vote and decided to adopt no. 3 if possible, no. 2 if not. In afternoon we had practice roll call in south field by order of Nips. I think to practice procedure they would adopt if prisoner escaped. Our count was one out, which was good for us but we found mistake.

Stews have been a lot better lately.

Thursday, September 17, 1942

Concrete in #1 ablution not set so closed all day. Working on emptying #1 and 2 pits but very slow and lost 2 buckets leaving us with 1 only.

Carpenters making ping pong table for Nips. Nips say will pay officers supervising work for Nips extra to ordinary pay. Went out in morning and found could not use road drain because of not complete so scheme 3 out. Dorney said he did not like #2 scheme and after discussion I decided to call another meeting of works, Docs and W/C and put to vote. Did this and after discussion scheme 2 was voted in. Roughed out scheme to discuss with Nips. W/C decided that 10% levy would be made on luxury purchases (even fruit) and used to buy medicine etc. I think officers should have been consulted and anyway Nips should be pressed to supply goods.

Heavy rain in afternoon and we went out and dug drains to stop huts flooding—rather enjoyable.

One of our boys died in hospital in Batavia today of diphtheria. Mac says Nips here seem even more upset than we are about it. They should be. At first they wouldn't send him to hospital after Nip orderly had seen him and said not sick enough. Then we had to buy serum ourselves as Nips wouldn't supply but then it was too late.

All cameras which were taken from us at Semplak have been brought here, with the exception of those we were forced to sell. The Nips are checking up on these latter and our old CC at Semplak may be for it.

Friday, September 18, 1942

Opened #1 ablution with stipulation that people take off their shoes before going in and F/L Dane volunteered to see they did. However one officer, F/L Furze, would not and insulted Dane so I closed them down again.

Funeral today and some of our chaps were allowed to go. Nip CC also went.

All wells very high again today. Saw Nips in morning and asked for pump they had promised to be rushed here. Put up scheme as chosen yesterday and he agreed but didn't know if they could supply bricks and definitely not pipes. He said start immediately. Thought we would have to do in concrete. He didn't hold out much hope for pipes to convert one latrine to ablution. Mentioned material at Semplak and he said he knew but transport and petrol very short. (good) I worked out quantities for comparative schemes in brick and concrete (doing new tanks in timber anyway) giving lorry loads required and submitted to Nips. Also asked them to urge morning oil and if I could do morning survey around plant and they said o.k.

Rumour: 25 of our officers and 500 men have been sent off island on 3 day sea trip. Rumour: to Borneo, and they were told not to take their heavy kit, mossy nets, etc. as everything would be provided. Nips say exchange of civilians has been made between Australia and Japan. Hope they don't move us off this island. Maybe they sent them to do a job or expect an attack on Java.

Saturday, September 19, 1942

50 new Nips came and were billeted in our end hut. They are raw recruits direct from Japan and hardly know any drill. They are taking over guard duties. Obviously Nips need all seasoned troops they can for other fronts. All Warrant Officers and old guard going tomorrow. Only Interpreter and one Warrant Officer stay. Recruits were issued with rifles and ammunition.

Nip CC and Interpreter said they would come over for dinner one night when we complained about the food. They said we can cook it, so why can't we? We explained we're used to cooking beefsteak and can't cook rice decently for so many with our poor equipment (44 gal petrol drums). Rice has been terrible lately—some say it is flour rice but it tastes rotten.

Nips must be terribly short of petrol. Our lorry went to Batavia today and took some of our lads to canvas shops for petrol and they took some out of lorries which brought recruits.

New Nip orders taken from book posted. Main points we salute all officers and duty Warrant Officer and armed sentries but after that only persons of own or senior rank. We cannot punish any offence. Later they modified this verbally to say we could award fatigues for minor offences which would be punished by Nips.

Started trench from wells #3 lats and took levels for same. Opened septic tanks which were in fair condition although there was sludge inside the outlet baffle. There is no fall to put trap into. Adjusted level after changing hairs.

Dinner 8:15 due to late delivery of meat again. Played liar dice at night.

New recruits aren't regular soldiers but attached civilians.

Sunday, September 20, 1942

No lorry again today to get new material to start tanks etc.

Old guard moved away today.

Took levels and set grades for overflow channel from #3 latrines. Also got cover off #1 septic tank which is in fairly good condition although all tanks are seething with maggots. Arranged to have #2 ablution closed at 9 tonight so we can start concreting tomorrow morning.

Cricket is going well. Two games going all the time. Getting basketball backboards made today.

New Nips were making everybody stand up this morning every time they passed the cricket field so Mac went to officer about it and he promised to straighten it out. One of new guard causing trouble this afternoon. He was wandering around the huts making everybody bow. He had a white arm band but don't know if he was duty officer or not. Clulee wouldn't bow but after argument he did in front of Erks a dozen times—very humiliating. Nip also rang gong for parade at 6, an hour before time but Mac straightened that out. Mac seeing officers about it all tonight. Looks as if these new blokes trying authority stuff. Nips were pests all night. They made everybody stand up and bow every time they walked past outside the fence and one chap inside was running all around the huts doing the same thing. They slapped one officer and some men. Finally when we saw them coming we turned our backs on them and walked into huts. Later they made the fire watchers turn out the lights and go to bed (after we had got specific orders the first day to have one light per hut on and have watchers.) They kicked one of Erk's fire watchers and tore pants of another with bayonet. CC and two Interpreters were out all evening so nobody to complain to. At 10:30 50 more of new Nip Erks marched up and there was a lot of running round at the house. Nip in afternoon stopped church service to make everybody stand up. Nips were yelling out commands all night at top of voices. They are certainly keen but they must have been pumped up with a lot of anti-British propaganda. New Nips were moved out of camp and into own quarters today.

Monday, September 21, 1942

Concreted 2 ablutions and set levels for rain drain through sports field.

Mac went over today to clear up saluting orders and make complaint about how guards were carrying on. He reported that he has won most points. He naturally referred to orders Nips had issued and got decision. He said there would be trouble if slapping continued as some-one would hit back and then there would be an enquiry. New amended orders are same as before except that we all must salute the Nip that patrols inside the fence but they promised that his patrols would be cut down to a minimum. We must salute all armed sentries when outside the camp. Erks are to salute all Nips when they are outside the wire and those of equivalent rank, or above, who come inside. Even then, one of the sentries walking in a party outside insisted that Mac salute so finally Mac went with CO to see Nips. Nips said he didn't have to and sent a man to tell Nip so.

Later we were ordered to parade at 5:30 for saluting practice but this was postponed until tomorrow. Nips were out getting practice later. Found out it was Nip Major who has come with men last night hence all the scurrying. He thinks he tore strip off CC for being away with Interpreters and no one to receive him first night new Nips here. When Nips said we had to have hair cut, we said we had no clippers. They promised to supply but still waiting. Nip Major said we must all go inside hut after lights out at 10:00 p.m. We still haven't got paid for work done for Nips. Erks on latrines are now getting paid too. Rates are Erks 10 cents, Sgt. 15 cents, officers 25 cents per day. The Nips say they have the cheque. In fact they had it for about week but say they can't get it cashed. I suppose their printing machine has gone haywire. Meat didn't arrive until 6:30 so dinner was not til 9. In meantime played liar dice.

Nip recruits had real workout today. They drilled in morning, afternoon and also practiced at night. They are quite good and very keen. Nip W/O slapped a couple of them for dropping their rifles. No further word of officer's pay. Lads are working on allotments every morning and afternoon now, even Sundays. 80 out to work today.

Rumour: Hong Kong has been taken by Chinese.

Wednesday, September 23, 1942

More wood delivered today by Dutch or Yanks. One of guards tried to make our chaps bow from other side of fence but they wouldn't. Officers had eyes right etc.—drill Nip method.

Arranged method for flushing open ditch from #3 latrines well with fresh water.

Nip stopped me talking to Weekes through fence. Nip officer came into camp today and saw method for disposing of H2O from #3 well and saw condition of bad water. Wog from Water Works here again fixing taps. Says he is going to call once a week. Says his boss okayed scheme to turn 1 of #3 latrines to ablutions. If Nips give us authority asked Mac to tackle Nips about it once more, especially since officer had seen it. One of Nips let off rifle in their quarters and had to stand outside at attention after. Got packet of "makings" (to make cigarettes).

Mac asked once again for pump and Nips said it's coming!!

Thursday, September 24, 1942

Started party in digging drains from corner each hut to east on order CC. Put overflow pipes in #3 latrines wells and tried flushing scheme—okay. But flushing slow in getting down drain until channel becomes water logged.

Nip guards prowling around camp at night. Made everybody put shoes under bed and turn lights out at 9:45, including fire watching lights. Officer was out again when this happened.

Rice good today all round. They dried it out more.

Sunday, September 27, 1942

50 men and Mike on ditches to #1 and 2 latrines. Making bridges for #3 latrines and setting levels. Fixed gate valve for flushing #3 latrines.

Nips say pay to officers being still discussed at Headquarters and probably get something definite by end of month. Announced on parade today that pay for work done for Nips inside and outside camp between 5th and 20th will be tomorrow. At last it's come!! I understand Nips $20.00 short in pay but they said T'dapa!!

Found out chaps that had been working hard on latrines construction had not been put on pay lists after Pat promising me they would be put on occasionally.

Still no oil or pump or material for latrines. Two of four taps Wog bloke fixed 4 days ago have broken again. No work outside today.

Concert very good tonight. Kalasati crowd have 2 very good singers plus we have a good band now of sax, violin, guitar and drums. F/Sgt. Williams very good on sax and I hear he's excellent on piano.

2 new batmen started today. Old one willing but no brains at all.

Monday, September 28 1942

Pay day for men who had worked for Nips from 5th to 20th. I got 50 cents and I do more work than anyone in camp. Lots of complaints. Some who have done no work got paid and others who were out 6 times got 10 cents. The permanent fatigues, latrines flushing and cleaning. Cooks naturally kicked because they volunteered for these jobs when others too lazy and now they suffer for it but most of them are being fixed up okay. Men get 10 cents, non-commissioned officers 15 cents, and officers 25 cents day. Anyway we have got our first pay so Nip assurance that officers all get paid same as Nip corresponding rank probably okay and we will eventually get it.

Cards in triplicate which will go to England finished at last and I hope they are dispatched right away. They give name, age, rank, occupation, civil life, father's and mother's names and addresses, next of kin to be informed, date and place of capture. Nips have now given us another form to fill out in duplicate—don't know what it is for—or info required. It looks as though we are going to fill in as many forms as POWs as we did in Air Headquarters. I'm glad to see the Nips have red tape. It gives us a chance.

Digging ditches for wash water from #1 and 2 latrines to wells of same is finished. Can now bail out wells or pump if Nips ever supply one they have promised directly into wash water. Also putting in more bridges at #3 latrines. Two more taps broken today. Showed Nips and again asked for supply taps and washers. Nips made STC chaps run around sports field 10 times today at noon 'cause they had cut holes in huts at bed heads—470 yds. once round. Only about 3 finished and we complained before that it was too much on POW food. Most of them collapsed. Nip W.O. ran with them and kept pushing them. Some Erks were supposed to run as well but didn't turn up! I think that's a better punishment than slapping but Erks are in such poor condition although they could improve if they would take exercise.

Rumour: Nips have asked for list of RAF and one of VAF so regulars can be sent to Japan.

Tuesday, September 29, 1942

Word from Nips that everybody must have hair cut to 1 cm by order Nip general. Air Vice Marshall is supposed to have his hair cut as well.

Our CO has ordered lights on at 7 in morning and we must be on parade at 7:20. This is because Nip had to wait about 30 seconds this morning for roll although Nip himself didn't complain. After all they rang gong for parade too soon according to the time they gave us. The people running the camp, however, are terrified of offending the Nips and consequently our day is that much longer and God knows the days are too long already. Mac says Nips told him yesterday that British and USA governments had agreed to a payment of $75.00 a month to each POW officer regardless of rank and they were just waiting for the Dutch government to agree before they paid us. This is good news although how the Dutch government, which are now in England, can hold their decision, I don't know—perhaps this is just an excuse by the Nips and they tell the Dutch that they are waiting for the British to give okay and so on.

Mac asked if we could send a morning party outside camp and they agreed but still haven't got any oil. Officers deciding whether Erks should be given Physical Training or not—long discussion and argument and finally decided officers should be given instruction in drill—

and then take flights in same—so some P. T. It boiled down to giving Erks drill instead. Won't they like that.

Erks started planting seeds—onion, beans, cucumbers, and radishes, yesterday and also manuring from dairy. Pay was issued in new Nip notes.

Wednesday, September 30, 1942

Word from Nips at 6 p.m. that 156 more men coming in tomorrow. The number is building up and still waiting for material to do latrines, pump, conversion of #3 latrines, etc.

Quite a lot of aircraft activity (singles) lately. Out with party and F/L Cartrell on a/m work around camp. Conditions very good and only one breeding place found. We collected all husks and noted all other breeding grounds. With the new bunch moving in it doesn't look as if we are going to be moved out of here very soon. Nips are going to let us buy milk from the dairy farm on which the camp is situated—25 cents/litre which is fairly good. If our pay comes through I'm going for this milk in a big way 'cause I'm sure it's okay at the farm as the farm seems clean.

Bailed out wells of #1 and #2 latrines.

Basketball hoops are finished today. Found thousands of mossies breeding in wash water tanks. That is why they have been bad around here lately but Nips still not producing oil. Told Doc and showed him but he didn't seem much interested. Poor Erks without nets will be in a bad way soon.

Officers had drill while I was out on morning survey.

Large convoy of new tires going to Batavia last two days—probably from factory at Buitenzorg.

Dinner at 8:00 due to late arrival of meat.

Thursday October 1, 1942

Milk delivered in afternoon quite good and right out of cows. Daily 20 cents/litre (nearly a quart). Our mess is going to get bottle a day between 10 men.

Mac got question of pay to permanent fatigues settled today. From now on my 4 men will get pay every second day.

Nip officers saw mossies in wash water tank today and said would try and get oil but cover them with attap. Pointed out they would get in through valve channels but they waved this aside. Showed them trenches we had dug in preparation for new tanks but they didn't bite re materials. Deepened wash water channel from #2 latrines to take overflow direct from well.

Got first shot of Nip vaccine for dysentery, diphtheria and typhoid along with rest troops. Tomorrow vaccination starts for bubonic plague which I understand is common on east end of island.

Cartrell collected husks we gathered yesterday. Put quart of coconut oil on #2 wash water tank at 7 p.m. to try and kill larvae.

156 new chaps moved into camp today. They are English gunners from Timor and came by boat with Aussies. 1200 including all at Sourabaya and by train to here. Their ship was bombed by a Hudson while in harbour in North Timor but missed luckily. Last British raids on Xupang, near where they were in July and then only one or two raids—the last one on day they left. At first Hudsons came over but given rough handling by Nips so fortresses used with better success. Nips used to raid from the drome with 27 bombers and 27 Navy Os with long range tanks, but not lately. 600 Aussies with original troops still fighting in hills of Timor. They harass the Nips at every opportunity.

Their Brigadier was taken to Australia by Flying Boat and destroyer came in one night and took some officers. They are being supplied by air. Six are RAF officers from Java. They got to Australia by lugger. They have had a lot of sickness, beri-beri, scurvy, cerebral malaria, tropical sores. Forty-two have died. Food has been poor—no vegetables. They had to build their own camp, including huts and just wandered around until men were beginning to disappear too often. Six officers with bunch and Major. Nips must expect attack on Timor if they removed all prisoners. There's nothing else startling about new blokes. At times they could supply 200 out of 1200 for work.

First milk delivered today and reports are it's quite good—not skim.

Nips told Mac tonight that officers will be paid in next few days. Officers will be paid equivalent to Nip officers without field services but they will only be allowed—up to Capt., 10 pounds per month—Major to Col., 20 pounds and Air Rank 30 pounds. The rest is to be put in the bank for us. Of all the screwy ideas. What in H__ use is it to us in the bank? We certainly can't help out the troops on that payment whereas we intended giving about 150 each which made 3-4 pounds a month per Erk. Also that is money our families may not get, that is, if our government has agreed on this. Still it will be better than nothing, although some say they will not sign for full amount until they get it. We claim 10 pounds not enough and officer here agreed and said he would try and get increased. This is to be expected because the more we get the more we spend and more rake-off for Nips.

Friday October 2, 1942

Oil we put on #2 tank no good so emptied tank today. #2 ablution closed down all day and night. Mossies also in tank #1 but not so many. Put quart of peanut oil on this tank at 4:00 p.m.

Our mess had first fresh milk today and was it good. Our mess are ordering 3 litres milk each day but they say they can only supply 20 per day. Morgan was in our mess so we had blow-out at tiffen—jam, nuts, margarine, milk, bully beef, peas and beans, biscuits.

Docs Morgan and Dawson moving to Batavia. They are starting a complete field hospital there for POWs under a British major and 7 doctors. About 6 medical orderlies also went. Nips say intention is to put all sick cases in this hospital. So it looks as though they are recognizing Red Cross.

First troops inoculated against bubonic plague.

We paid back the 35 pounds the officers were paid today so we can expect our first 10 pound monthly payment (for Sept.) immediately according to Nip promise.

Nips produced largest stock of medical supplies yet two days ago. Mac says hospital is same one our chaps have been going to, only now to be run by our own doctors.

All Dutch doctors, orderlies, cooking staff, etc. are sailing tomorrow according to Nips but don't know where to.

Dinner at 8:30 and three days' meat ration. Second stew I can remember not thickened by rice.

Chaps from Timor say reason more didn't go to hills was a lot sick and Nips threatened to shoot sick if others tried to escape.

Milk only 20 cents a litre which is quite good. Paid mess fee up to next Friday—$1.72 (Singapore dollars). Bought a pair officer's coveralls at $2.00. They may have been made for me they fit so well.

Saturday October 3, 1942

Everybody has to be inoculated for bubonic plague today.

Rumour: Nips told officer in charge of Cook House that he was only issuing him with a week's supply of rice because we're moving out of here in a week.

I don't know if these two items tie up or not. They may intend moving us off the island or some place where plague is common or maybe there is an epidemic that is moving this way.

They seem anxious to protect us from disease but that may be to protect themselves. Anyway these inoculations are certainly a good thing.

All of #1 wash water tank doesn't work so we'll have to empty it. Twelve anti-tank guns going up country in morning with troops in convoy.

Boys planting banana trees in allotment.

More orderlies to hospital.

Still no anti-malaria oil from Nips. Nips now saying all medical staff coming back. They're getting as bad as our Headquarters changing their minds. Also the reason we are rushing these inoculations is that Nips are afraid stuff will not keep. Had bubonic plaque inoculation at 3:00 p.m.

Doctors came back from hospital at 4:00. Dutch from hospital were supposed to have sailed at 7:00 morning but at 3:00 in the morning Docs were told Dutch were not going and they would be coming back to camp. Dutch doctors have been doing wonderful work. They have been making yeast and vitamins and producing very good food out of the same rations we get. Nips at hospital, however, even make patients get out of bed and bow. 1000 POWs (Yanks and Aussies) have been sent off islands but no RAF. Dutch were told they were being sent to Singapore.

Yank ship with 1,500,000 pounds of stuff was unloaded at Lorenzo Marques and picked and delivered stuff to Hong Kong and Singapore and there is some to come here. Docs say injections we are getting being made in Bandoeng. Conditions in camps at Tanjong Priok very bad and a lot of sickness. There are over 300 cases in the hospital and 120 of these are dysentery from Tanjong Priok camps. Latrine situation very bad as they are using bucket latrines and dumping into sea at night. Troops are allowed to bathe in bunches of 200. Their pay situation is same as ours. Also treatment by Nips same. Some POWs in jail. Some in schools (CAS) and other in camps at Tanjong Priok (coolie lines). Say harbour now usable.

Two officers and two Sgts. who tried to escape in Nip plane from Tjilatjap soon after arrival there were later shot.

Sunday October 4, 1942

Soap issue from Nips today—same as last time. One piece, 2 inch cube for one month. Also got tobacco issue for 2 weeks yesterday—about $1\frac{1}{2}$ ounces—terrible Wog tobac.

Toilet paper issue is behind time.

Nips sent over another form today. I just finished filling in printed form in duplicate giving name, POW number, unit, nationality and on bottom, welfare which we don't touch. Can't hazard what this is for.

Nip colonel made visit around camp and shook hands with our CO. Yesterday's inoculations don't seem to have affected anybody much. We sent out Erks to work and I had #1 wash water tank emptied again to get rid of larvae. Going to leave covers off to see if mossies still breed. There were Gulcine eggs in tank.

For the last 3 days have had Warrant Officers checking on Cook House and found have been a lot better, especially in amount of vegetables. Cooks must have been guzzling a lot of vegetables before.

Had Harvest festival service and I gave egg and banana. Nip guards have toned down a lot and hardly bother us except on last round after 10:00, especially if officer is out.

Asked Mac to ask Nips again for buckets to empty wells. Still haven't those they phoned for urgently a month ago!! Doc says to be effective dysentery inoculation must have third injection. We were only going to give 2 so Doc going to ask for more stuff.

Monday October 5, 1942

Bailed out #1 well again today. Finding mossie eggs on both tanks again. After rain in afternoon hundreds of maggots migrated out of #1 septic tank so took cover off to let sun in and that stopped them. Later rain started them again but next day they had all disappeared. Asked Mac to ask Nips again about timber to cover tanks and buckets to stop rain getting into tanks. He said he got the usual answer that they had been ordered and were coming.

Second payment to troops today for work done and not quite so many complaints now that permanent inside fatigues getting paid every second day. Nips returned the triplicate card in the afternoon to have troops number put on and few comments, etc. and said we had to work through tonight until they were finished. Worked till 12 but still didn't finish so cards still haven't been dispatched to England yet!!! Other cards also returned to be typed, not our own handwriting as previously ordered.

Third inoculation for dysentery etc. for first batch troops; 1.5 cc which the people are feeling.

Heavy rain started 5:30 and continued into night. Camp a quagmire and you pick up clay on your feet—and no paths in camp doesn't help. The latrines and ablutions are full of mud. Played bridge during rain.

Tuesday October 6, 1942

Found mossie eggs in both wash water tanks again. Took trap off #2 tank to see if eggs would be washed down drain. Trouble is pieces of meat etc. would also go down as people don't clean their plates in the bins first.

Didn't get my milk order of 1 litre per day due to big demand. Usually give ¼ litre every second day which I give to mess, as they also don't get order. Docs have ordered all milk boiled. New food arrangement comes into effect today. We are going to get stew and rice separately at tiffen and dinner. Same total. Docs brought this idea back from hospital with them. Meat is partly cooked evening before so it will keep overnight.

Nip CC told Mac today that Nip internees had been exchanged for Dutch and that Nips had been badly treated by Dutch so he was going to punch Dutch prime minister. This may only be propaganda so they have a manufactured excuse to ill-treat us.

Wog bloke here again today. We asked him re new shower scheme and he said he was ready to start but had not received orders from Nips. Therefore Nips had taken no notice after they had promised to put it up. Wog bloke only gave a small bit of leather for washers and exchanged 2 taps. Had to bail #1 well again today.

Very heavy rainstorm at 5:00 which flooded some huts slightly and nearly blew down No.1 hut which is still leaning badly. Asked Mac to ask Nips re more petrol tins and wood.

Wednesday October 7, 1942

New Cook House officer appointed and I think he is going to be good. He spent a lot of time in Cook House yesterday. Also told white cooks he is going to try and do rice the way the STC boys do it and they, of course, said it couldn't be done. Other people, especially the administration have always taken the cook's word for it but this chap says, "Well, you're going to try." Oh for more people like that. All through the RAF in the Far East the officers in charge have reminded me of Pasteur's instructions: "Have no patience with people who doubt everything in order to have an excuse for doing nothing." Good luck to the new officer. The stew was good at night and plenty meat left for tiffen stew tomorrow.

Cards are now complete for sending to England and in Nip quarters. Cleaning up ditches and deepening etc. because storm yesterday caused flooding in some huts. New Cook

House officer wants ditch down centre Cook House floor—same game as Malaya. Last one said he didn't want one, promised to conc floor if lorry produced, but no channels!!

Fixing well covers 1 and 2.

Played bridge from 5 to 8. Milk now shared among all that want it according to numbers in messes. Think I will get ¼ litre, 2 out of 3 days.

Thursday October 8, 1942

No lorry today although Nips asked for it. 3 taps broken already since man here.

Took trap off #1 tank 'cause lots of mossies in tank and none in #2 tank since I removed trap. Took 6 sets mossie eggs and put in tin with wash water. They were laid during last night.

Nips had ceremony, I think, of reading proclamation from Emperor on day ten months after start of eastern war. This happens on the 8th of every month. Noticed Nips bowed head when officer reading 'cause they shouldn't look upon the Emperor as signified by paper.

No work today. CO lectured 3 of us about being late on parade.

Good stew at tiffen and good rice. More power to new Cook House officer.

Heard today field postcards next forms to be filled in. That will be godsend when Muriel gets one of those to say I am well. Godspeed them.

Rumour: big tank battle in Queensland and very amusing—the Nips claim to have ruined Sydney bridge by torpedoing centre pier!!

Friday October 9, 1942

Put attap cover on #1 septic tank and filled around it with clay to stop flies getting in. But I don't think it will keep rain out. Removing surplus earth from drains.

Three more cases dysentery sent to Batavia. Now sending all cases there.

Order that Nip orderly officer (ordinary NCO) with white armband and no gun will be coming into camp occasionally and must be saluted by everybody.

Reading *Life of Pasteur*.

At nights now usually have walk around with Dorney and then sit outside and talk about war, our experiences during war and training etc., til lights out. I usually get in 3 or 4 exercise periods a day.

Guards a lot more friendly now and no face slapping. Sometimes when they come round we start to get up and they motion us to sit down or stay seated. Other times they are very particular that we stand and bow properly. Like last night when they raised a rumpus because one officer stood up with tin between his legs that he had been sitting on. But there are only a couple of the guards that are still obstreperous.

Nips gave issue of oz of English tobacco (coarse cut gold Bravo and Capstan). I suppose they were no use to Nips who use no pipes.

Cards to go to England still not away. They still want civil occupation enlarged upon. "Merchant" not good enough. They want to know "tea and tobacco merchant" etc. Also student of what etc. So goodness knows when they will get away. This is third time they have come back. First for RAF number, which they didn't want at first, and also trade written in full—e.g. A.C. 1.

Sunday October 11, 1942

Nips want to know who haven't shoes, hats and long pants and of course speculation is rife as to why they want this info. It looks to me as though we may be going to Formosa or Japan eventually.

Fixing ditch round hut. No boys working. Bridge at night. Not feeling too hot having headache especially after smoking probably due to inoculation.

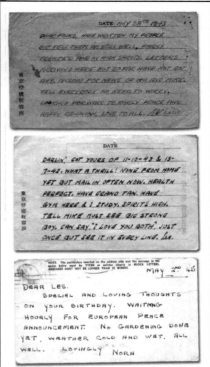

Postcards to Muriel and other relatives which were handed in to the Japanese camp commander but not sent for months or years, if at all. As a consequence, relatives were unsure for years whether Les was alive or dead.

Meat and vegetables came in today. On Friday we kicked about it, saying only two days' meat ration received as we never get it on Sunday. They said it was only two days so to save face had to bring it in today.

Monday October 12, 1942

Nips say those only having 1 shot or no shots must have one today. So either stuff is spoiling or they wish to move us soon.

Had vegetable stew at noon. Put up basketball backboards.

Got paid at last on scale 10.00 up to F/L, 20.00 above. We signed for full amount shown on Saturday. They told us the remainder would be banked for us and would move when we do. We're all to get bank books and can draw on our account by making application to Nips but I don't suppose they will let us draw much. I signed for $62.50 although I didn't like signing for money I didn't receive. Still I need the money and we will be able to buy more food now to augment our diet. We were paid in new Nip notes—hot off the press. Our CO says besides the bank money—62.50—60.00 a month is deducted for food. Some nerve if that is true! $2.00 a day for this food!! I suppose they could keep up a month for that!! And they can't take anything from the Erks!! If they took $120.50 off my salary in England that would be so hot as it means much less for Muriel, and I certainly don't need much. The question is will the English government say we have had the money or not? They don't seem to consider wives and kids at all since everybody gets same amount.

Big rush to buy things in night. Fixed chair into deck chair.

Big news this morning. Nips say 500 to go on 15th and another 500 on Sunday. They don't say where to but unofficially one of them told Mac Japan and I suppose it is. It looks as though they can't hold this island and are taking everybody off it as with Timor. No indication yet who is going first etc. Order that those that had second inoculation Saturday to have 3rd today—boy will I feel that!! Basketball all ready now. Darn it. So we move again. Personally I would rather stay. There is always the possibility of being rescued from here and if we go to Japan we are there until the end of the war and things may get tough as that nears. It would be heartbreaking if this place was taken soon after we left it. It will be spicy in Japan too at this time and that's what makes me think we will be going there, since they asked who had long pants. Had 3rd T.A.B. etc. inoculation today and it's not so good.

Wednesday October 14, 1942

List of those to go in first 500 being made out. Different reports say I am going, I am not, Dorney is, and soon. Eventually I find I am to go and Dorney isn't which is too bad but this may be altered if application is made to Nips. They were divided into 51 trades and they seemed to pick mostly (90%) technical men (English etc.). All STC are going. Seems to be complete unit: e.g. cooks, carpenters, plumbers, sick unit, etc. No W/C down and no permanent RAF personnel. Actually poor bunch of officers going. No idea where we are to go, maybe Japan, Batavia, Malay?? I don't think we would take the STC to Japan. At 4:30 we all had to go and get blood tests on slides to give to Nips but plates were not ready. Also no indication yet we would be going tomorrow. Had blood slides made for 100 after 7:00.

No pupae have appeared yet in mossies.

Thursday October 15, 1942

Blood tests for 500 finished by 12. Didn't go away until 4:00. At 7:00 p.m. Nips said 500 must produce samples of stools by 8:00 in morning. What an impossibility!! They gave us envelopes for it. Nothing definite today re going.

Finished book, *Life of Pasteur* today—best book I've ever read.

FROM JAVA TO JAPAN BY BOAT: A DEADLY VOYAGE

Friday October 16, 1942

Played basketball against STC—they beat us badly 'cause we didn't have enough subs. At 12:30 W/Cs called to Nip quarters. Came back and said first 500 going tomorrow afternoon. Plus all to parade at 2:00. At parade they said parade at 8:45 a.m. with kit. Officers what they can carry and one suitcase. Walked to Meestercornelius (8 km)—men what they can carry. W/C going to ask about carrying blankets, mossy nets. They said ship journey and pick up heavy clothing (which we ordered) en route as it hasn't arrived. They wouldn't say how long journey for, but looks like Formosa or Nippon. Stool sent in this morning. Nips say have to carry blankets, etc. Last orders parade at 8:00 morning with kit and move off at 11:00. 20 officers in first list (later reduced to 18 when 2 medical officers pulled off list). Bought pack off Collin for 3.50 and packed at night. Pack and blanket roll and suitcase.

Saturday October 17, 1942

Parade at 8 a.m. and kept there until 9:50 while Nips checked numbers and kit. Then we were told to leave kit. This wasn't so hot as I had my socks etc. in pack and hadn't fixed suitcase. It was an awful rush from then on. Not much time but I managed to get things fixed although not much time for fixing feet for march. No Aussie or N.Z. officers to go—they seemed to be keeping them until last or keeping them on isle—maybe to exchange. March started on time but officers were allowed to put all kit on lorry—this wasn't much help though because I carried airmen's pack. Heat was terrible and Erks, who were all trying to carry too much started to jettison packs in first ½ mile. However lorry managed to pick up all this kit. Two Dutch Medical Officers joined us on march. They were from camp near Bandoeng where 15,000 Dutch. I developed 2 blisters very quickly but we all made the station—5 miles. I had to look after my kit from there.

The CC had spoken as though big packets would be put on boat as not wanted on voyage. A wait at station and then by train to Tanjong Priok. Arrived first station at 1 p.m., then Tanjong Priok at 2. Left there at 3 in morning after filling water bottles.

The walk to the ship was Hell!! About ¾ mile carrying all kit but only 3 cases were left. Later three poor Erks had to go back for these, as they wouldn't send a lorry. We didn't get on board (last of RAF) til about 5. Some Dutch prisoners came behind us and some of them went on in middle of RAF. In all there were 1000 Dutchmen from Sourabaya, 500 from Bandgeong and 500 of us—2,000 on a 4 or 5000-ton cargo boat. It would make the Altmark look like a pleasure cruise. We were all put below decks in top and second holds. Top holds had been fixed up with continuous wooden shelves, dividing them into 2 bunks, 3'6" high x 10' deep. Each man has about 1'9" x 5' x 3'6" high for himself and luggage. Dirty matting on beds. Also about 200 Nips billeted with us but they have more room per man. The bottom hold is not partitioned but the Dutch are herded into these. They have sitting down space only. The heat is terrific but the hatches are kept open, thank God. Except that those in bottom hold get wet when it rains.

We got one loaf for supper and one for morning per man. Water very scarce and everybody taking out of tanks on deck which was later declared undrinkable so if it carries disease we all have it. There was a tea queue but right around ship. We are allowed up on our own portion of deck until 12 midnight and later they let a few up at night for air.

Latrines are wooden structures on deck—5 cubicles for 1000 men and 1 for dysentery and 2 for Nips. These discharge over the side but can't be flushed (with hose) when ship is in dock as they discharge over side. Smell is terrific and old faeces lying about on floor.

Ship didn't sail until 7:30 morning of 18th. Lights are provided, strung along bunks. Ship is *Singapore Maru* and seems very old although engine smooth. Does about 8-9 knots. Met Dutch officer who said some Works Department people were on same POW camp as he on isle near Tjilatjap including Harrison, Cameron, Acton. He says more RAF are POW at Kerto. Slept at 12 quite tired out.

Sunday October 18, 1942

Bread in morning, and tiffen at 1:00 and dinner at 6. From now on tenko at 7:30 and breakfast at 9:00—tiffen at 1:00 and dinner. Tenko at 9:00. Lights on all night. Meals are all the same but quite good, in fact best meals since POW. Rice (good, dry stuff cooked in 4 large steam cookers) and stew and tea for every meal. Stew quite thick with vegetables every time and fish and meat alternately. Not much stew per man but enough with rice. Dishing out rather muddled at first but gradually organized. Brought in buckets for 20 men each. We were usually short tea but made out. We had extra tin stuff we brought with us.

Passed Nip convoy of 11 ships and 2 cruisers. Conjecture is we're going to Singapore but nobody certain. Nip guards are civilian recruit type and quite nasty at times. Some are from Makasuru, our Batavia camp.

Nips gave us slips before we left showing our bank credit (mine 52.50.) Nips have great affinity for watches and collect dozens. They get quite peeved if you don't take them off and show them. But once they have them, you don't often see them again, although they do pay

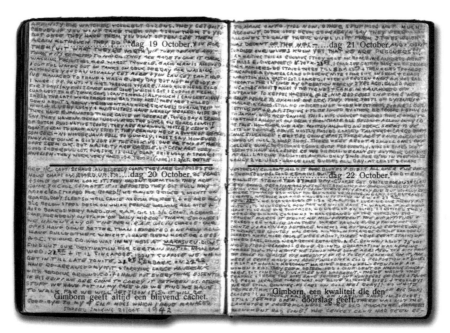

Pages from the first diary describing the boat trip from Java to Japan. The entry is an unusually long one, dated Sunday October 18, 1942.

you for them (not what they are worth). If they do take anything and it is reported to Nip CO they are made to give it back.

Washing facilities are worst trouble. Each man is allowed 1 cup full of water out of tank on deck per day for washing although you can usually get more and you can get salt H2O. I've managed to wash and shave every day but not my body and I wore one pair of pants and shirt through voyage. I had mild head cold for 3 days (the first since my nose done) which I got, I suppose, from chap next to me. Thank God I can't smell!! Although I can certainly smell the latrines which show how bad they are. They are swilled down about twice daily. We hadn't had much sickness during trip which is very lucky and my blisters have nearly healed.

Nips say they have evacuated Timor because of disease. Sourabaya crowd say they haven't been inoculated. The Dutch on board consist of native troops. They are an awfully motley crowd and don't seem to have any spirit. They remind me of a bunch of beachcombers. No wonder Java fell so quickly.

I must say they are doing a good job of the cooking. One or two of their officers seem okay but majority are rabble. Nip crew are very good, cheerful lot. Purser is jolly chap, friendly and speaks English. They work very hard and Officer in Charge troops (Nips) is 2nd Lieutenant. In charge of Dutch is Capt. Schaub, an elderly chap. They are supposed to have chaps on board up to 86 years and some of them look it. They haven't been told they are going to cool climate. It is reported they got full pay after 60.00 stopped for board!!

We played bridge 2 nights on board. Don't sleep so well 'cause no room for feet. And we are only 3'6" below steel deck—on which people walking all night and also boards very hard. Our RAF Officer in Charge is S/L Grant, a grand chap, formerly on staff of *Daily Mirror*. Thank goodness we don't have any of the permanent RAF W/C in charge. Our officers have done better than I expected and nearly all have pulled their weight. I have been more or less aide de camp to our CO who was in my mess at Makasuru. Didn't find out our destination until Wednesday 21st and it is Singapore. I don't suppose we will get in till late tonight—21st and disembark on 22nd. Have rearranged my kit and carrying large haversack with bedding around. CO has offered to carry it and I have put everything essential in his grip and we are going to carry it between us. Other stuff we have put in my case and if we have to walk far we will jettison it. So it will be good-bye to my 4 golf mugs which I have managed to hang on to till now. Other stuff is not much account.

Dutch officers from Sourabaya say they were allowed to have their wives visit them 3 times which was decent of the Nips and I don't suppose our wives know yet that we are prisoners!!! I am writing this as running story while on board. We anchored about 15 miles east of Singapore at 5:30 the 21st. I could see Cathay Building which brought back memories. We stayed there until 8:00 a.m. on the 22nd and then moved toward Singapore. A Sumatra came up during night and poor guy was sick on deck and chaps on bottom hold hatch got soaked. I woke up frozen and next morning had bad throat, the first since my operation 2 years ago.

Sailed past Singapore about 7 miles and then turned and came in and anchored off entrance to Keppel Harbor at 12:00. Nip Red Cross ship came near and sent people to examine our sick. They took tests of dysentery and malaria cases. Still no indication of when we get off. Seems to be lots of shipping about. We passed loaded tankers and cargo boats going to Singapore and empties going east. There are 7 ships anchored around us including 2 hospital ships. There were about 4 small ones off Collier Quay. Ships coming and going quite frequently. Nips on board don't seem to have had orders re our disposal. We can't get anything definite at all.

Latrine facilities awful. Only 3 water closets for 1500 in 4 holds and only 2 urinals. Hence long queues all day. At least 3 chaps yesterday couldn't hold it, poor blokes and did it all over the deck and themselves.

Food remains quite good. Rice, small bit stew and tea 3 times day. Guards get obstreperous and slap Erks around occasionally. Few cases dysentery on board caused by chaps eating raw vegetables. Terribly hot below during day and early evening but usually gets cooler toward dawn. Not too bad when we're moving. We lay off entrance Keppel harbour all night and moved into docks in morning of 23rd.

Rumour is both—getting off and RAF staying and joined by other British troops and going on to Japan. Nips are saying this. Nips change orders thick and fast. Sometimes allow us on deck, then chase all us below and allow only 10 at a time. However, we are mostly allowed on deck.

The first stopover was Singapore, a place Chater and a number of other RAF had evacuated in March. It was now under Japanese control, and he noticed a number of major differences.

Friday October 23, 1942

We disembarked at 1:30, RAF first and lugging our heavy kit with us and wondering how far we would have to walk and if we would have to leave our suitcases. We lined up on dock and I noticed they were rebuilding Godowns and cleaning up the docks. On subsequent march, it struck me how different the Nip attitude and procedure was. In Java they were taking everything out of the country and making defence works or extensive repairs only to dromes. The country was being milked. In Singapore rubble has been cleared away, more people were about. There were great stacks of ruined cars. Docks were being repaired. A R.C. runway about 75 yards wide extending across Grove Rd. onto reclamation was nearing completion—this is the thing we should have done ages ago. The Nips had the sense to realize the necessity of it and get cracking on it. There were a great many navy ships about including a good proportion of civvies and a lot of naval and merchant marine personnel. Even some Nip women and kids. They seemed determined and confident of holding Singapore. But somehow Singapore was different. There wasn't the traffic and I hear the Nips have shipped out hundreds of trucks, cars, as from Java. The place was not alive, although buses and trolleys were still running. No cars on Collier's Quay!! No white people!! Most of big shops closed!! Although majority of native shops and suburbs still seemed open. There was not the laughter and the cheerfulness of the old Singapore. Raffles monument had gone! The Cricket Club had been repainted but seemed dead and the only life on the Radang was what seemed a Military Youth Movement. The famous Raffles Hotel was occupied solely by Nips!! Signs of bombing everywhere and yet the damage did not seem extensive.

There were a few planes at Kallang, mostly passenger. In fact the air activity over the island was practically nil. Where are the Nip planes? I should have thought the island would be packed with them, as a reserve! And the residential districts—I saw Grove Rd. and East Coast Rd. about 1 house in 6 was occupied. How different from the old Singapore where you couldn't get a house at any price. Garden and tennis courts neglected. But I'm getting ahead of myself.

We waited on docks til 3:30 and were told to remove all our kit. Thank goodness we weren't going to be made to carry it. I'm afraid I wouldn't have got very far with all my stuff. Then the sick dropped out and we started our march. We had about 100 connected to our party of 500. We marched along the Dock Rd., Robinson Rd., Collier's Quay, Beach Rd. and Grove Rd., past Kallang Drome and on to East Coast Rd. We rested twice for $1/2$ hour each and altogether marched about 11 miles. The rumour that we were going to Changi looked correct. Some British troops who passed on a lorry said we would be okay. My blister broke again and I was glad when the lorries picked us up again on East Coast Rd. I was also glad I had brought my water bottle with me!! The luggage lorries passed us during march and picked up some more sick. We stopped the lorries opposite Changi jail and my heart sank. I thought we were to be pushed there. We started again and finally ended up at Changi. The guards on the march were very decent and gave us long rests. We learned later we were the first bunch that had to walk.

Conditions at Changi amazed me. Our troops seemed to be roaming around at will. Finally we were divided into groups of 100 and taken off and fed by troops at Changi, the Nip guards fading, or in other words we were turned over to our own brother captives!!! We were given a good feed and shown our quarters—a tented camp. But believe me, even that looked good after that ship. Dave and I managed to get a shower in the officers' mess where we fed and was that water good!! It washed the thoughts and dirt of the ship off us like a cloak, and we began to live again although I will say the lads had stuck it well. We were well organized on this trip and therefore showed up better than the Dutch who were mostly native troops and thought of nothing but their bellies. We hadn't our luggage the first night because it had been taken to the wrong section and we couldn't get at it.

Saturday October 24, 1942

It seems our troops have been at Changi since the capitulation. They all marched there in a body. The Nips have been taking them to Singapore in groups for working parties and there they lived in the evacuation camps (Alexandra etc.). The food has been very fair up until the arrival of Red Cross ships and supplies of food, boots, about one month ago. Since then they had been living like Kings with bully beef, meat and vegetables, condensed milk, sugar and greens from their own gardens.

They were administering themselves under different groups such as 18th Division Area, Southern Area, Australian Area, Northern Area, Indian Troop Area. These areas had a headquarters each who were responsible to command Headquarters. All full colonels and above had been sent to Nippon except General Heath who had been allowed to stay 'cause his wife was having a baby. So he was in command and dealt with Nips and passed orders down. Roll calls were passed through usual channels twice a day. There was still all the red tape and paperwork however. They don't seem to get away from that even in captivity. But they hardly ever see a Nip and are free to move around in their own area as they like and can go to other areas through ferry service—an officer going between two areas carrying a white flag and you attach yourself to his party. Some special people have their own flag.

Roberts Hospital has now about 25,000 sick, mostly beri-beri, dysentery, diphtheria etc. They have a lot of beri-beri due to polished rice from Siam until recently when they started drinking the water the rice was cooked in, thereby getting the vitamins.

We heard today that we were to leave by boat on the 26th again which didn't please us. Over 300 were buried in Changi cemetery who had died since capitulation. That was a lot for 50,000 white and 20,000 Indian prisoners. Our 20 officers were farmed out to different officer's messes. Some were treated very well and slept and ate with their hosts. Unfortunately our group of seven didn't. We were more or less treated as intruders. The officers, (gunners), didn't offer to let us sleep in their rooms, even on the floor. They were living in permanent brick Warrant Officer's quarters with push and pull showers, baths, etc. about 3 to a quarter and living in luxury. There was one room with a bed vacant and they didn't even offer our CO that!! We even had to ask if we could wash there!! My Gawd, if I had been in their place, I would have offered my bed and slept on the floor. We had to line up and draw our food with the men and ate in the Sgt.'s mess, as they didn't offer to let us eat in their mess, although other groups did and gave them extra food. The food was good due to Red Cross extras. They have their own canteens but order week ahead.

We tried to get some of our Java money changed, but no luck. Some of the other Java parties had had theirs changed by a canteen and the Nips said they would exchange it. They gave it to the Nips and are still waiting for the exchange money!!

I spent Sunday morning getting medical supplies for our two Dutch Medical Officers. But I did manage to get quite a lot which will be handy if we have another sea voyage. Also made inquiries from Division Adjutant re possibility of writing up cards for sending home and he said he would see in his Headquarters who could get in touch with Command., etc, etc. I could see that we weren't going to get cards written if we left early because of red tape. The people at Changi had written postcards home in June and they had been received by their people according to the Portuguese Red Cross man. Their nominal rolls had been received by British government so their people would know, whereas I don't think the rolls of the people caught in Java have gone yet.

Also asked if there was a chance of having boots issued to our troops since Red Cross had brought in a lot and the Changi people had mostly been issued. They said there was none left but day before we left they made another issue to their own troops!! And they all had had the benefit of the Red Cross, while Java people had not had a thing.

I found out the evening before we left that a great many letters had come on the Red Cross ships for British POWs. These were being censored at Changi jail and then given to records office for distribution. There were some there, records office, addressed to RAF personnel in Java and one of the officers of the previous RAF party from Java who had passed through had gotten one. When I finally asked the records officer if there was any chance seeing if there was a letter for me that night, and he said no, I said, could he see by 7:00 next morning if we were due to leave early. He said he couldn't find out before 10:00 in the morning because he didn't get to work until then!! I could have socked him to Hell. He promised to look when he got there and if there was one to send it to where we were parading in hope we would still be there and if not he would give it to one of the 2 officers in our party who were coming with next party. We left early in morning so I don't know if there was a letter. They have a records office at Changi giving all they know about people that were in Singapore towards last. It's compiled from all sources such as parties like ourselves giving info.

Air Vice Marshall Pulford and Rear Admiral Spooner are both dead. I spoke with W/C Aitkens who was on their ill-fated party. I saw S/L Tayor after finding out he was in Changi. He has put on weight. I often wondered what happened to him. It seems everyone just cleared off and left him, without telling him. I was certainly glad to see him well. The only Works Department person was Linge who had come through months previously with S/L Hardy and RAF party and had gone on by sea. Linge, of course, was at Tajikmalay when I left and that party went to Malang and then Batavia from there. I wanted to call on Taylor again but didn't get the chance.

Civilians have been put in Changi jail including about 60 women and children. Certainly tough on the latter. There's some talk of repatriating them and I hope it's true. Must be awful for them and they aren't to blame for the war and are no use to war effort. So why shouldn't they be repatriated!! Thank Gawd Mu and Mike got away safely!

There are about 3000 civvies in jail. Some have been taken out and given jobs running essential services and paid $50.00 a month! And they charge us $60.00 for our grub. They have education libraries, all sports and other facilities at Changi. However they have been shipping them out 650 a day for a while now. Some have a six day train journey in cattle trucks to Bangkok. Others say a 2 day journey and 50 mile walk to camp in hills. Some of their people were taken up country some time ago to build a camp. It sounds like Cameron Highlands which would be nice. Anyway they are all going to be moved in the next ten days and I think they may be going to different places. They say some of the Changi people have gone on sea trip, at first some Aussies, but then no Aussies. It looks to me as if they intend to break up all the units and mixing us up—we are mixed with Dutch. They told all Changi people to send all sick people—walking sick—on sea trip as they were going to light duties??? Other parties from Java were allowed to pick their own parties—we seemed to have got the dirt again because Nips picked us and took no account of friendships etc.

I hear Nips are stripping houses of furniture, fridges, etc. and sending to Japan same as from Java. Still, those things won't be much good anyway if the war lasts very long. Taylor came and saw me night before we left as I didn't get another chance to see him. Told two lots had arrived from Java since us, but were in another area. Also another RAF party of 500 was still at Changi who had arrived week before us. Looks as if they are getting all POWs out of Java and Singapore.

My weight on the 26th was 165 dressed. So I've lost very little since Semplak.

Notice Sikhs standing on guard with rifles about Changi. Was told they had gone over to the Nips with their captain. Only such have done it of native troops. 90% of Indian troops loyal. The Sikhs I saw looked like Jagas, mostly, which I'd seen in Singapore. Anyway, all POWs have to salute them and it goes against the grain.

Monday October 26, 1942

We had to parade (Dutch and ourselves) at 10:00 a.m. for a check count. Evidently the count in the different areas of Java parties didn't check. We'd spent all night re-arranging numbers into 50s, so when Nips arrived at 12:30 they soon checked us and we got away by 1:30 but were told to get back as soon as possible for stool tests, "by the order of the glass rod." Back in p.m. and lined up according to our new lists in ten groups of 50. Dutch were still on parade and didn't get away until about 4 p.m. when VIPs arrived at 3:00, didn't like our grouping and wanted us in order of our original lists from Makasura which has all officers but two and all NCOs first. Also 2 other groups arrived, A and B, from other areas. There was only the RAF in our 500, but other groups were 500 Dutch and 700 RAF army and US sailors.

Finally, they only rodded 200 of our group and sent the rest back to camp so it looks as though our group is to be broken up again, leaving only 2 officers and Jones who is sick. All sick are to be left and we are to supply 50 more from our party to stand by tomorrow to fill in for those falling sick. I had diarrhoea very badly today and put it down to figs I had yesterday. Anyway, a good clean-out will do me good as long as it's not dysentery. One thing to hearten us was that no party had been sent from Changi by foot. They had all been given lorry transport. We were told to be on parade again at 6:30 in the morning of the 27th, with luggage ready to move off. We were finally "rodded" and then hung around until 6:45 before we were allowed off. The night of the packing we handed our roll to officer's records so he could enter all our names and also gave my home address to him and Taylor in hope they would get a chance to let my people know by postcard.

I had wanted to swim today because organized swim parties are allowed every Tues. but didn't get the chance. It's now been 8 months since I have had a chance to have a swim!! Packing in semi-darkness cause Changi only allowed so much light. Dave and I slept in—last two nights on stretchers.

Tuesday October 27th, 1942

Felt rotten when I got up at 5:30 and went to w.c. twice before breakfast. Also had headache and felt weak. I didn't know up til last minute if I should drop out or not but decided to stick it. I wonder if it was a wise choice??

We got on parade around at 6:40 and I took two more visits to w.c. Nips arrived at 7:00 and we were all loaded into lorries with luggage, 25 to a lorry and left at 8:00 in the morning. I had to get three more men from camp to make up 1200 total. Arrived at the docks at 8:45 and hung around. Our group finally collected together—the original 200 and other 50 were marched away and rodded. This rodding must be a travesty because they certainly couldn't get results of slides of these men or us either. I suppose we all have to hang off Japan for few days until they test again. Then these 50 joined to other two groups to make them up to 700 and 500. At 11:30 we were told to place all woollen, textiles, rubber goods etc. in one parcel and other things like watches, money, etc., in another, to leave on docks. We thought they were going to deprive us of latter but then they explained we were to go on a disinfection ship, to be disinfected and our clothes also. This gave us the impression we were going on a decent ship to Japan with a bit of room.

As there were only 1200 of us, started disinfecting at 12:00 noon in groups of 100 while rest waited. I began to feel a little better as day went on, but hungry, because I couldn't face breakfast. Disinfection on ship was pleasant experience. We went in, took our clothes off, and put them, and our textiles, which we had brought in sack and put our name on it. They were then pushed down chute. Our feet were sprayed and we came on ship. We kept our towels and were then taken to a room where large disinfecting baths and one hundred of us piled in for 10 minutes. It was formalin, warm and satisfying. Then showers of fresh water, dry, and wait on clean mats til group in front collected their things. Then our clothes and kit were sent up on lifts and we dressed and went back on docks. Kit had been pressure disinfected. Our disinfection finished about 5:30.

Then embarkation commenced. S/L Grant had been on board and said ship was dirtier and smaller than the one we came from Java on but we would have "top berths." We were the last on board at 7:30 and found Nip CC had changed everybody about after they got on and we had to go in dirty bottom of aft hold, a terrible hold, very dirty and damp. There were 3 lorries in there also which took up a lot of room. Prospects looked bad and the 1200 of us were herded into the two aft holds, there being about 500 Nip soldiers in forward holds. The OBFs managed to find place in top hold at back—a black den—and Dave and I and two others went under Nip CC's bed space which was supposed to be reserved for us but which finally had 13 officers crowded into it instead of six, two from each group. It was only about 9 ft. wide and sleeping in two files meant a lot of overlapping. I should think it was the most crowded section of the ship and certainly the hottest 'cause my head was only 3″ from the engine room. Sweat poured out of us and they said this is to be a 30 day trip!! I wonder how many will get there! There were Yank officers in this section, one from Houston, two from the Artillery Battery.

We had some rice and tried to get some sleep. Rain soaked poor chaps who were sleeping on deck and those on bottom hold hatches. Everyone felt pretty low. Of our 1200, 18 were officers, 14 other ranks, 50 NCOs and rest STC lads. But I'd sooner have them than our own Erks. They're cleaner speaking and better behaved.

Wednesday October 28, 1942

Left docks at 9. Sailed west, then back through docks and anchored off Collier's Quay at 11:00. Took on more vegetables and tin stuff on 29th and all Thursday. Heat terrific and you couldn't stay below deck without getting soaked with sweat. No real organization on board for collecting food, washing dishes, etc. Fresh water was put in 3 tanks on deck, but used up immediately, a lot being wasted. Dutch use big tins full every time they go to latrines!! We had our meal in our cubby hole dripping sweat and hot tea made you sweat more.

Friday October 30, 1942

Sailed at 10:30, thank goodness, in convoy of 5 ships but no escort!! From what I could see at least 3 were POW ships but they were better off because they hadn't been waiting on board nearly 3 days!! Maybe our other 250 is in same convoy and perhaps even some we left in Makasuru! When we got underway Nip soldiers in fore hold took nearly all life belts and said if we were torpedoed, only Nips would be saved. While we were at anchor off Singapore, two vessels I took for minesweepers were patrolling the channel and I saw three mines blown up in a very short time and also one was exploded just in front of one of ships of our convoy. I don't know if these are our old mine fields they are still cleaning up or their own which have broken loose.

Saturday, October 31, 1942

Got soap issue today but it's like giving a cow a wrist watch 'cause we have no water to wash in. There's only very little drinking water and the three tanks which are filled whenever they are empty are used for filling the tea pots by a hose. A lot of inconsiderate people use the water out of the tanks to bathe with in the middle of the night letting most of it go to waste. So the Nips quite rightly are very strict with it now and we have to put day and night guards on it because it still goes. I managed to get a couple of salt water baths. They wash the vegetables with a fire hose of salt water and a few of us grabbed it and turned it on each other. Boy was it refreshing! (I usually get one of these a day because I park near the hose connection.) Read *Rebecca* on first part of this journey. Also got toilet paper issue of US newspaper but Dutch use rare water!! Got cig issue of 90 for 1200 men!!

Dutch filling in triplicate cards which we did at Makasuru. Ours, or one copy, are travelling with us, according to Dave. I wonder if the copy for England has arrived there yet. Changi people wrote postcards in June and Red Cross people say 11,000 got home and also the nominal rolls of POWs in Singapore.

Nip CC on board read us from Nip news sheet about two naval battles on the 25th and the 26th. The first, in the Solomons and the second at Santa Cruz, (he said in the S. Atlantic) in which US lost two battleships, four carriers, five cruisers, eight destroyers and twelve transports. One battleship, one carrier, one cruiser and six transports damaged only. US lost 600 planes, Nips 100. He said he was sorry but didn't look it. I'm afraid it just ran off our backs as we had seen in other Nip papers which altogether claim they've sunk more naval vessels than US possesses!

List of American POWs at Mitsushima camp, including POW number, rank and group number, recorded in F/L Chater's diaries.

Monday November 2, 1942

Sighted 3 small islands to east in p.m. Nips say we will arrive off Saigon at 3 p.m. tomorrow but will not go upriver and will be convoyed by small battleship (destroyer) from there. We are allowed free run of decks and can sit on superstructures aft of bridge. They say we will probably stay off Saigon two days, then to Taiwan, thence Japan.

Plane flew over convoy yesterday.

Vegetable ration getting small. Nip CC says we will be put in camps in Nippon after being searched and officers will have separate section. No sign of warm clothing we were promised but maybe we will pick it up in Taiwan. Weather a bit cooler today. Prices of things in Singapore very high now—eggs 12 cents, wog cigs 25 cents, sugar 90 cents a pound, matches 17 cents a box! So we were quite well off as regards prices in Batavia.

Tuesday November 3, 1942

Arrived off Mekong River which leads to Saigon at 11:00 a.m. just half hour over four days from Singapore. Three small ships already at anchor there. Small coast town with good bay and quite good houses, like summer resort but no docks. Rest of our convoy left at 4:30 and it certainly didn't please us to be left. Why must I always have the bad luck. I am the only Works Department person on this trip, the other one from Batavia, (Cullen) being left behind in Singapore (sick). There's a chance that Linge may have preceeded me though.

Two French ships followed the convoy and then Nip destroyer and French sloop anchored in bay. Nips say we have leaking boiler tube and going up towards Saigon tomorrow to get fixed, and may hold us up for a few days, which means that many more days on this damn boat!

Wednesday November 4, 1942

Sailed at 7:30 and entered Mekong River at 9:00 in the morning. It is a meandering river about a quarter mile in width and seems very navigable as we went at a good clip, sometimes close to bank. Banks were very low-lying and mangrove swamp which I should judge to be all under water with high tide, few fishing vessels on river but it seemed deadly quiet as though the plague had recently passed that way. Further up the banks began to show signs of habitation such as 2 or 3 clusters of native huts and paddy fields. Native sailing vessels all seem to be hauling wood up river and you could see places occasionally where the wood had been cleared. Hardly any birds noticeable.

I am feeling okay. My cold is now cleared up. My eyes were really swollen for 2 days but I think it was sunburn as I got my shoulders burnt at same time. They are nearly okay now. Ankles are also swollen but I think also burnt 'cause walking around in tennis shoes on hot decks all day. The doc says it's a sign of beri-beri—(lack of vitamin B) but I'm sure it's not in my case because we didn't have polished rice in Java.

I wish we would hurry and get to Japan cause things couldn't be much worse there and at least it will be cool. I've had enough of the eternal heat of the East and the change of climate should do me a world of good.

Anchored off two oil stations at 1:45 after a half hour stoppage. So, allowing 8 miles per hour, we had come about 33 miles up river but about 18 miles as the crow flies. No dock facilities but Texaco oil station which has been taken over by Nips. Destroyer passed us and went on up river. Don't know how much further Saigon is but looks like port 4 or 5 miles up river but I don't think Saigon is on the river so probably just the port of Saigon!

Anchored all day and later welding set came on board so it looks as though leaky boiler to be cause of stopover.

Qualities of meals have deteriorated. Breakfast—rice and 2 small pieces pumpkin and water pumpkin boiled in. Tiffen—rice and few slices tinned sliced potato. Dinner—rice and a few pieces vegetables in stew poured over rice and if you're exceptionally lucky a piece of meat size of small walnut.

By the way, a Canadian, P/O Morris, sleeps next to me.

Tie up about tea this p.m. Nips said at first we wouldn't get any but after they got theirs they allowed us to line up and everybody got their own tea. Nips say we use too much water but people pinch it out of tanks at night to wash in and wash clothes—being very selfish and not considering or caring that it means the curtailment of water supplies for everybody. The tanks are only supposed to be for drinking water. In other words we're not supposed to wash at all. From now on we must wait til Nips have had their tea and washed up before we can start to draw our tea. Trouble is all cooking for ourselves and Nips is done at our end of boat in 16 cookers in very restricted space. Also tea box and washing up box making a terrific bottleneck for 2000 men! There's not nearly the organization on this boat that there was on the one coming from Batavia as regards cooking and drawing of food. The Nip CC doesn't seem concerned or interested.

I slept on deck during night and it was quite chilly but the air was grand.

Though F/L Chater tried very hard to keep his spirits up, it was not always easy. In the trip from Java to Japan, twenty-five young men died of dysentery or diptheria in the crowded ship. The following entry relates the ship's stopover on the Mekong River.

Thursday November 5, 1942

Had wash in river water by hauling up side in my collapsible bucket. That bucket has been a lifesaver. We draw tea for our 12 officers in it. It was grand to have a sort of shower.

Bad day for morale altogether. Anchored in river all day and heat terrific. It was almost impossible to stay in our cubby hole or you would be bathed in sweat and stench. Terrible! On deck sun beat down and there was no shade—a terribly long day. Air below is foul, smell of sweat overpowering. Two water boats came along river and loaded us up with water so maybe now we will get a wash. I think most wearying and spirit-breaking day since captivity. Ankles quite swollen and legs weary but I'm sure it's not beri-beri although that is first sign. After all I've had no polished rice except at Changi and we had stuff to counter it there. The people who have been at Changi would be first to go. Think due to heat and hot deck and wearing tennis shoes. Doc says to eat more meat, vegetables and fruit. What a laugh if it wasn't tragic.

We asked Nips if they wouldn't put dysentery cases on shore at Saigon—one poor lad is terrible—just skin and bones. I've never seen anything like him and he got that way in 8 days. They say it's French territory, therefore they can't put anyone ashore—rumour is that's why we didn't go up into port and why Nip soldiers not allowed ashore but Nip destroyer went up river and rumour said POWs from Hong Kong were put out at Saigon.

Opposite: As a conscientious officer, F/L Chater kept meticulous records of not only his boys but of many other prisoners in the camps, including Chinese, Dutch and American. The lists included name, rank, regimental number, POW number, unit, and any other pertinent information such as cause of death.

Left: List of American POWs, identified by camp number, army branch, full name, age.

Believe me, I looked longingly at that French shore—within easy swimming distance. What would happen if we appeared in Saigon. Would we be interned by the French or turned over to the Nips?? Many were debating that today, I'll bet.

The Nip CC bought a lot of pomeloes and cigs today and then sold them to us. Pomeloes at 25 cents each !! What a price!! But I bought 2 'cause I figured they would do me a lot of good. Cigs were 10 cents package of 20 and there was enough to give packet per man.

There's been a lot of natives in boats collected round our ship all day. They are peddling fruit, beer and cigs and some of the Erks are trading sweaters, blankets, etc. for stuff. They'll be the first to holler when they get cold, I bet.

The latrine arrangements are poor but not quite as bad as on the other ship. 2 urinals and you never wait more than 15 minutes mainly because we are allowed on deck all day. 4 out of 6 w.c. (1 for Nips and 1 for dysentery) for 1200 men. This is not so good especially as there're a lot on board with diarrhoea. More vegetables came on board today but I don't know if we'll see any of them.

Rumour: we don't move until day after tomorrow—that will be Hell. Evidently we are now awaiting another convoy as welding seems finished. 5 merchants and 3 warships went downstream today.

Now sleeping very fitfully but I don't suppose that will hurt me. It's too hot and the boards over the steel deck are not very even or soft and also it's too crowded and when someone moves it wakes others up.

If you don't think about the future you get along. But once you start to think, the future looks so gloomy that you're bound to get downhearted. The tendency is to sit in the hovel and mope and sleep and feel sorry for oneself. You also curse the people who got you in this mess and talk about it to other people, feeling as you do—have I gone over the tale and asked why we were disembarked at Java at all when there was no work for us and so much we could do elsewhere—I never did a stroke of work in Java and neither did the rest of the Ministry Works Department!! Still it's too late now! It's not so much the war as the shambles in this world after this war that worries me! I wonder if Mu has started the school in South Africa. I hope so because it will occupy her mind. I hope she doesn't let her health go because mine is as good or better than when I left Singapore originally. If I could only get some word to her!! Maybe we will be allowed to write as soon as we get to Nippon.

Friday November 6, 1942

Started moving down river at 1:15 p.m. Thank God we don't have to spend another afternoon at anchor in this lousy Mekong River. Had another bath in river water as we were moving. Rain squalls bad at night. Usually a lot sleep on deck and if rain drives them down there's nowhere for them to sleep and also sends those sleeping on bottom hatch covers scurrying. All they can do is sit round for rest of night. If they can find room to sit!! Alleys and passages are full of sleeping bodies at night. It's almost impossible to get up stairs after 8:00.

We are anchored about 5 miles out from river mouth in place we were at before. At 5:30 2 destroyers there and big convoy came in from sea. (Singapore?) In evening I took 8-12:00 p.m. watch to see nobody pinches tea because if they do we don't get tea for breakfast. None of new ships seem to be POW ships although some have been used for trooping, by deck fittings.

Saturday November 7, 1942

Thirteen ships and 2 destroyers now at anchor—it looks like a big convoy for Nippons. One destroyer left toward Saigon—convoy of 11 ships including ours, and one destroyer sailed at 4 p.m. A sigh of relief as we got underway. I think everyone will be glad to get to Nippon and see the last of this trip.

We struck rough weather right away and soon a lot were sick. Our ship didn't seem to pitch much, but yawed and rolled a lot. Perhaps because we were heavily loaded. Our bottom holds are full of clay and gravel, reddish substance which some say is bauxite. Ship jumping about all night and things dropping off the shelves besides rolling against each other so didn't get much sleep.

Nip CC says everybody must remain below deck this trip because if subs see all people on deck they would take it for a troop ship and go for it in preference to rest convoy. I don't see that it's any argument because an allied sub is going to torpedo it anyway. Torpedoing is now in everyone's thoughts. We can't forget it 'cause the Yank who sleeps next to me won't let us. He was torpedoed on the *Houston* and is worried about getting it again. It would be bad luck to be sunk by our own sub, but it's all in the game, I suppose. Although we wouldn't have much chance if it happened. It's rather a blow having to stay below in this rank atmosphere. We can only go up to get tea and go to latrines.

Sunday November 8, 1942

Eight months POW and still not settled. I'm certainly weary of moving round. How I wish they had left us at Semplak!! Sea a bit calmer today. Actually we got on deck quite often as they were not strict with the stay below rule. I think actually it only applies after about 5 p.m. when subs usually take their sights. I think we only did about three miles per hour during storm last night, but seem to be doing better now.

Monday November 9, 1942

Doing quite good clip during night. *Buried Corporal Allan this morning who died during night*. He died of dysentery and he was the one I mentioned earlier that looked so bad. The number of dysentery cases is increasing. There are now 20 with 40 other cases diarrhoea. Naturally latrine facilities can't cope especially since only one w.c. for dysentery and some are going 6-10 times an hour.

Medical stocks also getting low. Nips have been asked for more medical stores but they haven't anything but disinfectant. No more dysentery serum left and only few pills. Of course when I got medical supplies at Changi I only got for our group—500—for a 30 day trip and actually only half of our group came, so we should have had plenty. Unfortunately Dutch (500) didn't bring any supplies (except to feed their bellies), and other bunch of

British RAFs, Yanks and army (500) <u>forgot</u> their medical stores—the most important things to bring. Asked Dave to ask Doc for list of essential things we want so we can ask the Nips if they will get at Taiwan.

I feel okay myself. Did few exercises and deep breathing late at night. Slightly warmer today. Nips not sending everybody below til 6-6:30 now. My ankles are now back to normal so it wasn't beri-beri.

Another run in with Nip CC re water. He says there are 800 Nip troops aboard and we use far more water in proportion to what they do. But he doesn't realize that all cooking, cleaning, and utensil cleaning water comes from tanks at our end. He says we can't have any more water now but can have tea four times a day. But Dutch still using water for latrines as much as even later in day and also for washing. I should think easiest way to stop usage is not to fill the tanks but they keep filling them when they're empty. Should think they could use one tank for salt water and Dutch could use that for w.c. because more is used for that than drinking and washing. Anyway, I wouldn't trust water for drinking with so much dysentery aboard. However, still nothing definite re usage as usual and Dutch have been told to go ahead by their CO and our troops have been told they mustn't use it. I wish the COs of the groups would get together and settle things once and for all.

Nip CC says he can give more disinfectant but no other medicine. He promises to see if he can get some in Taiwan but I doubt if he will bother. He doesn't seem to want to be bothered by us at all and refers everything we ask him to the sailors. One of our lads traded an old Elgin watch today for 3 bottles whisky, 17 packets cigs and 40 yen. Nips are always after wrist watches which makes me think that the ones they get in Nippon are not much use and when they go back they will make money on the ones they got from us. One of the Nips on another boat had a whole suitcase full. Of course lads take far under the value for cigs and food. I've still managed to hang on to one Mu gave me. When I tell them it's a present from my wife they don't press me too much which is decent and shows they realize the sentimental value. Trouble is now everybody says things are present from their wife if they want to hang on to them and Nips are getting a bit sceptical. Rumour: we will arrive Taiwan on Friday and stay 3 days. Dutch are to be dropped at Nagasaki and we go on (I hope so). When we get to Nippon we get beer and cig. issue like Nip soldiers.

Tuesday November 10, 1942

Two weeks on board—it seems like two years—and only one-third of journey completed. This ship will be a writhing mass of disease if that speed is not exceeded. Dysentery patients are mostly too weak to get to latrines and pails are provided for them but some of them don't even get that far and they're an awful mess where they are lying on the hatch cover. Up after hatch is also messy and flies are getting thick there and the food for that hold is dished out right next to them. No wonder cases are spreading but you can't expect anything else. There's no room to isolate them although we've managed to collect them in one place and we spray disinfectant over hatch cover frequently. I can see nothing for it but to take dysentery cases off ship at Taiwan but the Nip CC doesn't give much encouragement on that point. He says he only has jurisdiction at Batavia, Singapore and Nippon.

Shaved in tea water and showered in sea water. I usually get one shower of sea water a day from hose with which they clean food buckets. It's very refreshing even though you can't soap and it doesn't take much dirt off. Most chaps given up shaving but I find feel better if I do and can retain my self respect!

Sea still fairly rough and ship rolling a lot but not zigzagging any more. Nip told me tonight 10 day trip from Saigon to Taiwan—hope he's liberal!

Meals bunched together now at 8:30, 12:00 and 4:30. I don't know why—maybe to get us to bed earlier. Nights closing in earlier so we must have travelled east a lot. Meals very poor now — breakfast, 2 pieces bread, fruit, (mushed, and size of walnut) and other meals rice and a few potato slices with couple minnows if lucky.

Wednesday November 11, 1942

Armistice day — what a travesty!!

Boiler tube has gone again so we have to supply stokers day and night now. We have been supplying three shifts of six men, four hours each and they get shower in fresh water and a good meal out of it. I'm going next time it's our group's turn and get some exercise. Nips are still getting quite good food — vegetables, noodles, etc., apricots.

Thursday November 12, 1942

Convoy broke up today. Seven ships and destroyer went off in northwest at 12:00 noon leaving 4 ships including ours. We travelled north all day in straight line. Nips say two and three days out from Saigon are dangerous areas — that's why zigzag then. From direction they took presume rest convoy going to Hong Kong and if so judge we are still 500 miles — 4-5 days — from Formosa. There is now a distance counter on our boat and we are leading the convoy of 4 ships. We registered about 5 miles per hour average so will take 9-10 days total for our journey. Weather still rough and screw out of water/time. Not sure what part Taiwan we are going to. If in north, it will not be until later that we arrive but then we won't have so far to go on next leg.

Friday November 13, 1942

Last Fri 13th I was also on board — the *Empire Star* — but under circumstances a little more cheerful.

Another death from dysentery this morning. One of the Dutch. He went off very quickly and was buried in morning. More dysentery every day and no medicine now.

We started to move a little quicker during early evening and by nightfall other ships were out of sight. Read *Synon Times* new Singapore paper of 15-17th October. They say Lieut Commander Horswell has died of dysentery at POW camp at Osaka so it looks as though that's our destination. They say he was one of 200 survivors of *Lisbon Maru*, a POW ship that was sunk in East China sea by US submarine on October 1. I wonder if S/L Hardy's RAF 400 were on that boat?? It's certainly hard luck to be sunk by own allies, but it's all in the game. Nips in these papers stress that US lost a lot more ships in Solomon battles than they announced (three heavy cruisers and *Canberra*). They say nothing about Nip losses.

Weather got very rough again in afternoon and rainy. Trouble brushing teeth these days. Water I won't trust except sea water and usually do them once day. Big trouble is I haven't been to w.c. for about seven days and yet it doesn't seem to bother me. I've never been like that in my life before. I think lack of roughage and intense perspiring has a lot to do with it. But I think it's a good fault on this ship.

People who have sailed these parts say they've never seen anything but calm. Just our usual luck to have it stormy and have the journey made too long.

I've only changed once since I came on board (17 days) but there's no water to wash clothes, and besides they would be just as dirty in no time.

Saturday November 14, 1942

Did lot better speed during night — 100 miles between 6 p.m. and 9:30 this morning. We are doing about 7 knots now and sea is calmer although weather still squally. We may get in tomorrow at this rate but Nip engineer says maybe tonight.

Forty-seven cases dysentery in our people now. I think lots of Nips have been seasick too. Trouble is to find room for the sick. We are still using the buckets but even then faeces are dropped on stairs and deck, etc. by poor chaps who can't make it to the w.c.s. Nip doctor on board now alarmed by dysentery. Says he is going to try to get us all fumigated at Taiwan and try and get sick ashore. Trouble is it's the ship that needs disinfecting as much as anything. Everything you touch is covered with dysentery germs—the stair rails, taps, anything—it's a miracle everybody hasn't got it.

Weather got rough again in afternoon and night and speed dropped. Nips said we just missed typhoon which struck Philippines.

Flies very bad in hold and must be crawling with dysentery. During night very little sleep cause ship rolling and pitching badly and screw out of water half time causing terrific vibration. We are under steering assembly and that makes a terrific noise during bad weather like battery A.A. guns.

Sunday November 15, 1942

Weather bad again this morning and speed slow. Nips say we should get in tomorrow. I hope so. I reckon if they don't get the sick off we will all have had it.

I took a turn shovelling coal in coal hold today, from 12 to 4—enjoyed the exercise although work tough 'cause we're short handed. Had good meal, or I should say better than average at 1:00 and while having it Chief Engineer came up and said come up to his quarters after off duty and have supper. I had lovely bath at 4:00, and then a grand meal with Chief Engineer. Ate omelette, pineapple, biscuits, bread, glass of brandy, and good tea as well. He wanted to trade his stop watch for mine and I suspect that was the reason for treat but when I explained my wife had given it to me he didn't press and didn't get nasty. He seemed decent fellow.

To realize how many sick, we have to provide 3 shifts of 6 men and 3 of 4 men (30 men) for stoking and we could only get 26 out of 180. Nearly all STC lads are seasick and a lot of others who haven't dysentery. An officer in our bunk has been sick for about a week and vomiting into bucket in front of us!!

Monday November 16, 1942

Slept very well last night and this morning had good relief (first in about 8 days). I think the fruit, etc, which I had last night did the trick. Officer next to me went down with dysentery during night. That's getting close to home! He has moved closer to other cases.

Land this morning on starboard side!! At last!! We should be in today!! Sea a lot calmer now. Anchored in Takao Harbour at 1 p.m. and then moved alongside docks at 4 p.m. Drizzly, dreary weather all day. We haven't seen the sun now for a few days.

Another Dutchman died of dysentery this morning so we had a corpse to present to the port authorities. But they took it ashore in quick time which should speak more than words re conditions on this ship and I hope it impresses on them the need for getting the sick ashore. Some of them in bad way. Ship's doc was given list of sick which is 180 diarrhoea and dysentery cases and most of these will turn into dysentery.

Also gave Nips list of things: milk, fruit, etc. and asked them if they would buy them for us for the sick. We would pay for them. After talking and reminding CO re list medicines required they didn't give it to the Nip doc before he went ashore so if they get it now they will be lucky. Doc going to see about getting sick ashore.

Tried to get watch for Chief Engineer but so far no luck.

Weather quite cold now so I will dig out my sweater. It doesn't look as though we're going to be issued with the warm clothing we were supposed to pick up on the voyage.

Nip doc came back last night but would give no definite news about getting sick ashore but everybody is hopeful.

A lot of air activity around here. 6 good looking Med bombers travelling fast came over us and 9 fighters have been up practicing with a Drogue.

Tuesday November 17, 1942

3 weeks on this Hell ship and still at least a week to go. Chief Engineer said two days in port and five days sailing if good weather. Twenty-eight new sick cases today, dysentery mostly!!! At this rate we will be in mess by the time we reach Nippon—those who do! Blow this morning when Nippon doctor said nobody would be taken ashore. It's just plain murder for a lot of the sick. I can't understand their attitude. They say they have no camp or hospital for British soldiers!! The Nips will be getting it soon and then perhaps they will realize the seriousness of it.

Fruit, biscuits and vegetables are coming aboard but I doubt if any of it is for us. Some sort of watermelon came on but Nip collared them. Coal and H2O are being loaded and should finish tonight. H2O from hydrants on dock. Food terrible now. I don't see any of sick improving on it. Rice and bit seaweed stuff every meal. I eat it but I'm hungry immediately after again.

I slept very well last night with no rolling in engines, etc., although we were crowded having one of the docs in with us who hadn't slept for 4 nights.

Cold and dreary again. *Another death this p.m.!! RAF chap from our group.* Our 2 M.O.s doing wonderful work but it must be heartbreaking with no medicines. Nips gave us free issue of 20 watermelon and 450 bananas. But they won't go far among 1200 men. Also got 250 oranges which we are keeping for the sick.

Nips gave order—nobody to go forward of the engine room superstructure so they must be wary of disease themselves. Nip doc is going to phone his hospital again today after we again pressed for getting sick ashore and for medicine. So there may still be hope. Nips said free issue for sick today and tomorrow cigs and fruit coming aboard which troops can buy.

P/O Morris down with dysentery today. He sleeps opposite me. Other P/O Morris, (Canadian), next to me, now recovered and back again.

Wednesday November 18, 1942

Two more deaths during night and another before noon. One Dutch and two English. Surely all these deaths will have some effect on the Nips!!! Besides them taking extra precautions to protect their own troops! Seven deaths now all told!! And more to come according to Doc. Nips came on board today with two bottles disinfectant and two stirrup pumps and did ship in half hour. I don't think that will do much good 'cause we were down doing same, while we had disinfectant, many times a day.

They had A.A. practice today on Drogue.

Another death at night—total now 8.

Nips brought on packet of toilet paper and wanted to sell to us for $3.80!! And the whole ship suffering from dysentery and running short of paper. More fruit and sugar came aboard—100 kilos which we bought out of imprest and gave half to sick and divided remainder among 3 groups—gives about two spoonfuls per man!! Oranges we also issued, about 1 per man, and bananas also. Cost of oranges 5 cents and bananas 3 cents each. It's made a big hole in our imprest but I think this is certainly an emergency warranting it.

Moved P/O Morris to sick section tonight.

Takao Harbour a beauty. Very narrow opening and large inland harbour. Very extensive docks with rail facilities and large number of go downs, I should say bigger than Singapore docks. Also construction still going on. Loading which not done at docks done by Chinese coolies loading into tonkangs. These coolies carry terrific weights, two of them lifting up a 44 gal drum. They also load quickly. There seems a terrific amount of industrial buildings and engineering works in the district but little transport—most moving done by bullock cart and coolie cart. Harbour looks like it was originally an inland lake and was made by digging short, narrow channel out to sea. Very busy there, being about 50 large merchant ships in all time and others coming, going all day. Also large seem like coaling docks outside harbour.

Thursday November 19, 1942

Moved out of harbour at 10 and went up west side of Taiwan. Anchored 6:00 p.m. off island off west coast of Taiwan—about 50 miles up from Takao. Nips say moving again tomorrow morning in convoy. If only there wasn't this eternal stopping and waiting. We have been anchored about half the time on this boat.

We still have received no medicine from the Nips. Our Doc asked Nip Doc today and was told to go away as he had "No time for you." So it looks as though besides refusing to take sick off we don't get any medicine either. Rumour: dysentery among Nips in forward hold. Things very bad now. Chaps scared to attend sick and feed them. But we managed somehow to get enough volunteers. Med orderlies have been wonderful, especially Dutch. Not so many new cases today probably because of cold.

I have to wear sweater and shirt now to keep warm, although still in tropics. I suppose after living near equator for 3 years any change in temperature will be noticeable. I have bit of sore throat too.

Spent morning sorting out sugar. Meals now rice and water, melon, stew—2 pieces, the size of walnut. It's good to have a bit of sugar however.

Friday November 20, 1942

Still anchored. *Two more deaths during night. One Dutch and 1 RAF. Total now 10. One of our C group in afternoon, making total 11 deaths.*

Started moving at 1:00 p.m. in afternoon and were joined by convoy of 4 more ships and destroyer which came from Hong Kong direction. At first moved with good clip but later grew very rough and slowed us down—I hope we don't hit bad weather all this last leg. It means more sickness and probably more deaths in delay in reaching port. Nips say they had 30 deaths and 40 cases dysentery up to Taiwan and their sick were taken off there.

Saturday November 21, 1942

One more death (Dutch) during night. He was sitting on bucket and fell into bottom hold cause sea so rough. But he was pretty bad case before. Very rough during night and a lot seasick again and very little progress. P/O Angus Morris again sick and also Henderson from our billet. Dane, Gees, Dunlop, Mack, now all have dysentery started. Scarlett quite bad. Making deal with Chief Engineer for some food for sick in exchange of gold cuff links of S/L Grant. He agreed to our terms and we are to see him tomorrow.

Stoking today from 8 until 12 in the morning with Grant and Smith. Hard work but good exercise and didn't hurt us. Doc got some disinfectant and pills from Nip doc at last!!

Was able to do some washing after stoking but nowhere to dry it. Had some fish, other stuff of Nips for lunch on stoking shift.

Things very bad in sick hold during rough weather. Buckets fall over—chaps with them— they are so weak. Buckets fall down into bottom hold crowded with men. No wonder the disease spreads. About 10 buckets are kept going day and night with dysentery cases which shows how bad conditions are. Of course the buckets are only thing because chaps too weak to get up stairs and in any case only five w.c.s there and they are always full up and half dozen waiting with diarrhoea and others of rest POW. Our chippie fixed up board to stop people from falling over but not very successful. But can't get any material from Nips.

Sea very rough all day with strong head wind. Also very cold. Hope it isn't much colder in Nippon—I dug out my golf jacket and that helped.

I think dysentery spread by rice baskets which are not properly cleaned. They are just swilled with salt water which doesn't nearly remove all old rice and then they just stand and flies can get at them till next meal. Heaps of chaps can't wait for w.c.s and do over rail and some don't get that far. Consequently your shoes are full of germs, so we take them off before entering our hovel but then someone puts his on yours and when you go to put yours on again, you get germs on your hands and so to your mouth. That's one of innumerable ways of spreading. Cold weather should keep down flies but it is not that cold below and the place teems with them. I think they are the main source of infection.

Sunday November 22, 1942

Weather improved bit during night and moving better now. Destroyer went back to look for one ship which not visible this morning. Saw Chief Engineer this morning and he says come back to clinch deal tonight.

Another death this afternoon—total 13. This chap died very quickly having been up yesterday. Rumour he died of diphtheria.

If so things will be in a mess with chaps crammed together like they are. Doc not certain but thinks he died of diphtheria. He can't tell for sure without a microscope. Nips disinfected their abode above us with spray and later whole hold was done. There must be a carrier aboard cause Doc says incubation 3-6 days. We can only hope that it wasn't diphtheria. Doc had everybody with sore throat gargle but as usual it made mine worse. *Another death from dysentery in evening (English). Total now 14.*

Weather a lot calmer and making about 7½ knots. Also first sun for weeks which was very welcome cause it's been getting really cold. Bright moon and cold in morning.

Breakfast rice and rice water only. How can you expect sick to improve on that? I've had pain in stomach all day and rumblings. Looks like I'm in for a case of diarrhoea. I pray it's not the beginning of dysentery! Also had headache. Played bridge last two nights.

Monday November 23, 1942

Two more Dutch died last night. Total now 16!! Nips say when we get to destination we will be inoculated, rodded, etc. and some will go to Kobe, some Yokohama, Osaka, etc. Diarrhoea worse this morning! But head not so bad. Sea calm and making 9 knots. Sun bright and warm but cold in shade. Full moon at night and cold. Nips say no exchanging now for gold etc. probably because of disease. Another case of diphtheria in afternoon in hold among dysentery patients. Doc got some M&Bs 693s from Nips and gave shots to bad cases. Some have improved a lot but thinks only temporary. He says stops running but doesn't cure. However it might allow them to eat and sleep a little, building up their strength so they can renew the fight. Surely they will get immediate treatment as soon as we arrive. Rumour: we won't land for 4 days. *Another Dutch died in afternoon—17.* Strong rumours Dutch getting off before us and when we get to our destination the rest of us will be split up.

Tuesday November 24, 1942

F/L Groves died during night. He is young officer of our "C" group and rather a brilliant chap. He had had a sore throat for a couple days and yesterday it got a lot worse, although he was walking round. Doc says it was abscessed (septic throat), and he was going to lance it today. It grew during the night however and choked him. *Another RAF died in evening—19.* Very cold on deck today in the wind. I'm now wearing woollen sweater, shirt on top, and golf jacket over all, shorts and slippers. Many chaps haven't long pants and we haven't had those we were promised when we left Java. Those that were at Changi long enough managed to pick up warm battle dress, etc., but we weren't there that long, nor did we have Singapore money.

Food terrible now, practically only rice. I think we can expect a lot of pneumonia soon. All throats were inspected today and Doc says no more diphtheria cases.

We saw land today between 8-9 p.m., to the hour when I predicted it. We should be at Hiroshima by tomorrow night late (if we are going there). There are all sorts of rumours to where we are going so we'll wait and see.

Wednesday November 25, 1942

2 more Dutch died during night—21. Got very cold during night and cold today. Now in inland sea. *Also 1 Brit died during night—22. Diphtheria patient died 12:00—23.* Nip CC says when they dock they will take off all sick and rest will be rodded. Then we must wait on board until results of rodding show negative. Doc says 2-4 days incubation period for dysentery before you can tell from rodding.

Probably get in tomorrow which must be Hiroshima. Nip CC says when he gets back to Java he's going to put in a complaint saying they crowd too many on this POW ship. The food is not good enough and there is not nearly enough medical supplies. There's certainly plenty of grounds for complaint and there's ample proof in the sickness and number of deaths we've had. He's also going to see if people on board during quarantine can buy things.

Very cold up on deck and below today. I'm sure I don't see how some of them stand it without long pants, heavy coat, and some without blankets even. And most of the Dutch have never been out of Java! If we are not supplied with warm things on our arrival, I can't see many lasting the winter.

We anchored at 5 p.m., the Nips saying because of minefields. I put on longs today—too cold in shorts. Rest of convoy has now left us. Don't know just where we are.

Thursday November 26, 1942

Sailed at 6 a.m. and seemed to get into open sea again.

Yank died during night (Alderman)—24. This chap has put up a terrific scrap having been given up by the Docs over a week ago. But his mates have nursed him and given him tinned milk etc. and it's a shame that he died on last lap. Anchored off Moji at 1 p.m. Nip Docs came on board and rodded sick and said 46 going to hospital ship which is anchored alongside. Rest are to be rodded tomorrow at 7 a.m. and we are going ashore in afternoon. He doesn't know where we go from there but he says all POW ships stop here. Weather a little warmer in harbour.

Another RAF died this p.m.—25. There are dozens besides those going to hospital ship who can't walk so don't know what happens if we are to march anywhere.

Friday November 27, 1942

Rodding to start at 7 a.m. but didn't til 12:30. Gale blowing with showers.

One Dutch died last night—26.

Started moving into Moji Harbour at 10 a.m. Docked at 11:45. Started rodding 12:30. C group first off at 4 p.m. 190 of us walked to ferry—about half a mile, including some very sick. 7 of our sick were left to go on hospital ship. I carried sick man's luggage and also gave arm to sick man. We picked up rice and fish lunch on way. Nip with us who spoke perfect English (or should I say American). We were on ferry where all good—(obviously a civvy ferry) for 20 minutes and arrived at Simonoseri at 6. Then walked about a mile on covered overhead way from docks to R.R. station. I was supporting sick man all the way but felt quite strong. Nip (civvy) gave chap next to me pack of cigarettes. By the way, when we got off first ship customs went through our packs and stamped all cigarettes, cigars, tobacco and cards. This struck us as very funny, as though we were trying to smuggle them in.

Left Simonoseri at 7:00 in train. Nip says be on this train til 6 p.m. tomorrow, then one half hour walk then another train maybe all night. Can't figure where we're going but must be off Kyusho Isle. Train accommodation good with 3rd class carriage. Plush seats. Trouble is only 1 latrine and big line-up. Lot of boys very weak. Nip says we were day late coming in and it balled up their schedule. Says we're going to open new camp but didn't say where. When I told him we were technical people he was surprised they were sending us to this camp. We always get the tough breaks—have to open new camp with all these sick on our hands and that means a long wait before relatives informed, before letters allowed home, buying and changing money etc. Red Cross facilities will have to be started though Nip says they are operating in Japan. Coach cold at first but warmed up. Some new cases stomach trouble occurred during night.

Saturday November 28, 1942

Had to get off at Himeji to change trains at 5:45 in the morning. Stood out in cold on square after moving out of station until 9:00 a.m. Nip got us hot tea and we had cold Nip lunch basket consisting of rice and fish and other unappetizing stuff. We also had this for a lunch. Off again on another train at 9:00 a.m. Local stopping at all stations. At 10:30, we pulled into Kobe which at last tells us where we are—on the main island. At 11:00 a.m. at Osaka. At 11:40 morning Kyoto. All along this district an immense amount of heavy industry. Smoke stacks always in sight and at times a forest of them. If we're going by train until tomorrow morning we will be at least as far north as Tokyo.

Another death in train this afternoon at 2:15. Total, 27. Unloaded him at one of stations en route.

Ask Nip (Yank) about postcards, money, etc., but he said nothing to do with him—up to CO of camp. All industrial plants seem to have additions under construction. Nagoya at 4:10 p.m. Unloaded at 6 p.m., at, I think, Cyoti. Walked five minutes, I carrying luggage and supporting sick man. Then got on 2 electric cars which were crowded and only had 1 lavatory. We unloaded again at 8:20 at I don't know where. Then began the worst journey of all. We went up one side and down the other of a steep hill on a single file path. The journey took until 9:45 p.m. People were carrying their own luggage and supporting sick men. The journey must have nearly finished some of the sick, especially after the food we have been getting, and some being sick for three weeks. A lot of them should never have been allowed to start the journey. I was carrying a heavy haversack on my back along with my bedroll and my suitcase in one hand, supporting a man who could hardly breathe because of asthma with the other arm. Finally someone took my case and I carried the sick man. The Nip guards were very decent and carried a lot of our luggage and a Nip lieutenant carried a man on his back for a long time. Everybody made the journey, although I don't see how!! We got on another two electric cars and had a 15 minute journey. Evidently a landslide, or construction of a new tunnel was the cause of our little walk.

We got off and they asked those too sick for further walk of five minutes to fall out. (The rest of us moved off at about 9:45 and marched into a camp about 10:30). We all then lined up and all had to sign an oath promising not to try to escape. The new CC (a lieutenant) read out an address saying this was #3 Tokyo POW camp and that we would be treated according to international law: "But," he said, "we are at war and there may be a lot of things here you will not like." In other words, we would treat you according to international law if we weren't at war. Our spirits went up and then fell again. He pointed out hopelessness of trying to escape and said we would be shot if we tried. During oath they wouldn't let the sick go to latrines. The main trouble, however, was the extreme <u>cold</u>. It was below freezing and a lot of lads weren't dressed for that kind of weather. We also had some officers in late 40s and the whole trip was a bit too much for them.

We were next marched to our new homes. At any rate, they were better than the ship, but terrifically cold. Frame structures 180' by 20' by 14' to eaves built of ¼" rough cut weatherboarding with cracks at frequent intervals. There was a ceiling of same wood and a 6' centre way. A continuous bunk ran each side 1'6" inches from floor and another top bunk 6' above that fed by 12 ladders. The whole hut to accommodate 120 men or each man to have 30 square feet. Not too bad!! 7 electric lights in hut and on bunks layers of grass matting and on top closer woven matting. Quite soft. In centre 3 pits round where we must smoke as no smoking anywhere else in camp. They are to be used as charcoal fireplaces also. We were then issued with 5 blankets each and it's just as well as they would otherwise have been greeted by a bunch of corpses in the morning.

Also given 1 cotton shirt, 1 pair English service slacks (denim) and one heavy service tunic or type. These latter must have been Red Cross issue because some were made in January of 1941 in England and tunics were of all units by buttons. Size varied but my tunic and shirt were small. Some of tunics were latest battle dress and may have been captured in Singapore. We were told to detail one firewatcher each hour and to leave 2 lights on. These orders from Nip sergeant in broken English in husky voice.

We found out there are 85 Yanks from Philippines here who arrived two days ago. They have three officers with them. The camp is still under construction and our huts are only ones finished. (And they just have earth floors) We were told roll call at 5:30!! and it was then 12:30!! So we're still not to have a rest after two days on train with no sleep. We told sergeant this, saying boys very tired etc. and mostly sick but it didn't seem to have much effect. Anyway we all tumbled into bed and were soon asleep in our clothes still. We have been sleeping in our clothes since leaving Taiwan to keep warm and I'm sure many of them have not had their clothes off since then.

MITSUSHIMA CAMP

Sunday, November 29, 1942

We were called out of bed at 5:30 and it was very cold. Later I found ice in the middle of the day!! After roll call we asked if boys could rest today but Nip sergeant said nothing. We hung round until 6:30 and were then given breakfast consisting of stew (vegetable), mostly liquid, but certainly more than we have been getting to date, a mixture of mostly barley with little rice. No tea or water. There was plenty for everyone but it was same old stuff. We all stuck into it because first hot meal since ship! We then hung round some more, not knowing what to expect. Finally we were all paraded outside, including all sick who could be made to stagger. The sick were pitiful but it struck no chord of sympathy in Nippon's breast. In fact one was struck with a stick and sank to his knees. They then divided us into five groups, fourteen each in care of a NCO. The officers were kept separate (first signs of segregation!). The groups had then to change quarters, each one getting a section of a hut to hold 40 men. Officers were given a section at the end of one hut.

Next we all had to strip naked in below freezing weather and be weighed. Height, chest and foot measurements taken outside! Still, it wasn't too bad and the very sick were done in bed. One of our officers has diphtheria now!! And nearly everybody has a sore throat.

Dinner at 12:00 again, stew and barley rice. In afternoon we had to fill in forms in duplicate given same details as on our cards which have accompanied us!! I don't know what they want that for unless it is to compare with our cards. Also continued measurements. S/L Grant asked sergeant if he could see CC about medicines, toilet paper, postcards, etc. Sergeant said he would see but left Dave standing and didn't return. The CC doesn't speak English and it's going to be very difficult to get anything. I can see that. There was ice on water tank at 12:00 noon today.

Supper at 6:30—stew with very little meat content—some vegetables and barley. Now getting mixture of 85% barley and 15% rice which is change from eternal rice!! And I suppose better for us. Evening roll call at 7 p.m. and they chased us to bed immediately after and boy was it cold. Nearly everyone has cold and sore throats and although I had slight sore throat in morning, not so bad during day.

Monday November 30, 1942

Boys were lined up and marched off to work at 7 a.m. Few left behind were put to work in camp. Officers were not taken out to work. Sun appeared from behind hills at 9:30 and it got quite warm, in fact I stripped and had bath in open but water very cold. First time I had clothes off for over week and half.

We had one-quarter loaf of bread at breakfast in lieu of barley. We get bread 3 mornings in 10 and it's a welcome change. Asked Nip Interpreter for charcoal for fires in huts again and he said he would see CC. Also asked him for toilet paper, shop, etc. Very small bit fish with stew at night. Terribly cold and dismal hanging round huts.

In afternoon officers were sent out to work. They also made all officers get out of hut and dragged sick ones out too, even tried to get P/O Bruce out who is at death's door and can't stand up. They tried to push him out and then evidently thought better of it. Sick officers were sent back but rest of us and men went off to work.

Men from #2 hut were weighed and measured during noon and as tiffen late, they got none. I missed my second helping. Pains in my tummy but think just wind. Especially as passing wind and belching all night.

Worked in quarry all afternoon pushing crushed rock down to tracks to be loaded on to buggies. More about job later!! Work not hard as had rest while trucks being loaded but hard on shoes. Our boys spread all over and work under Nip civvies with only one or two guards scattered about. Working hours 7-11:30, 12:30-4:45 with 15 min. break in morning and afternoon. Some of lads working very hard came back tired but feeling good and to bed after roll call at 7:30.

Tuesday December 1, 1942

P/O Bruce died this afternoon. He was one of MVAF and has been with us since Wanerasa. Deaths now 28. He died of diphtheria but has had dysentery as well.

So we have diphtheria with us again!! And only 6 beds away from me!! Nips don't seem much concerned with death, although Nip doctor appeared today and made cursory inspection. Nips produced disinfectant and few aspro tablets, 130T—that's only medicine. Not much use against diphtheria and dysentery!! If we don't get medicine soon there will be a lot more deaths. We have 57 sick out of 190 and Yanks have 40 out of 82!! Surely the Nips will soon realize they can't get the work out of us this way.

Still trying to get interview with CC but no luck. I think he avoids it on purpose. It's a hopeless cause—everything must go through Interpreter and then we must just wait. CO sent in letter today asking for attention for sick, toilet paper, postcards, etc. through Interpreter. Nips say at present this place very difficult to get supplies to but this will improve. There's certainly no Red Cross supplies here. Ask for charcoal etc. every day but none received, although Yanks have had three issues and we have been promised it many times.

Officers were told not to fall in for work this morning but after men had marched off we were called off and set to work digging drain in camp. Going very hard as digging in crushed rocky stuff. Some of officers over 50 and they can't stand that, although I didn't mind. Civvy Nips stood over us and kept us hard at work at all times. In afternoon carried gravel which was very heavy. Two of our officers had to quit because they couldn't stand it. Still it is something to do, but they said we would be treated to international law and that

December 1942. F/L Chater is reading the bible at the first burial service, Mitsushima camp. Note the POW numbers on the backs of the seated men.

says <u>Officers don't work!!</u> So the first break in international law occurs. Nip guards okay except not Interpreter who dragged out sick. Other Nips seem more curious than hostile.

Rumour: officers to get some more administration buildings as quarters when camp finished. This is divided into small rooms. Nip doctor given list of medicine we required and I hope when he returns to his base tomorrow he sends back that medicine so we can do something for our sick and cut down deaths. All throats were gargled this evening with KMNO 4 because of diphtheria death. Scurvy now breaking out quite badly. The Yanks are the worst sufferers from this but some of our lads are getting it. It starts with lips scabbing, tongue splitting and throat swelling. Yanks also have lot beri-beri.

We are in valley with river running through it and entirely surrounded by mountains. Being on the south side of the valley we don't get the sun til 9:30 in the morning and lose it again at 2:00. This will improve during the summer but we won't need the sun then. We cursed the sun a couple of weeks ago at Saigon and now it's our Saviour when it comes up!!

Wednesday December 2, 1942

Buried, or I should say, cremated P/O Bruce today. We had to carry box he was in up mountain about mile to crematorium. Someone is to go up tomorrow for his ashes. He was given Nippon service by a Nippon priest at camp first. Had 3 wreaths from firms on construction here and soldiers of camp. Service was chanted by priest who kept striking on bell and then Nip came and burnt punk sticks on bowl in front of him.

I was appointed #3 hut commander by Nips today to see boys get out to work. Get up in morning ready for roll call. Every 5th day I am CO I must make out forms showing number of men sick and number at work, etc. Nips gave us forms for everybody today which are sort of time sheets for payment of troops, so troops are going to get paid. Nothing said about officers' pay or how we are going to spend money we do get.

Officers are not asked to go to work today though and Nip says no officers work now so our letter must have had some effect though I can't say I like this hanging around a cold camp all day with nothing to do. No books, no facilities for sport, learning Nip or anything and even if we do have dictionaries, etc., it's just too cold to sit still. It's impossible to sit and write or read. You must keep moving. Poor sick who have to get up and go to latrines during night nearly freeze.

We had a curry stew at noon and it was very good. More vegetables now than we've got since POW but mostly a radish (white) which I think causes wind and some diarrhoea. I know I've had wind and pains in stomach for last two days. So cold at night you dribble and pillow is all wet in morning and throat is also sore every morning, but this goes away after breakfast.

Although officers don't go to work now they won't let us go to bed during day, and don't know why as that's the only warm place there is except for small wood fire contractors build and round which few of us huddle like pictures you see of refugees from floods, war, etc. They don't seem to be making much effort to finish the camp. There are only about 3 carpenters working each day and they jump from building to building and they do work like blazes and certainly shove the place up, but very jerry-built—the slightest wind could blow it down.

They're supposed to be putting in a bath house with a boiler for warm water and the boiler arrived today. Most of Yanks have lice from lack of baths and although none of us have as yet, I shouldn't think it will be long, as most of us haven't had a bath since we left Singapore. I don't see the bath house being ready for awhile yet, then with 600 here we won't get one very often.

Thursday December 3, 1942

Cpl. Cross died today—No. 29. He died of pneumonia and I shouldn't wonder getting up in this cold to go to latrines with his dysentery. Still no fires in our huts. Thick stew at tiffin and bread issue of ¼ loaf per man this morning. Stews not bad now but all same, and barley every meal except on bread morning days.

Pay sheets not working yet, although eventually they will—starting <u>today</u>. Nip came in at night and said phoning hospital and to pick 4 men to go to hospital in case accepted. Also to send 5 samples stools with them of 5 more sick. This was good news and looked as though visit of Nip doctor was having results, although a good deal more than four should go!

It's so damn cold I can hardly write but must keep up diary now. Can't sit for very long though. Nips said F/L Dane and Veepal (STC) must be two to go.

Some old Nip boots issued to some of men this morning but not nearly to all those that need them. Half Yanks have not even socks and I don't see how they work without them. Luckily I have hung on to my stockings and still have a few pairs.

Funeral service for one of the first men to die at Mitsushima camp, December 1942. The civilian company for which POWs were forced to work sent flowers for about the first three casualties. After that, the bodies were simply placed in a wooden box and taken to the crematorium where a few words were spoken over them.

Friday December 4, 1942

We are called out every morning at 5:30 but Nips never get round for roll call until 6:15. So we stand and freeze the rest of the time. I can see no reason for getting up before 6:00, but orders are orders. It's dark when we do get up. Stew is making me get up to go to latrines three times a night and it is cold. Sleep with all my clothes on except tunic and even then feet are cold, especially since hut is so jerry built and doors swing open all during night.

Nips at 7:15 said four men and orderly to catch 8:00 a.m. train to go to hospital. This was good news so we got them ready. Journey will be in warm train and will last until 6 p.m. so looks like Tokyo. They say will be cured and back again in week. (Oh yeah). We fixed Dane up but I don't think he will last. Then the four men had to be carried—up hill—for 15 minute walk to station. They don't even dig out their sole lorry for the occasion but they at least got on train okay. Hope to get dope from medical orderly who is coming right back.

Rumour: Nip told Yank we're only here for 2 months and then change for other group. I hope so! But don't believe it. Anyway, if they don't get us some medicine, decent food, (fruit, milk, sugar, etc). we won't be here in 2 months, only our cremated ashes.

Nips took Bruce's ring and watch and said sending to England!!

It rained today and boys were sent home. Thank goodness. If they hadn't been and had got wet they would all have died of pneumonia as there are no drying facilities. Nip Interpreter kept out of way all day so we couldn't tackle him about anything. Came in at night and signed pay sheets for yesterday and today. Up to date with diary now, but awful struggle!! Eventually pay sheets signed for all days worked since arrival.

Saturday December 5, 1942

Nips allowed us to cook barley meal for sick who can't eat stew or other barley. It's made by boiling ordinary cooked barley and tastes like Roman meal. Trouble is we can't get sugar enough for it. Nips put a little sugar in it but not nearly enough. Still sick ate it and enjoyed it far more than they did stew. Salt salmon at noon which is a welcome change. I have slight diarrhoea but I think it's due to a lot of stew.

Cpl. Skeleton "Chippy" died today. Deaths now 30. He was a good worker and cheerful chap. It's tough luck because it's just through lack of medical supplies and attention, diet. Doc says all this diarrhoea is scurvy and not dysentery because no temperature. He's probably right because we've had nothing out of which to get vitamin C. All vegetables are boiled even though we're getting lots now — we're probably not getting any fruit now at all. Skeleton probably got pneumonia at last from running out to latrines. Can't get at Interpreter at all. He runs away saying he's busy whenever you go to request anything, and it's heartbreaking. You see lads dying in front of you and you can't do anything about it.

Cpl. Bullock who went with sick to hospital came back today. He says they went to Matamoto Hospital about 145 miles N.W. as far as he could judge. Hospital framed building with plaster but he saw 11 Docs and they started in fixing sick right away but diet for them was not so hot. They arrived at 3 p.m. with one hour off travelling time, 6 hours actual travelling. Saw no other POWs. Dane and Veepal stood journey well but not too good when he left. When they got into hospital they read out order threatening to shoot them if they escaped. And they couldn't stand up!! More and more sick at camp and still no medicine at all, although someone saw big box with Red Cross come into camp.

Sunday December 6, 1942

Diary at last up to date. I had pains in my stomach and diarrhoea last night. Also sore tongue today. Hope I haven't got scurvy.

Nips brought in shovelful hot embers last night and said we could have a fire. We were allowed to collect small wood scraps but when we lit them it smoked the hut out because there are no vents in the top of the hut. And the same thing happened today.

Another death this morning — total 31. He had diarrhoea (Gnr. Mackey) but finally died of diphtheria — so we haven't seen the last of that.

In our weak condition we are prey to everything that comes along. One of Yanks now has appendicitis. I don't know what the Nips will do about that. He's in a bad way.

S/L Grant sent in another letter to CC stressing need for medicine and toilet paper. Have also asked for special buckets for washing dysentery patients' clothes. At present they all are done at same place as dishes washed. Keep asking for this but nothing done.

Very cold today and no sun. I was Officer in Charge of camp and also fire watcher at 12:30 at night. Miserable day 'cause nothing to do and yet you can't keep still or you would freeze to death. I thought Java was bad with incessant heat, but give it to me now!! Cold weather is okay if you're dressed for it.

Another Nip doctor from Matamoto arrived at 8:30 p.m. He is going to inspect sick tomorrow. We all hope that something will now be done towards getting medicines, serums, etc. At least he talks which is more than the other one did. Says he has isolated a new bacteria from four sick already in hospital and that it attacks those who are not fit. This may be only propaganda, of course, but he's inspecting all our sick and ordering some to work.

Monday December 7, 1942

Nip Doc examining all sick, sending some to work, and giving others so many days' rest. Says parasite causing all diarrhoea. Trouble appears in stool. Says we can't get any fruit because of war, but I have seen thousands of oranges while travelling in this country. Says to give scurvy patients juice of raw radish and raw cabbage. We are getting enough vegetables now but all in stew form and that kills the vitamin C. He doesn't say anything about supplying us with vitamin C or B tablets. Says we should chew raw carrots but so far the Cook House won't give us these. Think some of our chaps to go to hospital. Nip Doc says four chaps who went to hospital from this camp are getting better which is good news because they were in a bad way. Shows what good food, warmth and proper attention will do and I hope sets example to people running this camp. So far boys have had no time off although Nips don't seem to be working last two days, probably celebrating anniversary beginning of war.

Rumour: we won't get any more bread—that is blow because we look forward to that. Can understand not getting flour although I should think they could make barley bread.

Just had look at some of chaps being examined—stripped by Nip Doc and some of them, especially Yanks—are in a shocking state—just living skeletons, nothing more, suffering from beri-beri and dysentery. Yanks CO is suffering and Nip Doc has promised him vitamin B injections every day. You can understand people getting thin when they go to the latrines 3, 4, 5, times an hour.

It's hard to put on paper the conditions that prevail. If people aren't around when food is dished out they just don't get any. It's not a case of saving some for a pal. They're like a bunch of wolves, nearly all common decency such as sick first has disappeared and it's now every man for himself. You can understand it in a way when they see chaps wasting away and dying. It must scare them and they naturally tend to ram away all the food they can lay their hands on to prevent wasting away.

Control of men is more and more difficult from officers' viewpoint. Nearly every order is carried out insolently. Our sick averages 40%, the Yanks 55%, which is terrific. I don't see how they expect to get much work out of us at that rate. They don't see that plenty of good food and warmth is best way of getting good work out of us.

I don't know what Nip coolies eat but they are terrific workers and shift immense weights and stick at it all day. They don't see, however. that we were in a very weak condition when we came here and also that most of us have never done hard manual labour while the Nips have been at it all their lives. They give us no time to build up our strength. Hence more and more men can't stand the pace.

I don't know if I mentioned it but filling I had put in at Semplak came out on 28th November. I asked Nip Interpreter at the time if there would be any facilities for repairing where we were going and he said no, he needed his teeth fixed and couldn't get them done. So it looks like false teeth for me if we don't get out of here soon!!

Six were picked to go to hospital by Nip doctor—2 diphtheria cases nearly dead (Casey) and haven't had anything to eat for weeks were put down as 7 days' rest then go to work. The irony is they won't be alive then!! Whereas hospital treatment now would save them. Our Doc is to collect medicine he requires daily from Nip medical orderly. He is not even given it in bulk. Sun marvellous today but only from 9:30 till 2:30!!

Altogether medical inspection bit of farce. Nip Doc examines nearly all men and gave them varying time: rest, then examine and go to work. Some very sick are to go to work tomorrow, for example, Street. Others, not very sick, get week's rest.

Tuesday December 8, 1942

A year since war in east started and it hasn't been much of a year for me and, I imagine, mine. Also 9 months today since I was taken prisoner!! My heart is still fair but must crack soon under strain and poor food. If it does—hari kari!! I've had diarrhoea now for about week but only go about 3-4 times a day—I don't think it's a disease but just change of climate and diet. Everybody now has a certain degree of it. Some of sick sent to work this morning had to return which is what we expected. Street, doing light duties around camp, collapsed. My feet sore today on soles. Don't know what causes this but I don't think anything serious. Doc says nobody to go to hospital at Matamoto which means three diphtheria cases remain in camp and we don't know if we are going to get serum for them. Soon we will all have diphtheria at this rate. Going to make No. 1 barrack a hospital (without fire!) and putting 70 of the more serious cases in first. Yanks to move to No. 2 hut where there will now be 101 and some from No. 2 to No. 3 (my hut) making 91 in that. Sensible idea but if some of our chaps don't get medicine soon they will pass out.

At noon today all diarrhoea patients had dose of salts. They were then told they were to have nothing to eat for 24 hours. They could only take the liquid from the stew. This is recognized treatment for diarrhoea.

Nip doctor says we are to get boots and socks soon. Says can't get sugar or barley gruel. Also says can't send letters home and didn't seem to know much about Red Cross supplies. Says he is going to arrange for toilet paper when he goes back.

Had lots of onions in our stew at noon. Still have salt which was brought from Java, which helps, although at rate other officers are using it (without asking) it won't last much longer. However I told them off about it because they had as much chance as I of bringing it.

It looks as though even when we do get a shop, there's no fruit, sugar, etc.

Big flap at camp this morning. Nips made us clean out camp saying Tokyo commander was coming. Asked Dave to get letter ready to hand him re Red Cross, letters, etc. but he got here before it was ready. Just looked through huts and went away. Didn't have any badge, rank or recent star so maybe civilian attached.

Nip doctor says snow at Matamoto now and will be here soon. Coldest month here is February, according to him. Says we are high up in mountains which accounts for intense cold. After supper all sick were transferred to No. 1 hut. We had arranged for filling up No. 3 hut from No. 2 and Yanks to go from No. 1 to No. 2. After half doing this Nips came along and started pushing Yanks into No. 3. We asked him if we could do our original scheme and he said okay so started reverting to that. Then, another Interpreter came along and changed back again so we now have Yanks in No. 3 and terrible mix-up over tenko at night, sending people to hut and dragging them out again.

Put diphtheria patients in small building at back as isolation.

Wednesday December 9, 1942

Bread in morning so rumour no more bread—Balls! Rumour we will only be here 2 months then we move out but I can't see it. Why all this building etc. if going to do that?

Gnr. Casey died today—32—one of cases Nip doctors said to have seven days' rest and then work.

I thought they were signing his death warrant. Buried or cremated in afternoon. Another journey up hill with 15 men carrying him in box. These men are paid and it happens nearly every day so Nips losing by treatment and consequent deaths.

First snow flurries. It brought back memories of Canada and when I used to rush and dig my sleigh out of the cellar at the first snow. First snow not so pleasant now!!

New Nip here today who dug officers and others out of barracks and made them work all the time and rapping them with sticks.

Weather miserable and no sun. Seems to be a lot of civvy type soldiers here now—a lot of yelling and slapping.

Diarrhoea patients are always taken out of hospital and lined up outside to take medicine which is cruel in this cold.

Thursday December 10, 1942

Very cold last night. Heavy ice film 1″ thick on buckets. (I was cold all night with 5 blankets and ground sheet on top me). But I'm right next to the door which is bad. Water pipes were all frozen in morning so could get no water to wash or wash plates or cook stew so had cold fish meal and at tiffen same as last night.

Some Nip medical officers around this afternoon. Also a full colonel. A lot of sick were dug out and made to work round camp during visit. Now have not nearly as many sick but two men collapsed on job today and carried back dead out with cold and weakness.

Officers working round camp again. My hands so cold I can hardly write but must keep going. Funny thing I had my first wet dream two nights ago—for about six months!! Of all places and times!! My diarrhoea seems to be better now as had first bowel movement in two days and seemed nearly firm. Put on a pair of my shorts under long pants today and better. I must make some mitts soon as my hands frozen and chapped to blazes. Been darning socks for last 3 afternoons which is very difficult when hands are so cold.

Still not getting any fires in huts except sick hut sometimes. Must go to bed after tenko at 7 p.m. but just as well cause nothing to do and too cold to do it if there was. So everybody glad to get into bed.

Sick and medical officers dragged out to do coal shovelling this afternoon Still no sign of any result from our letters to CC. Shoes and socks now big problem. Nips have issued some of their army type to some of worse cases but, of course, they have only small sizes. They say shoes and socks coming but they always say that.

Friday December 11, 1942

No work in morning. In afternoon cleaning up two new barracks. Later Nip CC came up and said men not saluting him and to announce at tenko. Also said we could move into new barracks in walled in section. Ten of us in a room with one door but hope warmer. At least we will be eating separately. Also said officers could go out on job to keep healthy but need not work. This was good thing and says we could go in batches. Asked Interpreter re Red Cross and he says coming but can't do anything yet because camp not finished!! I don't know why!!

Appointed Sgts. and told them their duties. Nips read out new rules, evidently got out by new I/C Nip W.O. medical orderly who seems good chap and knows what he is doing. Boys to wash after going to latrines, or meals, keep out of sick quarters, gargle in morning and after p.m. tenko. This is all very fine but half the time there is no water due to frost.

Had to put boxes out of each hut and fill with water for fire protection. But put too close to hut in my opinion. If the buildings ever start here there won't be any stopping them.

I was Officer of the Day today.

Today got raw onions at noon, raw carrots and parsnips. Stew of vegetables at night but vegetables very badly cooked. Barley at night but also far undercooked.

Bit warmer today.

Asked Nip Interpreter if we could have special meals for Christmas and he said thought so but not sure.

Saturday December 12, 1942

Nice and warm in our new quarters but also think weather warmer. I had pain in my tummy all night probably due to all the raw vegetables I ate yesterday. Had good w.c. this morning and pain gone.

Officers work at cleaning up in morning. Sixteen Yanks kept back to do washing this morning but were working, cleaning camp. I asked about this yesterday. Also working on camp in afternoon. But anyway, there's no hot water to be got in the camp for clothes washing and I tried washing things in tap water (35 degrees F) and you can't get the dirt out. And besides, there has been no soap issue. It's very seldom you can get a kettle full of hot water after a meal and that pumped directly from river to high level tank is undrinkable. I'm afraid if it was we'd all be dead by now!!

Sgt. Stannard died this morning—33. He got diarrhoea last day on boat and had it ever since. Nip gave bad diarrhoea cases Yank equivalent of M + B today and he may have been too weak to take it. He collapsed in latrines.

Nip medical orderly says reason medicines hard to get is English, Yank and Dutch supplies running out. (I don't know if he means captured or Red Cross) and they have very little of their own. I don't think I mentioned it but the Nips produced some diphtheria serum 2 days ago and a diphtheria case was given a shot. He seems to be doing okay now. Anyway, story couldn't get serum in this part of the world all balls!!

Nip made issue of one cotton sheet, single bed size, per man and 1 pair cotton long drawers. Will be handy but can't imagine Nip army issue fitting me. My feet got sore on balls today. Wore my tennis shoes to see if studs in others were doing it and at first I thought okay but later very sore. Must be chilblains or lack of some vitamin. Breakfast and tiffen—stew—very weak and just a little cabbage and onion.

Sunday December 13, 1942

Spent day in bed as feet too sore to walk on. Dutch Doc inspected them and said probably due to cold. Feet now thawing out and hence pain. Terrific heat coming off feet all day.

Nip Second Lieut. Doc here from Matamoto and says two of the people we sent there have died. One was Williamson, but Dane still okay— 35.

Nip CC around in flurry in morning and wanted to know why, besides 50 sick in hospital, there are 50 sick in billet. We explained that they weren't allowed to go and see Doc in hospital and Doc also sick and couldn't be expected to run round. Said only way would be to have men sick in billet inspected in morning before working and pass as fit for work or not.

They kept saying camp would be finished in a few days and then boys would all get hot bath (nobody has had a bath since arrival here) etc. and everything would be lovely in the garden—inferring we weren't cooperating with our end by letting boys shirk work. We tried to explain that the lads had had a very rough week with poor food and were weak and not able to stand up to continuous labour. But nothing would appease them so Doc inspected as many as possible yesterday.

Monday December 14, 1942

Cal Wake died and 1 Yank (Burke) this morning—37. This is far higher death rate than on board ship. The facilities for cure are very little better than ship and they must also fight cold. Nip Doc inspecting everybody again today—if it's the same as last time, ordering people to go to work in seven days, who die at end. It won't be much help. Now have two diphtheria cases and doing okay cause have serum. Nips brought in charcoal last night for a fire.

Nips say we will have fire in all huts soon. Every hut got bit of charcoal last night. Stew this morning terrible. All vegetables being raw.

Monday December 21, 1942

This is now December 21 and I haven't touched the diary since the 14th. On the15th in afternoon I went to bed feeling chilly and weak. I developed diarrhoea with nightly fever and have been running ever since. So happenings will be run together more or less. On 17th the Tokyo Commander of Prison Camps came—a full Col. with other staff. The lads were brought back early from work and had to line up outside administration building at 9. They were then drilled in Nipponese and let go. Called back again about 10:45 and finally he

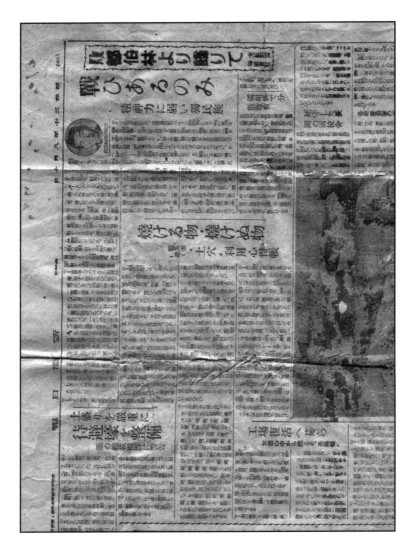

A Japanese newspaper, similar to those sometimes seen in the camps, which Les Chater was determined to learn to read.

came. He inspected them then made a speech saying, as usual we mustn't forget we were at war (as though we could), and that it was Japan's intention to exterminate our countries. But we were prisoners of war and we would be treated as such. But Japan was short of a great many things and we would not get eggs, bacon, milk, etc. (we more or less knew this). We must obey orders and work hard and not try to escape. Not very encouraging to us.

Then he inspected us in our billets. (I was sick in bed of course). After, he called out the officers and had a friendly talk with them. He said we would probably only be able to buy a few things at shop such as towels, hankies, bread and candy. We were getting better rations than the Nip civvies. He said we would not have to do menial duties but he would like to see some of us go out with men leading parade. We asked if there was separate camp for officers and he said no. Only for Generals and that was same as this. We brought up tobacco ration and he said would be seen to. He said couldn't buy wood from outside as on rations, same as army reservists. When asked about Christmas, he said holiday and service would be arranged through CC. When asked about learning Japanese, said we would be issued with sheets and also would get daily Nipponese newspaper. Said we could change money and could buy "daily necessities of life." Re Red Cross—said there had been lot of talk about it but nothing done. Re English books, they were scarce in Japan but they were being collected and would be distributed in our "Red Cross parcels." Nobody knew what he meant by latter. Opportunity would be given shortly for us to write home so after that interview you can bet we felt better!

Chris Power walked round with him and picked up following, mostly from Interpreter, same one that brought us here!! Said other camps were colder than this, some being issued with eight blankets and all had snow. Said men were working on roads, factories, anything at all. We were only camp allowed fires. This camp was very inaccessible and if they did get us things it was almost impossible to get them to us. Said bread was becoming part of staple diet but could not get flour now and fish getting hard to get. Nips are trying to get POW to eat more barley as more vitamins in it than rice, said he'd never seen a poorer body of people than we were when we got off boat. That seems to be lot from the Colonel's visit.

On 14th Interpreter came in with large forms which COs have now got to fill in. They were pay sheets for two months and they had been transferring data for men's pay sheets to these and got tired doing it. More work for us, which we wouldn't mind except we've got to do it in cold when men are here. Later he said could fill in from data collected on working parades which means can do during day.

Officers were hauled out to work on the 14th and I got kick in shin for not stooping to pick up frozen stones. (I was kicking them loose). On 15th Interpreter came in at 8 p.m. and wanted immediate data about ships we came to Japan on to phone to Tokyo!! P/O Scarlett told him bad food, no warm clothing, medicine, etc. I hope the account enables others to have a better run and hopes of survival when they get there!!

Cpl. Singleton died on 17th, a Yank. Yesterday, J.M. Smith, and we received word that all four who went to hospital are now dead, so total is now 41.

So F/L Dane is dead!!

Today, Nip took out postcards and waved them in front of lads and said they were soon to be issued: "Now go out and work hard!!"

Tuesday December 22, 1942

Feeling better today. Got up at 10:45. Only got up twice during night. Been taking bismuth tablets (2 three times daily).

Food has been very poor lately, most of the vegetables being raw and rice ration has been greatly cut. I'm sure boys aren't getting enough rice these days. Actually meals today were better—curry stew for tiffen and couple small bits meat. First meat in two weeks. I think reason vegetables aren't being cooked is because of scare of beri-beri and scurvy. Since Nip being here vegetables uncooked and it's not so good when you get them that way nearly every day. No bread since 15th. Nips promising us bread, cake, baths, cigs, etc. for Christmas. I imagine still no facilities for warm bath. I haven't had my issue shirt off since I came here. Now sleeping in that, sweater and socks and pyjama pants but damn cold.

Sickness was awful. Had sickness all night and went to w.c. maximum of 20 times in 1 day. It was awful squatting in w.c.'s in sub-freezing weather and then just getting back into bed and having to get up again. You have no control over your bowels and most of the time I just made the latrines. Most of chaps miss out at least twice during sickness and make mess and then they have to undress in freezing latrines and there's no facilities for washing clothes. Some of lads have been going for weeks like this and get too weak to get up. I know I felt damn weak after 7 days. You have pains in your stomach all the time. I think the main thing to do is to keep eating to keep your strength up. If the sick in this camp could get good food for a few days I think they would all get well. I'm sure eggs and bread could be got and perhaps sugar but nothing gets done. They must have dry, plain, rice, uncooked etc., and sometimes its very difficult to get hot water.

Great excitement at night. Interpreter said we would be allowed one postcard and letter of 2 pages, one side only, every 4 months. We are to say how well we are being treated by the Nips and how sick we are of the war (this will be true, at any rate). We will be issued with paper, etc. on Christmas Day.

Wednesday December 23, 1942

F/L Ackland getting worse. He can't get up to go to work now.

Working bit round camp in morning, sharpened razor for Nip and one for myself. Nip came in and asked me to shave him with razor I had sharpened for him which I did. Sid Marvin fixing watches for Nips now and gets brazier in our quarters to do it, which makes it nice during day. But don't know how long this will last.

Took over #3 hut again tonight. Men now have to number in Nip.

Stew a bit better today but not hot and not so much of it. Nip now giving up his left over food which is very fine. Last night chicken (bite each) and good rice. Their stew is always cooked.

At 4 p.m. Nip Interpreter told us to get out drafts of postcards and hand them in by tenko (7:00). We did, saying we were fit, anxious to see end of war, being treated kindly and well!! And we mostly asked for marmite, cocoa, bovril, oxo, saccharine and food concentrates to be sent. Interpreter said draft sent as sample asking for these was okay.

My diarrhoea about same—3 times a day. My appetite back to normal now.

Thursday December 24, 1942

Filling bath house and put fire in boiler. Got fire going well but found bad leak between concrete and pipes. So fire was put out and water emptied.

I'm feeling better now and appetite back, although still loose. Interpreter appointed P/O Dunlop O/C bath house and said light fire 9:00 in morning and officers bath at 12 noon, then Sgts. etc. Tenko not until 7:00 a.m. and Christmas Day holiday.

We are getting left overs of Nip food being brought in by Nip guard. They have very good food and one day some chicken.

Friday December 25, 1942

What a Xmas!! I hope it's the last I spend under these conditions. Had normal breakfast but curry stew and bread for tiffen. They also issued 10 cigs per man, for which we signed. We didn't get any carbon and haven't had any now for five days. Tiffen at night had meat stew tasting like venison. Lads not getting enough boiled water to drink now. Some have been five days without a drink and many meals there is no water at all.

We were all dragged out and weighed again today and I should say the results would shock them. Most of the lads look like skeletons. I know my weight has dropped a lot, especially during last week. Not a quiet day of rest for lads at all.

Filled baths (a concrete box 20' x 10' x 3') which is heated by flue pipes from boiler and started fire. Interpreter then made us put out fire and clean out bath, then fill and relight fire. Finally bath was ready at 3 p.m. and officers climbed in. It was grand. You rinsed yourself with buckets, soap, then wash off, then climb in and soak. It's hard to get out but after we all felt better. Interpreter came along in middle and raised Hell because we had got in before telling him. But when Dunlop had gone to see him he was asleep. Also it seems we were all to have our hair shaved off first and there was a row about that. Actually the bath was going til 6:30 but not everybody got one.

The cakes and oranges didn't turn up. Postcards were issued in p.m. at night. We had a big fire in front of administration building as we had asked for yule log and Nips dragged every-body out but only very few got near the fire. We sang carols and other songs and danced around. Tenko was not til 8, but we all wished it was earlier because we weren't enjoying it. And so ends Christmas Day, 1942.

Saturday December 26, 1942

We wrote our postcards today. I asked for concentrated foods, vitamins, etc. Told people not to worry and addressed to Mother. I hope we get home before the postcards. Oh yes.

Yesterday Nips brought us in copies of *Japan Times Advertiser*, a Nip paper printed in English. Dates—Dec.4, 5, 7, and 8. The news was interesting and very cheering, especial-ly of our big attacks in North Africa, scuttling of French fleet etc. This was best Christmas present in lot.

Two oranges per man were issued today. Stew good again at night being full of meat. I was Duty Officer today. We all had to turn out in afternoon and clean up garbage bins. Boys' shoes getting very bad. Some walking in stocking feet and now working in water. Nips have issued Nip army shoes (second hand) for those with small feet but those with size 9 and over are out of luck. They keep saying shoes and socks are coming from Tokyo but they never turn up.

Sunday December 27, 1942

Handed in our written postcards in morning. D.O. says Interpreter has discarded about 120 because we run sentences over 1 line. This means only about 80 got through. Some however who ran sentences over got okay so we don't know exactly why they were turned down. Only four officers' cards out of sixteen were accepted. Mine was turned down. It is certainly hard luck when we haven't sent any word home yet. We haven't given up hope yet. It's no use putting in a letter to the CC because it must go through the Interpreter and he won't listen to any complaints. We still don't have any toilet paper issue and it's getting serious. We haven't had any carbon issue for nearly a week now, so all freezing. Nips hard to fathom. One day they will slap you and next they are nice and give you cigs.

Great excitement in afternoon 50 packets of 6 smaller packets (total 300) Red Cross parcels came in. Marked for British and Dominion POW Far East, South African Red Cross, from Lorenzo Marques. The Nips opened one and there were 2 packets sugar, tin of margarine, bacon, gelatine, biscuits, marmalade, soap, chocolate bars and other things. They were put in store and we are all looking forward to an early issue. It has cheered us up no end.

Days getting colder and sun not so often now. My diarrhoea cleared up now and going once day but still loose. Thank God I got over it. Rice short these days and poor troops aren't getting enough to do work on. But we were told if we complain against food it would be cut.

Yank was caught breaking into stores and was beaten up badly by Nips. Then all his clothes except shirt and pants were taken away and he was thrown into guard room. The officers had to take an hour each during night guarding him and was it cold standing in open! He deserves all he gets but it will probably kill him with the cold as he has no blankets.

Monday December 28, 1942

Red Cross not issued today. Asked Nip Doc this morning and says will send toilet paper. Interpreter grabbed me and took me into bath house. He talked with CC for awhile and then he told me to fix leak. I asked him for tools (hammer, chisel) and he said haven't got, get from boys. They seem to forget we are POWs and expect us to carry everything around with us. Don't seem to have any tools round here and I don't know why they don't chase contractors to do the job they messed up. Anyway, we shoved some concrete into vicinity of leaks and hoped for best.

Sick increasing again. No wonder with this cold and food shortage. Sick quarters nightmare because so cold and those with squitters have terrible time getting up and going in to cold latrines. In fact, it is killing them.

Tuesday December 29, 1942

Coldest night yet, I should say. About 15 degrees frost. No water as all frozen up, so no wash, and no dish wash. Cutting paper for Nips today to cover cracks in buildings.

Nip medical orderly left tonight and Interpreter came round huts telling us to thank him for what he had done for us.

New Nip guard appears quite decent and with Dave doing sketches for them and Sid Marvin fixing their watches the "Shokos" do quite well with cigs. They even brought in their left-over rice and stew in morning for us. They will give cigs just to look at pictures of your wife. They all want to see wife's picture, her nationality, how many children, ages, etc. Storemen says we get Red Cross parcels on 1-1-43. Let's hope so!! Helped do up bundles of Nip canteens which they appear to be shipping away.

Food very bad today. Cold meals at breakfast and tiffen and weak stew at night.

Wednesday December 30, 1942

Bad show at breakfast. Just as food dished out Interpreter who was Nip Duty Officer, got men out of billet to do Physical Training. Then of course, food got cold and as they were coming back in to eat it they were turned out again to go to work. So most of them didn't get any breakfast to speak of.

Two more deaths during night. Total 43. F/L Ackland died of dysentery and Almaroff of shock after hysterics. (He was recovering from dysentery). I went to Ackland's cremation and it was ghastly. He was just a bundle of skin and bones and it was unbelievable. They put him in the urn and put wood and charcoal on him. His ashes will be collected later.

We unpacked Red Cross bundles. I hope it means they will be issued soon. The Storeman says January 1, 1943.

Cold meal of fish and rice and onions at tiffen and at night barley and onions raw. Reason for Nips using all cookers to do cakes for themselves for New Year's Day. But certainly hard on lads—also no hot water to drink.

Bath day and bath was ready for officers at 4, but Interpreter said not hot enough. Asked him to look at it again at 4:20 but said he was busy. Then he came and called us to bath just as our food was dished up so we had to leave it and come back to cold food. Putting men through bath very slow as tie-up in small dressing room. Water also gets cold as people get out to soap and swill and bath must be filled up with cold water. We put through about 100 and none of the others wanted one. This took from 5:00 to 7:30, so how they expected us to run 260 through, less sick (40) from 5-8, I don't know as the place is too small.

Interpreter raised blazes with tenkos in p.m.

Thursday December 31, 1942

Window in Cook House broken by #2 billet man, so cooks lined up all of that billet and punched them. Then punched V.O.D. and D.O. Captain Hewitt. Hewitt started off to see CC to complain but was headed off by #1 cook and Interpreter. Letter or no letter re this! They were going to make billet go without food re this but Hewitt persuaded them not to, saying only one man had broken window. Officers were shortened very much on our food issue in the next few days. Have had no bread since 25th. Looks as though finished. Announced at tenko holiday three days.

Tunic and slacks issued to every man. They are of light silky material to suggest type used by factory worker. Told by storekeeper English issued with 5 blankets while Yanks 6. He promised to have one more for English.

Lots of Nips going away on leave for three days, including Interpreter. Went to bed 8:00 on New Years Eve!!! One of Nips brought in some saki (wine) for us. Sometimes Nips very decent and then turn around and bite your head off. You can never weigh them up.

Friday January 1, 1943

New Year's Day! Let's hope this year will see peace again! Tenko at 7 in morning—all issued with 5 cigs. Understand present from contractors. Also had bath this morning and all others that wanted one. Nips celebrating and all drunk. Supper very late owing to #1 cook passing out with keys to store on him!! Didn't think we would get any!! Meals poor all day so cold ones.

Red Cross parcels issued to all (255) today. Thank Gawd. That leaves 45 in store—we signed for 300 earlier in day. One was nearly empty and two more only partly full. This pilfering must have taken place in England, however, because outside wrapping of 6 parcels was okay. We agreed with Interpreter on this. Boys spirits very high due to parcels and bath. They were even saluting the officers!! Whereas insubordination and bad language to us has been terrible.

Each parcel contained, with slight variation—1 tin of tomatoes, margarine, pudding, meat and vegetable, syrup or jam, cheese, biscuits, chocolate bar, creamed rice, bacon, meat paste, condensed milk, 2 sugar, 1 bar soap. Most of boys ate the lot on New Year's Day.

I was O.D. today and Interpreter said during holidays all cracks in billets must be pasted up with paper strips officers cut. Got paste (rice) from Cook House and boiled in boiler in sick quarters. This boiler was put in by order of CC to boil water for sick and cook up stews which are sometimes uncooked. Got most of #2 and #3 billets finished today with struggle as most lads too interested in parcels.

Sunday January 3, 1943

At morning Tenko 27 sick or in bed in #3 billet. Nip Officer of the Day raised Hell and beat up those in bed who did not have permission from Doc. This difficult as can't see Doc til 10 morning sick parade. But obviously a lot swinging it. Then put 22 of these in guard room, taking away tunics. Officers had hour shifts guarding. I had warned boys this would happen as number reporting sick at tenko was gradually increasing and yet they got up for food and most went to work. Hut commanders had only right to say who stays from work for 10 a.m. sick parade. Boys in guard room all day, without food, and in cold.

Mitsushima camp, January 1943. F/L Chater is taking tenko, his back to the camera. The village is situated in the hills beyond.

CC around and scurry to clean up camp. Also ordered all officers billets to be papered and sent five men to do. They, of course, couldn't make pinprick in it and had to keep going to Cook House for more paste. I spent most of day pasting my section.

Cotton socks issued to all men today—one pair—no heel type so size doesn't matter.

Monday January 4, 1943

Twenty-two in guard house all night and officers guarding them. Didn't let them out until all boys ready to go to work and then sent them to work without food. So they had no food for 24 hrs. Trouble is some genuinely sick suffered because of other lazy ones. We tried to get Nips to let Doc see all in guard room to say who is really sick but Nips said no. One man collapsed while going to work.

Both tiffen and supper cold meals, raw radish and rice, and raw cabbage, fish and rice.

Tuesday January 5, 1943

My right knee weak. Don't know why. Think I might have twisted in bed.

Cpl. Street died of diphtheria. He had been sick since boat with diarrhoea. Total 44.

Nips say if any not up for tenko who haven't seen Doc, Duty Officer will get guard room. This not so hot on officers!!

Our postcards, or some of them, still on Interpreter's desk!! So doesn't look as though our people will get them for a long time if at all! Cook house has run out of barley so we get rice every meal. Rice more palatable but issue now very small per man. We barely get small bowlful each. Good stew at night with meat. First good meal for a long time.

Lot of thieving been going on with Red Cross parcels but hard to trace. Caught one chap this evening. Interpreter returned.

Wednesday January 6, 1943

Interpreter says nobody, now, to be sick at tenko. If sick, they are to move to sick quarters before tenko. When asked re 45 Red Cross parcels, said these would be issued in about 8 days to those with most diligent slips.

Got English newspaper of Jan. 4th yesterday. Not much news, especially of N. Africa so it looks as if we have cleared that up. Huns reinforcing Pantellaria Island. Nothing re Russia or Far East.

Good stew at tiffen. Uncooked at night. Rice issue still low.

Thursday January 7, 1943

Out getting wood for kitchen twice today. Papering billet. Knee about the same. Weather really colder now than when we came. If you wash your plate and leave it for 5 minutes in the billet, the spoon is frozen to it!! This during day.

Twenty-one stoves and fifteen slightly smaller ones in the store for about week now. Nips say two each are for billets. If so I wish they would hurry up and install. When you ask the Nips when, they say "asita".

Yank died today. Total 45.

Still no shoes. A lot of boys down to socks.

Friday January 8, 1943

Food still short. Barely level bowl rice each meal. Tenko 7:00 and holiday. Supposed to be bath this morning but all water frozen up so couldn't. Details carrying water all day in buckets from river for cooking. No water to wash or clean plates, or do teeth. I'm lucky if I get my teeth done once day now.

All men weighed (stripped) and inoculated in right breast for dysentery. 10 English, 10 Yanks and 10 Chinese and 8 Indians had head and leg measurements taken. God knows what for!!

Inspection by CC in afternoon. We all had to fill in sheets showing all our personal effects. Interpreter says this is to protect ourselves from thieving so we know what each man has. At inspection we were asked what we needed most. Toothbrushes, paste, towels, soap, toilet paper, cigs were mentioned. They asked how many needed boots. Number—65. All agreed food quality okay but all said not enough. Told him less than one small bowl per man per meal. Also asked for salt and concentrated foods. He said reason so much diarrhoea was not chewing food properly. I told him they had not enough time to chew before work. He wouldn't listen to this and didn't pass on to CC. He said we would get more rice, giving each man heaping bowl full but I think there was a stipulation and that was when number of sick grew less, rice issue would increase—it wasn't quite clear. He said we were living under same conditions as Nip soldiers, (no fires) and eating same food and Nip soldiers weren't sick. We know, however, we don't get nearly as much food as Nips, or such good quality, 'cause sometimes we get Nip leftovers given us. And I also pointed out that we were all weak when we came because of boat trip but he wouldn't listen.

Nip CC insistent that pasting in our billet be finished as from now on weather would be cold. God help us if it's going to be colder than it is now. Wood detail in afternoon. Looking at myself when stripped for weighing gave me shock. I've lost a terrible amount of weight—mostly, I suppose, when I was sick. Too bad cause I was in good shape when I left Java.

Re postcards, the Interpreter is still going over them checking the English and he has one of our medical officers helping him so the rejection idea was just to scare us originally.

Everybody has lost lot of weight. Some of them look like skeletons!! Interpreter says last clothes we were issued with are to put on over others to protect them.

Saturday January 9, 1943

Big do at tiffen. Wash place was dirty so Interpreter lined men up in two lines and made men slap each other for about 15 minutes. We couldn't explain that since water still frozen there was no way of cleaning. Terrible job cleaning buckets and of course, no drinking water last 2 days and no water to wash.

Rice issue still short so increase hasn't started!! Bit of barney in officers' mess at night. Major Cory, (Yank) who has been dishing out rice, has been giving himself and friend far more than share. Had meeting and decided mess orderly would do dishing out each day and use measure.

Stoves were moved to each billet today (two each) but not installed. Still this is the first step! Nips brought in lot of tin sheets and evidently make pipes on job.

Monday January 11, 1943

Gave list of things we wanted to buy to Interpreter but he didn't seem interested. Rice issue to men now very meagre. Three buckets for 96 men!! Less than bowl per man. They can't last long on that. Stews also getting thin as vegetables running out.

Rain all day so no work for men. Some men issued with Nip shoes in morning but still a lot running round with no soles, especially large sizes.

Had all men out and Nips were hitting them in the afternoon because they were slow getting out for wood detail. Did pasting today.

Tuesday January 12, 1943

Big rush when news that Maj-Gen medical officer visiting camp tomorrow. Officers were rushed out to work and we cleaned up billet. Rice issues still very short. My knee still groggy but not quite so bad. Weather colder. Men making stove pipes but only stoves yet installed those in administration building. My w.c. visit first in 48 hours and nearly solid. Number of sick still about same—40 in hospital and 6-8 light duty men. Yank taken to hospital 2 days ago with appendicitis.

Wednesday January 13, 1943

Morning very cold but sun. Medical officer turned out to be a captain. Asked one of men in sick quarters if he could eat Nip rice and he said yes, but didn't get enough!! Good show, but I don't think it will make much difference.

Wood detail in afternoon. Shaved.

Barley, rice and few vegetables came in today. For evening meals, some barley and some barley mixed with rice for other meals. This is blow as think barley causes a lot of diarrhoea and can't make rice cakes of it. Rice has been welcome change even though not much of it and we have been making rice cakes in cans which go good with Red Cross stuff. Nips sold us 2 packages sweets at 11 cents each tonight. Very welcome, although small. Hope to get more. We managed to have wood fire every morning and evening which is godsend because we can have tea and cook Red Cross dope.

Thursday January 14, 1943

Stoves now installed in all billets. But issue of coal only 1 pail per billet—2 stoves per day. Men can only have stoves on from 5-7:00 a.m. Officers 4-8:00 p.m. We had ours going tonight and it was grand. Everybody was able to keep warm, especially feet which hitherto were always cold.

Nips say many more shoko coming here. This seems funny place to bring them. Putting more cookers in Cook House so looks like more men are due. Issued more overcoats to us today. Old Nip army pattern with hood. They are very welcome too. Nips say they are for when we go to Tokyo!! Which I doubt.

I was sick all day with chill. Not much sleep at night. Bath day and water very good. Afternoon—150 had bath.

Nip CC called Dave in today. Said those officers who want to work to fill in petition which would be sent to Tokyo. Put down what you want to do. Can't make us work according to convention but we can ask to work at our trade. We talked it over and decided to petition although it may mean separation. Still, if we could be moved from here it would be grand!!

Friday January 15, 1943

We had to fill in another form of name, nationality, unit, rank. Had to take all kit of deceased to Nips yesterday. Say valuables must be turned over to them to send to families. Also clothes—only our bodies are our own.

Still soft in w.c. Knee still bad when much walking. Everybody cooking rice cakes now and they are very good. Done in tin cans from Red Cross packages. Took list of chaps needing shoes—60 immediate cases. Started shoe repairing today. Two men and P/O Marvin. Nips supplied all equipment and leather.

Saturday January 16, 1943

Issued shoes today—30 pairs. I could have got a pair but none big enough. Shoe repairing well under way. Weather not too cold. Stove grand at night. Gave Nip medical officer 20 yen to get cod liver oil tablets. He produced them at 9 p.m.—150 each. He is going to nearby town tomorrow and wanted to know if we wanted cod liver oil with malt and sugar. We said yes and advanced him 70 yen.

Sunday January 17, 1943

Quiet day. Sawmill just re-opened after two-day shutdown and got little wood. Not pouring concrete any more and lads say all they are doing now is clearing up so looks as though rumour work shut down for two months is correct.

Stews very thin now. Probably four bits of vegetables per man. Rice ration still low with barley mixed now with breakfast and tiffen. Cold meal—fish (very small portion) at night.

Monday January 18, 1943

Nip medical officer turned up with 17 bottles of cod liver oil and sugar tablets—120 per man. Also got vitamin tablets for Yanks.

STC lad caught stealing and we handed him over to Nips. Given 20 days guard room which should just about kill him and we have to stand guard with 1 hour shifts every night. Nips say anybody found trading with civvies will be given heavy guard room and to report any civvies trying to.

CC put our wood fire out at 11 this morning. We have been allowed to build wood fire from morning tenko til 4. However admit mistake to keep on sunny days and have been telling chaps so due to shortage of wood.

Just rice with roots in at tiffen—level bowl! Don't expect men can last long at that rate. Diarrhoea patients in hospital only get two meals rice, gruel per day. All along meals to sick have been poorer than ours. I think Nip idea being to make people stay out of there by so doing.

Tuesday January 19, 1943

S/L Grant asked by Interpreter to stay in his office all day and do his work. One consolation he may get some "gen" out of it!!

On duty guarding at 7:30. Nip guards treated me decently giving one cig, 2 biscuits. About 4000 cigs and candy came into camp yesterday and rumour there would be an issue to us. Nips have lots at night and say we get no issue. Impossible to get cigs or tobac (hay) now. Nips smoke hay in small bowl pipes, pea size, and keep filling, getting about 2 drags full.

Tenko at 6 p.m. to allow Nips to attend cinema.

Still fairly loose, but not bad, once day. Put in my petition to be allowed to work.

Wednesday January 20, 1943

Shock re remaining Red Cross parcels. Only 36 now in store!! Cory asked Interpreter when they would be distributed and he said the Nip CC ordered the first distribution of 255 and there would be no more!!! So that's that!

Chau went on sick parade in morning and our Doc said he was fit to go to work in p.m.!! So we must guard again!!

Thursday January 21, 1943

Guard changed and one of old ones came back. New guard seems shy.

Officers allowed stove til 8 p.m. and we still have wood fire for cooking in morning til about 10:30 and from 3:00-4:00.

We cannot buy any cigs no matter what we offer!!

Friday January 22, 1943

Postcards sent to Tokyo. Dave says think all went as big stack. Thank goodness although it will still probably be months before they go!

Boys with diligent slips allowed to buy 1 bag candy.

Interpreter had us in front of administration building doing drill.

Boys were paid today. From stamped sheets. None got what entitled to. Made about 2.50 yen for month. Medical officer brought in more cod liver oil, vitamin C, cough medicine, salve, cost me 12.80 yen but worth it.

Duty Officer today.

Saturday, Sunday January 23, 24, 1943

Having "benjo" at tenko and Interpreter sent for me. Told me that no reason for not attending him. They don't seem to realize that when man has diarrhoea he must go in hurry and can't hold it. Stop taking oil to see if causing diarrhoea. Food now far better since new First Cook. Stews cooked, more rice!!

Tenko at 5:30 and at 6 p.m. Don't know why. Interpreter got all officers to write, without reserve, impressions of war in East!

Using very little Red Cross stuff now since food better.

Discovered I had lice so four of us took off shirt, sweater and underpants and boiled. Now wearing 2 short sleeved shirts and cold. Got lice from Yank officers who brought it to camp.

Interpreter produced sandals about size 5—wooden with straps—worth about 10 cents and asked us to buy, saying especially made in Tokyo for us out of Nipponese kindness. Of course they were no use to us and he wanted 70 cents and 25 cents cartage a pair. We refused to buy and there was Hell to pay. CC was there at time. Hewitt was slapped and we were told we wouldn't be allowed to buy anything else. Ordered no fire in stove tonight. Think because of this.

Persistent rumours we are leaving here February 1.

Had hair clipped today by order of Nips and find it very cold.

Have bad, dry cough.

Still loose but only one or two daily. Sure it's barley. Diarrhoea patients getting wheat.

Monday January 25, 1943

Rice gruel now. Very good but not enough.

New Nip medical officer very helpful and conscientious. Allowed fire in billets again.

Nips gave drink saki to boys with diligence tickets.

Having party so must be Nip festival.

Tuesday January 26, 1943

Holiday. Bath day and I did policing.

360 pair of South African boots—army pattern—newly arrived in cases marked Food for Br. and Colonial POW, Far East. Addressed to Tokyo, Red Cross delegate. Hope they issue them soon as lots of lads nearly in bare feet, especially large size. Shoe parade at meal time. (Everything is done then and meals must wait and consequently cold). Each person only allowed to keep 1 pair shoes!! Slippers and all others turned in. No Red Cross shoes issued.

Speech by CC at 3:30 and issue diligence slips. Then allowed to buy cigs up to 2 for slips. Officers issued with 2 cigs each. I was in bed with bad throat and missed issue.

At night bonfire and those with diligent slips allowed to buy up to 2 packets biscuits at 10 cents. Entertainment around fire more to amuse Nips than our chaps who in outer ring and cold.

Tenko 8:00. Hell raised because some drifted back to billet.

Wednesday January 27, 1943

Lost voice due to bad throat. Nothing much doing. Wood and water fatigues. Chap from sick quarters caught stealing rice from kitchen at night. Took blankets from him for hour. Made all sick sit up while identifying.

Throat painted last two days.

Stews nearly always cold because in window half to one hour before serving. Also Nips now calling officers for fatigues at meal times!!

Nips come to us for all tools etc. pliers, spanners, hammers, paper. I don't know how they expected us to get those things to here! They don't seem to have anything on the job.

Thursday, January 28, 1943

Good thick vegetable stew at noon. Stews have been thin recently. Other meals thin.

Still no voice. Did washing. Think have few lice again but can't find. CC and visiting officers made inspection.

Nice Sun.

Man found with stolen goods put in guard house for one night only!!

Chap who hit NCO reported to Nips and let off with warning!

Sgt. Holmes died of worms and one Yank of diarrhoea. Total—47. Yank's name Krause.

Friday January 29, 1943

Officer of the Day—asked Interpreter if could try to fix frozen pipe to administration building and taps on wash stand. He said okay. Asked for pipe wrench and he produced small adjust spanner only! Started fire under exposed place between Cook House and shoe shop til 4:30. But still frozen. Changed 10 yen note with Nip paymaster. Bought Yank canteen cup.

Much joy when rice and barley mixture for supper in lieu of usual straight uncooked barley. Very good. Hope this continues. Think it result of Nip medical officer telling CC diarrhoea caused by barley and CC's talk with cooks in afternoon. Also each barrack got 6 buckets rice, $^1/_2$ again as much as usual! Boys can live on this even though stew uncooked!!

Think 2 deaths yesterday due to colder weather.

Saturday January 30, 1943

Voice still gone. No sign issue Red Cross boots.

Food still keeps its improvement. 65 kilos rice and barley mixed for evening meal though vegetables in stew not cooked.

Fire under water pipe all day but still no sign running.

Had my sweater and towelling shirt stolen off the line. Searched kit of two suspects but no luck! Now only have Nip issue long sleeve shirt. One or two lice crawl occasionally but not many.

No fires allowed in billet today. Reason given that Officer of the Day had not asked Nip Officer of the Day when we could light them, but we had never been told to ask them that. This seems the only way we get to know Nip orders and it's the hard way. Nip CC now making practice of visiting Cook House during issue of evening meal. He sure is going to make certain we get a square deal on them. I don't think he knew just how little we were getting and how badly cooked it was most of the time.

Sunday January 31, 1943

One of STC Chinese died of pneumonia. Total 48. We will have to be careful of this disease. There are 2 more cases of it and Nips say February and March worst months. They purchased vapour spray for its treatment and officers paid for it.

Weather about constant. Freezing at night and only thawing when in sun.

Monday February 1, 1943

Officer of the Day, Sacamota, made us put out wood fire in billets. This bad blow because ours is the coldest billet. We had been having fires from tenko—9:30 and from 3 to 4:15 to cook tea and orvel and rice cakes. Wrote letter to CC asking if we couldn't continue these fires pointing out cold billet. They let us buy tea but nowhere to brew it. We did all fatigues round camp although according to convention we shouldn't. Offer to purchase wood. Dave took letter to Interpreter and for once he was reasonable. Said Officer of the Day had stopped it, not him. ??? Promised to hand letter to CC. Later he said he showed CC and he had said could have carbon fire for cooking gruel in morning and in afternoon and for tea. We have to buy carbon at 2.50 yen a basket so now our fires are on authorized basis.

Shoe issue today but still of old Nip repaired shoes. Making chaps wear shoes too small for them. Why no issue of Red Cross shoes and parcels?

Very good stew tonight. CC asked Dave if he liked it.

Put in 25 watt lamps through billets.

Interpreter told Dave could not buy clothes or food but would buy him other things (including cigs) when he goes to nearby town at the end of week!!

Tuesday February 2, 1943

Fire in morning again. Thank goodness. Stoves not lit til 5:30 because Officer of the Day not to be found. No coal issue. No thawing fire. Dave bought one basket carbon at 2.50 which might have to last many days.

Left leg badly swollen at ankle and above. It was very sore last night. Had vaporizer treatment. Cough bad during night.

Fire on water pipe again but still not thawed out. Food remains good.

Lots of rumours from job and guards—Roosevelt and Tojo having conference and signing papers and soon we will be packing and going home.

Wednesday, February 3, 1943

Heavy snowfall during night and day—6″. Rain later. Sent lads out in heavy snowfall some with hardly any soles. They didn't work but came back again after 2 hours very wet.

Stoves allowed in billets but not allowed to draw coal, only burn slag (if you can). Cook asked for wood detail from no. 3 billet but they were so long coming he got mad and got all men out of billet standing in rain for nearly hour. Officers got wood.

Had another vaporizer bath which doing me lot of good. But still no voice!! Acquired Yank mess kit.

Nearly all officers have squits today. Four of them didn't get to latrines in time. One person sick twice so I took his guard duty at night. Think because fat in 2 recent stews which our stomachs not used to.

Power came out of hospital yesterday.

Had bath today and changed clothes.

Thursday February 4, 1943

Officer of the Day today. Still no voice. 2 doses carbon for squits. No benjo today. Left leg and ankle swollen away up today but not painful. Doc says lack of proteins or kidneys. Face also swollen.

Ace came out of hospital.

Very wet underfoot as snow melted. No sun. Lots more diarrhoea. (Oil in stew??)

Boot parade but no Red Cross issued.

Three people sick so had to do guard duty—8:30.

At p.m. tenko now Doc inspects light duty and says who can stay in. Sent one chap with infected foot to work. Lads all hate him and think very pro Nip and he does get lot of privileges—own room and fire all day. CC told him he spent too much time in his room and said he must spend most of time from now on in hospital. Orderlies in hospital (4) very strict and uncivil but they have a tough job.

Had numerous squabbles in hut re shoe issues, overcoat and green suit issues, methods of dishing out food.

Drawing slag for stoves now and terrible trouble getting it to burn. Bickering in mess increasing daily. I suppose it's understandable though.

Gunner Mitchell died today of diarrhoea. Total—49.

Friday February 5, 1943

Late food issue to no. 3 hut because two orderlies late. Say trouble caused by Nip orderlies that all light duty being moved to one end of hut.

Wood at sawmill hard to get now cause civvies taking good tailings as they come off saw. Wood mostly wet and bad for Cook House. Think they would put in store but say no. Had Red Cross apple pudding in p.m. CC in Cook House every morning dishing out meals. Taking real interest in food now and quality and quantity retains its improvement.

Sun grand from 9:15 to 3:50. Quiet day. No Interpreter.

Saturday February 6, 1943

No guard duty tonight, thank goodness. Very hard to get wood now and vegetables not quite cooked. Roots and carrots only stew now. With few leeks.

Derr, Yank, died today of diarrhoea. 50. Officers and L.D. (light duty) men in camp had to carry coffin up icy mountain. Fell down twice and body rolled out amusing Nips no end.

Dave and I cleaned out stove pipes. Stoves at 4:30 and CC let men draw good coal, not slag, as we have been, which wouldn't burn.

Interpreter away on leave.

Sunday February 7, 1943

Heavy snow 6" during night and rain all morning. So no work. Had bath and 3rd dysentery inoculation. Weight 7 kilos—154 lbs. Lost 17 lbs since Semplak. Bowel looseness worse and changed clothes to try and get rid of lice.

In afternoon had fire drill. Men formed and officers from camp to station up hill. Then passed boxes, sauce, etc. (150 at 30-40 lbs) to camp. Very tiring work. Voice still gone. Reason is trying to settle disputes in barracks. Taking one dose carbon each day. Leg still swollen but not sore. Many lads have this. Doc says due to lack of proteins, called edema.

Rumours: war over. We landed in Denmark and Norway. Still fighting in Africa.

Monday February 8, 1943

Bags of candies issued to troops and officers at 10 cents a bag. Five wood trips in morning. Good dry wood so food cooked. Very good curry stew at night. Big rice and stew issue. Interpreter Officer of the Day, so no stoves til 5:30!! Interpreter raised Hell about officer's barracks and said all blankets to be folded and place kept tidier. CC said we are quite good but wish to cut time of bucket passing in half.

Tuesday February 9, 1943

Still loose and leg swollen. Interpreter said men to be issued with toothbrush and powder tomorrow to last two months. Also one bottle ink and pen for 33 men to last six months. Men had to fill in form showing what Nip clothing gets issued. Officers fill in form to buy toothbrush and powder, and pen and ink.

Stoves at 5:00—no sun and six wood details. Very good rice and stew issue cause of this.

I was medical officer today. Interpreter came around with Nips in blue uniform. Told us we could only cook at meal times. If we wished to see him we must go and rap on his window first. Next day's Officer of the Day must go at 5:00 a.m. to his office for orders.

Letters home, issue of razor blades and toilet paper was raised but he said no order re these yet from Tokyo.

Yank who had been at Matamoto Hospital for a month with appendicitis returned. Said very well treated. As good as Yank hospital. Food good such as bread and jam, eggs, etc. Diarrhoea patients here got 10 eggs in stew between 20 men. We have had no bread since Christmas.

Interpreter said can't buy anymore cod liver oil as CC wants us to put money in bank. Might as well have no money.

Interpreter says going to have athletic meet in month and wants suggestions for events!

Another tooth filling came out. Doesn't look as though we're going to get treatment. Looks as though I'm due for false teeth when I get out.

Nips say Roosevelt dead.

Wednesday, Thursday February 10, 11, 1943

Guards changed. New ones seem friendly—Nip's celebration day. Founding of Nip Empire?

Bath day, but not for me, as Officer of the Day. Yesterday. I reported for orders at 5:00 with Follows—two officers to go out each day as observing officers for diligence, slackness and dangerous workers.

Toothbrush and powder will be issued to men and issued today. Hewitt and Faulkner observed today. Hanchos and Officer of the Day to report each day at 5:00 unless no orders.

Sgt. Frances, Yank, died of malnutrition. Total—51. Found my sweater and shirt among his effects—this was one of suspected men which I had searched. Must now boil them all again.

Leg very swollen but not painful. Throat now practically better. We are now in charge of Cook House as far as cooking goes and Sgt. Rice is chief cook. Beans and rice at noon and <u>very</u> good.

No orders at 5:00 as Interpreter went to village as Nips celebrating. I got permission to light stove and draw coal at 4:20 from under Officer of the Day. We were taking from slag tip and he made us take from lump coal—good show.

Some men in at 3 p.m. lately as on piece work.

Friday February 12, 1943

Fifth Wedding Anniversary.

Four officers on funeral party. I was kicked when I wouldn't get up to go, pointing to my swollen ankle. Trip up mountain was bad and icy and many men flipped. We skidded coffin up last bit. Nip who kicked me later tried making up, giving me butts etc.

Gary and Dave saw Interpreter and complained about officers being called out on detail at meal times and S___ fatigues. Had long talk and threatened to write Tokyo. Interpreter said he would consider. Also mentioned me being kicked. Later CC called Officer of the Day, Blanchard, and through Interpreter said he was very perturbed about number of deaths and asked him his opinion, saying he had Doctor's. Said that he had increased food and sickness increased. Blanchard said we needed more protein, bread, nuts, fish and meat as we not used to present diet. CC said we should masticate rice 20 times and not have so much liquid. Mustn't mix rice and soup and must wear sheet around middle. Said people dirty in bath and we said no soap so he asked for list of people without. So it seems CC okay and Interpreter has been fly in ointment. Later Interpreter asked Blanchard to attend him in his office.

Kai-Ho at 5:00 and told about sheets and toothbrushes and powder were issued to men. Officers to get tomorrow. Fires at 5:30. Officers decided to put in letter to CC further to

Blanchard's interview giving suggestions for cutting down sickness. Officer said pleased officers going out on job although couldn't force them to. Officers who had gone out say not too bad, just walk about.

Year since bombing of *Empire Star*.

Saturday February 13, 1943

Since our complaint Nips asked us to do fatigues nicely and have had light duty men doing water-carrying although we still do it.

We put in letter to CC with 5 points apropos Blanchard's interview.

1. Remaining Red Cross packages should be issued to sick.
2. Thicker soup with flour added.
3. Issue Red Cross shoes to boys who can't wear Nip shoes.
4. Want European doctor used to temperate zone diseases.
5. Ask for more Red Cross packages to be sent from Tokyo.

Interpreter has said he would pass to CC and made following comments on the five points.

1. Red Cross packages were being issued. (Note—only milk, sugar, tea, biscuits have been issued and still many in store).
2. Might be able to thicken soup.
3. Waiting orders to issue.
4. Said 300 more POWs coming here and may be Doc with them but none in Tokyo.
5. Would see about more Red Cross packages.

Had injection for typhoid. Bath tenko at 7 a.m.

Interpreter said tomorrow holiday. Candy will be issued to all at 10 cents. Food very good now. Beautiful thick curry stew.

Wood detail. Now clear mountains for last week and have till 4 p.m.

Had orders re fire drill.

Sunday February 14, 1943

Hunter, Yank, died. (malnutrition) Total—52.

Holiday. Promised tenko at 7:00 a.m. At 5:30 fire drill gong sounded. Boys had to turn out and form bucket chain from river to bath house and fill bath. Cold morning and not too good for boys.

Had bath today and changed shorts. Still have lice but stick at them and not too bad. Can't get hot water to wash clothes. Interpreter away for day so quiet in camp. No candy issued today although promised yesterday.

Left leg and ankle very swollen. Nip Doc says beri-beri!! Still very loose and going 3-4 times a day. Cutting down on stew to see if that improves me.

Officers not issued with toothbrushes and powder as promised.

Monday February 15, 1943

Nip doc here and stores officer. Only 136 out to work as sickness increasing. More in hospital. Hunter's funeral today but only one officer required as detail kept back.

Tuesday February 16, 1943

Cpl Tucker died of diarrhoea and Travis, Yank, of pneumonia. Total—54.

Spent morning in bed to rest leg and because of squits. Leg better.

In afternoon officers hauled out to carry coffin again amid much shouting. Very rough trip with L.D. men only. I helped carry coffin there and back.

Nip summer orange issued to all men who have to pay for them. Very sour orange but I enjoyed it. Nip doc says they contain vitamin B and C. Officers got 4 more oranges later from Nip doctor who bought for us. We also got vitamin B tablets. He promised us more. No candy issued yet but toilet paper (about 200 sheets per man) issued at 11 cents each. At last we have our toilet paper which we have been hollering for since arriving. It's a blessing even if the men have to pay for it.

Nip Doc argues all swollen legs and faces are beri-beri. Our Doc says kidney trouble or lack of protein. Bean issue after p.m. meal. Like boston beans but sweetened. Four dessert spoons each. Very good. Nip doctor also got us 1 bottle vitamin C liquid and is going to try and get more. Nip doctor examined men with swollen legs and ordered 26 to stay off work. One day later Interpreter made them go to work.

Wednesday February 17, 1943

Started giving carrots with meals instead of putting in stew. This will give vitamin A and C. Vitamin B in 2 doses issued to all men. Officers pay for this.

Travis's funeral and officers and L.D. men again performed.

Only 124 to work. Fifty-five in hospital.

Bath again today. We have been asking for more carbon for two weeks but still not received. Tenko at 5:00.

Nip doc says Nip nationals getting badly treated in US but not England. Sent to Alaska without having proper clothes and sick having rocks rolled over them.

Blanchard fixing CC wireless but high wave. I was also in Interpreter's office and keep asking about Red Cross packages—food etc.

Thursday February 18, 1943

Rain at night and today so no work. Officer of the Day.

New forms issued (150 total) from Tokyo. Long things asking for our reaction during fighting, etc. I didn't fill one in as only 10 for officers. Went to office with Cory and while there visiting I should say Paymaster Nip started talking to us in English and asked us what we wanted. We said more beans, meat, fish. More clothes so boys could change. Issue of Red Cross boots as some boys nearly barefoot. Oranges, more Red Cross parcels and issues of remaining ones to support us. He said all camps have only one issue of them. We told him we had only one pay day and were well overdue and he seemed surprised. We asked for more bread. He listened attentively and said bread was scarce. We would get more fish but not more meat. The "Smiling Sergeant" kept making cracks and in the middle of our conversation the CC came in all smiles. The "S. Sergeant" said something and immediately his whole attitude changed and he ordered us abruptly back to our billets!!! So evidently we were letting the cat out of the bag on some points—I hope it produces results!!

Still no candy so it looks as though the Nips have decided to eat it themselves!! Tenko at 5:00 last two nights which is good because those that wish it can go to bed. Bean issue at noon.

Boot parade but not Red Cross boots issued. No wood at mill.

Friday February 19, 1943

Fifteen cases of oranges came in. Rumoured for us. Still no wood at mill and position getting bad.

Beans, spoonful of each all meals. Fish at noon.

Saturday February 20, 1943

Went out on job as observing officer upstream. Would have been okay except my leg was very bad. Till ten spent in hut near fire then walked around site. Had talk with Nip civvie who was a civil engineer. Told me dam 40m at bottom, 10m at top, 50m high, 59m head. 4—20,000 kw units, total 80,000 kw. Main dam has not started yet but one coffer dam consisting of log frames and threaded on rods and filled with rocks and concrete facing. Wall about one yard thick on upstream side nearly complete. Bypass channel complete and river is now running through it. Dredging main dam site has just commenced. Scheme is well thought out and will take about three years to finish. Dam is on section straight then the river takes a U bend and Power House is on opposite leg of U. In between is hill about 400' high. Tunnels driven through hill take water to turbines about 5-600' away. Most of the excavating done by hand and blasting and moved by L.G. (light gauge) railway on flat trucks with removable tops. Most Korean labour who shift colossal loads on their backs. Our lads loading trucks, carrying poles, pushing down loose material, etc. Some of them working really hard. Work from about 7:20 to 11:15 and 1:15—4:15 with two 15 minute breaks. Very tired when I returned and not feeling too good.

1800 lbs Irish potatoes, 2 cases fish blubber and 2 cases biscuits came in. Boy do those spuds sound good but actually we get enough starch in the rice. It's proteins we want.

At night the pump broke down and number 2 cook came and asked for Blanchard and flashlight. We told him we had no flashlight. He then went to see Blanchard in Interpreter's office and he said no use going down without flashlight and anyway he couldn't go as he was fixing radio. Cook then came back and asked Scarlett, Dunlop and Kessel if they had flashlight and when they said no he hit each with his fist.

Kit went to see Interpreter and he said please excuse all mistakes and said same to Cory when he went to complain later. Started to put letter to CC about it but never did. Big wigs in blue uniforms around job today but didn't inspect camp as we were told they would.

Sunday February 21, 1943

Our rations cut in half today by second cook because of yesterday's rumpus. We complained to Interpreter but he said could do nothing. Luckily men in billets turned up trumps and produced enough rice to keep us going. Cook collected tools and went down to do pump himself. But at night came and got Blanchard to go and have a look at it so may be okay tomorrow.

Weather definitely getting warmer now and sun clears hills till 4:30. Blanchard is to go with cook in morning to fix. No water to wash anything with so officers have to take buckets to river and wash and then haul water from house 600 yards away.

Two wood details but mill cutting special timber so very little and poor tailings. Spent day in bed as leg away up as yesterday and not feeling so well.

Stew thick with spuds and meat at p.m.—what there was of it.

Monday February 22, 1943

Bit bigger rations.

Blanchard working on pump all day with two men from works. Officers cleaning buckets, hauling water and wood.

Cpl. Aindow died of diarrhoea. Total—55. Officers on funeral detail on p.m. and carried coffin whole distance and back with L.D. carrying wood. Path very bad with ice and had to drag it up hills.

My leg away up and sore so saw Doc and he said it was dry sipalas and I should move into hospital for cure and my diarrhoea. Decided to stay in bed in billet and started therapol treatment at night. Also new carbon, opium, and bismuth mixture three times a day for diarrhoea.

Word from Interpreter that money (foreign) to be changed and money handed in. We took it as voluntary and I did not hand any for Nip yen.

Pump still broken. Blanchard said section out of water.

Tuesday February 23, 1943

Fire grates taken away. Looks like end of stoves and weather still cold. Put in letter to CC through Interpreter complaining about treatment of officers—(kicking me on sore leg, etc.)—and manner chasing us about on fatigues. Eleven trips to draw water for officers.

Chandler, army Pte., died of diarrhoea. Total—56, and five officers only available for funeral. Also had to do bucket washing. Officers' food back to normal now. Thank goodness. No time to ourselves at all due to fatigues.

Pump still out of action. Rainy today.

Spent day in bed and had 3 doses therapol (Nip equivalent of M and B) 693 sulphur pyrodine. Leg painted with iodine. Ring around calf and above swelling and swelling painted with ichthyol. (Fish bones boiled down) A very sticky substance. My leg lot better with rest.

Wednesday February 24, 1943

Holiday. In bed all day and continued M and B treatment.

Diarrhoea bit better. Officers had water detail.

Thursday February 25, 1943

Still in bed. Leg lot better. Nearly normal.

Pump still broken so bucket washing and water carrying although five men kept back to help.

Had steak and tomatoes from Red Cross box at night. Fish at night. No beans for two days but radishes.

No stoves last two days. Major Cory made Sacho of No. 3 hut. Thank goodness I got out of that.

Friday February 26, 1943

Doc seeing about having stoves a little longer. After all, CC said we could use them to heat up water bottles to put on stomachs. Stoves at 5:00.

After refusing Officer of the Day, Interpreter said could now write letter home: 2 sheets, 1 side, 100 words max. 500 letters. Max 5 words a line, 25 letters. Stationery issued. Copy to be made and handed in.

2 oranges issued. Tangerines! Beans again, stew only. Potatoes and carrots now and thin. Sick quarters getting bread two days now and sick decreasing slightly. Place very dirty though and no fresh blankets when people with diarrhoea dirty them. Hence they have few blankets and feel cold. Facilities for cleaning very inadequate. Blankets and clothes boiled in big cauldron if wood available, but this doesn't clean them and faeces still on when thrown on line.

Leg now normal and went off therapol this morning.

Still no Red Cross boot issue. Theory—waiting till fires finished and most boots being repaired have been burnt or they don't want their own people to see us better shod than they are.

Saturday February 27, 1943

Henrickson, Yank, died of kidney trouble. Tan Teck Wah (STC) died of pleurisy. Total—58.
No move to fix pump and water situation bad. Men have no facilities for washing at all. Latrines are dirty and smelly as can't clean them. Five men kept back for bucket washing and water hauling. Stoves at 5 p.m.

Morning in bed. Diarrhoea about same.

Sunday February 28, 1943

20 oranges issued. Stoves 5.

2 funerals and I helped carry box all way both times. Feeling good in myself.

Large load of rice came in and no barley. New boiler for boiling water which burns sawdust now working and okay.

New coffin (box) appeared bigger than old one but old one so filthy we didn't mind.

3 loads coal came. Fish tiffen and beans twice. Leg up slightly. Some letters handed to Interpreter today.

Monday March 1, 1943

Wood details, good dry wood. 125 to work.

Boiled sweater. Officer of the Day. 2 oranges. Stoves 4:30!!

Mess bought tin for boiling clothes in.

Roberts (Yank) died of diarrhoea.

Officers with swollen legs injections of Ca Cl 2, (20cc at time, into the veins of the arm) every second day and 1cc Vitamin B1 (Metabolin) every day from medical sergeant. Scarlett, Rhys, Mack and myself to take course. 75 yen each time for Ca Cl 2 and 3 yen for box metabolin (10). Course has done Cory a lot of good.

Tuesday March 2, 1943

Funeral detail.

Dinner of fish, rice and stew of whale liver and fish—very good. Tomorrow holiday and inspection by CC. Pump working okay and got lot of camp cleaned up. Started draft of letter home. Changed under mats of bed and shook blankets. Dust was inches thick in and under mats which are old grass carriers.

Wednesday March 3, 1943

Cleaned up hut etc. and CC said good after inspection.

Fish at night. Beans regularly now at least once daily.

First 100 letters to go Tokyo by 12th. Holiday. Cig issue of 5 per man and 10 to officers at 8 sens for 20 which officers paid.

Had bath and complete change. Still have odd louse but doesn't bother me much. Nearly all officers have them now.

Shaved 3 Nips and permitted to buy 20 cigs. Everybody weighed and I am 69.8 kilos. Slight drop.

Thursday March 4, 1943

Gunner Cole and Smith (Yank) died of diarrhoea. Total—61. Buried Smith.

Officer of the Day. No fires. Tenko 5:30 morning. Liver and carrot stew tiffen. Fish water soup night. Had first shot Ca Cl 2 and Metabolin.

Drafting letter.

At p.m. tenko 6 men with "most diligent" tickets got drink of saki.

152 at work which Interpreter says good but he still demands more. Says this worst camp and if more men work will increase rice issue. All meals now about 50/50 rice barley mixture and usually wettish like Semplak. Made wet to increase bulk according to Sgt. Rice. Soup now mostly soya cake, liver, fish etc. as vegetables nearly all gone.

Have been doing stomach exercises last 2 days and have hardened right up.

Friday March 5, 1943

Teas (Yank) died of diarrhoea and Ginther (Yank) of malaria. Total—63. Two funerals and only twelve men. Very rough work.

Still solid. Good liver stew at noon. Fish night and 2 oranges.

Dave did % working graph for Interpreter which shows steady increase lately but numbers at work only figures Nips go by and they don't consider 63 have died.

Saturday March 6, 1943

Funeral.

155 at work in morning. 153 at work in p.m.

Interpreter told Doc when he went to plead for stoves, more men work, then can have stoves. But Smiling Sgt. says Tokyo has ordered no more stoves and Cook House etc. must now weigh all coal and wood used. Looks like coal shortage in Japan.

Rumour fish liver all gone but three good stews. Thickening with flour helps.

Pump broke again.

Had 3rd shot B-1 and second Ca Cl 2.

Rumour rice issue to officers to be cut but still okay. 44 kilos rice noon and 64 night.

Leg swelling down at night while up again during day. My face swells up occasionally by morning showing protein deficiency or kidney trouble. Have prodigious appetite and taking cod liver oil candies at 6 a day.

Clearly, F/L Chater became increasingly concerned with the number of men at work both in the morning and afternoon. Threats were constantly being issued against the POWs when work numbers fell off. Often privileges such as the amount of food dished out, the handing out of Red Cross parcels, shoes, cigarettes, etc. depended on the numbers who showed up for work parade. Therefore, from now on in the diaries, the number of workers out that day appears. Obviously Les felt keeping track of this was part of his responsibility as an officer, and also, to document for reference, should the need arise.

Sunday March 7, 1943

Pork and vegetable stew and flour noon but only piece of pork each.

No fatigues. 156 to work but shoe shop closed so increase at their expense. Rumour it closed 'cause men wanted at work and no more leather.

B-1 shot today. 36 hours between w.c. and still solid.

Handed in letter for home.

Dry mix for supper at night. Trying out new scheme. Beans, vegetables, soya are mixed and given us dry. Not quite level white bowl. Effort to stop diarrhoea and night urinating. Some have to urinate 9 and 10 times. I go 3 to 4 times a night and it's not so hot getting in and out and going out in cold. Think lot of colds due to this.

Monday March 8, 1943

B-1 and Ca Cl 2 shots. Observing and lots of climbing up river but felt fine. Got tea and cake at p.m.

Cry of lads on job is always "More rice." They really work hard. Some are breaking granite with picks which have sort of hammer head at one end and are very badly balanced. They only get two 15 minute rest periods a day. Work, including marching there and back (⁄ mile down river), mile up river. From 7–11:30 and 1–4:30. Eight hours. Others load trucks with heavy stones and gravel stone mixture which is very difficult to handle. Others carrying and loading cement; others shovelling and pushing mixture down banks. Four in machine shops. Still no sign of rice increase although more men at work. Promise looks like old "asita" stall. Dry meal at night again and fishy soup at noon, but liked it.

Nips say if peace not declared now we will be here 5 years!! Lots of rumours about, so something happening.

Kai Hoe damage to Nip property including issued clothing whether accidental or otherwise. Must be paid for. From 11th working day will be nine hours—rather hard on lads on this food.

CC in our billet and said very untidy. Last warning!!

P.m. tenko 6. No stoves. Played bridge but rather cold. Paper for second 100 letters issued.

Tuesday March 9, 1943

Vitteli (Yank) died of diarrhoea. Total—64.

Cleaned up quarters due to CC warning.

Can get teeth fixed in village. Only cleaning about once every two days due to difficulty of getting pure water. Dave got his tooth pulled out and Doc had couple filled.

Ordinance Nip Lieutenant here again. Same one Cory and I talked to last time. Cory saw him and he promised to try and get more tobacco for us.

Interpreter says tomorrow holiday and he is going to try to get rice issue increased because more men at work. Also cig issue. No. 2 and 3 billets are going to be rearranged according to the groups they go out to work in.

Pump cutting out again.

Started squitting again. Dry meal at night and bit more. It is to be regular night issue now.

Wednesday March 10, 1943

Holiday. Nip anniversary of defeat Russian fleet. We all had to parade and salute Tokyo.

Billets changed and Yanks, British, and STC all mixed up. 10 cigarettes issued per man for which they paid at 15 s.

Grand meal tiffen. Beans in rice, thick liver, vegetables and flour. Stew and salt fish. Probably because of Nip officer who has spent long time in kitchen. Rice issue in morning to be increased by 20 kilos making 64 kilos. Thereafter rice increase will be at morning and supper with big meal at supper. Thank goodness rice increased at last. Thickened fish stew p.m. Medical officer went away yesterday so no shots. Guards changed yesterday.

Second 100 letters sheets issued p.m. Nip visiting officer took tenko p.m..

One of guards very anti with Blanchard over taking shoes into billet and gramophone not fixed.

Squitting again and not feeling extra but continuing exercises.

Thursday March 11, 1943

Started 9 hour work day. Tenko in morning at 5:30 and work parade at 6:30.

Officer of the Day Compton.

Nip officer took tenko again. Kit observing and talked to this officer. Mentioned only 5 cigarette issue, lack of boots, 60 had died since leaving Singapore due to undernourishment and weak condition on arrival and then having to work hard. Also arrived in tropical kit. Also lacked soap and officer said, Japan short of soap and men would have to borrow from each other. Kit said men have none to lend and one in Red Cross but would not last long. Would be okay if we could get Red Cross package every month. I tried to get a shoe issue but Nip officer said in two days.

At noon two L.D. men were sent out to work in slippers three sizes too small, with their heels overlapping about two inches. Nip CC was there at time but said nothing. Nip officer took tenko p.m. and took numbers of those badly needing shoes. There were 60 of them and also those without overcoats and green suits. One whose shoes were bad they called okay.

Walking on the broken granite on the job tears the shoes to pieces in a few days. Mine are on their last legs and I'll never get a pair here to fit me unless they issue the Red Cross shoes. Also asked how many no soap—180 last time he was here. After tenko he called sachos and the L.D. issue and they issued 120 bars of soap to those without. This is to last men two months for self and clothes!! Soap had evidently been in store at all time!! Hospital issued with 10 bars for doctor, medical officer and patients!! Speedo ordered bath filled at night but when told it would all leak out, cancelled it.

Visiting officer said two officers must go observing every day. I told him we were sent back for funeral details and water fatigues, but he said must have two in any case.

Officers to buy soap but not till next time!!

Arranged to go observing with Dave in morning. 3/4-hour tenko!!

Friday March 12, 1943

Caught chill yesterday and fever and diarrhoea during night. Feeling dizzy so Blanchard took morning tenko and I spent day in bed.

Bath started but stopped again to save coal.

Dave hit by Speedo when he told him only supposed to be two observing officers after Speedo asked where third was. He complained to Interpreter, but as usual could get no satisfaction.

Dry meals continuing at night. We boil kettle and have tea and rice cakes at 3 p.m. each day and now keep fire on for evening meals now that no stoves. Still using stuff from Red Cross to put on cakes. Regular scramble making these cakes over morning fire and cooking gruel. At times very amusing and at others tempers flare. Have wood fires every morning which we light immediately after Nip Officer of the Day out of hut after morning tenko and keep them till about 9 a.m.

New working hours started yesterday. Tenko 5:30 morning and breakfast. Work parade 6:30. Finish morning 11:30. Work parade p.m. 1:00 (tiffen about 11:45). Finish 5:00. Supper about 5:15 to 5:30 depending on tenko which is usually about 5:15 which early tenko is good for men cause they can go to bed after supper if they wish.

60 pair of Nip split toe rubber shoes issued to men but still no large size even in these and still no issue Red Cross shoes!! Boys don't mind split toe shoes when they get used to them but those with big feet still can not get fitted. 158 to work but Interpreter's only cry is "More men work!! By any means."

Saturday March 13, 1943

Bath ordered and probably last one for good while as remodelling and going to use some of bath house as kitchen. Starting morning going to cook in open till kitchen finished. Interpreter asked Blanchard to submit plans for oven to cook bread for whole camp. Gave him about 3 hours. Sounds good, but is it??

Visiting officer has now gone. Rice increase not noticed by officers but is by men. They get six whole buckets between 90 men. We get $^2/_3$—$^3/_4$ bucket. Second cook seems to have it in for us.

Half day in bed. Feeling better but diarrhoea still bad. Bath in afternoon.

Tenko 5:15, 126 at work. Officer of the Day now to be on 3 days same as Nip Officer of the Day.

Asked Interpreter if we could play bridge at night as we had been stopped by guard last night and he said okay. Also asked if light could be kept on later in morning so we could see to eat and he said he could arrange.

Cooking outside. Rice drier and dry meal p.m. Two faggots, fried batter, at noon. Stews now practically water.

Interpreter asked for all officer's letters.

Sunday March 14, 1943

Wood details. Feeling better and diarrhoea not quite so bad. 162 at work. Fair stew.

Two permanent L.D. men with weak hearts sent out work.

Plans for oven sent in. Work on Cook House going well. Using boiler that was used for boiling out diarrhoea clothes in new Cook House for rice. Medical Sgt. back and had two shots. He said I could see Interpreter re getting my teeth fixed.

English paper of 16th Feb. tells of German retreat in Russia. Discussions between Turkish and English officials.

Monday March 15, 1943

Observing Koreans working on job. They carry immense loads on their backs in carriers and in slings for two men with pole. They say they are conscripted labour.

Slapped for being late in p.m. for work parade as I was at benjo.

CC around in afternoon on job. CC very angry because he said men aren't working hard enough and if things don't improve he will cut rice issue. Personally I think boys working well on food. From now on must not wear battle dress to work as think men too hot while working. It's going to be very cold in morning and late p.m. without battle dress and more will be into hospital with pneumonia. CC complained about men not wearing sheets. Appealed to medical orderly re wearing battle dress and he said men with colds could wear battle dress.

Bean and meal only for dry meals and vegetables getting very short. One and a half batter rizoles at tiffen.

All men vaccinated in group 4. Four officers taken to village by Interpreter and had teeth fixed.

Tuesday March 16, 1943

167 men who wore battle dress were slapped by Interpreter at noon. When told, medical officer had said it was okay, he said no excuse as May Ray CC ordered and must be obeyed. Also said officers could not wear overcoats when observing. Said we could buy toothbrushes, powder, razor blades, note paper, pens, pencils. When told men did not have much money as they had only been paid once, he said only men with money could buy. Later men's pay sheets given to Blanchard to make up. Officers got out list of stuff we wanted to buy and Interpreter had it here in an hour. I got toothbrush, safety razor blades, paper. Very cheap. Razor 22 s and 75 s tax!!

Resumed injections.

Wednesday March 17, 1943

165 out to work.

Tomorrow is payday for men for two months and sell cigs. Men allowed to buy razor blades. Tomorrow also holiday.

Mess orderly. No fatigues.

Feeling better—leg still swollen slightly but improving.

Eel stew twice. 32 cartons cabbage came in. Nip lieutenant visited. Probably CC of another camp.

Thursday March 18, 1943

Holiday.

Men paid for Jan. and Feb. They were paid 1 yen a day but 90 s deducted for Government deposit. Officers not paid.

10 cigarettes per man and 20 for officers sold.

Vaccination inspected. One out of four of mine took.

Fish tiffin and dry meal with eel at night.

Very warm day. You can sit in sun stripped and not feel cold. Temperature range very great although it doesn't seem to freeze at night now.

Friday March 19, 1943

Marvin back from hospital and 14 officers now in mess. Now free of lice since took off flannel shirt last bath day.

169 to work. Quiet day. Dry mix morning. Troops getting 6 buckets of rice at times but officer's ration very poor.

Sgt. Lawley died, diarrhoea. Total—65.

Saturday March 20, 1943

Nip sock issue to men and officers. Latter pay 8 s a pair. White socks, no heels and not warm. Dry mix.

Rain during night and morning while men work. Foolish to send men out and Gangers, the Nip foreman, didn't expect them because they didn't turn up till late and had to look around for work. Men got wet so were allowed stoves. Officers refused stoves by V.O.D. but later O.D. said we could as two observing officers got wet. Nearly row with V.O.D. till he found we had permission from O.D.

Dry mix at night. Wrote up diary as had got long way behind.

Nip read out of Nip paper to us. Huns had crossed Ronetz River and had bombed London and Algiers. Latter good news as we must have captured it.

Did washing of two shirts and five socks. Spending a lot of time darning socks.

Observing plays Hell with socks and shoes.

Sunday, March 21, 1943

Marvin back in hospital in bad way with diarrhoea. Made rather a mess in billet twice not being able control himself.

Observing in p.m. as Scarlet not feeling up to it. Funeral in the morning.

New printed form from Tokyo re punishment of POWs. For attempting escape, hitting or disobeying guards, etc. mostly capital punishment or prison to 10 years.

167 out to work.

Dry meal mixed with rice at noon and dry meal at night.

Monday, March 22, 1943

Observing up river. 166 at work.

Rainy in afternoon and some men got wet although I managed to keep fairly dry as had Dave's raincoat.

Men issued charcoal but officers got none. Interpreter says only interested in men as they work and officers don't so he doesn't care what happens to them!!

Bean and oyster soup night. Tried fixing Nip soldier's watch.

Possession forms we filled in awhile ago returned for amendment.

Officers took out stoves from 1-2-3 and officer's billet.

Tuesday March 23, 1943

10 cigs to men and 20 to officers sold. Cig issues now quite frequent and I think outcome of ordinance officer's visit.

Oyster fritters yesterday at noon but I could only find batter!!

Took rest of stoves out of camp so it looks as though stove time now finished.

71 pair Nip rubber shoes issued.

Seaweed, soya cake with rice at noon. Thick gelatinous seaweed and flour stew at night.

New form appeared to be filled in giving schooling, Branch service, special jobs done, etc. Twenty-six to be done each day and questioned by Interpreter thru Blanchard.

Thursday March 25, 1943

165 at work. Overcast in morning. Drizzle during night.

Officer of the Day. Gave permission to wear jackets.

Another Red Cross box issued to Doc. He gets one for sick occasionally but sick only get sugar, milk, butter, tomatoes, tea—so what happens to rest? Suspect medical officer and Doc clean up.

Wood details. Kai Hoe night. Starting tomorrow new working hours:

Get up at 5 in the morning and breakfast immediately.

Roll call at gate at 5:50. Start working at 6 in the morning. Tenko officers and sick 6:00 a.m.

Finish work 11:30 and tiffen then. Work parade 12:50, work 1:00, finish 4:30. Kai Hoe 5 p.m. Supper 5:15. Tenko 7 p.m.

Must use latrines on job. No jackets to be worn. Guard changed on 27th holiday. Actually, finishing time p.m. first given as 5 p.m. which would have made 9 and ½ hour day. But this was a mistake, thank goodness.

Medical Sgt. back from Tokyo. Only trouble will be longer day and 7 p.m. tenko too late. 5 p.m. tenko would be good so boys could go to bed after supper. We tried to get changed but Interpreter said no!!

Sent out 2 L.D. men in p.m. and 170 to work. Said if they got sick to come back!!

Doc was talking to Medical Sgt. and he said diarrhoea patients in Tokyo work but they work in factory. Also they have better food as this place hard to get at.

Pages from Sanseido's New Concise Japanese-English dictionary. Japanese words are spelled phonetically using the English alphabet, then written in Japanese, followed by the meaning in English. Les was able to build his own dictionary from this, and thus read Japanese newspapers.

Interpreter says L.D. men get salts but no rice unless they go to work. But they will get fed o.k., if I know anything.

Gave L.D. men going to work special tags.

My diarrhoea a bit better.

Dry meal, beans, rubber, oysters at noon and I had major share of syrup spread. Also dry meal at night with beans in rice and sweet seaweed. Plenty rice in p.m. but not at noon. 170 at work in afternoon.

Mending stockings.

Friday March 26, 1943

Observing. Started new working hours.

Beans, rubber and oysters with rice at noon and plenty. Some did not like this. About 50% prefer beans, etc. separately. I rather enjoyed it.

Cold for boys at 6:00 working without jackets. Fine later.

Fish bone and seaweed stew at night. Heads and tail of fish which Nips have put in our stew. Terrible! Some officers don't touch. Vegetables practically nil now. When boys got in at night meal held up until their numbers in working groups sorted out!!

170 at work.

Told men pleased with the way they were working and CC pleased also. He was on job in morning.

Kai Ho Holiday tomorrow and physical inspection will give more rice!

New guard very affable and free with cigs.

Saturday March 27, 1943

Holiday—or no work day. There is more chasing about in camp on these days than on working days. All weighed, (71.8) Height—(185.7) Chest (97) Grip (70 and 55) Eyes (20) Hearing (okay) Colour Vision (75%) taken.

Meal held up till 1:15 till this finished! Also time for running—50 M with 50 K weights (16) and lifting weight above head (2). One officer, 47 years old, collapsed under former. No wonder!!

Three fish bone and seaweed stews. Terrible.

Nip guard says fighting soon finished.

Cigarettes issued. 10 men and 20 officers. They certainly are dishing them out frequently now. Medical Orderly.

Details given above put on form. Still filling in other forms giving unit, etc.

Sunday March 28, 1943

170 at work.

Fish at noon and fish water. Rain at night and sent men out in drizzle in morning. Then heavy rain set in and boys got wet and came in about 10. They were allowed carbon to dry out but officers were not although two observing officers had got wet. I tried to buy carbon for officers but he said it was impossible!! Rain in afternoon so no work. Word that Nip Major Second In Command of Tokyo prisoners' camps coming tomorrow and big flap starting to clean up camp. Men with raincoats (60), were called out and cleaned up. Interpreter gave them 30 cigarettes to divide!! Attitude of Nips seemed to have changed lately. Not so much chasing us round or yelling at us. More cigs!!

Rest of men were then ordered out to wash soiled clothes from sick quarters at the river. It will be a wonder if they don't get sick with diarrhoea. Also had to cover garbage which had been dumped near main gate.

Supper not until 5:45.

Interpreter inspected quarters at 3 p.m. with CC. Later Interpreter apologized for sending men out in rain!!

New guard very decent. Sgt. handed out 40 cigs at one time!!

Feeling o.k. but still going 4 times a day.

Officer of the Day.

Simpson died of diarrhoea. (Yank). Total—66.

Monday March 29, 1943

P/O Marvin died of diarrhoea and syphilis. He had been in hospital a month and just came out and then back again. Total—67.

171 at work.

Interpreter questioned Indians and Chinese about how they liked Nips and if they liked Nips better than English, etc. Very queer—maybe they intend to let them go!!

Seaweed stew two times—poor.

Inspector Major here at 10:00 a.m. Hurried inspection and couldn't speak English so we couldn't ask him anything so very disappointed.

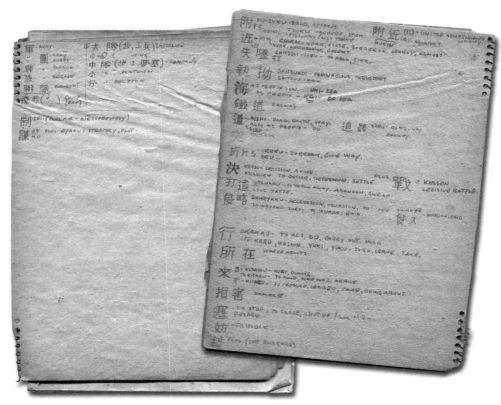

Pages from a Japanese dictionary created by Les Chater himself. He studied Japanese writing so that he could read the Japanese newspapers for the war news.

Officer of the Day.

Stew at noon special. Pork—soya cake—roots.

Wednesday March 31, 1943

170 at work.

Observing officer. Nip soldier with me all day and spoke quite good English. At night I cut his hair and shaved him and he gave me 20 cigs!!

Only 27 in hospital now! 3 officers lost appetite so plenty of rice.

Dry meal, beans and roots with rice at noon.

Officers had 4 hour fire drill on hand fire engine and they enjoyed it! Very amusing.

Thursday April 1, 1943

Had fire drill in a.m. and p.m. Quite good idea and fills in time. Very amusing at times too when hose gets tangled round wheels but lot of nattering at each other.

No observing in p.m. because drill and Interpreter says none for week because of these drills.

Rain in morning and boys got wet but weather cleared in p.m.

Dry meals with roots, pork and beans every noon now.

New Cook House came into creation. Due to food at 5 a.m. and tenko at 6:00, cannot light our fire until 6:10, so cold meal. Cooks showed Nips how to make gravy and we are all going to get some tomorrow.

Friday April 2, 1943

Cold and clear last night.

Fire drill a.m. and p.m.—3 hrs!! Interpreter quite decent to us. Interpreter says he may have to go back to his regiment as he can't make himself understood to boys because his English is so bad. Also his conscience bothers him as he now finds since he stopped slapping and bullying boys they working better and more at work! Something certainly has changed the attitude of Nips. I wonder if Germany is collapsing. Some of Nips say Germany no good and Nips not friends with them any more!! Five Maki fatigues and at last a bath!!

A one star Nip was showing me his dictionary when the CC came along. He bawled Hell out of him, I don't know why. Perhaps they have been told they must not fraternize with us.

NCOs told they to get 15 s day.

Saturday, April 3, 1943

Holiday and order all boys to sleep in afternoon!! What a difference from usual holiday. 10 cigs sold to men and 20 to officers after bit of arguing.

Interpreter says Nip Col. in charge of POW camps who was here before is coming at the middle of or end of this month!! He is the one who promised us English papers, bread, etc.! Also Interpreter thinks war will be over in a year but he didn't say who would win?? There must be some reason for their change in our treatment.

Nip who was bawled out yesterday was in again today inferring he was not afraid of CC and didn't know why he was picked on. He is a student and fed up with army life and wants to get back to school. You find all the intellectual Nips like that. They are fed up. The non-intellectual types seem satisfied because they probably see that when soldiering is done, they have nothing to go back to!!

Darning stockings in spare time these days!! Must keep all my stockings intact!!

Flour gravy at noon to put on rice and very good. Also fish. Beans and roots with rice at night and lots of rice. Played bridge.

Sunday April 4, 1943

Rain nearly all night and all day and boys didn't go out to work!

Poor root stew this morning and very wet rice. Wet rice and beans mixed at noon.

Terrific appetite these days. Seaweed stew at night. Very poor meals lately and hardly any vegetables. Some officers noting signs of scurvy—i.e. sore mouths.

Fresh issue bar toilet soap, tooth powder and toilet paper to all men and officers.

Talking to Nip soldier at night who says Russians hold Stalingrad. They are fighting in Gibraltar, not fighting in Africa. Nips are bombing Australia. Says he will bring paper in tomorrow. Difficult to understand the Nips as they speak so little English and we may misinterpret his meaning.

Monday April 5, 1943

Red Cross stuff arrived. 900 lbs dried pears, 150 packets of malted mabela at 5 lbs/pkt, 1,152 corned beef 12 oz. tins, 48 pair Yank captured shoes.

174 out to work. Cleared in afternoon

Started translating Nip Malay dictionary. Nip Officer of the Day says if anybody caught smoking outside billet cigarette issues will be stopped.

Tenko for men has now been outside for two weeks.

Poor food again. Couple roots in soup in morning. Beans and couple roots in rice at noon and rice and pork (one piece if lucky) and bread stuff (2) and noodles (12) in soup.

Officers' pay sheets for Jan. Feb. and Mar. made up by Blanchard so looks as though we're going to be paid. Men's March pay sheets also made up.

Took lists of our Nip issue clothing, our boots and blanket.

First cook came back.

Rumour: Nip ex-service (wounded men who more or less run the camp) received papers calling them up for service in the Solomons. One Nip showed our lads the paper.

Tuesday April 6, 1943

174 at work.

Interpreter and Blanchard working on cards we made out in Java and ones we recently made out giving unit, education, etc. and comparing them. Lists of all men giving own clothes: overcoats, tunics (2), slacks (2) hat (1) raincoat (o) boots (1) blanket (1), made out and handed in. Additional items—undershirts and pants added to list!!

New Medical 3-star Sergeant and supposed to be Doctor arrived and is to stay.

Very good dinner at noon. Rice, gravy and dry mix, beans, roots, soya.

Washed clothes. Sunnyish. Bridge. Stew at night.

Had diarrhoea again and wind last 2 days.

Gunner Charman died of diarrhoea—68.

Wednesday April 7, 1943

Funeral and 6 officers went although men had not gone to work because of rain. Some went at 9:30 after rain stopped.

Medical officer and guard changed and sorry to see them go. They have been really decent to us. Best yet.

New form to fill in giving list of things own army issued to us—me none.

Sort of spinach soup in morning, beans, soya cake (little) with rice noon. Barley with rice lately has been poor quality, dirty and with big roughage which has made our tongues sore and I think responsible for wind and diarrhoea.

Darning again! Stockings beginning to rot!

Colonel not coming now till end of month. New guard round tonight with old and seemed decent. Nip soldiers said sorry to go. When men came in from work they were lined up and about a third to about a half numbers were called including most STC and engineers. Kittsel and my names were called among the officers. Blanchard and Interpreter sorting out from our cards last couple days has given rise to many surmises such as those whose names called will be going to work in factories in Tokyo, as those chosen are engineers. We are all going and will be divided up.

Thursday April 8, 1943

174-5 at work.

Sent men out to work at noon although drizzle later developed into heavy rain and men got soaked and came in early.

Bath with little water as water leaked out due to concrete flue pipe joint.

Greens soup in morning. Dry mix with rice at night. Fishy green soup at noon. Had beef and vegetable tin at noon and not extra good.

Cool day.

Mackie learning Nip bridge. Opened Red Cross margarine.

Friday April 9, 1943

W/O Coker died diarrhoea and buried in afternoon—69.

20 cases onions and some roots arrived, thank goodness for former. Greens soup this morning and dry bean mix at noon. 2 K onions and 15 K root soup at night.

Snooze this morning.

172 at work.

No fire drill last 3 days.

Doc making bread in sick quarters by steaming in boiler from barley flour and local purchase yeast and B.P. fed to sick patients and supposed to be very good.

Bridge.

Saturday April 10, 1943

172 at work.

Rumour: all leaving in four days but not consistent with arrival of vegetables and five loads of coal which officers unloaded.

Fire drill with water from water tower to demonstrate to CC and pump actually worked well since we fixed it with our tools.

Very fine day and washed boiler suit which Sgt. Rice had and towel (latter first wash in 5 months!!) Going round without shirt! Frost at night—what a change in temperature.

Bridge. Dry mix at noon.

Sunday April 11, 1943

Hays (Yank) died of diarrhoea—70.

Mackie fatigues. Cloudy.

Cig issue—10 to the men, 20 to the officers!!

Shaved and hair cut for Nip. Paid 10 cigs!

Dry mix, beans, fish and roots at noon. Root and onion stew in morning. Thick onion and root, gravy with rice, at night. Very good.

Funeral p.m. Officers called for pay but found mistake in sheets and sent them back.

Order bed at 7 p.m. and until then Interpreter permits music, as if men feel like that.

Breakfast getting earlier and earlier. This morning called at 4:35!! Makes for H__ of a long day and sit round in cold from food till tenko at 6 in morning. Then we light fire till say 9 p.m. or go to bed. I usually have wood or some fatigue in morning. In afternoon I sit in the sun and read or learn Nip, and do washing fatigues. Tea fire 3:00 till say 3:45 with rice cake. Then learn Nip etc. till 4:45. Eat till 5:15. Then sit and talk till tenko 7:00 or play bridge. It's the monotony that gets you, same thing every day!!

Nip guards in tonight talking to us. Had trouble with one trading wallet with one of the men for cigs. He got wallet and was going to get cigs, so he said. I know he would not get the right kind.

Monday April 12, 1943

Rain at night and heavy rain earlier in the morning. 50 boys did not go to work.

Had weight lifting for all men again. I did 9 times!! I was first last time.

Went on same form which has been inked in and some figures changed.

Seaweed and onion stew morning.

Paid today:

Month	Wage/M	Bank Deposit	Messing	Total Net	Pay
Jan	122.50	56.82	15.68	72.50	50.00
Feb.	122.50	58.34	14.16	72.50	50.00
Mar.	122.50	56.82	15.68	72.50	50.00

Cleared in afternoon but troops did not go out to work. Big load of rice and barley came in. Dry mix beans and onions at noon. Onions and root stew in the evening.

Tuesday April 13, 1943

Bitner (cook) says the other day Interpreter told him men in this camp are going to Tokyo. Bitner said yes, he had heard that, whereupon Interpreter said where and when was he told this rumour. He shut up.

Recreation parcel came in donated by neutral people for POW. Interpreter says more coming and also newspapers in few days. Parcel—1 uke, 2 mouth organs, 2 chess sets and boards, 5 books "Japanese in 30 hours" and 2 English, Nip dictionary, 12 packs cards. Interpreter kept one each of books and 6 packs of cards as he says Nip soldiers have no cards but we have to sign for all. Men can only use in officer's billet and only when permitted so there is a catch. Can only use on afternoon of rest days!!!

Tried to repair clarinet for STC lad but no springs.

Onion stew morning and noon. Dry mix at night.

Ordinance officer who has been here before arrived.

Wednesday April 14, 1943

169 at work.

Tenko 8 p.m. and men allowed to use recreation facilities. Some good playing on guitar by Fernendez. Bridge.

Onion stew in the morning and new and dry mix at night.

Fix boiler for lousy clothes behind sick quarters.Wood details. Did a lot of washing.

Cold as H__ last couple nights. Cloudy in morning and clear p.m.

Jackson,(Yank) died Ephritis—disease of kidney where kidney stops functioning. Total—71.

Some shoes issued but not to officers. Went to see Interpreter re shoes for officers and asked if we could buy them. He said no shoemakers here and all shoemakers now doing war work but he would keep in mind and see next time he was at the next village.

Lads divvied in and bought guitar which Interpreter bought at next village for 52 Y.

Thursday April 15, 1943

170 at work in a.m.

2 digging fatigues up to station to bring shovels but "Speedo" would not let us buy anything.

Signed for 3 months' pay—Jan., Feb., Mar.

Fine Day!!

Dry mix at noon. Onion and seaweed soup at night. But seaweed was mouldy and bad and cook made them wash and use it!

Making paper bags.

Friday April 16, 1943

Funeral detail—five men held back.

167 at work in a.m. 168 in p.m.

Filling paper bags with sand but mostly broke as not dry.

Started Nip lessons from book.

Entertainment night till 7 p.m.

Ordinance officer left.

Dry mix at night. Thick onion, root and pork (2K) noon. Onion soup in the morning.

Brought flowers from funeral.

Lot of men getting hurt on job.

Grand day!

Monday April 19, 1943

167—10

Officer of the Day.

Drizzling in morning but sent men out. Then heavy rain and men came back.

7:00 a.m. Interpreter told Major he would allow entertainment in afternoon if someone would present him with handkerchief!!

Heavy rain until 4 and entertainment allowed.

At least 2 men sent out with no soles in their shoes.

Dry meal at night. Onion stew in the morning and onion, fish and root stew at noon.

Bridge in the afternoon.

Rumour: Nips in Bombay and fighting Singapore and we've captured Java, Borneo, New Guinea.

Tuesday April 20, 1943

168—167

Officer of the Day. Fine.

2 lorry loads turnips or white radishes came in. Officers cutting off tops and cook said no rice for us cause we left off too soon.

I ruled form for 1st Sergeant.

Cigarette issue 5 for men and 20 officers which we paid for. Dissension among officers re issues. Were given cigs.

Radish stew at night and fish. Onion stew at noon. Plenty of rice these days.

Men got out of bed to receive pay at 9:30. Didn't finish till 11. Told must have finished by morning tenko.

Payment men for March screwy as usual. Blanchard does most of preparing of sheets as Nips get tangled. Men work identical days and get different pay!!

Lots of wooden clogs and stationery came in and put in store. They seem large. Are they for us??

Wednesday April 21, 1943

167-166

Got more books from YMCA including 3 *Tokyo Times Weekly* which disconcerting since campaign in Africa evidently not finished and not very satisfactory!!

Officers tying up radish tops. Looks like we are to get them in our soup.

Radish soup in the morning. Dry mix with few beans and radishes at noon.

Tenko at night not till 7:45 by Interpreter who had gone to village, but to be expected.

Fine day and went round in shorts, getting sun tanned. Still cold at night probably due to height but getting warmer at night.

Shaved Pigface who promised cash tomorrow—I wonder?

Friday April 23, 1943

167. Fine.

Tied up radish tops in store room and cut up radishes rest of day!!

Wooden clogs issued to all so it looks as though we don't get Red Cross boots.

Bundle English *Tokyo Times* came in and went to administration. Ten bundles of potatoes came in.

Twelve letters from England arrived to see if men were at this camp, but alas none were. Anyway, letters have started to come in!!

Everybody weighed <u>after</u> supper this time. My weight now 75.4 Kilos.

Letters are from England and seemed to be for army men who are stationed in Malaya. They are dated 24th Sept. 1942—7 months!! Names were same as men in this camp but not for them. Some Red Cross supplies came in from America!!!

Thin radish stew in the morning. Dry mix at noon and curry stew at night. Less stew now but thicker and I think better idea!

Pump broken and no water.

Saturday April 24, 1943

166.

All day installing new pump and motor unit to feed water to camp. Nip fitters didn't know much about it and got everything ready before realizing fittings were different. No water all day!!

Kai Hoe says tomorrow holiday if sunny.

Very heavy work on pump and fatiguing day.

Flight of 24 bombers over today which is very unusual and most in one unit by far which seen since arrival here.

Blanchard had long talk to CC through Interpreter. CC asked how did he think we were being treated and Blanchard said better than before and that reason was that camp wasn't ready and CC said that was so. Asked if he would take up Nip nationality if Nips won and said "No, once English, always." Asked what he thought of Churchill and Roosevelt and also Nip way of living here. Blanchard said that he thought there was a big gap between ruling class and workers and CC said only apparent in this out-of-way place and not common all over Japan and really big middle class.

Definite none of the letters from England are for anybody here. Disappointing and discouraging if letter must go to all camps to find receivers. Thank goodness not many Chaters.

Thick curry stew for supper with little pork.

Sunday April 25, 1943

No work day!!

Bath since pump started working at 10:00 this morning.

All billets cleaned right out and blankets and mats and undermats taken to river bank and sunned. All belongings taken out of billets and latter cleaned thoroughly. Good idea and although tiring day should be done once month. Amount dust which had accumulated on beds was colossal!! Suppose this has to do with Colonel's visit.

600 *Nippon Times* newspapers printed in English issued to us varying from 21 March to 19 April 1943. More papers are coming!! Looking through papers, main points are position in South West Pacific seems unchanged since we left Java. Germans starting offensive in Russia after being driven back by Russians and meeting stiff resistance. Amount of sinking by U boats colossal according to their papers and I admit they are alarming. On the other hand we have air superiority and are giving Italy and Germany H___ from air. Position in China about the same. In N. Africa Germans only in Northwest corner of Tunisia and the rest of North Africa is ours although this is disappointing as had hoped this section had cleared up long ago. Burmese India border stable and Nips claim to have defeated English attack and annihilated English army. Papers are mostly propaganda and very little extra news. Mostly articles on bad position of Anti-Axis countries, dissension among them, big sea losses, bad economic position and unpreparedness as against happy position of countries captured by Nips—and their increased production, etc.

Monday April 26, 1943

Picked up radishes which dried in sun and cut up lot more. Took most of day.

Stew three times a day of radishes mostly with potatoes and onions.

In Kai Ho say light duty and medical orderlies to catch 100 flies a day and give to Interpreter. No water to be drunk out of tap unless boiled!! And we've been drinking it all along!!

Japanese guard, name unknown.

Japanese guard, name unknown.

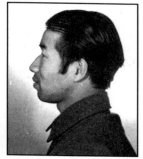

Tuesday April 27, 1943

168 at work in morning, 166 in afternoon

Picking up radishes as few drops of rain fell. Packing old rice containers. We seem to be working steadily for cook now.

Curry stew with beans at noon and usual radish stew in the morning with addition of our fish at night.

Went to local dentist at night and had 2 teeth filled. Dentist very good and filled with amalgam!! Only charged 150 y (60 cents) per filling!! He had equipment as good as any I've seen and fillings were two which had come out. This is last place in world I would have expected a well-equipped dentist. He said rest of my teeth okay which is relief. I hope I can go again for periodical check.

Wednesday April 28, 1943

170 at work in morning, 169 in afternoon.

One tin bully beef per man and 150 lbs dried pears for camp to be issued tomorrow on occasion of the Emperor's birthday!! Also Nips asked us how to cook mabela so we should get that in morning. Told them do like porridge and not mix with rice.

Leg still slightly swollen but does not bother me. I have trouble if I wear my shoes cause they always were slightly on the small size, although biggest I could get and now with warm weather feet probably swollen little. Usually go round now without stockings all day and wear sandals I made at Semplak or Nip wooden clogs. This is okay and not too cold now but too much walking, especially in sandals, makes my feet sore. Anyway, it saves socks. Sandals have been godsend.

Still squitting and heaps of wind although only go once or twice a day which is below average here. Cutting down on eats and find it helps, especially with wind. Soup flavoured with soya sauce products gives lot of wind and also cutting down on that. Morning soup is now standard, it seems—radish, mezore mixture and very bloating.

Sunny, hot during day and now getting tanned. More men getting sick with fever. Seems to be a lot of this fever, and it's not malaria. Some called Dengue but no Dengue mosquito here and I thought that this was not reoccurring.

Getting quite a rice pot belly and can't do any of my shorts up. However, hope to soon get rid this when we leave this place.

Glare from sun very noticeable here too but I have 2 pair sunglasses so well equipped. Some lads are getting in early these days as on contract—piece work. Some get in at 2:30!! All seems quite cheerful.

Number in sick quarters now going down although no L.D. increasing. Not getting bread from barley flour now since Nips say baking powder too expensive although officers have offered to buy!! Still giving wet rice.

Flowers in these parts now in full bloom and must admit they are beautiful—types I have never seen before and mostly wild, from shrubs. Lads bring them in from job.

Fixing clock for cooks. Doing clarinet and making fly swatter.

Thursday April 29, 1943

172 at work.

Emperor's birthday but no holiday!! Heavy rain at work parade so lads didn't go out but rain stopped later so they did work at 7:00 in the morning!!

Issued 1 tin bully per man, 150 lbs. dried pears to men. Still 750 lbs latter in store. Pears very good and not really dry.

Spent morning fixing clock for cooks and also doing clarinet. Flies getting bad now and dangerous to eat outside.

Troops allowed Entertainment night. Fine afternoon.

Third cook who has been down on officers at times and good to us at other times and who seems to run Cook House is going away in a couple of days and is being replaced by Pig Face! May be good or bad for us. Time will tell.

Issuing mabela by putting only one lb. with rice for whole camp each meal. This is CC's idea and of course is just wasting it. We each get 1/227 lb. per meal!! CC tried trial cooking of it in Cook House with sugar on it and said "Hiroshi" and when it was suggested we have it the same way the sugar shortage cropped up and we certainly can't get sugar. However directions say mix salt with it as breakfast food and surely they can get salt enough!

Two good meals today. Two of long fish per man at noon and one large piece of mackerel fried in batter per man at night. Very good and men enthusiastic.

Practically clear of lice now but get a couple occasionally. Fixing shorts and letting them out! Bath.

Guard changed and sorry to see old ones go as good shaving and watch-fixing customers. Rumour: Turkey has entered war on our side and from bits in paper just issued, it is probably true! If so, war must be going our way.

Friday April 30, 1943 + Saturday May 1, 1943

Poor meal at noon with roots in rice only. Don't know what has happened to bean issue last couple days. They still have plenty.

Modifying forms we handed in giving our civic jobs and special qualifications. Are they going to move some?

Most of radishes we cut up have gone bad and have mould on them. Officers had to sort and wash to try and remove mould which, of course, is ridiculous. Then put all out in sun again. CC's idea about cutting up so couldn't blame anyone else.

Pig Face now second cook and he is not too bad. Shaved him today on 30th.

STC lad was given 10 days guard room for fighting. His opponent went to Nips and is now in disgrace. As usual officers have to guard him during night, so 10 more interrupted nights ahead.

Pay sheets for men made out.

Looks like we get mouldy radishes soon as those which weren't out, although still okay, are few.

Cigarette issue 5 men, 10 s—20 officers.

Sunday May 2, 1943

My second birthday as POW and feeling quite optimistic today. I shaved 3 Nips and collected 30 cigs, 24 of which I gave away to officers. Holiday today and bath.

Poor meals but dry mix at noon and less beans. Fishy stew at night.

Boys cleaned up camp at night. Officers tying up grass, vegetable containers.

Fixing Nip watch which gaining. Also looked at Sgt. Rice's watch but pretty hopeless.

Monday May 3, 1943

170 men at work.

Fixing watches for Nips.

Started small garden in front of our billet as instructed by Smiling Sgt. Tomatoes and watermelon to be planted from seed but seems late in season. We could have started long ago. Have to haul earth as camp built on rock fill—given three days to do.

Still getting 1 lb. mabela in rice per meal.

Four cases Nip rubber shoes came in—2 with split toes and others evidently made especially for POW as not split toe and big size—some even big enough for me. Officers asked for some but Glass Eye said for working men only and none for officers. Issued to men today. At last big enough shoes!!

Seven rabbits, six does and one buck came in and two each issued to No. 2, 3 and officers billets to look after but nothing given to feed with!! Kept two in small box 3′ x 18″ x 18″!!

Notice latrines were crawling with maggots so anticipate blue bottle invasion shortly. Special fatigue picked up radishes at night as it looked like rain.

Dave sick so did 2 hours guard duty.

Wednesday May 5, 1943

Dry mix at noon. Working on garden.

Case of dried blood protoplasm came in on 4th from American Red Cross—a bit late!! If it had come sooner we wouldn't have had so many trips up the hill!! In a way it's a good sign that Yank Red Cross supplies are getting through. Hospital working well these days probably because Doc sick!!

169 at work.

CC presented me with packet of cigarettes when I picked up a butt!!

Fixing Nip watches.

Dry mix at noon. Mackerel soup and radishes. Taksan night. Now eating heaps of radishes every meal—those which had gone mouldy. I suppose they want to use them up! Even dry mix is full of them. 200 Kilos mackerel which came in being put down in mezor!

Lads from No. 3 billet had to stand attention for 1 hour at night in drizzle because one man would not number loudly. Jones as usual.

Thursday May 6, 1943

Interpreter back.

Hauling earth for garden. Lads bringing infinite variety of wild flowers lately. I've never seen such an infinite variety and such beauties.

Have itch and rash in crotch quite badly. So got ointment from sick quarters. I shaved my organs, bathed in hot water, and put on ointment but it still itches at night.

Two cases Nip Red Cross medical supplies came in with American case.

Fish stew at noon and at night and usual radish in the morning. Saw them cutting up the mackerel—it's beautiful fresh fish but it's boiled to little bits in soup so you can't see it and soup is lousy with radishes.

At night tenko lads had to show what they had in their pockets and also produce purses. When the Nips found out only few had purses and some kept money in barracks they ordered them to make paper bags and carry money on them so it wouldn't get stolen in barracks.

Nip "Haiti" brought me watch strap. Fixing Nip watches.

Put radishes in sun again as going mouldy.

Friday May 7, 1943

Smiling Sgt. ordered more earth on gardens so all day hauling. We ordered to make paper bags to carry money if we have no purses and carry on us.

Prisoner released from last 3 days of his sentence so don't go on tonight.

Cigarette issue brought up and Nip phoned for some which will be issued tomorrow.

Had ¼ tin bully in p.m. and was it good!!

Cut hair of two Nips and shaved one.

Lads had to show purses they had made.

Meal same as yesterday. Getting sick of radishes 3 times daily.

Lads as they came in were to have teeth inspected by Doc to go to dentist, but 5 out of first 8 had bad ones so they stopped.

5 sacks Haricot beans came in.

Gave to Nips list of people with mossie nets and they said they are issuing to all men. I brought mine with me so okay but I shouldn't have thought they would be needed at this altitude.

Dave O.K. now.

Saturday May 8, 1943

Officers issued 36 cigarettes each. Orders to be issued tomorrow.

Shaved Nip and Sacamoto.

Tomorrow holiday.

Major asked if could get another issue corn beef, pears, tomorrow, and also change method of issuing mabela. But Interpreter said no. Also asked if we could buy shoes (Nip) for officers but also no.

Pay sheets for men rushed through but no pay.

Rice figures decreased—figures later.

Finished early for garden to have pig waste tomorrow as fertilizer.

Dry mix noon.

Sunday May 9, 1943

Rest day. Put manure on garden.

Asked for bamboo and material to make fly swatters and Interpreter said look for in camp and use paper. When I pointed out that none were in camp he said boys bring in "asta". How they are going to get paper I don't know!! Flies getting very bad now!!

Left alone today. Officer of the Day. Finished first tin bully with Dave.

Shoemakers still in camp. Had mine half done but wearing slippers all time now.

Fixing Dave's watch.

Men issued 200 packs cigs.

Playing volleyball with basketball from Semplak.

Interpreter had some of our chaps in administration giving concert. He said we're going to have entertainment every Sunday now and Dave made arrangements. Say officers to buy new instrument every month.

Dry mix at noon, radish stew in the morning long fish at night.

Chap caught stealing mezor from Cook House and visions of at least month's guard room, but Interpreter let off very easy. Beat him up with fists a bit and then he had to walk through billets with sign on him saying, "I am a sergeant but I am a thief who steals the mezor from Cook House. Would you mind laughing at me for my conduct?" Lucky for us. A chap who fights gets 10 days. I think Interpreter does not want to report to Tokyo as this supposed to be best disciplined camp.

Have been loose for couple of weeks now. Also had spots on thighs and organs which are very itchy at night. Not lice bites, but I think other mite, probably fleas.

Tuesday May 11, 1943

175—173. Officer of the Day.

Dry mix separate from rice at noon. Cleaning up beside sick quarters.

Sending out more men every day, especially L.D. men. Doesn't matter if Doc says they aren't fit and really I can see why. Some who Doc said couldn't work were sent out a while ago and most of them are still working.

Officers had to do some saluting practice at night and are to do for 10 minutes after morning work parade. Colonel In Charge of Prison Camps supposed to be coming on 20th.

Interpreter questioning all boys on job and in camp on following lines and entering on sheets. Have you been sick and what with? Are quarters okay? What were you doing before you joined up? What do you like to do best?

Today officers were questioned by CC through Interpreter. Asked me if I minded fatigues in camp and I thought he said "Are you fatigued by work?" and said "No." He jumped at that and then I saw what he was driving at and said I didn't mind fatigues. Asked me what I did as civil engineer and I told him. Asked me what I would like to do best here and I said "Work on pumps."

He told F/O Power he was going to send him out to work with boys tomorrow as he was volunteer! He objected and then he asked him if he could work in kitchen. He said no to that. He then asked him if he could do medical orderly and he said yes. He could learn from Doc very soon.

Told P/O Dunlop he was too young to do office work and he could go in kitchen. Looks as though they are trying to put us all to work on site before Colonel comes!!

Rumour: all over in Africa.

Wednesday May 12, 1943

175-172 and 4 shoemakers.

Did bit saluting practice ourselves in morning. Did a lot of washing.

Sirens went at 10 p.m. and blackout. Don't know if raid or practice. Hope raid, but doubtful.

Thursday May 13, 1943

CC lined up sick and said they must go out to work. When pointed out nobody in camp to do fatigues, said officers could do! But Tokyo Colonel said officers would not be required to do latrines. L.D. men to line up at 9:00 a.m. tomorrow!!

Finished mouldy radishes in morning. Now I may be able to have soup but mezor is sour so I don't touch liquid anyway. Squits improving but now using sulphur compounds since first ointment did not work. Filling has come out of tooth again.

Two boxes Nip medicine came in. Hospital now has more medicine than ever before and fewer patients—14.

Rumour: Tokyo and Osaka raided last night. *Tokyo Times* dated May 10 indicates North Africa now cleared up and Russians doing okay!

Sunday May 16, 1943

Rainy.

Men's pay sheets for May made out. Officers paid for April. 50 y given and 57.32 y put down as deposit. Messing 15.18 yen. Total 122.50 yen. Said May issue of cigarettes and cakes will be on the 20th.

The Colonel is supposed to be coming then. Told how to arrange kit and had inspection for same.

More YMCA entertainment stuff came in few days ago but went into stores like everything else. Includes ping pong kit and cards.

Had fires today but Interpreter said nothing.

Itch still bad.

Soup now potatoes, roots and little meat. We are getting 5 minutes command practice every tenko now. Issued one cake (size of silver dollar) on Monday.

No work day. Bath. Entertainment.

Interpreter says American Red Cross has given $150.00 for use to prisoners but cannot buy cigarettes or food or medicine etc. Use for athletic and entertainment and musical instruments, etc. Asking men for suggestions. Will be godsend because can buy high bar and other gym equipment.

Some of seeds up.

Monday May 17, 1943

Working all day making table for medical sergeant.

Mike's birthday!! 5 years old now!! Wonder how old he will be when I see him!!

Tuesday May 18, 1943,

181. L.D. men still going for walks.

Working all day on another table for medical sergeant.

Meat stew at noon and dry mix at night.

Five watermelon seeds showing. Things seem to grow very quickly here. Some barley is completely headed and potatoes well up.

Bundle came in wrapped in *Tokyo Times* dated May 31, 1942. I think it is new issue of *Tokyo Times*.

Fine.

Asked medical sergeant to take watch to village to get main spring but he came back and said no main springs here.

Planted tomato plants.

Wednesday May 19, 1943

181. Fine.

Making 20 ashes boxes for cremated men. Think for last 20 men who died as they didn't save their ashes and probably have orders from Tokyo to send them. They will get ashes out of kitchen I suppose. Made quite quickly and would be okay if Nips would leave you alone, but they all must come around and use the tools. Reminds me of Tom Sawyer exactly and they're really only a bunch of kids.

Now get 1.7 lbs rice mixture per man per day. Mixing meal with rice now and deduct that much rice. Mix now is :

	Breakfast	Noon	Night
Rice	22.00 kilos	25.00	22.00
Barley	28.00 kilos	27.00	29.00
Meal	9.00 kilos	6.80	6.80
	59.00 kilos	58.80	57.80

Meal is divided between soup and rice and would be okay in soup except spoiled by sour mezor. Using spuds quite quickly now. Two fish soups with spuds and roots. Morning stew is now spuds, rice and mezor and meal. Rice varies — sometimes wet and sometimes dryish.

Nip tools are used differently from ours and poorer material. Saw has cross cut on one side and rip on other and cutting stroke is when pulling towards you. This is quite sensible because saw is in tension when cutting as opposite to ours and I suppose everybody has had English saw bend on cutting stroke in camp. Can also see line better and saw to it easier with Nip saw. Saw is smaller and used quick, short stroke. When planing cut as pulling towards you but can also used as pusher. This also quite sensible as longer stroke and can hold easier with knees.

Forms showing men's working days each month now to be brought up to date from four months back. This means a lot of work and can only be done from working cards which are stamped daily by hanchos on job and again when they come in from work. Think Tokyo ordered this. We stopped stamping originally because Nips failed to provide sheets.

Lorry load of rice and barley came in. Cory asked for mabela to be given us in quantity but CC said no, the men would get too many vitamins at once!!! And at home we have this straight every p.m. Not getting any now.

Cigarette issue: 10 men, 20 officers.

Thursday May 20, 1943

186. Cool.

Nippon Times up until May 2 came in. From these it looks as though decisive stage is being reached in European war. Turkey seems to be with us which is very suggestive of which way wind blows. North Africa nearly cleaned up. We have definite air superiority in Europe and are raiding Germany and Italy extensively.

Finished making boxes and started on ping pong table.

Dry mix at night with no beans. Have not had beans now for about three days.

Haircut.

Friday May 21, 1943

185. Hot. Inspection by Naval Officer.

Working on ping-pong table. Officers have to pay 25 yen for saw which has been broken!!

Name of meal they put with rice is Kibi, a millet grown in Machuko. Notice in latest paper. A/C Maltby announced by British as captured so God knows when F/Lieutenant will be notified to next of kin.

Roots finished noon meal. Turnip tops going to start to use in morning. Stew three times today. Potato and roots in morning, same at noon with soya cake and potato and soya cake at night.

Officers had to give impression of reading article on bombing of Nip hospital ship as reported in *Tokyo Times* and also on General Yahagi's speech that Japan plans operation on grand scale and Britain and America will surrender.

Tools taken away so couldn't work on ping pong table in p.m.

Sunday May 23, 1943

Fine. Holiday. Bath.

All day making letter box for Nips so couldn't work on ping pong table.

Cigarette issue 10 to men, 20 to officers.

Entertainment day. Shaving and haircut for Nips.

Kit inspection for men of all service clothes. (khaki shirts, etc). The number is to be divided between all men so have equal amounts, so those who have lugged a lot of stuff this far now lose some of it. This does not appear to apply to officers.

Monday May 24, 1943

186.

Guard changed.

Rain but sent men out and when rain got really bad they came in again at 10:30. Out again in afternoon but rained heavily so they got wet again and came in early. Really, no need to send them out as there's not a lot of work to do and they get in early nearly every day.

Speedo wouldn't give me tools until late so couldn't do much on ping pong table. Working in shoe shop and building house for pump motor and switch.

Horse and cart brought in green tops like young parsnips. They are not bad if cooked long enough.

Tuesday May 25, 1943

187.

Rainy but men out to work.

Another cigarette issue of usual 3 issues in 5 days!!! Why??

Officers had to write impression of three articles written by Yanks in POW Camp at Mukden, Manchoukud: one letter of appreciation for things done by Nips to improve conditions which he states were very bad, letter of Yank who offered service to Nips especially in Philippines and poem against Roosevelt. These articles were given us on paper clipping from Tokyo but the interesting thing was an article on the back saying Tunisia had fallen!!! Looks good now and second front not far off in Europe.

Lots of visiting officers today. One civilian officer and a major and W.O. The Major spoke good English and was very decent, cheerful chap. I'm sure he just dropped in unannounced. He shook hands with us all, told Yanks they fought well in Bataan, asked all ranks civil occupation, said war would soon be over and we would be going home. He said to learn Nip and asked men if they had had letters from home and seemed surprised and said same thing to CC when they said no. It does seem strange we've had no word. Things look pretty good was the attitude he took up, especially since things look so black for Germany with the fall of North Africa. He seemed to hint at negotiated peace.

Had another run in with Speedo re broken saws. They are his private property. I went to see Interpreter re them and told him they wanted us to do work for them and then pay for saws which are broken, although Nips used saws at the same time—but could get no satisfaction. Ping pong table held up by Speedo in meantime. Went and got more wood for table and planes sharpened.

Felt rotten at night with chill and took aspros.

Bridge every night now.

Bought raincoat from Sgt. Rice for 15 yen.

Thursday May 27, 1943

Cloudy.

Radish top soup morning and noon and p.m.

More tomato plants planted with flowers on! A bit late, I think.

Rumour: Nips sunk battleship, cruiser and several destroyers on April 24.

Some 150 letters arrived for us but only about six for men at this camp. One begins to wonder when one will get a letter. Tie up seems to be in many names with same initials, like "W.H. Brown." (Ten letters). They all bear regimental numbers and it doesn't seem as if the office of sorting at Tokyo has these numbers although one copy of original cards with regular numbers on was supposed to go to Tokyo!! There is a letter for S/L Grant and we are all waiting to hear from it. Three of six letters which hit are for Yanks which gives me hope of letter from home soon.

Lots of policing areas have been divided up.

More postcards have been issued and we can turn in 50 per day. Can have 30 letters per line. Local CC has added stipulation that we cannot ask for clothes, concentrated food or medicine. The very things we want!! Still I think they are the things that will be sent anyway. Other stipulations are no reference to Nip troop movements etc. and no economic references. Must print legibly in ink but can sign in ordinary signature. Letters not issued to men tonight.

Not getting <u>any</u> mabela now!!

Friday May 28, 1943

Cloudy and occasional rain.

Letters still not given men. Mental torture!! When asked for them Interpreter said he must check first but he is making no effort to do so. Dates are Sept. and Oct. 1942. Eight months to get here!! Woe is me!!

Dry mix noon. More Red Cross stuff for us arrived. 13 100-lb. sacks sugar, 2 150-lb. sacks salt, 11 crates each 48 1-lb. tins M and V containing peas or beans, 5 boxes each 4 7-lb. tins cocoa, 8 boxes dehydrated soup mix. All from South Africa Red Cross. As usual it all went into Nip store so Nips will have good feed and God knows when we will see any of it. Still some of original Red Cross boxes in store after 5 months!! That is, if Nips haven't cleaned it up. They have been seen with some of it many times and some of our chaps have been given things from them!! We have only had the one issue of bully and pears and they have been here 2½ months!! And there's enough for 6 issues!! It's a damn shame!!

Still squitting and itch worse last night again. Eye still bad and Doc said eyelash infected at root.

STC lad caught bringing dry chili powder into camp, which he had bought from Korean. He was let off by CC because he is Diligent Worker. (I think because they don't want to send report to Tokyo as this is supposed to be best disciplined camp). A bit of humour entered this case when Interpreter explained that this powder is also known as "Excitement powder" otherwise known as Spanish fly!!

In Kimo it said anyone buying from civilians will be severely punished.

One of Yanks carried in from job after going violently crazy!! Three officers have to guard him tonight and I was one of unlucky ones drawn. It's a wonder more don't go bats.

One of chaps in sick quarters has pneumonia and Doc asked for Red Cross package for him and was told none was available!! This leaves 23 packages unaccounted for. Out of the 45 left after new issue. Does it mean no more left?

Fish soup (small dried type) at night.

Medical Sgt. later got Red Cross packages.

Saturday May 29, 1943

187. Fine.

Domestic soap issue to men.

Talk to Nip guard and he said Nazis "very sick" and "finish this summer." They are short of steel, mag., Al., etc. He is not concerned however as he says Nippon then wait and when we come they sink our ships. However, it looks good if Nips believe Germany will go under soon!!

Boys in good spirits these days.

I have cold bath every fine day now and is it cold. Right out of river!!

25 more English books issued to us. Pretty poor and ancient stuff including Tarzan and Mars series. Asked if newspapers could be taken to sick quarters and Interpreter said he would ask CC. He said books could not be taken to billets. This is foolish because there's entertainment only once a week for a couple of hours and men can not read book in that time.

Major asked for issue of Red Cross stuff and Interpreter said impossible!! That is his stock answer to everything we ask for now.

Finished card writing—this time to Mu's folks—and handed in.

Sunday May 30, 1943

Fine. Rest day. Officer of the Day. Bath.

Fixed drain. Got cigarette issue—10 men, 26 officers.

Shaved Interpreter, Sacamoto, and Medical Sgt. Made table.

Asked Interpreter for Red Cross stuff and he said impossible to issue, only CC could issue. Asked if he could ask him tomorrow and he said he would see.

Tenko 7:00 a.m. Entertainment. 2 small salt fish soups.

Speedo wouldn't give me the plane to do table for M. Sgt. so latter took wood and had it planed.

List of Red Cross Medical Supplies which came in 23/4:

Sulfaanilamide	5000 Tbl.
Acetylsalicylic	3000 Tbl. (aspros)
Sulfanilamide	3000 Tbl.
Quinine Sulphate	1000 Tbl.
Cod liver oil	3 pints
Chloride-o-Lime	3 bottles
Kmno4	4000 Tbl.
Nicotinamide	100 Tbl. (Vitamin C)
Tannic Acid Ointment	4 lbs.
Marpharson and H2O	
Bovril	40 oz.
Iodine	45 Ampules
Ether	15 lbs.
Pediculosis Exterminator	2.5 Ltr.

Monday May 31, 1943

190—189. Fine but cloudy. Best working number yet.

Made table for M. Sgt. without tools needed. The Nips just tell you to make table but do not give you all necessary tools and wood and expect it to be done in an hour!!

Nips really put out about something in Nip newspaper. Found out Yanks had recaptured one of the Aleutians, Attu. Nips claim they used 20,000 against 2,000. They were "brassed off" all day, even jovial cooks. Nip, at night, said he couldn't tell the true position of Germany as Nips were with Axis. That is certainly significant!! He said they had plenty of food and Russia hadn't but he expects Germany to cave in this year as he said a couple of nights ago.

Asked Interpreter if they would issue bully beef today and he said impossible!! I pointed out that work parade is the best yet and boys were doing their best and then asked if we could have letters from home. He was doing officers impressions and he said he had forgotten letters!! Asked if I could help him with letters and he said later. Gave example saying last letter man had before he was a POW may have said his wife was ill and he would be worried till he heard again and that it was cruel to withhold letter. He said, I see. I asked later if I could help and he said he was busy!! (Doing impressions.)

Doing wood details with cart with Scarlett each day.

Officer of the Day.

Second cook looked at rice buckets p.m. and said Taksan and then cut rice issue for morning by 10 kilos!! It seems they have run out of meal which was replacing rice but they haven't put equivalent rice back. Figures were:

	Breakfast	Noon	P.M.
Rice	22.00 kilos	25	22
Barley	28.00 kilos	27	29
Meal	9.00 kilos	6.8	6.8

Meal finished and no rice increase.

Tuesday June 1, 1943

188. Rice 9 kilos (meal) short and therefore wet to make it go further.

Officer of the Day.

2 fresh fish stews today—3-4 lb fish like salmon, very good but salty and oily and I think make me squit.

Made bridge and writing table getting wood planed by carpenter. Working in administration.

Playing bridge every night now.

Asked Interpreter why rice was cut and he said he did not know!! Asked him if we could have original rice figures replaced now that meal finished and he said "Impossible!" Asked what he meant by impossible and he said, "I do not know!!" His two stock answers to anything now asked. Asked him if we could have letters today and he said "No!" Whereupon I blew up and said, "We have 190 men out to work, the best yet, and boys doing their best, and you cut their rice and withhold letters and you talk of Nipponese gratitude!!" Then he told me to leave.

He sent lad who has bad rupture out to work today. This STC lad was ruptured on job last year lifting heavy rocks. He didn't consult Doc and when I sent for latter he was in bed and didn't get up in time. In the afternoon they put this lad in kitchen with orders he is to be worked hard all the time. He is to get up every day at 1:30 in the morning and no rest all day like other cooks. He is to get level blue bowl of rice every meal (as well as soup) and is not to taste anything else or he will get beaten up.

Wednesday June 2, 1943

187-6.

Two fresh fish soups.

Interpreter sent to our billet by CC to explain things after reading Blanchard's impressions on articles by Yank POWs in Manchoukud. Blanchard had pointed out that the camp was probably like this one with a lot of deaths, small issue of Red Cross stuff and tampering with latter. Interpreter said CC had asked him to explain:

1. Red Cross boots had not been issued 'cause they would have been ruined in 4 months on rocks on job and then they might not be able to get any more and we would have had nothing to go home in! This quite reasonable to Blanchard although he thought there would be plenty more coming.

2. Intention was to issue Red Cross food in small quantities at long intervals, keeping it mostly as reserve as war was mostly at sea and blockade and it may be difficult to get food in future. This also reasonable. When asked about pilfering of Red Cross food by granted men, he feigned ignorance but Blanchard told him we had proof in many cases. Blanchard told him he would tell Interpreter immediately if we found it happening again and he agreed. But two empty bully beef tins were found in the Interpreter's own basket the other day!! So he knows about it!! Blanchard said all boys knew about pilfering and were mad. Obviously they are all windy that these will get to the Colonel. He is to be here between 5th and 8th. If we get chance, however, they will get to him anyway.

Dave asked if he could see handwriting on envelope of his letter and Interpreter opened it, read it, and told him everybody okay and would issue tomorrow maybe!!

4 bundles each onions and cabbages came in.

Feeling chill so had temp. taken—102. Balls also sore and afraid rupture but Doc says no. Either gonorrhoea, T.B. or lack of women—I prefer latter and probably so since I haven't had a wet dream since just after we came here. Had no urge for months, in fact since capture. Painted my balls with iodine and gave me aspros.

Cards home all handed in but Interpreter has not started on them yet!! Dave got his letter and one other chap his at night. They have to make copies first. Only about a half sheet and says "About all I can say is we are all well." Postmark was Sept. 42—nearly 9 months to get here!!

Officers get paid for May, usual 50 yen with 56.82 yen deposit.

Cory saw Interpreter re rice cut and he promised to take up with CC in morning.

Thursday June 3, 1943

187-6 out to work. Showery.

Felt better but stayed in bed. Officers fixing drain. CC put rice issue back to normal and 3 kilos!! They certainly want us satisfied when Colonel comes.

Figs. Now	Breakfast	Noon	Dinner
Rice	31	31	29
Barley	26	28	29

Dry fish mix, no beans at night, not getting many dry mixes now, or beans.

Blanchard copying letters, mostly written Oct.1942, and infer they have had no official news of us. No food shortage in England, address Japanese Red Cross, Tokyo, one sheet sometimes written on both sides.

Fixing watches and sleeping. Feeling fair.

Saturday June 5, 1943

CC saw our fire and said "Iki-Ni." In Kai Hoe said wells in officers' billet are to be filled in. No more fires. So our morning fire and our 3 p.m. tea fire are at last finished but they have had a good run. No more Quaning". We will miss this part of our constitution!!

Sports meeting to be held on the 13th and I am to arrange it. Colonel will be here definitely on the 11th. Tomorrow is a rest day.

Helped Pollock with refrigerator.

Rumour: Nip envoy leaves Tokyo at 10:50 in the morning for neutral country for peace conference!! This told by civvy to work honcho and hence to boys. Hope so but doubt it.

Monday June 7, 1943

Cloudy.

Poor vegetable soup. Mostly daikon tops at noon, dry mix, onions, daikon tops and a little cabbage at night. Daikon tops every morning. Vegetables are practically finished. Also clearing store for Col.'s visit. Getting our tea now by putting leaves in kettle and getting hot water from kitchen. Officers had 15 minutes saluting and Nip command practice.

Interpreter said I was to make out events for Athletic meeting, making signs and posting them up all over camp.

Today's resolution is to "Improve your health" etc.

Latrines now cleaned by details using them.

Tuesday June 8, 1943

Cloudy. Very hot last night even with only two blankets. Used sheets for first time.

Sirens went at 8:00 a.m., 12:00 and 4:00 p.m., but just practice, I fear.

Chap said he saw one Nip give another some dried pears but not certain enough to report.

Moved empty sacks and barrels to station.

Three terrible soups today. Daikon tops, and 2 daikon tops and seaweed.

Washed clothes.

Wednesday June 9, 1943

189 to work.

Cloudy and showery.

Morning—daikon tops. Noon, dry mix with beans (few) and hardly anything else. Fresh fish soup and onion at night but little fish. A case of fish came in today. 2 loads of coal arrived and officers emptied it. Officers built flower beds.

I started making letter box for Interpreter after finally getting plane (well nicked) grudgingly from Speedo and only 15 nails. Had to leave this job for notice board for S. Sgt. and had to plane off his letters too before correct. Speedo took saw and hammer so I couldn't finish the letter box.

Two cold showers, one blanket and sheet last night and pyjama pants only and quite warm.

Colonel now inspecting at 8:00 a.m., for 4 hours on the 12th.

In Kai Hoe I had to finish letter box today and do latrine doors tomorrow.

Everybody is to do their best to make a good impression at inspection so this is the best camp in Tokyo district.

Saw Interpreter re tools at night and told him I would not be responsible 'cause Nip "Haitis" taking away all the time. He called Speedo who gave me a saw but not a hammer so I didn't finish the box.

Thursday June 10, 1943

Nip W.O. Doc here.

Col. now coming on 13th !! So is the 12th a rest day?

Daikon top soup in the morning, cabbage and soya cake and onion soup at noon and onion and daikon top, dry mix at night.

Making more flower beds.

Interpreter woke us up at 9:30 to put our shoes under the bed. Then got officers out at 10 p.m. to throw logs down bank up near bridge!! I think this is revenge against civvies for putting logs there on the pathway, as he said, be quiet.

Dentist in camp to fix a lot of boy's teeth. Looked at mine at 1:00 in the morning. I am to go to his office in the village to get teeth fixed tomorrow night. I showed him where his filling had come out.

Fire drill.

Friday June 11, 1943

Making duck boards for M. Sgt. Making terrace at the side of sick quarters.

Sports meeting postponed till 20th.

Dry mix at noon, onion and soya cake. Onion gravy at night.

Speedo presented Cory with a form and asked him to sign for 300 Red Cross packages three days ago. Cory amended the number to 255 and initialed.

Officers working on official regulations for POW from Tokyo which are to be mimeographed and handed to us. Interpreter said if we are asked when we got them, say months ago. Oh yeah!! Obviously we should have had these ages ago. Also if we are asked about the camp, speak well of it!! Oh yeah!

Went to dentist at night and had 2 fillings (amalgam).

English khaki shirts arrived and went into store as usual!!

Saturday June 12, 1943

Rest day.

Soya cake only in soup in the morning. Small beans and onion soup at noon, like gravy and very good. Dry mix, onions and daikons, at night.

Cigarette issue, 10 per man, 20 per officer. Cake issue, 1 man 6 officers.

Feverish activity all day. Making flower gardens beside our billet and beside sick quarter.

Hot day. Bath.

Making boxes for Speedo.

Inspection by CO. Col. will be here by 7 :00 in the morning now!!

Men paid for April and May. Sheets were given to Blanchard at night and they had to be made out and men paid. It was10:30 before we finished.

Flash!! Col. will be here with 4 aides at 7 in the morning but will go through books in 40 minutes and inspect camp at 10:00 a.m. or inspect later at 11:00. Cory is being instructed as to what to say if Colonel asked him about camp but he says he will just tell the truth!!

Ordinance officer and one other here.

Sunday June 13, 1943

193 at work. Best yet.

Warm.

Sgt. Portsmouth died at 7 p.m. of diarrhoea. Total—72. If he had to die, too bad we didn't have a corpse to show Col!!

Camp spic and span before chaps went to work. Lots of flaps. Colonel arrived and was served with Red Cross cocoa and we hadn't had any yet! If he takes Red Cross stuff, we can expect people here to pilfer!! Made his inspection at 9:00 a.m., and then visited works. Had about five other officers with him but our old friend, the Yank Interpreter, was not there. Worse luck. He retired from army 'cause of ill health. Col inspected us in billets and made some remark about shoes. Unfortunately we didn't get an interview with Colonel but new Interpreter came and talked to Dave. However, our Interpreter was with him so couldn't put anything across except shoe shortage.

Interpreter said war news good and bad, which means opposite for us. Evidently things in Europe going good for us. Also said 700,000 letters for POW being sorted at Tokyo. That is very good news as it means an average of 20 each.

Colonel raised hell with CC cause sewing machine had been stuck in storage and not used.

I found out later, the inspection was a howling success. This camp had the best discipline and morale of Tokyo area camps.

Cig issue 10 per men, 20 per officers.

Had to go and play for Interpreter at night to soothe him. Interpreter said Smiling Sgt., Medical Sgt., Shoidisan and Sacamoto are all going about the middle of this month!! Glad to see some of them go, except Medical Sgt. who has been very good to us. Rumour: Doc is to be replaced by Nip doctor. Interpreter says he may also be going about the end of the month. Loud cheers!! He is worrying about his farewell speech!!

Practically hot water for soup in the morning. Fresh fish fried in batter at noon, for Colonel's benefit. Soup with 5 kilos of onions and 4 soya cakes at night. Terrible!

Interpreter said to Cory, he would ask CC for Red Cross issue tomorrow!! Inspection must have been good.

Monday June 14, 1943

Cloudy.

Six men kept back for funeral detail. Hewitt had altercation with Glass Eye re this detail. Although he was not V.O.D., he stuck his oar in when Hewitt took exception. Ordered him to kotski. Hewitt wouldn't so Glass Eye poked him in the stomach. Hewitt took him by the arm and said, come and see Interpreter. They went into administration but Glass Eye stopped inside and again ordered him to kotski. Hewitt refused and Glass Eye backed down altogether, becoming interested in working figures.

Funeral in morning and picked berries—raspberries and blackberries. Issue of 150 lbs dried pears and 1 tin bully per man. Bully beef boxes had been tampered with and were 6 tins short. The boxes open on the sides. They slid back boards and extracted tins. They even nailed an extra piece of board on the side. So obvious!! Also Col's example!!

Boiled water and sour mezor soup in the morning. Fresh fish soup at noon—not too bad. Artichoke soup at night.

Guard changed and agriculturalist Nip came in to say good-bye. Quite decent lad and says new guard is last one for this camp! Strange, although we certainly don't need a guard—we can't go any place. Perhaps they need the men!! Lots of old faces in new guard.

Tuesday June 15, 1943

Very heavy rain all last night. Showery in morning and only tunnel detail went out. Reason given that working place flooded!!

Sour mezor water in the morning. Bean dry mix at noon with bean fried in butter which has been here since the start and is now going rancid! That's what happens when they try and hoard. Still no vegetables come in!! Cory asked Interpreter for six more tins bully and he said okay. Long fish night.

Rumour: all Red Cross stuff will be issued to us in the next ten days before change in administration heads. This came from Glass Eye and Shoidisan. Two cases salmon and one meat came in.

Tried to find out from Interpreter if could buy prizes for sports meet but could get no satisfaction and he became interested in notice board. Always the same—never a straight answer.

Entertainment.

Thursday June 17, 1943

190 out to work. Clear.

Cooks say all hanchos and everybody but Glass Eye leaving. Same old morning soup. Dry mix with big beans fried in butter at noon. Fish, (salmon) soup in the afternoon.

Shaved Number 1 and 2 cooks. Nip razor for which I paid 1.02 and 3.40 tax very good.

3 loads Mackie.

Went to w.c. about twice today and softish.

Interpreter pulled a crafty one with Red Cross boxes. We were issued with 255 of original 300. Hospital had had about 13 since. Five were incomplete on arrival. Interpreter asked Doc to sign for remaining 40. He said no, hospital had not had that many but he would sign for 20 which he did. Interpreter then asked Cory to sign for 20 but Cory said hospital had only had 13 and he would sign for these not knowing Doc had signed. He signed for 13 which leaves only 7 unaccounted for by Nips!!

Had sing-song in cook's barracks until 8:45 and lads in fine spirits. Morale is certainly good. Working lads issued with rectangular rice boxes. God knows what for.

Friday June 18, 1943

Rain most of the night and day. No work.

Usual morning breakfast, fresh fish soup at noon and long fish at night.

Went to station to see M. Sgt. off at 4:30. New M. Sgt. looks quite decent and took tenko. Medical officer. Washed sheet. Made back rest.

Smiling Sgt. told Cory he is leaving July 8th and by August every army bloke will have left and camp will be run by 50 civilians!! Looks as though we will be on same basis as Koreans and it may have mixed blessings. We won't have the standing with Tokyo, I shouldn't think. Well, all we can do is wait and see.

Bridge as usual.

Saturday June 19, 1943

Morning soup as usual. Good rice and fresh fish soup. Mungo bean soup p.m. and very good like pea soup. 56 bags of rice and 60 barley came in.

Working on Nip watch most of the day. Got 7 packs cigs for it.

Rumour: lads going to live out when guards go!!

Mosquitos breeding in fire buckets.

Sunday June 20, 1943

189—185 out to work.

No rest day because of work lost during week due to rain.

STC lad, Kwek Tuck See, died of pleurisy after only two days' illness. Died 11:30 last night—73.

Officer of the Day.

Five men kept in for funeral detail. On funeral in a.m., weather fine.

Same morning soup which I don't touch. Mungo bean soup at noon was good. Fresh cod soup at night with no cod so we opened a tin of bully beef. Cory saw extra 3rd cook put tin bully inside his shirt from store and they have cocoa every day now. Blanchard told Interpreter he would tell him when he had proof of pilfering of Red Cross stuff but he seems to have backed down. I suggested we send letter in re this, but no support. I wanted to ask for check but usual, "it won't do any good anyway!!"

No bridge last two nights as Kit got offended when I pointed out his partner had made demand bid and he passed.

Monday June 21, 1943

187-5. Fine.

Same morning soup, dry mix with big beans at noon. Fresh salmon soup at night.

I was hard today at w.c.

Officer of the Day.

Interpreter said he was going to Tokyo tomorrow and would get me anything I wanted as I was shaving him but he couldn't get shaving soap.

Interpreter talked to Indians saying representative in Tokyo who wanted Peace but this had no effect on our lads.

Sgt. Rice says boys taking noon meal with them to work, in couple days' time, in boxes. What kind of noon meal will we get when men take out theirs?

Asked Interpreter if I could go with him on job next time to get high bar.

Tuesday June 22, 1943

185. Officer of the Day.

All men weighed and I was 79 kilos. I have been doing exercises every day now for two weeks and have taken waist line down though 1/5 of a kilo behind the heaviest in camp!!

Same morning soup, fresh salmon soup at noon after they scraped the maggots off!! Same at night with addition of fresh vegetables. Cross between lettuce, cabbage and very good.

In Kai Ho men to take noon meal out on job, day after tomorrow.

Sgt. Whitley given five days' heavy guard room for stealing overalls and officers guard as usual.

Not much of new vegetables came in. What ten school boys carried in, so grown locally.

Fixing watches.

Interpreter went to Tokyo to ask if he could stay here. We gave him a letter and asked him to give it to the Colonel which he promised to do.

1) Can officers buy shoes?
2) American or British Doc?
3) Regular and more frequent issue of Red Cross food to implement diet which has recently deteriorated.
4) Canteen.
5) Can we have regular issue of newspapers sent if we pay.

Don't suppose anything will come of it, but worth trying. I asked him to get me shaving, hair and scrubbing brushes, 2 volleyballs, guitar and uke capos.

Doc says they are taking most of the medicine away when army men leave!! I suppose we'll be treated by Nip civvy Doc then.

Wednesday June 23, 1943

182. Fine.

Morning soup same as mentioned but had some anyway. Good mungo bean soup with flour and butter at noon. Chinese cabbage soup at night.

Fixing watches.

Guard, CO and one other changed.

Some of tomatoes transplanted and they have fruit on!! They have come on amazingly but see no reason for transplanting.

Thursday June 24, 1943

184. Fine.

Men took out lunch of dry big bean mix. Boxes hold 2 level blue bowls. Onion and cabbage soup night and good.

Men like taking out meal as gives longer rest.

Talking to STC lad at night who is interested in weight lifting. Number 119. He has some grand physical culture pictures. Nice chap and think well to do. From Penang. He has some chest expanders which we are going to fix up.

Friday June 25, 1943

184. Fine.

Long fish and few onions at noon. Marlin soup and cabbage at night and good.

Fixing Nip watch.

We now draw our noon meal at 9:15 and it's cold by 11:30. Cooks won't let us heat it up so have fixed sawdust hot box which we'll try tomorrow. Got lot of stuff from village when went up to get cigarettes. We were to have an issue tomorrow but cigarettes had not come in. We are going up again tomorrow. I got a bottle of cod liver oil for 2.33 which cost 4.00 in black market. Also knife.

Night off from guard duty.

Saturday June 26, 1943

Fine.

Dry mix, onions and pork at noon. Marlin and onion soup (20 k fish) at night and very good.

Started moving fence back on river side of camp which gives rise to rumours. First cook is said to have stated 300 more prisoners coming in in 5 days. I hope not!! They don't seem to be able to keep men they have busy. One of hanchos on job is supposed to have said the same. On the Colonel's first visit the Interpreter said they were going to extend.

I put a shelf in the canteen and Speedo says they were going to use it to sell cigarettes and cakes. Can't see it used for this though as cigarette ration is handed to Officer of the Day and this is quite satisfactory and cake is only issued once a month if that.

Fishing has been going on in the river for the last month. Mostly 3 inch stuff but some carp and 1-2 lbs. caught.

Chap had leg broken on job when cable broke. Leg was set at Nip local hospital by Nip Doc and Bullock said set pigeon toed.

No rest day tomorrow. Probably, 28th or 29th.

No guard duty as prisoner has temperature.

Sunday June 27, 1943

Fine.

P/O Mack died of general weakness. Has been sick since arrival with diarrhoea. Funeral in morning—74.

Interpreter and Sacamoto came back. Interpreter brought mandolin from Y.M.C.A., bought strings for guitar and Hawaiian guitar pick set. Didn't bring me brushes however. I didn't think he would.

Interpreter sent Chris and Hewitt out observing today and Blanchard and someone else to go next day. Tomorrow rest day.

Big changes due. Sick and medical orderlies are to move to far end of #3 billet. #3 billet personnel to move to #1 billet. 3 hancho details to move to far end of cook's billet. Stores in middle bay, cook's billet to be moved to middle bay, #3 billet along with stoves. Blanket, etc. from officer's billet to middle bay cook's billet. Bedding to be taken out and aired. Tenko will be at 6:00 in the morning. Then food. I did sign for canteen and Interpreter said it will be open tomorrow but nothing to sell!! What a laugh. All things such as toothpaste, soap, cigs, candy, etc. which are normally issued by Officer of the Day will now be served through canteen. Cory and Power will be in charge of the canteen. Kinchi and one other brand of cigarettes to be sold.

Still moving the fence back along the whole side on river side. Something in wind. Looks like more people coming in. CC in our billet and indicating changes but couldn't get it. STC lad asked Sacamoto if we could swim in pool near bridge where river overflows retaining wall and he said no. I suggested he write out request saying I would observe and put it in suggestion box, which he did and also get a dozen others to do the same. I asked Interpreter the other day if we could and he said the river too dangerous.

Dry mix, beans and soya and pork at noon. Curry soup, onions and pork at night. Making a hot box.

Monday June 28, 1943

Fine. Making price signs for canteen. Smiling Sgt. says they moved fence to give more recreation room!

Issue of 250 lbs. Red Cross pears out of blue. Glass Eye explained if issued all once, we'd get diarrhoea, so they issue in small lots. Had wire removed and had been pilfered. I think that's why they issued so much.

Billets changed around according to last night's Kai Hoe but didn't affect us. Most of day making hot box.

Dry mix, big beans noon and long fish night. 3 cookies per man as well as 10 cigs, and 20 cigs officers issued in the usual way and not through shop.

Got more recreation things and told to display them prominently. Included cards, checkers. They had been in store a long time.

Men paid for two weeks in June. Granted men pushing things round in billet and throwing money about while trying to issue cigarettes, cookies and pay. Cory saw Interpreter about it but latter said CC gave orders. Interpreter said we may be here forever!!

Tuesday June 29, 1943

Cloudy.

Ingles (Yank) died and I think it was an accident—75. He had had diarrhoea badly for 3 days and had gone to w.c. on job. Evidently he had fainted and fallen back. His head had been hit by a log, and forced on to his chest and he had died of suffocation.

We went to the job and took him to the crematorium. Medical orderly, when he pointed out that some officers have no shoes to go on funeral, Interpreter said go in clogs and when pointed out they are no good, Interpreter said borrow other officers!!

10,000 cigs came in.

Sent 3 L.D. men out to work with cards. If they work they get paid but can rest when they feel like it. Good system, I think.

Cory got list of things Red Cross representative asks on visits and it is now apparent why all activity lately. Such questions as how much recreation room, (move fence back). Facilities for spending money? (Opening canteen). Inspection by officers tomorrow and obviously Red Cross rep. Interpreter says we must answer in favour of camp!

Wednesday June 30, 1943

Fine.

Made out a copy of questions Red Cross representative asked and also summary of Red Cross packages received and issued in case we get a chance to talk to him. He is to inspect at 9:00 in the morning. Also made remarks on other questions he may ask.

Dave and Blanchard sent out observing, obviously to get them out of the way. Blanchard was going out in slippers and at last they issued Dave and he with rubber shoes!! Later all officers got them but me. Interpreter told me to change with Dave at 8:30.

Canteen was all stocked up with cigarettes, cookies etc. in morning but cleared again as soon as Red Cross representative left!

Blanchard and I hurried into tunnel at 10:30 and we were kept there till 11:30. Found out Red Cross rep, a Swiss, had been on job during that period. So we were taken out of the way so we wouldn't see him!! Too bad as I had everything ready.

There hasn't been much progress on the job. Lads have not worked too hard and on contract most of them finish early.

Cod for noon and the same fried in batter at night.

Tunnels through mountain quite interesting. They are to take water from reservoir and deliver to turbines. They are about 30′ diameter and concrete lined. Slope about 1 in 50 at a guess. So they will carry fair amount water.

At noon we had a cold meal on the job. Some of the bosses are very good to lads and bring them things to eat. We had cucumber and soya sauce and tea.

Following things were brought up in interview of Dave, Cory, Hewitt and Rhys with Swiss Red Cross rep:

1) On policy of issuing Red Cross supplies: representative asked Nips and they said it was at the discretion of CC, that there was no time limit for issuing but signed receipts had to be submitted to Red Cross in Tokyo. Asked how they could tell there had been no delivery as we had evidence of it here, and he said only by receipts.

2) Could any authority overrule our Doc's decision about sending sick men to work, and after questioning Nips, representative said CC could overrule.

3) Asked if we could have Yank or British doctor and after asking Nips, the representative said none were available in Tokyo but they might be able to get one from another camp.

4) Hospitalization of operable cases and representative asked Nips who said Matsumoto Hospital is now full but Doc there was going to let us know when beds are available.

5) He said no exchange ships now available for Red Cross supplies and no supplies at present in Tokyo but expecting some soon.

6) Asked about officers doing fatigues they hadn't volunteered for. Answer from Interpreter vague and something about CC ordering them. Representative said as they hadn't ratified Red Cross convention, they could do as they liked re officers working! Asked that all orders for officers' fatigues come through Interpreter and he agreed.

7) Brought up question of beating up of people by granted men and Interpreter said he would tell them to stop this. Representative made it clear that since they hadn't ratified Red Cross convention they could really do as they like and all he could do was transmit our complaints to our countries through Geneva and it would boil down to reprisals.

Rep saw our library and said it was very small and he would try to get more books sent.

Finally the Nip major, who was with the representative, stopped Interpreter as he couldn't find out what was being said as local Interpreter couldn't follow conversation in English and thought things might be said which he didn't want said.

Representative brought through camp and made notes. Nips said our Doc here (Dutch Wog) was good and Dave said if you want to see how good he is look at number of deaths we have had. Nip major said that was due to our weak condition when we arrived which was due anyway to Nip neglect.

Later the four of them were called into Interpreter's office and CC and Smiling Sgt. there. They were questioned as to what they had said to representative as obviously Interpreter couldn't follow it. Hope Nip major brassed off with Interpreter!!

Later Dave and Cory were called back after the CC had left and were slugged by Smiling Sgt. so that Nips evidently didn't like the questions that were asked!!

At night granted men given talking to by Sacamoto and Pig Face and Ex. #2 cook slugged by him!! Didn't know what this was all about but funny as they had "rubber necked" Dave and Cory previously.

2 basket of carrots, 2 of cukes and 1 of runner beans came in.

Thursday July 1, 1943

Cloudy. Brought in wood and sawdust.

Shaved Interpreter who asked me where we wanted to swim and I told him in the pond near the bridge. He promised to ask CC. Also said "I'm willing to make better plan!!" Meaning, I take it, he is willing to help to make the camp better—but he doesn't act like it!!

Have been sleeping up top last 2 nights and slept very well as air good. Have been troubled by fleas lately which far worse than lice and can't catch them. They don't seem to trouble all of us.

Dry mix and beans at noon and thin fish soup at night.

Guard changed so report from Smiling Sgt. that last guard was last one was all balls as usual.

Friday July 2, 1943

188 at work.

Cloudy. Fried cod at noon and seaweed soup at night with little cukes and carrots on side.

Officers to make fish pond tomorrow for POW to observe and bring up fish!!

So far no ill effects from report to Red Cross representative.

Mouldy bread (1/3 loaf ea) fried in fat with smear of butter and couple grains sugar. This is for tomorrow's breakfast. Bread came in at night before Red Cross representative came and was on show for him. Nips would probably have had it but let it get stale as usual so we were given it. Still even mouldy bread is good to us although we don't get rice. Food lately very poor with lack of vegetables which I can't understand as plenty growing close at hand.

I'm not eating so much lately and waistline decreasing.

Saturday July 3, 1943

I am going to rig up weight lifting apparatus in billet.

Tomatoes making rapid strides and a lot of fruit appearing. Watermelons are a failure.

Interpreter made officers stand at tenko till billets finished but when Sacamoto came on we were dismissed at night and got away with it.

Sunday July 4, 1943

Rained most of the night again. Men went to work at 7:30 when it stopped but it rained in afternoon again.

Started fish pond. I'm very loose these days and go 4-5 times a day. Don't know what the cause is.

Mungo bean mix at noon and pretty poor—carrot, cuke, fried bean soup at night.

Four loads of coal came in. Big coal supply now. I suppose it's sent here when they can spare it, in preparation for winter.

Monday July 5, 1943

Showery.

Nip Doc here during the last two days. He asked to see Dave, Cory and Blanchard. In ensuing conversation following points covered. He said no big happenings in Europe. He asked if we had mabela and we said very little and had wasted it by putting in one lb. with rice. He said letters being sorted at Tokyo, after asking us if we had had any. Expressed surprise when he saw Nip summer clothes and asked if that was all we had. Cory said we have few clothes of our own. He went round the camp and we told him our interpreting difficulties and told him he spoke better English than our Interpreter. He examined sick and STC with rupture and we asked if he could have hospital treatment, which he did not promise. In general covered most of points covered with Red Cross Representative. He seemed decent but we suspect he was only asking questions from his own curiosity in the Nips.

Cook's inventory 18 sacks of rice and barley short. Must be usual Nip paper error as okay two weeks ago. Anyway, they are cutting 4 kilos rice and 4 barley each meal till deficit made up which will take 36 days!

Working on fish pond and they change their ideas every hour. We are doing hour shifts of three but some hard to get out.

Rumour: Nips getting H___ in Solomons because of our air superiority. Interpreter brought back medicines for troops which they asked for: Wakamoto (Vitamin B) ointment (for flea bites) and one other.

Black market flour being issued these days and can get nearly anything. Two sacks each of pumpkins, eggplants, cabbage and carrots came in. Big bean mix at noon with raw onions. Vegetable soup at night and very good.

Tuesday July 6, 1943

Cloudyish.

Officers doing up 500 blankets to send to Tokyo to be cleaned!

About 20 sacks potatoes, some onions and eggplant came in. No. 1 cook says vegetables now going to come in in small amounts of about two days' ration. This good as fresh.

Still on fish pond and tough digging.

Mungo bean mix at noon and sloppy and poor. Fish and vegetable soup at night with raw onion, tomato, eggplant and cucumber and very good.

Asked Interpreter if he had asked CC re swimming and he said no, he had diarrhoea—what that had to do with it I don't know!!

Leg okay now for couple months and no swelling. Eye also okay. Weighed on Cook House scale and 77 K with pants and shoes on.

Wednesday July 7, 1943

186 at work.

Had swim! And hope will get permission for lads too. Interpreter came and took me to pool near bridge and told me to go ahead. I expect he wanted to see what I could do and did I perform!! I hope it has good effect! Water was surprisingly warm.

Made table for chap in sick quarters with broken leg. Did a lot of work hauling big rocks for fish pond.

Vegetables in morning soup!! First time in months—some cabbage. 40 K potatoes in noon mix with raw vegetables on side and good!! Fish and vegetable soup with cukes and eggplant on side and potatoes in rice—good.

Quartermaster Officer here and big changes in diet. In morning 7 kilos barley only—no rice and taksan vegetables in dry mix—no soup (not missing anything). Some meals to be straight rice. Noon meal 44 kilos rice and barley and vegetables and beans in dry mix. Nobody to be allowed in Cook House now, especially major!! Guards in Cook House and given instructions. Rumour: to watch our cooks! Maybe they are to blame them for rice and barley shortage.

Hewitt, Sgt. Brown and Doc had interview with Nip Doc last night and following covered:
(1) Suggested diarrhoea patients be put on straight rice and Nip doc seemed surprised this not already done. Going to try.
(2) Hewitt said diarrhoea caused by barley and suggested it be ground. Nip did not think this possible.
(3) Stressed necessity of more vegetables, meat and fish.
(4) Suggested couple of men from each detail come in for noon meal as now it sometimes goes bad by noon. He will see.
(5) Said morning soups no good and want more vegetable.
(6) Can we have sugar issued to us in bulk so we can use as we like since we don't put sugar in soups.

Think this discussion may have some effect.

The Second Diary

LES CHATER'S SECOND JOURNAL, DATED JULY 8, 1943 TO JANUARY 14, 1944 is the smallest book. It measures only 7¹/₂ cm by 11¹/₂ cm by ¹/₂ cm. Also somewhat worn looking, but generally in good shape considering its age. It is embossed on the front cover with the word Notebook. The first five pages are blank, perhaps because F/L Chater was saving this space for official records of some sort. If we are to learn from his first volume, we know that this was what F/L Chater saw as his duty as an officer toward his "boys:" that is, to be a record-keeper. He recorded sicknesses and deaths, Japanese treatment of the POWs, their diet, important incidents at the camp, even the little news he was able to glean from reading reports in Japanese newspapers.

But uppermost in each man's mind, as it was in F/L Chater's, was the state of his own health. As he watched his mates sicken and die, one by one, he must have felt, deep within, a terrible fear for his own life. Some might consider it obsessive to be so concerned about the state of one's bowels, but this, for many men, was the surest way to judge their own health. A fine line existed between diarrhoea and dysentery, but once the more serious illness struck, life could slip away in a matter of a few pain-filled days.

Nonetheless, F/L Chater's positive attitude prevails in each entry of this diary, as it does in the other two. He is grateful for a good meal, a good swim, or a good talk with one of his fellow inmates or even a friendly guard. He is even grateful when his friends receive letters and he doesn't, commenting that next time he is sure to get a letter. If we are to list the reasons for his survival, clearly his optimism would be at the top. Consider too how this attitude influenced the others in the camp—including the Japanese!

Unlike the first diary, there are no commercial printed dates in this booklet, only a fine blue line 2 cm from the top of the page. F/L Chater's printing in this booklet is somewhat easier to read than the first book.

Thursday July 8, 1943

Fine weather. For a.m. 7 kilos barley, eggplant, cabbage, all in soup—2 ladles per man—no rice. Not much to go to work on!! Boys mostly ate their noon meal at kyukei so there is nothing at noon!! One hancho was sent to village and got rice for lads, and another tried to. Noon, dry mix, 22 K barley and 22 K rice with beans, potatoes, pumpkin and eggplant. At night, 15 kilos barley, 8 kilos rice with beans, spuds and pumpkin in rice and soup with potatoes, eggplant, carrots and tops, beans. Very good meal.

Went to get cigarettes in the village, but none. However bought a lot of things. I saw a lot things in the village which get black market at high price!

Officers on fish pond. Officers are to take out noon meal tomorrow to lads. They will get hot and fresh meal anyway!

Interpreter had men up to his office questioning them asking if they had experience on the following:

1) Experience in installing wireless and repairing on ships.
2) Installing and repairing small (500 w) transmitting sets.
3) Experience in automatic telephone exchanges.
4) Experience in telephone trouble shooting.
5) Experience in battery work, welding, machines or generally technicians.
6) Experience in research laboratories

No. 1—to go to Manchoukud

No. 3—Big cities employed by civvy firms.

No. 4—By telephone companies.

No. 5 and 6—factories

Some of these would be okay but not when bombing starts as likely to be in target areas. Only about one of our lads said he had experience. Most of them prefer to sweat it out here.

Friday July 9, 1943

Fine. Hanchos on job say going to organize rice pool as they figure boys are not getting enough to last two days.

138 at work.

6 kilo radishes and 10 kilo spuds in sloppy soup. Noon 22 kilo beans and 22 kilo rice with beans, onions, and spuds in dry mix and good. At night, 15 kilos beans and 8½ kilos rice with onions in mix. Very good soup with 16 kilos mungo beans, 10 onions, eggplant. Four bundles of eggplant, 3 cukes, 2 daikon and 1 fava beans came in. I made a cart and we took the noon meal out to men in buckets but balls-up at other end mostly caused by Nips wanting to do it their way. Tomorrow may put in boxes here and take out at 11 a.m.

Still squitting!! Haircut.

Rumour: heavy fighting in Solomons and Aleutians.

Interpreter went round billets at 10:15 and took names of all men who had left their sandals out.

Saturday July 10, 1943

Fine. Sloppy stew same as yesterday. Noon dry mix with large white bean (haricot) onions and eggplant with sweet seaweed, on the side. Night—mushy rice with little spuds and pumpkin and soup of eggplant, onion.

Took noon meal out in buckets and divided by billets as do in camp and okay although they got just over blue bowl per man.

Asked Interpreter if we could swim now and he said, "I cannot tell." Then I asked if I could go in this afternoon if Shoidi did and he said okay. Hewitt and Scarlett asked Smiling Sgt. if they could and he agreed. Went in at 2 p.m. and were having a great time till CC came along and stopped us, saying swimming only between 5 and 6. Later at Kai hoe he said swimming for all men from 5:00-6:00 and I am observing officer. Bad time as right after hurried meal unless we eat at 6 and then it's cold. Still it's a swim.

At tenko tonight, Smiling Sgt. lectured Nip guard for one hour while we were standing waiting. Chaps sat down so after tenko all marched to guard room (190). All but 60 put in guard house (about 25′ x 14′)—rest standing outside and no windows in guard room. Officers lined up outside and had to "stand and observe" although it was quite apparent we were also being punished even though we didn't sit down. Men asked for it because they had started to take liberties since discipline by Nips not so severe.

P/O Scarlett was slapped by Interpreter for looking up when Interpreter was talking to us!! We stood out till 10:45 and then two Erks were carried out of guard room who had fainted. Then tenko was called. We were given a lecture re discipline and let off. 5 hours standing, mostly in one place!! Boy, were we tired!! Still, we thought we were there for the night!

Sunday July 11, 1943

185 out to work. Fine. Officer of the Day.

Started new fish pond behind administration today. No rest day.

7 K barley, onions and spuds and fava beans in a soup! Noon—dry mix, beans, onions with eggplant on the side. Night—fish soup with beans and eggplant and spuds and beans in rice. Swimming from 5:00–6:00 but finished at 5:35 as all had had enough. 27 down altogether and grand. Quite well behaved as I have laid down rules. About 7 life guards in camp which helps me. It doesn't look as though I am going to have a hot supper as long as swimming is on as start just as food is dished.

New arrangements for tenko now. Billets line up according to working groups and each Hancho "Bangos" his group. Only one "Eyes Front" given (by Officer of the Day).

Very sultry at night and couldn't get to sleep. Mossies bad these days too. Cig issue usual.

Monday July 12, 1943

185 to work.

Hot and sultry a.m. Usual soup with spuds and fava beans. Noon spuds and eggplant mix with cucumbers on the side!

Chap caught smoking at wash stand by CC who threw pipe away and said no more selling cigs to POWs. His excuse was although pipe in mouth no tobacco in it. Interpreter said he would intercede for us as maybe CC was mistaken but troops are getting lax, witness guard room the other night. Also they say cheeking Hanchos on job, etc. They will soon lose all privileges they have!!

Seaweed soup and 1 bowl beans and spud mix at night. Vegetables came in. No swimming. Rain.

Men given talking to by Sacho re laxity obeying regulations. It was decided officers should tick off any disobedience.

Rumour: Russia and Nips at war—heavy fighting in Solomons where we outnumber Nips 20-1.

Rumour: Sicily nearly in our hands—we are moving our troops to Eastern Mediterranean. Huns made small crossings of Doneti.

Kumi Electric Co. to take over camp in 8th month.

Tuesday July 13, 1943

185. Hot. Officer of the Day. Swimming and very good.

Usual a.m. soup with barley—very good. Dry mix noon with soya bean and onion. Night soya bean and potato mix with onion and carrot soup—very good.

Washing soap issue to men. Working on fish pond and tough work in heat. Lads must be in good shape to stand so many hours each day at such work. Getting hotter now.

Wednesday July 14, 1943

Hot. No work on pool so fixing watches.

Interpreter called me in afternoon and said concert for all in new building up town. We were to make a program lasting for 3 hours starting at 6 p.m. and no swimming.

Some letters, (about 15) came. One for Kit and another for Dave. One for Sgt. Rice (Canadian!!) so looks good for me but none in this lot.

Concert in village cancelled so had swimming. Held impromptu concert in billet at night.

Interpreter told us he is leaving soon. Guard changed. Soap issue 1/2 tablet to officers. Smiling Sgt. says all army personnel leaving camp except CC. Sacamoto came back and I think he brought all the dope with him.

Usual a.m. soup with spuds. Soya beans and onion mix at noon and good. Beans and spud mix with onion. Spud and bean soup, curried and very good.

Rumour: Japan and Russia are not at war but relations strained. Sacamoto brought paper back for us dated July 7th which says vital battles in Solomons and Yanks have landed on Rendover Isle there. McArthur in New Guinea fighting in Aleutians. Mussolini made speech in which he takes full responsibility for war and says enemy very near fatherland. Looks bad for Italy. Wavell made Viceroy of India (Military dictator)! Very heavy bombing of Sicily and Italy. (Naples bombed 70 times.)

Thursday July 15, 1943

Rest day. Medical Officer. Tenko 6:40 a.m. Hot.

Smiling Sgt. says he is leaving soon and all army leaving except CC.

Electric Co. taking over and work Hanchos will run camp. This should be grand.

A truck load of rice and barley came in yesterday. Swimming from 1:00 to 3:30 and 75 men came down. It was grand and had basketball which makes good water polo ball. It will be difficult to get enough players however.

Usual a.m. meal. Dry mix, beans and onions at noon.

Saturday July 17, 1943

Very hot. A.m. same onions and bean mix and more at noon. Bean mix and blue bowl and one and a half white bowl per man with poor seaweed and onion soup.

Asked Interpreter if I could make copy of letters so we could issue them and he said Blanchard would do this in the afternoon but he didn't!!

No swimming as blood test for all for diphtheria. Also took throat swab test.

Cart sent to Tokyo so now have to carry food to men at noon. Also will have to carry wood. Tomatoes, carrots and pumpkin came in on hand cart.

Fire extinguishers sent to Tokyo so looks as though army is taking everything with them.

Papers came in from June 22 to July 4th—which say Russians have started offensive!! Seems submarine warfare has been defeated by new methods as hardly any sinking claims made and say will start sub warfare soon when discover new methods. Big fighting in Solomons. Churchill says when Europe cleaned up and settled will concentrate on Japan. Our bomber losses over Europe—6%.

Sunday July 18, 1943

Hot. Fixing watches. Carrying wood to kitchen now. Made box for Speedo.

All in camp at 4:30 ordered to swim!! Reason was cameraman (civvy) taking pictures for propaganda obviously. Tomorrow all POW are to be photographed separately, clean shaven with POW jackets and new numbers. Also going to take pictures of people in tomato patch and near fish pond.

A.m. soup same, onion and bean dry mix with cukes at noon. Onion and bean mix and onion and spud curry soup with cukes and tomatoes on the side at night. Hand cart vegs came in.

Only two letters issued so far to people who went up and asked for them!!

Paid today—50 y—deposit 57.26 y. Bridge every night.

STC lad had thigh broken when cable broke.

Rumour: Yanks captured Ravell.

Monday July 19, 1943

Cloudyish. Everyone had pictures taken. Also group pictures of musicians, officers in tomato patch and fish pond. One copy to go Tokyo and another home, probably Air Ministry. Had to shave off beards.

Cory and Hewitt allowed to send radiograms home. 35 words, two persons per month, Yanks only, (but they eat English Red Cross food!) "Friendly men" allowed to send first, then diligent men!

Went to village with Kawate and bought a lot of stuff. Interpreter said today Smiling Sgt. leaving on the 28th of this month and Interpreter a few days later—also officers may be leaving between these two dates for officer's camp. This may be move for better or worse. Looks as though they wish to conform to convention by segregating officers. Will have big load to carry with condiments etc.

Swimming but only 3 down but good.

Usual a.m. big bean and onion mix noon and good. Bean mix and pumpkin and daikon soup at night.

Tuesday July 20, 1943

Usual cig issue. Usual a.m. soup, bean and spud mix at noon. Bean mix at night with curried carrot and bean soup—good.

Rumour: we landed 300,000 troops in Sicily.

Interpreter said Cory and seven other officers moving to Tokyo with him in next few days. One Yank staying and four others. He will pick officers to go—worse luck!! Says fatigues we doing here contrary to International law and they may go from Tokyo to officers camp to read and study. Personally I don't know which will be better—to move or stay. Things should improve here when civvies take over but CO and all "granted men" are staying. Depends who stays. I would like to be with Dave anyway!

Closed books today and I was 8 yen up—pleasant surprise.

Fleas are getting very bad and nearly everybody has them. All except four officers are now sleeping outside our cubby holes but fleas are there too. They must be in the straw undermats. Officers spread all over billet and best thing is to keep moving.

Making boxes for Nips to send army stuff away. All bowls turned in (except officers) so don't know how men are going to be served tomorrow!! Men kept on hop. Started raining at 10 and we took out food in rain. Heavy rain set in and men came in after food. Eased up at 2:00 and they went out again. Rained little more and then stopped.

Wednesday July 21, 1943

Cloudyish, clearing later for swimming and did 10 lengths. Weighed and I was 74.3 K, a drop of nearly 5 K due to cut rations, not eating till after, and swimming. Most of lads down. My actual weight was 73.2 K as I weighed just before but they always add on.

Farewell concert tomorrow. Making boxes.

All letters finally issued and still doesn't look as though they are sure we are POW. Kit's letter dated June 27, 42!! A year ago. Dave's letter Dec. 3—latest date of letters Feb. 4, which is not too bad.

Had first tomatoes out of garden! Watermelons growing better last two weeks after bad start. Gladiolus flowering. Eggplants have produced fruit but were stolen!!

Officers now going about the 25th and CC making selection of those to stay. Everyone has own opinion of who will be left. Doc will be according to Interpreter. I say Blanchard, Hewitt, Rhys and myself. We all do work round camp. There will be plenty to do with only four officers and we don't know how granted men will behave when Hanchos go. Not much company during long winter days either!!

Switched rice and barley quantities between night and a.m. Better because we get soup at night anyway and didn't seem to make much difference in quantity of night meal. We are to get two days' notice if possible as to who is to leave. All officers to have shoes fixed tomorrow.

Thursday July 22, 1943

Hot. Moved to other side billet topside to try and dodge fleas but they found me!!

Usual a.m. meal but thicker. B.bean mix noon. Mungo bean mix at night with seaweed soup and a couple of small dumplings. Pretty poor.

Swimming and did 12 lengths—getting better. While I was swimming Interpreter came in and gave names of officers to go—those staying are Hewitt (Yank), Rhys, Dunlop and as I thought, *myself*. I was one out in my guess, probably cause all S/L rank to go. Blanchard asked if any chance of changing as he and Dunlop are friends but Interpreter said no. Tokyo Colonel had made selection—meaning I suppose, he had said so many F/L to stay. Well, so be it, I stay. It will be gloomy without Dave and the rest but those staying are not too bad. No more bridge so will probably have closer contact with men at night. Had concert at night by command and 1 M.S.

Interpreter said would probably issue Red Cross boots to those going but didn't know about Red Cross food. Packed all kettles away.

Friday July 23, 1943

Cool last night and I suppose nights will begin to get cooler now. Officers making preparations to go and rather makes one gloomy.

Exchange for foreign money handed in months ago given today.

£1—95 sen

$1 Yank—99 sen

5 pesos—8.75 yen

1 guilder—30 sen.

Seems all out of proportion. Oh well, I haven't any to come. Total handed out 328 y. All deposit money of going officers handed to Cory to give out—about 3,000 y. Then recalled again to administration building.

Interpreter gave speech at p.m. tenko. " You are all hungry and do not work as well. I am hungry too!!" (Oh yeah!) "And I am angry but new diet is summer diet and order from Tokyo! War will soon be over and then you will go home so keep your health! This best

Currency collected from the various places Les was located, including Hong Kong, Ceylon, and Japan. Token wages were paid to POW workers by the owners of the foundry in Kanose, but there was nothing to buy. This money is now worthless.

camp and best climate." He told Cory later they are going to island prison camp in south-west Tokyo, probably the one where the Germans were last war.

CO stopped all rice balls a week ago on job but mostly back again. Food terrible today as no vegetables have come in. Same in a.m. Dry mix B. beans noon and evening same as morning.

Five swimming and did 14 lengths easily. No party as promised but entertainment. Cigarette issue as usual. Officers going were told to hand all their Nip stuff in and then stopped them.

Saturday July 24, 1943

Going officers lined up and Interpreter said Blanchard and Hewitt change places. They all thought Hewitt to go but he meant Hewitt takes over entertainment. They then had to hand in all Nip stuff which was great relief to them.

Cigarette issue again. Two in two days. No swimming. Made hammock to stop fleas.

Farewell party night for Interpreter, Smiling Sgt., Medical Sgt. and gave us ½ gal saki. Drank toast to our health. Interpreter made speech in the p.m. tenko saying some officers going. Some you like. Some you may hate. Cory in reply asked for co-op with remaining officers. Officers signing autographs all night and entertainment till 8:30. M.O. going. Officers issued with Red Cross boots and are they good. Rather significant I think—want them to look their best. Lined up at 4 and had kit inspected—to see they are not taking any Nip stuff, I think. Then after all packed had to unpack again and be re-inspected at 6.

Food same as yesterday except got 2 doughnuts each with night meal. Our cooks persuaded them to do this instead of putting flour in rice. Did very well with presents today.

Shaving etc.

All officers paid for July—50 y—56.82 deposit. Officers all set to go by electric train all way—12 hours to leave at 7:10 a.m. when Interpreter came in at 10 p.m. and said would not leave now till 28th! So they have to go through it all again. CC gave them speech at 4:00 and said they had been treated as friends. I wonder how they would treat enemies!

Sending L.D. men out at 9 in a.m. and if they work, they will get paid.

Sunday July 25, 1943

Special meal a.m. for going away officers! Who didn't go away. Spud mix noon. Spud mix night and spud gravy. Watermelon came in! But still no more vegetables. Glass Eye said we could buy things in the village when we went up with No. 1 Parasite, but latter scared stiff and wouldn't let us. Glass Eye very friendly these days. I shaved him and he promised me corned beef and *sikit juji* also!

Swimming and did 16 lengths. Smiling Sgt. visits us frequently now and learns English. Says 1st cook, Glass Eye, Pig Face, Ex. No. 2 Cook and One Arm only granted men staying. Not a very good selection.

Fleas getting very bad now and some officers are not getting any sleep! I think my hammock is the answer.

Tomorrow is rest day. Tenko at 6:30. Glass Eye promises to buy things in Mura for us.

1st solid stool for months!

Monday July 26, 1943

Hot. Weather very hot now during day but cooler at night. Cubicle unbearable. Tried to get swimming in a.m. but wasn't allowed till 2 and only a few went down.

Rest day and not bothered at all. I had tummy ache slightly and went soft again.

Going away officers buying mess kits and the prices! What a difference. You could get any part for 5-10 cigarettes in winter time. Now the price is 10 yen for cups and bottles and 15 yen for mess kit with lid!! The old supply and demand.

Lots of chaps bringing in greens (old Canadian weed), washing and eating them, and they don't seem to hurt them. Usual a.m. and same at p.m.with dry mix and 3 doughnuts at noon. Latter was very good.

Some of granted men packing preparatory to leaving tomorrow: Speedo, T.B., Pig Face, Kawatasan. Sorry to see two of these leave as have been decent lately but Glass Eye coming round fine and he used to be worst in lot. Sacamoto asked me if I would buy Speedo's tools but I said no. I made things for Nips so they should supply tools. They were left on table in our billet. 65 yen was price. Hanchos passing round books for our addresses. I don't know what they expect if they visit us in future!

Tuesday July 27, 1943

Hot. Usually carry wood in early a.m. now, before 7. Sleep a little after dinner. Take meal out to men at 10:45 and fix watches and read and play bridge the rest of the day. Every time I fix one watch I get two more to fix!!

Granted men due to leave seem to have gone and tools are still on our table!! Ordinance officer and medical Sgt. here and rations increased. Meal we used to get put on at every meal—a sort of millet grain—17 K a.m.,15 K at noon and night—a substantial increase!!

Men very cheerful these days and spirits really high. Civvies in administration the last two days preparing to take over, I guess.

No fleas last night and I slept right through, not even getting up to pee!

Officers still leaving in a.m. as far as they know and have been promised Red Cross issue but don't know if to all men or just officers. All officers in front of administration at 6 a.m. tomorrow!! Persistent rumour: that Musso" has abdicated" which, if true, is very significant.

Pay sheets for men for December handed to us to be made out. Strange, as men paid for this month.

STC lad caught with mess kit, cup and tomatoes he had stolen and this reported to Nips. Hope we don't have to guard with only 4 officers!!

(Later) Yes, we have to guard and do 2 hours each but he only got one day guard room and no breakfast—they certainly are relaxing. Later another STC lad caught with ink and cod liver oil stolen. He was also put in the guard room but given two nights. All out of proportion. Had to pay for watermelon we had today—what a joke. Officers paid for all. Going away officers get 1 pack cigs as Red Cross issue!! and had to pay for them!!

Wednesday July 28, 1943

Hot. This time the eight officers got away—Interpreter and Pig Face went with them. Pulled out by electric train at 7 a.m. We and cooks went to station with them. Glass Eye brought kettle for us. He has certainly changed lately. Greets us officers as long lost brothers and he used to be most hated man on camp.

Cooks and medical orderlies utilized to take out noon meal now. Plenty of food for the four of us today—too much in fact! Looks as though we are going to be well treated.

Special a.m. meal for officers with hot cakes, noon mix spuds but plenty of it with extra ration. Men had boxes filled with cukes on side. Rice and spud and pumpkin stew at night.

Cleaned up billet. Hewitt removed all mats from their hovel in attempt to defeat fleas and reports it works. Place seems dead without other officers but don't notice it too much. Interpreter says he's coming back on the 30th and is leaving for good on the 1st!!

Rumour: new cabinet formed in Italy by order of the king. Also rumour: Italy has asked for peace. If this is true, it won't be long now. This winter should see the end of Germany since she obviously couldn't spare any men for Italy. Also big fighting in Solomon area.

Thursday July 29, 1943

More parasites working round camp now preparatory to take over by Electric Co. Didn't do any guard room last night as not called out!!

Get wood every day now for Cook House and I'm Officer of the Day.

No swimming as rain. I have been only one going down last two days but I'm determined to keep it open.

Rice and soup in the morning. Potato with butter mix at noon and cukes. Curry vegetable stew, spuds and string beans at night. Dry rice with butter. String beans came during the last two days and we got cukes yesterday.

Rumour still persists Mussolini given boot and new government has asked for 24-hour armistice.

Friday July 30, 1943

182—Hot. Cleared all mats out of our cubicle and washed it down in effort to get rid of fleas. Took off doors and windows and place grand now. Flies no worse than before.

Interpreter came back. Two swimming.

Eggplant soup and rice in a.m. Mix of soya beans and pumpkin at noon and mix and cukes at night.

Pump motor on fire and water detail at night. Time going very quickly now. We're finding so much to do. Cleaned billet through and it's better than it's ever been and CC said "Hiroshi!" Seems well disposed to remaining officers. Tomatoes came in.

Medical Sgt. left for Matsumoto.

Saturday July 31, 1943

182 at work. Interpreter told us he's going today and we can accompany him to the station at 3:00. I think Sacamoto is going also but Smiling Sgt. is not going today. Interpreter brought back a letter from Dave saying they arrived O.K. and are staying a few days before

leaving for other camp which has been reported as good. Met one Air Crew—only chap from Makasura who says everybody moved from there and Clulee had died.

Asked for cigs but they say there are none. Ten men kept back for water details as pump still out of order. Pump working in afternoon. First cook leaving Cook House to take Sacamoto's place. This will leave ex. 2nd cook in charge which is not so good.

Interpreter left at 3:15 and we saw him off with sigh of relief. One of the greatest tormentors gone!!

Rumour: new civvy Interpreter educated at U. of Washington, US! Rumour: it is a woman!

Parasites took over guard duty today and look funny carrying guns in their scraggy dress.

At night tenko Interpreter speech read and Smiling Sgt. said he and guard leaving tomorrow.

Fukijima Keitaro, (nicknamed Mushmouth) the Interpreter at Mitsushima camp, who was accused of beating American POWs with wooden shoes, clubs and other instruments. He was sentenced to death, later transmuted to seven years' imprisonment. (War Trials photo)

Sunday August 1, 1943

Hot. Found out how fleas got in hammock. Went to lats and when I came back my legs were covered. Fixing watches.

Mix in the morning and mungo bean soup. F. Bean and spring onions mixed with cabbage and beans on side at noon. Mix at night and onion and melon soup. Spring onion and tomatoes on side. Feeding very well these days. First cook seems to be still first cook as well as office job. "Little man" out on job now as chief hancho and our cooks seem to have running of Cook House themselves now. Food ration increased this a.m.

All officers set out to see Smiling Sgt. off but CC sent all but me back. Only 5 granted men left now. Sacamoto must have left yesterday some time.

Rumours but not definite Italy packed it in.

	a.m.	noon	night
rice	16	16	
barley	14	21	6
millet	16½	12	12
beans	14½	—	—
spuds	—	—	15

Monday August 2, 1943

Hot. A.m. mix with mungo beans. Noon, mix with long beans. Night mix with pumpkin and tomato on side.

New Interpreter arrived and speaks good English. Attended Davis Agricultural College in the US. Seems decent chap. Says twice Nips have sent ambassadors to US to ask for honourable peace terms and have been refused. This blow to us but must expect it. Says Nips will fight to last man. At evening tenko he seemed very nervous but got ideas over well— what a difference from last Interpreter. Also very polite to Nips, and us, bowing all the time.

Hewitt had run in with Yank L.D. man who wouldn't do work ordered. He took a swing at him and when he got cheeky he took him to the Interpreter. Nips pleased Hewitt hit him and put him in guard room and we have to guard as usual.

At tenko Interpreter said men getting lax in discipline and dress at tenko—in future punishments will be more severe. He said they must obey officers as orders given by them were from CC as we have no power to issue our own orders. CC says if we spruce up he will allow us to buy sweets, soap, etc.

Fixed hammock which broke last night. Granted men now take tenko. Swimming.

Talking to Interpreter but only thing worth mentioning is he promises to see if CC will allow entertainment every night. Civvies took over officially.

Working on fish pond.

Tuesday August 3, 1943

Rice issue at noon and morning, but 1 kilo to make up for shortage of 18 sacks which I mentioned before. Mix in the morning, noon and night, with gravy on side at night.

Swimming. Started to study physics book.

Came to our notice that some people are stealing Red Cross food from store. Searched suspected kits and found 3 tins bully beef.

Yank still in guard room asked Interpreter for cigarette issue but he says there is none at present. Chaps have become a little better at getting out for tenko.

Very little news but no news is good news.

This page illustrates Les's attempt to practice his engineering skills using the single engineering book in the camp.

Wednesday August 4, 1943

Interpreter asked Doc for names of people who should go to hospital. We officers discussed whether we should turn men involved in Red Cross thefts over to Nips and decided yes. Then the issue arose whether to question them ourselves first and I voted we should as innocent men may be punished and guilty get away if Nips took it all in hand.

Very tired as we didn't get to bed till 11 and did 2 hours guard room duty later. Yank to stay in guard room till CC says he can go.

Hewitt reported theft of Red Cross food to CC through Interpreter at 2 p.m. At 3:00 CC came to billet and in long conversation told us to find out who the guilty persons are from suspects, then tell him. Also he said he had kept the officers to run this camp who were hard working, obedient and other officers went to camp which had worse climate than this. He told us to do our best to run camp and although soldiers had been sent away he was still in charge and regulations are the same. He seems more amenable to us these days.

Asked Interpreter to see Red Cross stores more securely locked up. Yank still in guard room and Interpreter asked us what we thought best thing to do with him. Told him we didn't think he was crazy but this is not Doc's opinion. We think our present method best.

Ex 2nd cook is definitely in charge of Cook House now but a bit better than he used to be. I played cribbage with Rice at night. We found out who stole Red Cross food when one confessed and told Interpreter. Hardly any vegetables now in storehouse. Three potato mixes today with gravy at night. Mungo beans in morning mix.

Thursday August 5, 1943

Rain and no work. Did guard duty last night again.

Had tomatoes from our garden. Hewitt picked them and took to CC who said officers could have them.

I talked to the Interpreter and he asked if we ever bought stuff at the canteen. I told him it had only been open for the time the Red Cross rep had been here and we couldn't buy anything then. He remarked "That not so good." He said he would see CC re opening of shop. He said guards had told him men were buying things out on job and I said if they were, they were probably paying many times the value and since they didn't get much money, a shop where they could buy at current prices would be much appreciated. Suggested they might buy sauces, vegetables, and fruit in season if they were not rationed.

Entertainment all afternoon and night.

Martingale let out of guard house and CC told him he had been put in because he disobeyed his own officer's orders. Two men who stole Red Cross bully beef were sentenced to 15 days guard room. We put in a plea for leniency. The CC said if we hadn't, he would have sent them away for severe punishment. Hewitt was talking to the Interpreter at night and he mentioned us doing a.m. duty and how he felt this was a bad influence on the men as it led them to think we wouldn't turn them in. Also as much punishment for us. Interpreter said this was the C.C's orders and it was usual in Nip army as punishment to officers of unit whose men were at fault so it looks as though we continue.

Dunlop doing pay sheets and posting daily work sheets. Interpreter says he will supply paper, glue, etc. How different from Mush who expected officers to supply everything. I have all the tools now and it seems as though I am to keep them.

Shaved three Nips but got nil.

Potato mix a.m.and mungo beans. Potato mix and gravy at noon and same at night. Practically no vegetables left now.

Friday August 6, 1943

Very hot. Guard house duty last night but Interpreter told us we wouldn't have to do it again till further orders. I talked with Interpreter who seems to be an intelligent chap. Speaks good American and is a decided patriot. He studied psychology and philosophy I should say and converses well on races and their shortcomings. Told us what Japan is fighting for. An "East Asia federation." Says she would probably make peace if she could retain Philippines and Malay. Doesn't want India.

Rations of people in sick quarters cut to a third. What about poor chaps who have been hurt on job and who need food to mend broken bones etc!!

Pumpkin mix a.m., bean and pumpkin mix with cukes on side at noon but 4 kilos cut!! Fixed table and put in cubicle.

Saturday August 7, 1943

Hot. B. bean mix a.m. and noon with cukes on side noon. Potato mix at night with pumpkin soup. Meals pretty thin. Chap Pedder hurt on job when he was knocked off a platform by a bucket. Doc yesterday talked to Interpreter re cut in sick men's food and Interpreter said he would see CC.

Swimming and 20 down as water high. Did 14 lengths again (about ½ mile). CC said we could have entertainment every night from 6:00-7:00. When asked by us through Interpreter we had suggested 6:30—8:00.

Asked Interpreter if we could cut 6″ off legs of table as too high to write on. He saw CC who is coming to look at it. Interpreter spoke of gambling going on and said it must stop.

Chaps who have been skipping fire guard, etc., given fatigues.

Sunday August 8, 1943

Hot. Saw chap stealing tomatoes at 3:45. Chased him and although didn't catch him with goods certain it was Corporal F. Tried him at night but discharged him as there was insufficient evidence.

Morning meal cut from 16k rice to 8k and noon from 16k-15k. Meals were slim enough before. Hand cart of eggplant, F. beans, and tomatoes came in but all beans and some tomatoes bad and had to be thrown away!! Since Interpreter came civilian medical orderly has been at sick quarters. Operated on Sgt. Hepburn last night for piles by local civvy Doc at local hospital (dispensary).

Made out card index system for entertainment material.

Have been solid, once a day for last 3 days!! First time in months for such a period.

We still take food out at noon and it is dished out on job in hut erected for that purpose. Lads think food will increase from today as Kumi supposed to have taken over from today. Kumi is contractor doing job. However, food is still responsibility of army Quartermaster, according to Interpreter and Kumi has no say!!

Dunlop says number on camp gate now number 2!! If they have changed the number I suppose letters will go astray again. Told Interpreter next allowed letter home now month overdue.

Lots of new Koreans now on job and are being given strict army drill. They say they are treated as prisoners for first month. Anyway, they seem to be relieving our chaps of all the heavy work and lads finding things very slack now on job as regards work.

Meals today as laid down on August 1st with few potatoes in noon mix. Had discussion with new Interpreter this morning re Japan's intentions—quite interesting.

Monday August 9, 1943

Hot. 176 at work. Hospital numbers increasing slightly mostly due to accidents.

Bean mix a.m. Tomato mix, at noon with cukes and carrot. F. bean, curry soup with potato mix at night. Very good.

Interpreter said CC giving 300 parcels to troops, but wouldn't say what. We had to get out list of most diligent men to receive extra. Any man who had been sick immediately ruled out. Leader gave us 300 packets cigs which were usual cigs which we had to pay for!! Also about 40 sheets (small) of toilet paper. We paid for these too but later refunded as said these given by Kumi.

Tomorrow anti-flea day. All get up one hour early and take blankets and mats to river bank to air. Come back at noon and turn over. Asked him if I could eat in camp at noon. He said yes and later no, as couldn't get hold of CC to make decision. Men pick up blankets etc. after all get in at night.

Entertainment. Swimming. Cuke and tomatoes (hand cart) came in.

Tuesday August 10, 1943

Hot. Putting out of blankets went O.K. Asked Interpreter if men could leave off under mats and he said he would see. CC later said O.K. so we piled them in No. 3 hut. Everything went off smoothly probably cause Nips did not bother with it. Lads all sleeping on just top mats now. This will be improvement though don't expect it to cut out fleas altogether.

More vegetables, cukes, and pumpkins came in. A.m. and noon meals same as yesterday. At night, pumpkin mix with cukes on the side and eggplant and pumpkin thick soup. One Arm made speech at night tenko saying:

1) Before camp run by army and army officers and men. But now run by army employees (5 granted men).

2) Former administrators had now gone to war for first time while five men left had seen service in China and considered themselves better fitted to run job.

3) They did not want us to think they were slave drivers or wardens and want us to co-operate with them, and men with own POW officers to run camp smoothly, maintain health, obey orders etc. Must salute granted men at all times.

Jones (Yank) caught trying to dodge work by putting thermometer in hot water breaking it. Given 20 days guard room with reduced rations. CC called Hewitt and complained this is third case in only a few days. Hewitt said:

1) We have not, in first place, been treated as officers and men had come to disregard us and we had no control over them and could not be responsible for their actions. Also until new Interpreter came we could not take troubles to CC and all trouble could be traced to last Interpreter (Hewitt said language difficulties). Thought we could now handle men if we were allowed to punish small offenses and were backed up by Nips.

Noticed Brown working on job today. For sheer guts nobody on camp can touch him. About 6 months in hospital with diarrhoea and other diseases and life despaired of many times but always came up smiling. When he first arrived he was in latrine about every 15 minutes.

Men now seem to respect officers more since checking them on all offenses.

No swimming. Officer of the Day. Toilet paper and cigs issued.

Wednesday August 11, 1943

Hot. 181 out to work. Officer of the Day.

CC says V.O.D. and men hurt on job to be paid full time. Also as a result of Hewitt's talk with CC we are now committed to punish minor offenses ourselves without bothering CC. He seemed to understand our previous position and now states we are being treated as officers (paid and not required to work). Interpreter says some prisoners are working in factories on war work but by their own choice rather than carry stones etc. Thinks all, however, live in camps like this. Change in ration again to following kilos:

	A.M.	Noon	Night
Rice	8	13	4
Barley	14	21	6
Millet	16	12	12
Beans	10	—	—
Spuds	—	—	15

Sgt. Hepburn who was operated on for piles on the 7th is doing quite well.

STC lad operated on for rupture which he got on job months ago. Lot of cases being treated now at local civvy hospital. All accident cases taken there first and doc and nurse visit them in camp nearly every day. Of course they have no x-ray and broken legs set by guess and by God. Interpreter said at night tenko that men are now forbidden by CC to eat grass which they had been bringing into camp and eating. He said he knows food is short but it's short all over Japan!!

There was a small amount of earth to level after tenko but could not get 20 volunteers, although got about 15 which is better than we would have got 2 months ago. Officers got praise for leading work.

Officer of the Day and Medical Officer. Swimming and did 20 lengths.

Thursday August 12, 1943

Hot. 181 to work. Officer of the Day.

Asked Interpreter if chap who sustained rupture on job could be treated as accident case and be paid but CC said no. Cuts and things that are visible—yes. Also asked him if accident cases in hospital could draw books to read.

Bean mix a.m. Eggplant mix at noon with cukes. Potato mix, cukes on the side and eggplant soup at night.

One Arm took tenko at night and for the first time no official count was made. He asked me to announce that all were to "Bango" as loudly as possible then he had the bango and salute practice and then we were dismissed.

Friday August 13, 1943

Changed food ration again cutting down rice and adding beans.

	A.M.	Noon	P.M.
Rice	7	10	3
Barley	14	21	6
Millet	16	12	12
Beans	10	—	5
Spuds	—	—	15

S. bean mix in the morning. Pork, potato, daikon mix at noon and potato and bean mix with daikon and pork spud soup but very little pork at night.

One Arm thanked officers and NCOs for co-operation and stressed importance of tenko. Had Hanchos report at tenko and no bango.

Playing solo lately. Morale of troops and discipline greatly improved lately. Studying physics. Announced that accident cases paid from now on by industrial welfare of Japan. Also all men must have bodies covered at night and M.O. to go round twice a night to check up. V.O.D.s now to be paid.

Eggplant, sugar came in. Swimming.

Saturday August 14, 1943

183 at work.

Food as scheduled with eggplant and pumpkin soup at night. Tomorrow is rest day. Seems as though tomorrow is a general holiday in Japan. Studied most of day. New Interpreter making big difference in camp since we can get to CC anytime now with our problems and requests.

Sunday August 15, 1943

Rest day. Swimming at 2 p.m. Tenko 7 a.m.

Cook (little man) going to Tokyo and think for good as civvy seems to be learning workings of Cook House.

Troops not bothered at all today. How different from other rest days under old regime!!

Still getting lots of tomatoes from garden and big % being handed to sick quarters.

Entertainment in afternoon. Food as scheduled.

Loose again.

Monday August 16, 1943

Food as usual but men report very short. Nips fitting up steam shovel which they obviously bought as scrap from Yanks. Interpreter left in afternoon for two days' holiday and said hoped we would get along okay. How different from last Interpreter.

Koreans which have lately arrived do not have as good quarters as we have. Occupy some houses which are done up and fenced and they are locked in and tenko'd like us. They make awful noise some nights all through the night with stamping, hand clapping and singing same thing over and over. They get issued with saki.

Doc says Nip medicines packed when Nip M.O. left but actually still here. We have no disinfectant now.

Swimming.

Tuesday August 17, 1943

Cloudy.

Sgt. King died. He has been in hospital for about 5 months with diarrhoea and malnutrition—76. Buried in afternoon. Got back at 6 so no swimming.

Meat in noon and night mix!! With pumpkin and watermelon soup at night. Troops only got 3/4 blue bowl at night—pretty slim.

Studying.

Troops had to turn in all pairs of shorts but one and all army slacks. Don't know what the idea is as it doesn't seem as though Nips are going to use these since they said turn in any old pairs.

Thursday August 19, 1943

Nip Officer of the Day says if fire watchers don't get on job they will double those who need to stand guard. If okay for a month they will cut guard in half. One fire watcher now watches kitchen to see no stealing as they don't seem to have strong enough locks. Usual food but rumour rice is to be cut and beans and barley increased. Petition being got up by men to change our cooks as they say they are trading off food for cigs and money, etc. They are putting forward substitute names.

Interpreter came back and brought us mandolin and uke strings but no calculus books. Working on calculus today.

Swimming alone and 24 lengths!!

Rice cut again and beans and pumpkin increased. New figures have alterations in brackets on the 13th. Axes and knives have been taken from Cook House. They will be withdrawing chow buckets next!! Suppose Kumi will have to make up deficiency that army took away.

Cig issues further apart since army handed over. Doc gave lecture: "Chew your food." CC has ordered he give one each night.

Rumour: Nips bombing Timor!!

Friday August 20, 1943

Hot. Started copying out math notes.

Seaweed soup a.m. and seaweed, pumpkin and marrow soup at night. Mix as usual. Pear issue of 100 lbs (4 boxes.)

Kai Hoe camp not kept as good as used to be so must spend 20 minutes each night on cleaning and getting ready for inspection. If camp arrangement improves we will be allowed concessions??? Also all windows must be closed at 12 midnight to prevent POW getting cold.

Swimming—26 lengths. Hard again.

Glass Eye showed us bully beef box with only 4 tins in and indicated POW had stolen rest.

Saturday August 21, 1943

Hot. All boys searched when they came in from work but don't know what they were after. Took names of those with curry powder, pepper, etc. Interpreter slapped some of lads!!

Vegetables came in—7 pumpkins, 2 eggplants, 1 cuke. Thin soup a.m. and pumpkin and cuke soup at night.

Swimming 10 lengths but called back after 15 minutes!!

Petition to change cooks seems to have died natural death as Peil took case to first cook who said he would put anybody who got another petition up in Esso. All were given a long white cloth tag with number on to be worn on hat like pig tail. Said to be to distinguish POW from Koreans since we now wear straw hats like them.

Sunday August 22, 1943

Hot. CC asked me what I thought of a.m. soup. I said it was no good and didn't take it myself but couldn't speak for the men. However he gave orders to stop it and put ingredients in rice. We are getting a lot of beans now — 3 times a day and as rice cut down beans increased and diarrhoea has increased a lot lately, even Hewitt having it. He has not been eating soup so that leaves barley and beans as the cause. I blame latter as not fully cooked and very indigestible. I am loose again.

Got form from Interpreter to fill in showing total days POW, in this camp, number of days worked, number of days sick and cause of sickness. Looks like medical synopsis. One Arm gave speech at night tenko saying war was reaching a crisis. Nips were suffering privations, etc. to meet it. They heard Nip Nationals were not being well treated and they however were treating us by International law standards but could not keep this up without co-operation from us. Interpreter also read order form from CC which said we must wear piece of spare blanket around our middles at night in addition to other bedding. Also keeps repeating not to drink raw water. After all in bed, Interpreter came around and woke people up to see if they had blanket band on.

Monday August 23, 1943

Hot. All weighed. I was 74.2 K — same as last time. All boys down 5-6 K so food outlook not too good. 250 packets of cigarettes and 250 Hay came in. Also vegs, and <u>newspapers</u> — July 19–Aug. 10. Missing few dates in between.

Working on form for Interpreter showing number of days in camp, number rest days, number of work and number of sick days. More instructions issued by Interpreter re belly band. Only need wear at night as well as blankets but can wear shirts.

Grub short as millet has run out. The usual mixes with b.beans and pumpkin, and pumpkin and seaweed soup at night. Talked with Interpreter re diarrhoea. He says a lot of Nips now have this!!

Tuesday August 24, 1943

Hot. Shower night.

<u>Mu's birthday</u>.

Usual a.m. food. Curry mix at noon but only 3/4 box per man. At night fried piece of pumpkin each and b.bean mix.

Kai Hoe — 26th rest day.

Repeat about covering stomach and windows closed. M.O. to report on those not complying. We are to clean up camp on the 26th and air blankets on the river bank. The men must march in better order to and from work. No swimming last 2 days as pool very low.

Stoves, benches, blankets, etc. removed from camp.

Worked nearly all day on sick and work day report and handed this to Interpreter.

250 packets cigarettes and 240 hay issued. Interpreter said men who have least amount of sick days as shown on report I just handed in to be given extra cigs, etc. by CC's order. They will also be given privileges in future. Asked if CC could not give section Hanchos extra for voluntary work they do but Interpreter said no.

Wednesday August 25, 1943

Hot. Glass Eye searched in attic of 1 and 2 barracks and removed everything boys had hidden there. Also looked in our kits very roughly. We thought something funny. Then CC called us up to administration and said that there have been two more cases of Red Cross food theft and decided it was us. "Your nation decisively." We suggested putting guard duty on stores every night but he said he didn't think much of our race if we had to put guard duty on locked doors. He said he would give us till 8 a.m. tomorrow to produce culprits and if not would take second step. Ordered us to search all men's kits which we did but found none of the stolen stuff, although plenty of other enlightening things. Then we searched No. 3 billet and found 2 tins of meat and vegetables. The Stolen Goods!! But that didn't produce the thief. At tenko at night Hewitt asked men who had stolen the things to come forward and save everybody in camp from suffering and gave them until 7:30 p.m., then would announce in barracks if the thieves were not found. Anybody that could, should come forward and give information. However, 5 men did come forward and the camp was saved.

Thursday August 26, 1943

Hot—rest day. Tenko 5 and camp cleaning till 7. Blankets and mats taken to river bank and aired and also moistened by rain in afternoon

CC didn't turn up so couldn't report men who stole by 8 a.m.

Food getting shorter and men find they are getting weak after so many hours' work. But I think the heat is mostly to blame. The nights are getting cooler now—sun not appearing till quite late now.

Friday August 27, 1943

Hot. CC didn't call up men who stole Red Cross stuff as said wanted to think over punishment. Boys told not to pick up fruit or vegs outside as will be assumed they stole it.

Big stir today. Reported Germany and Russia negotiating separate peace and Yank and Russian ambassadors have been withdrawn!! Boys very downhearted as this would mean prolonged war but I refuse to believe it especially since rumour says we have landed in Italy and doing well.

Usual meals today with curried seaweed and marrow soup at night.

Swimming since pool up due to rain.

Saturday August 28, 1943

Hot. Sleepy in afternoon these days.

33 kilos increase in rice per day and no cut in anything else! Bulk beans in last 2 days. Tea and sugar (3 kilos) issued to lads at night. Meat also came in!!

Still copying out math. Swimming—20 lengths and speedo.

More "tabbys" came in and shoes changed tonight.

Four small details told to stay in this a.m. but later two sent out. Two in all day and they are going to get paid for it!! Meals same as yesterday only s. beans substituted for b. beans so look out for wind!!

Sunday August 29, 1943

Warm. 202 paid workers (including injury cases) out of 209—pretty good!

100 sacs of spuds came in. Spuds 60 kilos a sack. Spuds total 6,000 K!! Usual meals today with rice increase however. A.m. 13 K, noon 13 K, and night, 7$\frac{1}{2}$ K. Also no soup at night but fried pumpkin and very good.

Weight 73.3 K. Very windy last night and loose.

Still no action by CC on men who stole Red Cross goods.

Nothing further re Huns and Russians signing separate Peace so false alarm. Thank Gawd!

Monday, August 30, 1943

Another problem—wholesale stealing of spuds last night!

No wind so must have been soup that was doing it. Still a little loose.

Kumi responsible for rice increase of 20 kilos/day. <u>Candy</u> given but to most work days and diligence tickets. 126 packets. Usual a.m. and noon meals but boiled pumpkin with sugar and meat! Noodle, eggplant soup and mix at night.

Swimming but water low. Playing crib last few nights with Sammy and Quennel.

Tuesday August 31, 1943

Hot.

At last locks put on No. 3 and 4 billets (store rooms).That should stop spud stealing.

Boys told only to take necessities to work and can only bring same things in!! Means no more buying—maybe.

Eggplant three times today. Usual a.m. and noon bean mix and fried eggplant (very oily). Fish, seaweed—eggplant soup and mix at night.

Started Pinochle. Swimming.

Wednesday September 1, 1943

Hot. Lot of squits today probably due to oily eggplant last night.

Interpreter announced again we must close all windows and doors in barracks at 12 midnight to prevent colds and 100 men sleeping together in a barracks with 3 feet per man!! In spring they insisted on all windows and doors being open!!

Usual a.m. and noon mix with fish hash on side at night.

All men had to sew their number on their blankets. Sirens went at 6:45 p.m. and all lights in barracks turned out!! Also most of lights in village out. Their air raid signal is long blast evidently. (Opposite to ours.)

Thursday September 2, 1943

Warm.

That alarm was the real thing but looks different because all clear hasn't yet gone (8 a.m.). Interpreter says these air raids are a precaution and as long as lights on in billets do not throw beam outside we can have them on. This is a relief as I had visions of spending rest of night in darkness.

Food shows vast improvement. They now give our own cooks three days' rations and they have a free hand in preparing the meals. Tonight's meal best yet—big slice boiled pumpkin with soya sauce, big helping mashed potatoes and onions! Rice with red beans and onions and "taksan." Usual mixes a.m. and noon. Interpreter says increase in rations due to Japan's self sufficiency program and asked us how we liked meal whereupon we said <u>O.K</u>.

Wouldn't let us swim because it was raining and they said we would get sick!!

Friday September 3, 1943

Four years since war started!! It doesn't seem like it.

CC in Cook House and concerned over food. He asked how much men got at noon and how it compared with the most they had got. Told him about 3/4. Also asked if we could get anything in the way of extras we wanted and if we would let him know he would try and get it! What a change in policy.

Interpreter brought paper and envelopes for next letter home. We are to hand in ten per day and instructions same as last time except no copies required.

A.m. and noon usual mix. Night—fish and bean hash, pumpkin and seaweed soup. Bean and spud mix and pickled eggplant on the side.

Blackout finished but siren not blown. Rain in afternoon. Officer of the Day.

Rumour: Taiwan Bombed!!

Saturday September 4, 1943

Rain in afternoon but cleared for swimming. Pool up again. Officer of the Day.

Doc informed us he's leaving on the 5th for Tokyo POW hospital. Doesn't know if there will be an exchange or not. Well, we won't miss him. Two lads, Findlay and Robertson who are supposed to have T.B. going with him. Glad to see hospitalization of incurable cases commencing!

Big shock today! They issued the Red Cross boots to all men!! With the stipulation of course that we are not to wear them. Shoved out 214 all sizes and said those who didn't get fit could change in about 5 days. Asked men if they could wear tabis till weather got cold!! What a change! Asking them. We said O.K. of course! What a feeling to get a real pair of boots on one's feet! We shouldn't have cold feet this winter with heavy hobnailed boots. Of course rumour is now rife especially since CC said some time ago we wouldn't be issued with these until we were going away! Increase in food, letters and now boots—what does it mean. Hope peace representative is on his way to USA!! News unfortunately lacking these days.

Usual a.m. and noon mix although noon issue small french fried spuds, pickles, fish, onion stew and bean and pumpkin mix at night. Very good.

Running quite freely again but I think it's beans and big meal at night. Interpreter says letters can come in faster now. But oh boy the mistakes—about 1 in 10 correct—I have taken on a job of correcting and inking them. Find Yanks most illiterate.

Interpreter still harping on saluting but lads don't take much notice.

Sunday September 5, 1943

Warm—rest day. Nips want list of water bottles and own blankets men brought with them. There's something in the air. I hope we don't move actually. CC commended Doc for work here and said another doc coming here so doesn't look like move.

Usual a.m. mix, seaweed soup at noon and onion soup at night with mixed spuds and beans.

Hewitt asked for paper and pencils for troops but CC said no as Kumi was going to open canteen and they could get pencils and paper there. In fact didn't know why they had not opened!!

Swimming. Sing-song.

Monday September 6, 1943

Warm. Sun doesn't appear on opposite mountain now till 6 a.m. and at one time it was on camp at 6:30!! Morning and evening closing in and getting cool. Weather is really grand now.

New Cook House secretary (Kumis man) accused punk of stealing our rice (2-3 bags a month) by weighing bag in with our issue and giving us short weight. He hauled him up before the CC. Limpy looks like a good man.

Usual a.m. and noon mixes. Night, fish and onion hash, fish pickle, boiled pumpkin and bean mix.

Correcting and inking letters. Swimming.

Doc and 2 men with T.B. left in a.m for Tokyo Hospital with Glass Eye and we were allowed to go to station.

Rumour: landing on Italy. Also writing on a goods wagon passing through the station: Italy has accepted Peace Terms—"Roll on The Boat." However, I don't attach much importance to this.

Tuesday September 7, 1943

Showery. Swimming and pool up.

Usual a.m. and noon mix and potato and onion mash, seaweed soup and red bean mix. Cook 3 says Kumi rice issue hasn't come in for the last couple days.

Those reporting sick with diarrhoea will now be starved for 2 days and then put on special diet. Only 6 hospital patients now—what a difference from last winter!! About half of those are accident cases.

Interpreter questioning men as to their letters asking them why they think they will soon be home. Thinks they are getting news. Valerga had long talk with him and said if they had any news it was what they read in the *Nippon Times* or what came from Nip Hanchos. I think Nips themselves see red light or they wouldn't be so concerned about us getting the news.

Interpreter let slip we had landed in Italy.

Wednesday September 8, 1943

Showery. Swimming.

Had long talk with Interpreter re why men should think they're going home soon as it's written in letters. Told him because men are in good spirits due to good treatment etc. Also had another talk with him at night covering Japan's chances in this war. He gave long talk to men reiterating belly-bands and maintenance of health during coming cold weather, etc. Officers told to submit report on changes proposed for V.O.D.s.

Usual a.m. mix, onions and bean mix at noon with small pickled fish, which is quite frequent now. Egg and spud and onion soup and red beans, spud mix at night.

Thursday September 9, 1943

Interpreter asked us to make out list of things boys would like to buy if Kumi started canteen and CC would check. We said we would run the canteen. Interpreter said according to list he has, POW are allowed 3 to 5 cigs a day—we certainly haven't been getting this amount. Also allowance of toilet paper, 4 sheets per day, tooth brushes 1 per 3 months, face soap 1 per 2 months, washing soap 1 per month, tooth powder 1 every 3 months.

CC intends to stamp out diarrhoea or kill us all. He thinks increase in rations has caused increase in diarrhoea and says he will cut them drastically if necessary. Also all our diarrhoea patients must report sick and they will be starved for 2 days then put on light diet (cup of barley water per meal) until cured!! Also diarrhoea patients to be put in other end of our billet!!

New Doc arrived at 10:30 p.m., a British Naval Lieutenant, captured at Hong Kong. He had been head of POW hospital at Tokyo. They had rough treatment at H.K. and arrived here in Sept. last. He states 100 men from *Lisbon Maru* which was sunk got to China and escaped!! He saw our eight officers when they went through. They are going to an officer's camp which is the goods: batmen, Red Cross parcel every 2 months, radiograms, 500 books, bread daily, doughnuts weekly, chow on the whole—skoshi. In South Isle. Re other camps—some good, some bad. They have received more letters and Doc had 16!! He was in Headquarters and British officers do the sorting. Morale of all POW very high and doing things. Working in steel mills, unloading ships, etc. and other factories. More POW still coming to Japan. All officers, colonels and up, over in Formosa. Stocks of Red Cross medicines at docks but Nips hoarding and can't even get at Central Hospital. Central Hospital full of amoebic dysentery and diphtheria carriers who are quite well with few chronic diarrhoea and T.B. cases. Idea is to send all serious cases there from all camps. Food in camps varies. Some get plenty and others not. Food same as here and nearly all camps now in care of civvy firms. Some officers left at all camps like this.

First batch of Yank letters just arrived and ship leaving soon from Japan. Stocks of Red Cross food etc. at Lorenzo Marques, awaiting ships.

Rumour: Russians moving forward rapidly.

Friday September 10, 1943

List of things on order for canteen put to CC.

List of changes in V.O.D.s so seven V.O.D. to be billet Hanchos—submitted to CC and approved. Also agreed to allow us to move elements to break up troublesome cliques!

Veg stew poor and seaweed with mixes and seaweed soup. B. beans fried in fat—very good. Men very pleased with new Doc. Swimming.

Rumour: Italy surrendered unconditionally. Oh boy, if this is true!!

Sunday September 12, 1943

All letters finished.

I wrote home this time. Found out from Doc this No. 2 Detachment Camp not No. 3. Told Interpreter and he agreed and had to change all letters. Interpreter said CC had been on to him and said he was responsible for the discipline in the camp and discipline now poorer than when other Interpreter here. We talked to men at night and explained they would do better if they kept themselves clean and also billets and watched saluting.

Monday September 13, 1943

Showery. Went round job with Doc, Interpreter, Hewitt and Dunlop and got wet. Doc had asked to see working conditions of men. Job does not seem to have progressed at all. Dam site is still flooded. Has been for 2 months now since slide broke bypass channel. Don't seem to be doing anything about it. Men not as hard worked as used to be.

Doc asked to make report comparing this camp with others. Says they put Red Cross food to officers soon as they came in and they were issued almost immediately.

Boiled mashed squash at night. Usual a.m. and noon mix except a.m. beans separate.

Sunday September 19, 1943

Coolish—night quite cool now. Will have to have 2 blankets on top. Interpreter took 10 y notes to village to try and change so he could pay men. Said might take 2-3 days!

What a difference the new Doc makes. The men have confidence in him. Many cases he has diagnosed correctly which Dutch Doc was treating for something else, especially beri-beri. Has asked Interpreter if he could get rice polishings to give all men so much per day to prevent vitamin B deficiency. Has also asked for Vitamin B shots saying officers will pay if necessary. Interpreter is going to take up with Kumi medical orderly. Officers can buy these things for own use only.

Food very slim. Old thin mezor soup and mix a.m. Mix noon, pepper, meat (?), seaweed on side. At night mix and seaweed soup.

Still doing exercises every noon. Swimming.

Monday September 20, 1943

Interpreter says beginning tomorrow V.O.D. will have to go to work. Medical orderlies to do cleaning, or supervise the cleaning of the camp. Also all Red Cross food will be issued to officers and when they wish to issue to men, ask CC. Also at the end of the month officers to report on all NCOs as to suitability and those not considered worthy will forfeit their extra 5 sens a day. This will go into a fund to be given to those men with good work records. Interpreter said the issue of Red Cross food will stop pinching by administration Nips!!

Radiogram came in for chap named Clark but we have no one on this camp by that name. Yank.

Food weighed out at noon and seemed more even. Onion soup in the a.m. and quite good. Mix at noon and "skoshi." Bean mix at night. B. beans and meat on side and seaweed soup.

Interpreter got beaten up from 6:30 to 8:00 by "Gunzokos"—administration people—ostensibly for making announcement to NCOs after tenko about cutting poor NCOs, etc., without telling Nip V.O.D. and yet he was only transmitting CC's orders. They also accused him of being in sympathy with the prisoners, telling him not to forget he was still a Nip. This because he remarked not to hit a chap so hard the other night who we reported. He was sentenced to 30 nights standing in front of Guard Room naked and working during day. Obviously he couldn't have done it but they let him off after 1½ nights. It will be interesting to see how he reacts towards us now as we know he hates the administration people now.

Rumour: Roosevelt says war will be over this year and Churchill has promised Nips taksan senso then.

An article from the Saskatoon *Star Phoenix* giving Les Chater's status as a prisoner of war, eighteen months after actual capture—proof of how long it took for information on captives to be released. (14 Sept. 1943)

Tuesday September 21, 1943

Interpreter well disposed towards us today so beating hasn't changed his opinions.

Change came in today and we paid off half men at night. All remaining Red Cross food turned over to us except cocoa which CC said he had special instructions for, (actually they have been drinking it all along and I doubt if there's any left) and anyway other camps got it. We must ask CC when we wish to issue and issues should be made on Yasume days, etc. Sugar is to remain in store for time being and CC is going to think over its issue as we put in a strong request for issue all to men so they could use as desired. There were no raisins!! More details tomorrow. Bakelite spoons given to us to issue to men but told to hold as more stuff coming shortly.

Doc saw camp Cook House secretary re no more gobos, satomea and daikons as bad for diarrhoea and Colonel Suzuki had promised no more. Three loads vegetables came in during last two days.

Rain last night and pool up so good swimming.

Two tailors started work and I had pants let out and towel fixed. Glass Eye in good mood today. Civvy Nips now eat in new kitchen one of our chaps has built and he is doing cooking.

CC says from now on men to be paid twice a month and officers once. Also we have to return all over 50 y which we received on the 18th. (45.50 y).

Rumour: Chinese captured Swatow and we have landed paratroops behind Nip lines in China.

Wednesday September 22, 1943

Very cold during night. An alarming drop in temperature although I had an extra blanket I was still cold and in a.m. it was cold till about 9:30. It brings you with a jolt to the realization that winter is not far away and accordingly I started getting mending done and went through kit.

Eggplant soup and mix in the a.m. Mix at noon. Beans "skoshi" these three days but barely little more. At night, onion, mungo bean soup. Fried spuds and spud mix at night.

Swimming but cool when I came out. Cards at night.

Thursday September 23, 1943

Interpreter asked if we could swim at 2:00 from now on and CC said okay—from 2:00 to 3:00.

Paid again—for September—95.50 but had to give in 91 yen, 45.50, for August and same for Sept. CC then said we could not hold more than 50 y at any time so we all had to turn in any surplus over this. I turned in another 100 y. This seems to be new rule as Doc said they were paid 50 y a month.

Interpreter told me to announce to men they must be more efficient in saluting at gate, etc. Making garden beside No.1 billet. Put doors back in cubicle. Weigh day—76.4K. Up 3 K but scales fixed this time and probably correct now.

Saturday September 25, 1943

Yasume and boys left alone after half-hour cleanup in a.m. Tenko at 6:30 a.m.

Asked for bully beef issue but they said no but <u>could have 4 boxes of pears</u>. Worked out at 14 per man.

Interpreter came and <u>asked</u> us if we wanted anything in village. What a change! Brought back what we asked for and also what seemed cross between crab apple and pear—tastes like latter. Said he had ordered 40.00 y worth for the camp!!

Had one watch fixed in village already—new stem. First hot bath of season. Big concert at night as broadcasted and went down well. Nip Cook House secretary sang a piece.

Lot of vegetables came in and Cook House secretary told rice "presento." Big meals today. Mungo bean and onion soup and barley a.m. Straight rice and mabela mix at noon with same soup. Same soup at night with fried b. beans. Spud mix.

Put doors back in cubicle today.

Sunday September 26, 1943

Warmish. 450 packets hay came in. Also 250 of clothing soap, 220 notebooks, 300 toothbrushes, 211 pencils, 24 pen holders, 129 pen points, 7 bottles black ink, 11 red, and razor blades (result of our order, I suppose).

Made cage for pheasant.

Seaweed soup and mix in the a.m.; mix at noon, soup onion fritters and mix at night.

Going w.c. once a day now and slightly softish.

Doc has not been able to get much medicine yet. Nip M.O. went to town 60 km. away but they said he couldn't get any for a month. Local town Doc has been coming every day but now not going to and we are to send for medicine although we can't get much there.

Monday September 27, 1943

Rainy. Boys didn't go out to work till 7:30 because of rain and came back at 11 because of same. No work in p.m. and CC said officers, of their <u>own</u> accord <u>could have an issue of soup mix</u>. It wasn't up to much though. Usual a.m. soup and noon mix but few beans. Night—red bean mix, boiled pumpkin, small fish, mungo bean soup.

Issue of following to men: 1 packet hay, 1 tablet soap, 1 pencil, 1 notebook, 1 toothbrush, 1 spoon.

Making sign boards for Glass Eye.

Tuesday September 28, 1943

Cloudy but warmish. Have another garden to do—bigger than last and officers to do but we are going to set troops on it.

Not feeling so hot today. Squits. Had itch again and have had 3 applications oil for it.

Interpreter says troops can buy wakamoto (vitamin B) and is going to get orders.

Doing sign boards for Nips. Glass Eye says we don't need lights to do garden because officers are going to do this during day. We intend forcing issue—officers should do no manual labour.

Meat and b. beans soup at night. Very good.

Wednesday September 29, 1943

Warmish, swimming. We didn't touch garden and nothing was said. Troops finished when they came in from work.

Speedo doing more sign boards. Quartermaster coming on 20th and hence rush.

New assignment for people responsible for fire prevention. Sold pipes to lads. Collected money for wakamoto and nearly all troops wish to buy it.

CC asked to look at our deposit cards but think just to check how much he is supposed to have in bank.

Squits seem O.K. today. Itch also better.

Seaweed soup in the a.m. and mix but I hadn't any soup. Mix at noon with few s. beans. Same mix at night with gravy. Lot of barley and little rice in 3 days' ration, about a 5-1 ratio.

Swimming. Started taking wakamoto.

Rumour: Russians reached Dneiper and we are still at Salerno.

Thursday September 30, 1943

Three day issue food and rice and barley about same this time but very little vegetables, only 3 sacks of spuds and cooks say spuds in store going bad. Kamajo was going to start giving rice balls to boys today but CC stopped it—Gawd knows why!

Swimming 50 lengths—little colder today.

Another garden for lads to do—work all day and now when they come in.

Mix in the morning, blubber, seaweed and beans. Beans and spud mix at noon. Blubber and smelly meat and spud soup and red bean mix at night. Up to village with Interpreter and he let us buy what we wanted: e.g tea, sauce. Got 208 y worth wakamoto for troops. Only 20 K beans this issue.

Friday October 1, 1943

More beans came in and sack given to issue.

Interpreter asked if any STC lads showed leadership and we said no.

Spud and seaweed mix in morning and the same at noon and "skoshi." Beans on side and spud mix at night.

No sun, no swimming.

Rumour: CC didn't stop rice balls but when work hanchos asked if they could raise "Kamari" and give rice balls extra, CC said couldn't raise it but rice balls o.k. So some giving rice balls anyway.

Cigs getting hard to get and price going up. All cigs coming in now raffled and raffle mania has struck camp.

Reading Shakespeare and mending socks.

Saturday October 2, 1943

Cloudy—no swimming. Pool low.

Bean mix in the morning. Spud, seaweed mix at noon and beans. Spud mix at night and blubber gravy.

Interpreter said he would try and get a calculus book for us. Also asked for list of things men would like to buy—e.g. curry, pepper, pipes, etc. Looks like canteen (maybe).

Fixing socks.

Radiogram came from Penang for STC lad. First communication for one of them.

Clearly, the situation in camp has improved somewhat with the new Interpreter. These entries illustrate this very well.

Sunday October 3, 1943

Heavy rain during the night and most of the day so no work and called Yasume day. M.S. concert night but since hurriedly got up mostly singing. But Singh, dressed as a girl, went over big.

Pear issue 10 per man. Lot of pears found maggoty—kept too long.

Had to repair fence where we took earth away for garden. Had to be done speedo for inspection on 20th!! What a job. It looks like a patch work quilt and will draw attention from a mile away. One of the young soldiers in charge and must have it done his own way. Rather humorous—young kid telling a 5 year varsity engineer how to shore up a fence. Consequently now it is more liable to fall than ever.

Reading *Within Four Walls* and puts ideas in my head!!

Such a change—can get tabis changed now whenever men ask and last winter when boys really needed them it took about 6 tries to get Nips to issue a couple of old pairs which never fit!! Interpreter very friendly and helpful. Comes and asks us if we want anything every time he is going to village and talked to Hewitt till about 10:30 tonight.

Mix a.m. and noon and fried fish in batter, soup, and red bean mix at night with seaweed on the side.

Bath.

Monday October 4, 1943

Pool high and sunny so had a good swim.

Fixing fence again and putting labels on all buildings of fire wardens after which I was given tea and cigs in administration building!

Two patients with broken legs were to be taken to village hospital for x-ray but postponed. Why they didn't take them up months ago when legs broken to see if they were set o.k.— gawd only knows!! Took three men up and x-rayed the other day for T.B. etc.

Orders from Tokyo—every man to keep diary which will be sent home if he dies. Same restrictions as letter except can be 50—100 pages. Reason given is a lot die without anything to send home!!

Mix a.m. and noon (skoshi) and b. beans on side and spud mix at night.

Tuesday October 5, 1943

Very cool last night with two blankets on top and sheet.

Clear and sunny but air nippy. Long speech by Interpreter at tenko about few men who slack and disobey on job and threats of return to army administration (all conjured up). Took about half an hour to tell us this over and over again until stopped by instigator Glass Eye.

Took two men with broken limbs to x-ray at hospital near power house.

No swimming. Cigs now hard to get and 50-65 sens packet.

Mix a.m. and noon. (bean)

Wednesday October 6, 1943

Cloudy. Interpreter now brings watch every day for regulating. All Nips crazy for watches but Nip watches all very poor and unreliable.

Food very low now. Boys get only 2 white bowls at breakfast, less than box at noon and $2^{1}/_{2}$ white bowls at night. Can't expect boys to work on that. Interpreter said last night he was responsible for food increase. True when he first came but since then issue has dropped considerably. My weight is fairly constant now, about 76K.

Spud mix and seaweed soup in the morning. Mix at noon and bean soup and spud, melon mix at night.

At night tenko it was announced that there will be an inspection of men for Nip blankets, sheets, overcoats and ground sheets or raincoats.

Regular to latrines these days. Reading *Modern Spain*.

Rumour: have evacuated Naples. Biggest battle war between Kiev and Smolensk.

Thursday October 7, 1943

Cloudy and cool. Wore sweater all day.

Making 100 chevrons of red for people with lot of diligence tickets to wear and 100 of blue for those with best working records.

C.E. checking blankets, sheets, overcoats, hats, denim slacks, underpants, tunics, raincoats, pillows, once again (about 10th time). They always seem to lose the lists and can never find any old lists which were made out.

Volleyball and net and medicine ball given us. These were sent by Y.M.C.A. in May and as usual, have been stuck in storage where they have been ever since and have missed all the good weather when we could have used them!!

Notice that CC of main Tokyo POW camp inspecting here on 9th and as usual panic. Camp to be cleaned. Numbers on hats and tunics to be checked etc. and officers and NCOs to set example.

Thin soup and spud mix in the morning with coconut oil. Mix with coconut oil at noon and bean and meat on side at night with soup mix.

Loose. Left leg tender again today. Hope it isn't going to swell up like last winter! Must be bad circulation.

Rumour: Russians 40 miles from Polish border!! Huns in Crimea cut off!

Friday Oct 8, 1943

Leg about same and Doc gave me shot CACL2 and sulpha quanamide. Eye swollen today. I think it's a sty. General health of camp good these days. Last 2 days have not had one L.D. man!! And before that had only one for about month. Yesterday record day—203 paid workers (including accident "Kosho" patients) out of possible 207!!! In hospital 4 Kosho and 3 sick and 1 E.D. and 1 L.D. "kosho". Good omen for coming winter.

Camp cleaning today in preparation for inspection tomorrow. Nip V.O.D. congratulated us for cleanliness of camp!! How different from old times. Eye wash* being laid on as usual— new numbers, placards etc.

We have tea now every meal since we can buy tea.

No news of war in east for long time—things must be going badly for Nips.

Cool, cloudy, but still having shower every day—water chilly though.

Seaweed spud mix and thin soup in the morning; seaweed, spud and bean mix at noon and spud mix, cabbage and meat and flour thick soup at night.

Loose today.

(* wool pulled over the eyes, nonsense, fooling people)

Saturday October 9, 1943

Officer of the Day. Tokyo Colonel came at 7:30. Tenko not till 6:30 and men stood till Colonel came. He inspected men making them take off shirts, shoes, inspected finger nails. Seemed concerned about men's health. Also raised H___ about torn condition of men's clothing and lack of shirts, etc. Later he inspected the camp. He sat down and talked to the officers. He thanked us for good condition of the camp. He asked us what we wanted most and we said tobacco and he said something to CC and Interpreter told us he said see officers get some. He brought up question of letters and was surprised when I told him only 10 men had received them in this camp. He said there were 300,000 English letters in Tokyo!! Hope this produces results! Then brought up library and asked us how many books we had. We showed him what we had and he said he would send some more and change with another camp. Inspected camp and well pleased. Tasted noon mix and I think first mix he had seen as Doc says they don't have these in other camps. Went on job then. Saw men coming in early and didn't like this much saying men in Tokyo work longer—rather foolish of our chaps to come in early today. On whole, satisfactory inspection different from previous ones in that he seemed more concerned about our welfare and health which is significant. Also I think it raised the prestige of us officers.

Latrines about 10 times today but no pain—think just periodic clean out.

Mix in the morning and noon as yesterday and soup at night with cabbage and a little meat.

Sunday October 10, 1943

Heavy rain all night and day so no work. Hot bath. Officer of the Day, Medical Officer.

Asked for bully beef issue but CC said wait. Glass Eye issued thread and we are to sew our numbers on all clothes. Also he said officers only supposed to be issued with pillow, sheet and blankets and would have to turn rest of stuff in. That jolted us until he said only for Q.M.'s inspection and then he would let us have them back though we weren't supposed to have overcoats, etc. I don't know how we would live without them.

Squitting badly.

Men's pay received yesterday but as usual 70 y in 10 y notes which is no good.

No concert as decided having them too frequently.

Men with more than one shirt had to turn extras in to be given to those without any. Rather hard on those who carried all their stuff this far and are gradually being relieved of it.

Cabbage soup 3 times today and mix.

Rumour: we have taken Sardinia and Corsica.

Monday October 11, 1943

Clear. Interpreter said small pears which had been ordered for men now in and officers are to go and get them. He took us to the village and let us buy what we wanted first. He said it was their policy (or his policy) to allow officers to buy any luxuries possible!! What a difference from last Interpreter who did his best to belittle us and make our conditions worse. Also wanted to see us treated as officers. He is very deferential towards us. Maybe he sees red light and wants to keep on our good side for good word at end and he will certainly get it. Offered to let us have his monthly beer and saki ration which we jumped at! When in village he bought lot of things for troops such as curry powder, pepper, powder, razor blades.

This will constitute our canteen but Interpreter says most of these things he is allowing us to buy off his own bat and sell to troops on Q.T.

Small pears we went to collect turned out to be large juicy apples—oh boy. 806 of them at 10 sens each. We suggested 3½ per man and extras to section Hanchos, officers and other diligent men. CC said no—3 per man and rest divide between the 7 Hanchos and 5 officers! He is certainly pulling for us now. Recognition of our part in good inspection by Colonel, I think. So we had about 15 apples each, offered 12 to Interpreter and same to CC but they refused. Men very pleased with issue.

Big Glass Eye interfering in sick parades now and wants to send men out to work who Doc has told to stay in. But Doc stands up to him. Let some go out with promise they will be given light duty.

Cabbage soup a.m. and p.m. and 3 mixes with beans at noon and seaweed other two times and spuds. Small fish on side most meals.

Tuesday October 12, 1943

Clear.

Still squitting. Leg and eye o.k. now.

Cpl. James caught stealing from Cook House last night and another trying to get into store. CC peeved about it and just when we are beginning to get things for behaving—one or two always spoil things.

Glass Eye called officers out to spread shite taken from Nip latrine on our gardens (cabbage about 3" high now). Interpreter apologized and said these are not his orders but recommended we do it although he hated to ask us to. Said Nip "Shokos" do this themselves sometimes—so Hewitt and I did.

Got 900 packets H. hair and 100 packets cigs from Kumi. H. hair for men and cigs for officers (20 packets each). However don't know how long this issue is supposed to last since only issued two packets cigs per officer today. Doesn't look as bright as at first. Men got 1 packet H. hair each.

CC said re two men who stole, has tried Guard Room, letting officers punish and letting men off free and still stealing so this time troops going to be punished giving 1 blow with lath to each man on rear. So after tenko men stripped and punishment was duly administered and I think very effective.

Long talk with One Arm at night who says "Senso dami" and had apple feast.

Men paid for last half of Sept. Swimming but water coolish.

Wednesday October 13, 1943

Still squitting. 10–12 times day and not feeling so hot.

Dubbining flying coat bought for 12 y.

CC said men could read books and play games when they come in afternoon from work. Also asked if men would prefer bigger "kamari" and increase in pay from 10–25 s a day or stay on short "kamari" and pay. Said boys would be allowed to buy things (food—oh yeah—tobacco) and other items with extra money. We pointed out men would prefer to do extra work for extra food rather than extra money since with small amount food now getting just able to do present work. CC said getting more than Koreans and if we thought Koreans were better off he would change their jobs and chow for our boys but can't give our lads extra chow for extra work. Told us to get men's opinion and let him know in a.m.

Selling things from our billet bought on 11th as canteen. Men with no winter underpants issued with Nip lined ordinary pants—okay but small. Finished pay. Interpreter says keep as much small change as possible in camp as hard to get—don't we know it.

Thursday, October 14, 1943

Clear. Spent a.m. in bed as still squitting and not feeling so good generally. Started sulpha quanadine tablets. Two every three hours.

Put numbers on Nip clothes which liable to be recalled. Interpreter took our Nip underpants tonight and issued them to troops—I hope we get others to replace them after the inspection.

Another accident today—man hit by falling rock. Eight others went to help him and then there was a big rock fall where they had been working—if they had remained working they would all have been buried. Report going to CC about this.

Doc preparing report on food showing we not getting enough and beri-beri increasing. Five men to receive red chevrons for over 100 diligent citations and 12 blue ones for not missing one day's work. CC to present personally. He says he's going to give officers some sort of badge of recognition for good work we have been doing in running camp. Interpreter said we are well in with CC and it would be a good policy for us to do a small fatigue (like spreading shite) rather than have CC's good will lessened.

Officers went to village again today and brought a lot more stuff for men's canteen—e.g. shark oil, wakamoto and notebooks. Things coming around fine. Also brought back two watches which have been repaired—one with broken spindle.

Seaweed and cabbage soup—spud mix a.m. Seaweed and spud and bean mix at noon. Spud mix and b. bean soup at night.

Rumour: Russians attacking Kieff from west and south. They have crossed Dnieper and Pripet River, tributary of Onleder.

Friday, October 15, 1943

Made bet with Interpreter. He gives me 10 y for every month under 9 that Germany doesn't hold out and I give him 10 y for each month over 9 that she holds out. Hewitt bet him 50 y Germany is beaten in less than year.

Free issue of following to all: 1 bar good soap, 1 pen holder and 2 nibs, 1 packet tooth powder,1 bottle ink per section. Day after tomorrow Yasume and CC will present diligent and work chevrons.

Feeling little better today and number of trips easing off.

Doc put in report on food we are now getting, pointing out how little the issue was and how deficient in essentials like proteins, and vitamins. Put in report of CC's request re increase work and more pay, saying men would do more work for increase in food but not getting sufficient food to do increased work even for more money. Rice and barley "skoshi" for the next three days. Seaweed soup a.m. and spud mix, beans noon, b. bean soup and mix at night.

Saturday, October 16, 1943

Medical Orderly.

Cook House secretary gave us five more 60K sacks of spuds for today and the 17th!! That should give us enough to eat. Started yeast culture on the 15th and gave all men about 2 spoonfuls today for vitamin B and prevention of beri-beri. Lists given us of men to receive red and blue chevrons tomorrow. CC to present them and also he is giving a lot of prizes. Work Hanchos are also going to pick out men and give prizes.

Seaweed soup and mix, a.m. Seaweed and beans mix at noon. Fried spuds, spud mix and B. beans on side.

Feeling much better and diarrhoea gone.

Sunday, October 17, 1943

Cloudy, and showery. Hot bath. Rest day.

Prizes presented. Prizes to men with work records and citations. Prizes from camp include rest of things from Red Cross boxes and not much at that considering there should have been at least 35 full boxes and cigs and chevrons. Hanchos presented cigs, H. hair, medicines, few towels, etc. These prizes for period to end of July. Old number 3 camp day. We're now going to issue prizes every three months.

Firm today!

Tunics issued to troops yesterday (supposed to come from Hong Kong.)

Seaweed soup and spud mix in the morning. Ditto noon with bean mix. Spud mix, b. bean soup and mashed spuds at night. Another issue of yeast to troops.

No issue of Red Cross food although we asked for it.

Rumour: Bagdolio formed "ITI" government and declared war on Germany.

Monday, October 18, 1943

Warmish—rain during night.

Interpreter spending more and more time with us. Seems to be boycotted by other Nips.

CC came to our barracks looking for me and when I stuck my head out of bed, grinned all over his face. How different his coming to us and actually grinning when he found me in bed—he gave orders originally we were not to go to bed during the day.

Interpreter still persists that the war will last 10 years and Nips will fight to the last man! We argue with him every day but no hard feelings!

Pay for men for first half October received but as usual in big bills. Made table for CC.

Still loose but regular.

Tuesday, Oct 19, 1943

Finished table for CC and he is very pleased.

Interpreter asked us if men wanted tobacco issue and when we said yes, he arranged with CC—officers got 2 packets cigs.

Buried pipe to administration building 3' to prevent freezing this winter but still left some sections shallow and made joint with concrete so can't use taps for 2-3 days!!

Sent two more watches to village.

Seaweed soup a.m., and p.m. Seaweed mix a.m., bean mix noon.

Wednesday, October 20, 1943

Inspector Quartermaster will not be here till 27th now. Started wearing belly band again.

Wanted officers to spread human manure on garden again today. We took objection to CC who ruled if anyone made fun of us, report to him and he would deal with him. Also since gardens for good of all—all had to take turns—starting with officers. So we win again!!

Seaweed soup a.m. and p.m. Seaweed mix a.m. and seaweed on side!! Bean mix noon and b. bean on side at night.

Thursday, October 21, 1943

Officer of the Day. Men paid for first half of October. CC said to prevent black market all things will be made available in canteen but men must keep account of their expenditures beginning with this pay. Will try and get 1,000 packets of H. hair and 1,000 packets cigarettes per month. This is good step forward.

Seaweed soup a.m. and p.m. Seaweed mix a.m. Bean curry mix at noon. Spud mix and black beans on side at night.

Rumour: Nips have occupied one of New Hebrides.

Friday October 22, 1943

Clear and colder.

Wearing belly band and pyjamas at night with two blankets on top and two below.

Still having shower and exercise every day but water very cold. Regular but a lot of wind. Usual a.m. and noon meal and quite enough. Night spud mix with b. bean and pumpkin soup.

Nip CC ordered burning for cures now — going back to the dark ages! They'll be bleeding us next. This burning leaves scars too like vaccination marks. They're doing it for everything. Nip CC told Doc he hoped he would take up that form of medicine and Doc said he would have to if he didn't give him some medicine soon.

Officer of the Day. Started wearing socks three days ago a.m. and p.m.

Rumour: we started attack on Burma.

Saturday October 23, 1943

Coolish. Brought bed from top bay, where I've been sleeping all summer, to inside cubicle.

Rice and toho soup a.m., bean, seaweed mix at noon. Spud mix and seaweed soup in the p.m.

New green jackets and pants supplied by Kumi and given to men whose suits unrepairable. All "gunzokos" sick today as result of eating "mushrooms" after our cooks warned them they were iki ni". Interpreter came and told us CC had asked him to tell all he knows re gunzokos (their shady deals). He was on trail of a gold watch which some chap is supposed to have sold to one of them against the rules. Interpreter certainly has no use for them especially since they beat him up.

All men who have over 20 Y and NCOs with over 30 y to hand in surplus for deposit. No one came forward. Officers have to keep accounts of money they spend too.

Sunday October 24, 1943

Cloudy and cool — too cold for shower and throat not so good.

Gave Int. watch to take to repair. Watch inquiry still on. Food very "skoshi." This a.m. we got only one and a third white bowls so one of lads left his with us and we took to Interpreter and showed him. He took it up with Cook House secretary.

Seaweed soup a.m.; bean and seaweed mix at noon; bean soup and spud mix at night. Gonzokos gave Hewitt toho and then asked him to give them a box of mabela as they couldn't eat rice as tummies upset because of "mushrooms." He took it up with us and we voted 3-2 against giving it but Hewitt did anyway!!

Men's diaries all called in and gone over by Interpreter but afraid most of them not very complimentary to Nips especially after a.m. meal.

Monday October 25, 1943

Rain in afternoon so all men came in early — little better issue for next 3 days but still "skoshi". Young daikons, satomeo, and Chinese cabbage came in. Told Interpreter re mabela but evidently CC has authorized granted men to have this — they got more today!

Men getting all fixed for inspection. New Guard Room suits, khaki tunics, holes patched and clothing beyond repair replaced.

Last haircut 6 weeks ago. Shaving every three days and shaving soap lasting well.

Interpreter doesn't seem to have got to bottom of watch business so heaven help him if we can't prove it!

Reading today. We never have any fatigues now except occasional voluntary wood fatigue and carrying out of chow every noon which is rather pleasant.

Seaweed soup and spud mix in the a.m. Bean and spud mix at noon. Seaweed soup and spud mix at night.

Rumour: fighting in Celebes and Philippines!!

Thursday October 28, 1943

Clear and cool night.

All men now clean and ready for quartermaster's inspection on 30th. Colonel also coming. All men new work suits. Tabbys changed if desired.

Not much fuss outside Glass Eye's department. Our deposit cards returned stamped by CC so 10 y deposit (outside usual over 50 y) okay. Usually get lecture at evening tenko at which we stand and freeze while they tell us to guard our health, etc.

Big % of millet with rice and barley now and not too bad. Brings quantity up. Meals today the same as yesterday with Chinese cabbage on the side at night.

Red Cross boots fixed so we all have our correct size now.

Friday October 29, 1943

Lot running about today in preparation for inspection. Busy till 10 p.m. getting numbers to men to put on before a.m. tenko—last minute as usual. Handed in our overcoats, tunics and winter shirts—G.E. has promised to return after inspection as we not supposed to be issued with them.

Men to lay out everything on beds in a.m.—nil on shelves. Tenko to be 6:30. Food daily issue I suppose till after inspection. Mostly millet. Sun doesn't appear on camp now till 8:30—9:00 and is just clearing hill when setting.

Saturday October 30, 1943

Inspection by Quartermaster and Major from Tokyo—Colonel didn't show up. Doc sent note to chap in Tokyo by one of inspection officers asking him to try and get some letters through. Inspection very cursory—just walk through billets as far as we were concerned and after all the preparation!! Interpreter says he hopes we officers have a little rest after inspection.

Satoimo in mix 3 times and spuds, satoimo and cabbage soup p.m. and daikon and satoimo soup p.m.

Permission given to hold church service on Sunday between 6:30 and 7:00.

First news from home!

Sunday October 31, 1943

Oh happy day! Received telegram from folks. Received Tokyo October 6th. Shows they got my letter written March 7th which gave my POW number. I get a break after all. First to receive cable with exception one STC lad. Interpreter came in with it in morning, with cheery good morning which we grudgingly answered (sitting freezing). I couldn't believe it was for me. It says "Everybody well—cabled Muriel Preparatory School Ispingo Beach, Natal—Chater." What a relief to know Mu got safely to South Africa and also that she is doing something to keep her mind occupied. Looks as though she has adhered to her intention of starting school for kids from Singapore! And yet the reaction was a swing to depression, naturally, and crazy to go home. This cable also is first indication for all camp that our letters of March 7th got home!!

Limpy, Cook House secretary is leaving. He has been very good in his fight for better chow for us but can't get along with granted men. He exposed bits of graft to CC but since latter didn't seem to do anything about it, he quit. Hewitt talked to new secretary and says he seems nice chap. (He is going to Tokyo and promised to bring us some technical books so good start).

Rumour: going on to winter schedule tomorrow—tenko 7 a.m. and finished work 4 p.m. but nothing official.

Monday November 1, 1943

Lots of sweet spud vines came in—vines only. We have to separate leaves, shoots from stems. All are saved and I suppose we will get them in soup. We will soon be herbivorous animals—the Nips get the spuds.

Lads had to start on this separation when they came in from work after finishing their "Kamari" and were not very pleased. Didn't start tenko at 7 after all.

Burning of men to cure all ills still going on. Evidently it is an order from Tokyo or CC here has got special permission to do it. They use a small piece of fibrous punk size of pencil tip and apply on certain parts of the body. (Same place every night.) Burning leaves scars and some lads don't want it done but are ordered to. Have asked G. E. for our clothes back, (which were taken from us for inspection) but he says "chotamati."

Officers brought three sacks of cabbage from village.

Photos which were taken of all POW months ago given to us. Two prints per man, one to be posted in a book, the other given us and we can send them home with our next letter but I don't think many will. You never saw such a bunch of hardened criminals in all your life! I certainly won't send mine home. Gave the boys lot of laughs anyway.

Still getting our yeast every day using Red Cross sugar and it is doing a lot of good—no beri-beri in camp now! Millet predominates now every meal and rice decreases—half millet.

Solid today.

Fixing floor of our cubicle to prevent draughts. Asked Interpreter if we could put 3″ saw-dust down and he is going to ask CC. Sick increasing. Seventeen in hospital with three pneumonia cases.

Tuesday November 2, 1943

Still having showers daily but water getting cold!

Pay came in as usual—300 y in 10 y notes! How they expect us to pay men earning 1.40 y half a month, I don't know!

I put three blankets on top tonight with two below and mossy and sheets underneath. Taking warmed up rocks to bed which are very welcome.

Lads had to do spud vines again when they came in and were not very pleased. Either was I, being Officer of the Day and having to chase them.

Wednesday November 3, 1943

Sunny. Nip holiday (anniversary of some Emperor).

Got our shirts back from G.E. but that's all! I suppose we will have the same fight for every article. We are getting peeved and thinking of going to CC about it.

Finished vines today!! Lads had to get up half an hour earlier and take undermats from No. 3 hut and take to river bank to air. Then pick up—put under beds when they came in.

CC said we could have mabela issue (72 lbs) and 26 lbs of sugar and also tobacco issue.

Cabbage soup a.m. and straight millet etc., bean and onion mix at noon. Onion and cabbage soup at night, millet and mabela—one and a third cupfuls per man and was it good!!

Friday November 5, 1943

One Arm at tenko said now all men must wear winter trousers and jackets to work and going to and from work, work clothes over all. Can also wear overcoats to and from work.

What a change. Last Feb. when it was really cold they wouldn't let boys wear winter jackets and they were never allowed to wear overcoats out of camp. Officers still have no underpants, jackets or overcoats.

Shock today when Hewitt went to village with Interpreter to buy for canteen. Officers had put in approval list and CC cut off all vitamin medicines, (except wakamoto) and sauces, etc. One day he tells us he is going to treat us like officers and is going to give us special privileges and then this. Interpreter said it was just our tough luck being at this camp. Mood CC was in, I suppose.

Wore flannel shirt for first time and very warm although weather warmer today.

Interpreter has taken to wandering round camp and chasing O.D. to clean up bits of straw, billets, etc. Also he is complaining that men are not gargling every day so now he is making them do this (with KMNO4) before yeast issue. Doc is still pressing for medicine but only a little coming from local hospital.

Cabbage soup a.m. and p.m. Millet, rice, barley a.m. Bean. onion spud curry at noon. Soup mix at night. All men to get extra blanket—when they come from Tokyo. Other camps only have five but this camp is supposed to be colder.

Saturday November 6, 1943

200 sacks of pumpkin came in and a lot of sweet potato vines from next village.

Announced at p.m. tenko—tomorrow Yasume and corned beef issue.

All men to wear pants and overcoat to latrines. Fire guard to see all doors and windows closed and to enforce former. All to gargle at least twice a day. If anyone is caught stealing the whole section will be punished by beatings as last two suffered, except anyone who informs and he will be let off.

Interpreter also warned we must leave barracks cleaner. One Arm praised lads for working well—he seems only human Nip in camp. Always cheery and decent to lads yet one would think he has more cause than any of them to be ugly.

Usual a.m. soup and bean without oil mix. Bean and S. Ema mix noon. S. Ema mix night with cabbage and satoimo soup. Fried cabbage stems on the side and sweet red beans.

Cloudy. Interpreter came and got a list of library books saying they are to be exchanged.

Sunday November 7, 1943

First church service 6:30 to 7:00. Nips stopped it at 7 with "Taksan Owari." About 50 attended.

Hot bath and new system. Before it leaked so badly last section in had about 6″ mud in bottom to wash in. Now fill up and reheat after 2 sections. Very satisfactory.

Yasume but all boys had to get out and sort potato tops all morning and some in the afternoon. Also camp cleaning. Some sort of Nip holiday too.

Corned beef issue—one per man. 20 sacks of beans in. Dough buns and pancakes coming in but very expensive. 1.50 and .60.

Two cases chickenpox.

Monday November 8, 1943

Took out medicine ball and Interpreter made us put back saying we can only use it on Yasume." Keep our health!! Might as well put us into cotton wool! Interpreter now walks round camp and insists on cleaning camp and handling arrangements in billets and usually have lecture every night now on this. Things repeated a dozen times. Thinks we are as dumb as they are!! Also optional re wearing winter things on job. Anyone stealing vegetables outside is to be beaten.

Officer of the Day to see all men gargle every morning. Sick increasing—18 today and 7 "cocko", 3 pneumonia and 3 pleurisy. Colonel of East Corp. coming tomorrow.

Still no overcoats.

Fixed doors.

Tuesday November 9, 1943

Interpreter out early seeing if billets clean. Colonel arrived but didn't even inspect camp. Rain at night. Holding off till 10:30 a.m. and then rain in afternoon. Lot of boys got wet.

Issue for these three days—16 millet, 6 rice and 8 barley per meal. Cabbage soup a.m. and p.m. with boiled pumpkin and sugar at night. CC says if boys don't gargle twice daily no medicine will be supplied to sick but Doc says we don't get it anyway!!

Beans every meal for three days.

Rumour: war has ended.

Wednesday November 10, 1943

Order nobody allowed in Cook House without cause. Cooks not even to be in at night. (Beans, etc. will be locked up). Usual long-winded speech by Interpreter at night.

Two books received from Tokyo—Nip-English book and electrical technical. Interpreter scared stiff CC will find out they were ordered by officers. This country certainly ruled by fear of army.

Made steamer rack for Cook House. Lots of vegetables these days and I go regular to lats. 220 packets yellow H. hair came in and 1 packet per man issued. Still no sign change to pay men. Civvies sick of war—if they had say, it would end tomorrow. More dung spreading—this time by troops.

Rumour: Huns going to evacuate Kiev.

Thursday November 11, 1943

Glass Eye sent Interpreter to tell officers to spread dung again. Hewitt had long argument with Interpreter pointing out CC had made ruling last time that everybody was to take a turn and he finally refused to do it. Interpreter said you win and men did it when they came in.

Hospital cases issued with extra blanket. Nip Doc comes from village hospital to look at sick occasionally.

First fires allowed in billets on 9th as men wet but order for wood fire came too late and pits not clean. CC said we could pack floor of our cubicle with sawdust.

Issue for next 3 days—11 millet, 5 rice and 6 barley—only 22 kilos per meal. But we have one bag of pumpkin (39 kilos) per meal. However this won't take place of rice!!

First frost.

One week ago a Korean asked me the time on the job and said he was hungry. They are nothing more than slaves. They are far worse clad than our boys and they live in old converted huts with window spaces but no windows!! Their bedding is dirty and benjo arrangements vile. They are kept in by the fence like us but haven't nearly as much room. They appear to have a Guard House and are marched to and from work and have Nip Hanchos over them at work like our lads. However they don't seem down-hearted although all express the wish that the war would end and they could go home.

Usual a.m. and noon meals. Red bean mix at night with fried sweet potatoes and soup. Mabela given to sick (with sugar.)

More Nippon Times came in. Rumour: war will be over 7 months.

Friday November 12, 1943

Dates of *Nippon Times* handed to us Oct. 1-25.

Rumour English POW leaving camp but think all balls. Rumour some of guards leaving. Medical secretary left today but no loss. One of "Haitis" taking his place.

Due to skoshi millet etc. and a lot of watery vegetables, noon mix was very fluid and you could pour it. No good for carrying out to men. Going to try and cook vegetables first tomorrow and then put rice in same water.

There's something in the air with rumours and granted men talking.

Usual a.m. meal. At night we had mashed sweet potatoes on side.

Sun went behind hill at 3 p.m.

Saturday November 13, 1943

Got canteen stuff from village but Interpreter wouldn't let us buy anything on the side. (Not approved). And a little while ago he said officers could have any luxuries it was possible to buy—special treatment!!

Putting sawdust on floor of our cubicle to stop draught. CC then saw and said all men to do the same in billets tomorrow and I look after it. I told him there was not enough dry sawdust and he said to spread it in the sun.

120 bags sweet potatoes came in. Also a lot of daikons and we had to cut off the tops and hang them up like last time.

Usual a.m., cabbage and pumpkin soup. Noon mix dry with new idea of using sweet potato vine shoots and not bad. At night we had boiled pumpkin, raw cabbage, meat, cabbage soup, spud and red bean mix.

Got some trianon (M. and B. for pneumonia.)

Sunday November 14, 1943

Mabela issue of 2 large cartons came in and 15 K sugar for noon.

Hot bath. Yasume. Officer of the Day.

Tried three times in morning to start sawdust collection but guards would not let us out. Didn't start till 2:30 and only one barrack got sawdust in.

Had another non-denominational service. Everyone took bath on threat of Doc to give a cold shower tomorrow to abstainers.

More sweet potatoes came in making total of 270 bags!

Report Robertson who went to Tokyo hospital with T.B. has died.

Vitamin C tablets—6.33, .50 watch (Freco) 3.50.

Big meal at night, beans, spud shoots, toho mix, sweet potatoes, spuds and pumpkin in rice. Sweet potatoes boiled per man. Everyone had enough—also cabbage and pumpkin soup.

Monday November 15, 1943

CC in Cook House and tasted mix. He said it needed more salt and Cook House say we're not getting any.

CC said hospital could have small coal fire getting coal from Cook House in a.m. and p.m. Asked Interpreter for postcards. He said don't be surprised if more people move in to camp soon.

Lads had to haul sawdust and spread as they came off details.

Got more trianon for pneumonia and it's doing a lot of good. Now 19 in hospital!!

Daikon top and cabbage soup in the a.m. and pumpkin and sweet potato mix, beans, sweet potato and pumpkin mix at noon. Soup and mix and on the side mix at night.

Officer of the Day. Loose after 3 days solid.

Rumour: naval battle off Bouganville in which US lost 4 battleships, and 2 carriers.

Thursday November 18, 1943

Another clothing check. One chap borrowed a water bottle from another. When this was found out he was made to slap the person he borrowed from! Then Glass Eye gave latter a cigarette. Nip justice!

1.1 kilos at noon! More spud cutting. More cabbage and daikons came in.

Hewitt took bottle of live lice to CC to see if he could get permission to use boiler. CC was angry and said men must kill lice daily but no boiler!

Interpreter says all men must cut off moustache as only CC allowed this luxury!

While inspecting clothes Glass Eye found sweet potatoes on two boys who had pinched them during washing and cutting. He searched all kit. Space between billets was like a hail storm for awhile. Some slapping but that's all.

Friday November 19, 1943

Colder with north wind. I have been wearing a flannel shirt and gr. jacket only last couple of days. Tomorrow tenko is half hour later—6:30. Interpreter on about spud pinching and said he had not reported this to CC because he doesn't want all the section punished. But stealing still goes on.

Big noon meal. Mix in the morning. Usual daikon top and cabbage soup at night, also with boiled sweet potatoes.

We told Interpreter their papers print a lot of untrue stuff.

Got 700 packets of 30s H. hair and 300 packets cigarettes and sold one to each man.

Saturday November 20, 1943

Rumour: all leaving camp and another 200 coming in. Don't know how this would affect officers. Chaps had to move out of No. 4 billet (16) but they say this is so they can spread spuds out to dry as rest of billet is store room. Too bad 'cause lads had papered it all up.

No spud cutting today. Think they may be going to use up cut ones first. Still setting them out in the sun to dry.

1/8 inch ice on water bucket this a.m. High mountains had snow on them.

Usual a.m. meal and at noon mashed sweet potatoes. At night, sweet potatoes and cabbage soup and mix.

Interpreter says there have been three attempts to land in New Guinea (probably Bouganville) and we have lost eight battleships, and eight aircraft carriers (total 45 ships). Nip V.O.D. asked for list of people who had any experience flying or repairing planes! Several men handed in their names.

Sunday November 21, 1943

No service as Doc at dentist. Five men to dentist.

Interpreter started at 8 p.m. to interview men who gave numbers in last night as plane repairers. Must have had call from Tokyo to start this at this time of night so it looks like move for some!!

Got all men up at 10:00 last night to take potatoes in to administration when it started to rain! Ceremony of cut spuds this a.m. We took them out and spread them, then it started to rain so we started to cover them. Then we took some into No. 4 billet. Then we picked up some we had spread. They find cut ones are going bad quicker than whole ones. Sama sama" daikons in spring so they are cutting no more and using cut ones first. Getting seven bags of sweet potatoes per day! Rice and barley are short and there's been no millet for 3 days. 12 Barley and 9 rice at noon and 6 rice and 9 barley in the morning and evening. Thank goodness we have a lot of vegetables.

Took sports program to CC and he added seven events and said he wanted entries in by a.m. so I asked for entries at tenko and got an alarming number.

I also have to present a memorial service and a concert program in the a.m. so I am working on these at night. (Service has to be half to one hour long.)

G.E. issued an extra pair of tabbies to those working in wet! No word yet of wearing Red Cross boots.

Cooler today.

Monday November 22, 1943

Punk gave 60 K dried sweet potatoes per meal saying that is equivalent to 100 K whole. Still questioning chaps about planes.

Gave CC program for memorial service, sports meeting and concert and he vetoed. He wants cross made and said we could fly Yank and British flags so we're making these. We are also going to burn incense and blow last post.

CC says nobody allowed back in camp until 3:00 even though finished "Kamari."

1/8 inch ice on fire buckets in the a.m. Brrr. But I still only wear flannel shirt and sweater but put on denim pants today. Cold shower.

Friday November 26, 1943

Yasume and Memorial Day. Officer of the Day.

One year since Yanks arrived at this camp. Had memorial service for those that have died in the camp in a.m. attended by CC and staff and they didn't interfere in any way, even paying their respects in Nipponese fashion. They had two representative boxes of ashes covered by a Yank and British flag and paper bouquets.

Then we had our sports meeting in afternoon which went off very well with little interference from Nips. CC sat through whole show and was very amused at the Tug-o-War. He donated prizes (small) but spirit there and I think lads all enjoyed it.

Few had baths but water leaking badly.

Issue of M. and V. to all and 3 oranges (mandarin) per man. Big meals included bean and onion mix on the side at night.

CC got written report from 2 diligent and 1 "bad" man of each of 4 working groups about what they think of working conditions and how they could reduce accidents, etc.

Saturday November 27, 1943

CC ordered hospital to have stove! And only 5 in camp. I installed it. Sick decreasing and only 12 in hospital now including 2 "Koshus." New Doc is doing well.

Flour ran out so no yeast. Meals still big with taksan sweet potatoes including boiled ones at night and bean and onion mix on the side. 1K per man at noon.

Had cold shower. Frost every night now.

Told CC what's wrong with bath and asked for 4 men to stay in and fix. He is thinking about it. Still putting out cut sweet potatoes every a.m.

Officer of the Day.

Sunday November 28, 1943

Service. CC said I could keep 2 men back to fix bath.

List arrived from Tokyo giving new numbers for POW but lots of mistakes! My name has been given as Cater! I hope this won't mean my letters go astray.

180 K meat came in! Probably horse but looks good. Daikons coming in every day. 5 sacks of spuds given for 2 meals tomorrow.

Year since we arrived in this camp! Things have certainly improved since last winter. Can face this winter okay and hardly feeling cold yet. Have finished putting sawdust on the floor and CC ordered a section per day of the barracks to be done but I'm afraid it is wet.

Boiled sweet potatoes at night plus spud mix and bean and green mix and daikon, pumpkin soup. Putting 4 K polishings in mix for 3 days.

Rumour: Formosa bombed by 20 planes.

Tuesday November 30, 1943

Got heating unit out of bath but waiting for timber and cement. Job is lousy with it yet can't get it.

Interpreter read out note from CC giving bad treatment of Nip nationals in US such as rape of women, putting them all in jail pending building of camp (same as Nips did to our nationals in Singapore!) and they still are there 9 months later and shooting two Nip nationals who they said were escaping. However they say they still treat us well as in the spirit of Bushido. Asked 20 men to write to him about this news which they did in no uncertain terms.

Got paid 15.5 y and deposited 80 y leaving 27 y for expenses to Nips.

10 K meat in soup with daikons and cabbage at night. Also onion cabbage, bean mix and rice.

Thursday December 2, 1943

Orange issue 6¹/₂ per man. Also toilet paper issue of 36,000 large sheets and 4,000 small. 207 bars of washing soap given to officers to distribute to those without soap.

Interpreter at p.m. tenko says all men must have numbers on all green jackets back and front. Also 15 men from each section lined up in front of administration to receive orders for removing valuables in case of fire.

Tried to talk Interpreter into letting us do new work our way but must put in frame and pour box first, so got wood and cement at last and made frame and set it.

Oranges—2.07 y.

Monday December 6, 1943

Yasume.

Issue of 1 can corn beef and 1 meat and vegetables per man so looks like more Red Cross food coming in.

Working on bath. Cold again last night. More carol practice. A.m. tenko—8.

Tobacco and cigarette issue, 30 s.

Rumour: Churchill says no offensives until spring!

Tuesday December 7, 1943

Rain at night and till 11 a.m. so no work.

CC agreed to my idea of finishing bath which is same as original scheme.

Some Red Cross things came in. 16 Red Cross boxes, stockings, boots, c.beef, but all in small quantities. However boys say these only loose things and more at station. I hope so.

Lot warmer today.

Very good bean, spud, daikon and cabbage in the a.m.

Nippon Times came in.

Wednesday December 8, 1943

Officer of the Day. Finished concrete bath.

CC asked to see our expense account and I had to speed. Also asked to see money to check account.

CC bawled Hewitt out for spending too much on tobacco, saying he couldn't give to those who were sick with no money! Administration would care for those people and anyway if they don't work they shouldn't get tobacco.

No more Red Cross stuff came in so it doesn't look as though there is any more in the village after all.

Sunday December 12, 1943

Church service and carol practice.

Can't get water for tea from Pollock's Cook House anymore as Nip guards anti!

Punk says "taksan" letters have come in but Interpreter says he doesn't know about it.

Punk promised us flour to make pumpkin tarts for Xmas and rice balls and red beans!

Grouted bath and told CC probably be ready for next Yasume on the 15th.

Also asked CC for clothes and he "chotamati" as usual.

Fried bean, meat and cabbage mix at night. Barley predominate in mixes now and looser, but only once a day.

Oranges—Paid. 2.07. Cigarettes paid 30s. 3 toothbrushes—45 sens.

An account of individual expenditures by POWs.

Monday December 13, 1943

All to have haircut before 16th.

Daikons coming in nearly every day. Food still "skoshi."

Cold sitting up nights now. Sun doesn't get on billet till 9:45 and leaves at 2:30.

Had sore throat at night and during the night. But warm enough. Still only wear shirt and sweater. Gloves for all and socks came in but only issued gloves to outside workers and only those without, so officers didn't get any and my hands are cracking.

Having Patience Marathon.

Tuesday December 14, 1943

Lights out at 7:30 now.

199 working men including kosho—what a difference from last year at this time.

Had small fire in the bath house to set concrete.

Daikon and daikon top soup in the a.m. with bean and pumpkin mix. Bean, pumpkin and spud mix at noon. Night same as a.m. CC and Cook House secretary supposed to be foraging for food! Which now is getting hard to get.

Put first paper in bed.

Wednesday December 15, 1943

Yeast issue started again.

Rain in a.m. so made into Yasume and had hot bath. Bath great success and very little leakage. Only had to stop 10 minutes to heat at one period and water stood all night. Also didn't use much coal.

Warmer. Nips say last winter was very severe one and it certainly doesn't seem nearly as cold now or probably we're used to it.

Tobacco issue and cigs 30 sens.

Rumour: Cook House Secretary to buy 90 K meat for Xmas and oranges.

Carol practice. Had slippers made.

Sunday December 19, 1943

Measurements of all taken. Mine: chest expanse 103 cms. Waist 87. Foot 29. Taken by Glass Eye but don't know what for—it couldn't be for tailor made clothes!! They did the same a year ago.

Food skoshi these days but not too bad yet.

Service and carol practice. Rumour letters here again.

Monday December 20, 1943

Found out we are to be allowed bath now on 1st, 5th, 10th, 15th, 20th, 25th of each month unless Yasume day near one of these dates so started bath at 10 a.m. stoking myself! Very good bath and finished about 5:30 p.m.

Officer of the Day.

Food very skoshi now—only getting 2 white bowls in a.m. and p.m. and about .9 K at noon. Soups a.m. and p.m. but only seaweed and daikon tops and bottoms.

Tuesday December 21, 1943

Two parcels about a foot square arrived for Yank lads—seem to be put up by Red Cross and food—lucky devils.

More *Nippon Times* arrived—November 25th to December 13. Coming in frequently now.

80 K meat came in for Xmas but don't know how much Nips will get. Also dried fish and "grit." Nips pinched cheese, 2 pair socks and something else out of one of the parcels above. Tried to trace who did it, but couldn't. What a shame after waiting all that time.

CC says only a few in camp causing trouble but all will suffer if these don't behave.

Wednesday December 22, 1943

Officer of the Day.

Only enough sweet potatoes left for 3 days now then daikons and more daikons—still coming in. 100 lbs. rabbit came in and very good.

One Arm said at tenko a lot dying on each side on front but we would always be safe here. Then asked us where we would sooner be and we all said fighting—that stumped him.

Letters definitely here but all Yank and going to take 60 days to censor.

Fairly good meals these 3 days. Daikon and top soup in the a.m., with meat broth in p.m. Fried fish on the side at night.

Having carols stencilled.

Had cold shower! Weight 79 K.

Thursday December 23, 1943

Still not very cold. Findlay coming back with Punk from Tokyo Hospital.

No. 13 Yank caught stealing from civvy house and all of us beat him with sticks. We will be lucky if Xmas surprises not stopped—some chaps have no sense and this same man was caught stealing tea from sick man two nights ago.

Saw some of the letters—about 60—and Interpreter says there are five times as many so I may be lucky—some English although mostly Yank. Some getting 6.

CC has written out five precepts of our way of life which all men have to repeat after p.m. tenko.

54 new books came in and we catalogued them—look fair, mostly novels from hospital camp. Notebooks 40 sens.

Findlay came back. Findlay says we are sinking 2 Nip ships to 1.

Friday December 24, 1943

Bath.

Only gave us 21 K meat out of 170 K—stingy for Xmas. More daikons came in.

Rain till 10 p.m. but boys had holiday all day. Don't know why they didn't send them to work in the afternoon.

Sick in hospital increasing—now 5 pneumonia cases but trianon fixes them up okay. Four men operated on at Nip Hospital for cysts, boils. Doc says jobs not too bad.

Saturday December 25, 1943

Second Xmas as POW and very different from last one. Last 2 days very mild. Holiday.

Following issued: 16 Red Cross Boxes, 27 packets cocoa with sugar which were issued at p.m. meal. (This out of 28 packets which came in!) A tin of M and V [meat and vegetables] per man came in recently. 7 cigs and 2 packets hair per five men paid for out of Red Cross funds. Every man got big red bean patty and small pumpkin patty. Two fried fish in batter at noon with mix. Soups and mixes half daikons—worse luck.

Had service in the morning and sang carols and had a sing song at night. Lads very cheerful at night. Two oranges per man. Opened tin of condensed milk which I had kept from last Xmas's Red Cross parcel and had in cocoa—grand. John opened tin gold block tobacco and we smoked some. Nips left us alone. Let's hope next Xmas at home!

Monday December 27, 1943

Slightly cooler.

Glass Eye says officers get gloves and socks "asita" if haven't any.

Good issue of average 40 K meal—cereal, rice, barley, millet, "grit" but not much veg. Soup (daikon and tops) a.m. and p.m. and mix.

W.c. only once a day but slightly loose since sweet potatoes gave out but feeling okay these days.

Had to make list of numbers of men and ages. They also want list of bad characters in the camp (are they going to move them?) and good workers.

Friday December 31, 1943

Extra bag of rice from Kumi. Had cooks in at night till 7:30 with little sing song. Home brew and ether. Rather quiet New Year's Eve!

Tuesday January 4, 1944

CC says men can have wood fires for half an hour in the a.m. between food and tenko. Officers and cooks to get supply of wood in next five days. However, I don't think they will bother for just this little time as it will smoke them out and they will have to leave nearly as soon as they are lit. Meals large in grain but very little vegetables—40 K grain (very little rice) a.m. and p.m. and 50 K at noon. Soups have hardly anything in them—few daikons.

Buik raised row at night saying wash stand and lats must be cleaned at night and medical officer must supervise. However, if lats washed then they will get a coating of ice and there will be broken limbs. He is trying to run camp as usual—sure this is not CC's idea.

Letters now have to be translated into Nip so CC can read them. So God knows when lads will get them. What a torment!!

Friday January 7, 1944

Orange issue 3 per man. Oranges 58 s. Charcoal and burner 1 yen 46 sens, cigs—46 s.

Section on other side partitioned off with blankets and quite warm in a.m. and p.m. Different from last winter and cosy. Read there at night.

Making steamer for big pot.

Still not allowed to wear Red Cross shoes but so far feet warm with 2 pair socks.

Saturday January 8, 1944

8 tons of carrots at the station! Making cupboard for Cook House.

Coldest day yet—20 degrees. Pump froze up and nearly burned motor out.

1000 packs H. hair and 250 cigs came in. H.H. now 45 sens a pack. Cig and H.H issue formerly to officers only. Flour issued for bread on 10th. Putting with some of our homemade yeast on 9th and let rise. Red beans mixed with it.

Four loads of coal came in but can't use yet.

Thursday January 13, 1944

Warmer—did lot of washing. Officer of the Day.

Glass Eye holding clothing inspection last three days and made speech about it tonight probably to impress new Sgt. Latter took tenko a.m. and left early at night so Glass Eye's speech was wasted.

Searched one section for stolen 3 yen and 3 pairs underpants.

Have read *Girl in Blue Hat*, *Goodbye Mr. Chips*, and *Cage me a Peacock* lately. Also *Nana*.

Boys can have fires in billets p.m. if temperature -5 degrees C.

This photograph, of POWs from Hong Kong, was circulated after the war to illustrate the plight of POWs and attempt to obtain financial relief for them.

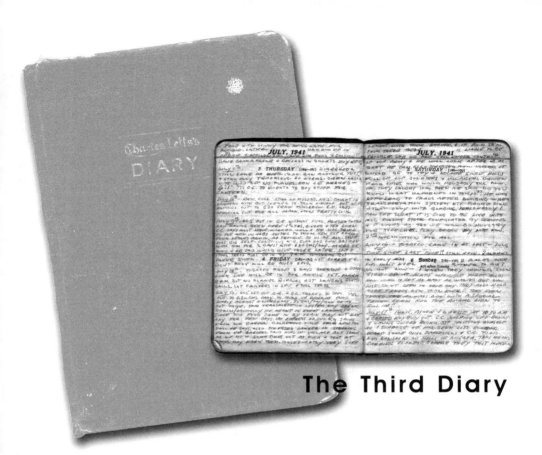

The Third Diary

THE THIRD DIARY, DATED JANUARY 15 1944 TO FEBRUARY 4, 1946 is Les Chater's final diary as a prisoner of war. It is blue leather, with, on its cover, an enclosed rectangle embossed in gold, with the words (somewhat enigmatically) "Charles Lett's Diary." Similar in size to the first diary, it is 9 cm. by 14 cm. by 1 cm. Printing becomes noticeably larger as the diary comes to its close. Mr. Chater's excitement as he sensed the nearing of the end of his imprisonment may be the reason for this. But it might also be noted that in this third diary Mr. Chater's health was beginning to take a serious decline. He had watched close to 80 of his fellow POWs die—men once as healthy and vigorous as himself. Indeed, he had often officiated at their funeral services, or helped carry their naked remains up the side of a mountain to be cremated. Though his battle to maintain his own good health had been a determined one, given the circumstances, it was a battle he was beginning to lose. Indeed, had his imprisonment lasted much longer, one wonders if Mr. Chater would have made it home.

Saturday January 15, 1944

Big wigs probably Directors of Kumi inspecting job.

No bath as boys not in till 4 p.m.

Lads searched by new Sgt. as they came in but nothing discovered.

CC says work cards not necessary anymore as paying done from sheets made out by Dunlop. Interpreter called in diaries to check money boys supposed to have.

CC asked for list of non-smokers so he could give them something else to spend money on.

Glass Eye slapped people wearing overcoats on tenko but not officers.

More leeks came in.

New Sgt. hasn't been around much although out on job and stopped our lads working with women and going through town.

Monday January 17, 1944

14 degree frost and cold. Had to put overcoat on bed.

Some of the lads saw Yank Red Cross boxes at station. Estimate 400 of them—great excitement.

Good grain issue next three days.

Lead from pump to water tank put underground.

Filling of river bank goes on and getting uncomfortably near our swimming hole.

Nip reporter asked us questions through Interpreter and we gave him straight answers. Do we like army or civvies? What did we think of the food? What do we think of the death of Yamamoto? And he said many people have the same opinion as us—that he was foolish to be flying in danger. What do we think of the Aleutian Campaign? How long will war last? What relations will exist between Russia and Japan? Would we be treated as heros?

And we asked him—what would happen if Japan lost? And he said there would be no Japan. But when we pressed him, saying, what about women and kids, he hedged.

Wednesday January 19, 1944

Yasume. Bath—went in twice.

H. hair and cig issue to men and 3 packets cigs to us—69 sens and H. hair—45 sens.

Our charcoal fire is very comfortable and I read nights till about 8:30.

Yank got another private parcel.

New Sgt. very well disposed. Lets troops have fires in a.m. and p.m.

Have High Bar going in barrack.

Thursday January 20, 1944

Pollack says Interpreter told him all those over 32 being sent home! What a hope! Still makes one feel good.

Sent Rice's watch to village.

Chap slept through p.m. tenko and didn't even get beaten up for it. Certainly treating us different now.

Sgt. said he is going to issue Red Cross parcels in 3 days. One per 2 men.

Issue about the same as usual. Only have to wash buckets at noon now as usually some rice or soup is left and they give it away to get buckets washed, also dishes. Get dishes done every night. Interpreter left till 25th.

Saturday January 22, 1944

Bread and fish.

Heavy snowfall and boys having snow fights!

All 38 x 4 Red Cross (Yank) boxes handed over to officers—going to issue next Yasume day?

Hard these days. Doing work for Punk.

Granted men very affable now we have Red Cross parcels! Had 2 tins Meat and Vegetables.

Sunday January 23, 1944

Slight thaw most of the day.

Not feeling too good. Bad throat. Bad left knee and weakish.

Hospital figures down a little—13. Lot of boils and infections lately.

Snowball fight between Nips and us at tenko, everybody jolly.

Weight 81.3 K. Heaviest man in camp again. Most weights up.

Wednesday January 26, 1944

Pump working at 2 p.m. Doc talking to CC and CC says he will think about letting boys wear Red Cross boots on wet days—says he was saving them till we went home.

Agreed to get more rice polishings, and sugar for sick. Asked if boil patients should have bread. Doc said yes. Also asked about yeast and Doc told him how to improve it. Some yeast pinched again last night. CC very interested in sick and food these days.

At p.m. tenko all lined up and Sgt. said tobacco now expensive and so boys could buy more following scheme which comes into force tomorrow. Usual "komodi" [quota of work for the day] will constitute day's work. Any extra cars will be paid for at 10 cents a car, but no man can earn more than 20 cents extra a day. Those not on komodi will get 5 cents per day if they stay—also cooks and inside workers. This extra not compulsory however. Asked boys what they thought of this and they said 16 cars enough and they would be too tired to do more.

Fish on side again at night. Plenty of food. Leek top, pumpkin, daikon soup.

Monday January 31, 1944

More letters came in—about 60—half for the English and <u>one for me from Mu.</u> Hope we get them soon!

Enjoying coffee, jam and butter from Red Cross Parcels. Also Chesterfield cigarettes and quite good—6 packages per man.

More books (new) came in—33—Yank and quite good, although one on How to Dance! Also *Nippon Times*—Jan. 1 to 13th.

Colonel coming on 8th.

Thursday February 3, 1944

CC ordered bath started at 11:30! Lit at 12:15 and ready by 2:30! CC said it was a cold day and boys would be cold but actually snowing. Boys got straw rain coats.

Saturday February 5, 1944

Those with only 1 pair socks to be issued with another. Soap issue (washing).

Colonel coming on the 8th announced at tenko.

CC says tomorrow Yasume and mabela issue. Punk sponging coffee and milk at night.

Sunday February 6, 1944

Officer of the Day. Yasume (Oh yeah.) Hot bath.

Nips running round like hens with heads cut off.

Tobacco and cigarette issue, orange issue, tooth powder and toilet paper (small), pen nibs, tabbies. So all men have 2 pairs and before you couldn't get any. Seven tins of bully in soup. Mabela (2 cases) with 15K sugar.

Water cut off in middle bath to fix pipe. Drain cleaned and general camp clean-up.

CC inspected at 1:00 and asked troops if they were getting enough to eat and they said no—would like full binto per meal.

CC turned over to us bag Red Cross sugar to be given to sick. (Nips had pinched rest of bag). 49 pkts. Red Cross Cocoa (out of 140 pkts.) 154 tins of corned beef also turned over. Nips immediately called Hewitt over and asked for "presento" sugar and cocoa and milk, which they got!

Took partition in No. 4 billet down and then had to put it back up!

Paid troops for all of January.

Monday February 7, 1944

Colonel came early at 3 p.m. unexpectedly and what panic—first thing they did was to come to us and borrow coffee, other two bags of Red Cross sugar, put in Cook House store. Ration for tomorrow raised to 57K—60K—57K for 3 meals—crafty.

Officer of the Day.

Colonel inspected feet at p.m. tenko but that's all. Nip Doc with Colonel asked Doc cause of boils and Doc said not enough protein and want more meat. Nip said lot of deaths from pneumonia at other camps and suggested sending Doc there but Doc said he didn't want to go and probably deaths from pneumonia due to lack of trianon.

Civvy came with Colonel and calling up STC lads and asking them questions—would they prefer British or Nip rule after the war. (Answer British). Would they like to return to Malaya? Answer—Yes! Are you willing to co-operate with Nips after war? (Mostly say they don't think Nips will be in Malaya then.)

Tuesday February 8, 1944

Colonel arrived at 9 and inspected camp at 10:15 but very cursory—went through without talking to us. Very pleased with sanitary condition of camp and few sick. (Only 5 in hospital yesterday). However there's the rub because has ordered our Doc to go to an Australian camp on the West Coast for 3 weeks where 25 died in January. Cold and misty there. Danger is will our Doc come back? We all hope so. Lads have every confidence in him and CC also. He can get things out of CC.

Nips "borrowed" cocoa twice and tried to again but Hewitt scared them last time saying he would get in wrong with CC.

Sgt. said he is leaving at the end of the month as there is not enough work here. Too bad because he's done a lot for us—fires in billets a.m. and p.m.

Civvy with Colonel supposed to be prince and has attended Oxford. Says he likes English culture but when war commenced he came home. Interviewing all STC asking them if they would co-operate with Nips and go back to Malaya. Getting straight answers and all lads loyal to British. "China Boy" says Chinese and only one face!

Japanese production microscopic compared with America, Britain and Russia. All say British will win and they won't go back to Malaya if it is under Japanese. Good for them. Hope Britain rewards their loyalty after the war.

Wednesday February 9, 1944

Colonel came back at 9 this a.m. but didn't inspect camp. Doc talked to him and he said Doc would be coming back in about 3 weeks. CC very pleased when Doc said this was the best camp. Doc also put in good word for swimming next summer if our pool is filled in.

Had tin of bacon. 16 degrees of frost at night.

Saturday February 12, 1944

Interpreter let me see my letter. Evidently Mu didn't hear a word about me till September 23, 1943. Something wrong somewhere. Worries me when she says she is not happy. Hope now she will look on cheerful side. My reaction on getting letter is terrible. You wish you were home and wonder how long it will be.

Doc got word he is leaving the morning of February 14th.

Food continues average although vegetables a little shorter. No trouble now with diarrhoea at all. Warmer.

Monday February 14, 1944

Letters given out! However had already read mine although reread it half dozen times.

Gosh how nice to have genuine letter from home. Hope Mu bucks up now.

Doc left and we went to station. He missed the first train.

Nice getting letter on wedding anniversary! By some of letters we find that some of the first postcards arrived home but I should say few of them—Damn Mush Mouth!

Wednesday February 16, 1944

Rest day—bath.

Tobacco issue and 1 package cigarettes per man with extra pack for work Hanchos. 4 packages for officers—.92s, orange issue, 3-4 per man.

Winter shirts and winter underpants handed to Rhys for issue. Men to have 2 winter shirts now and 2 underpants but, as usual, officers don't get any—can't figure it out. We were allowed to change our shirts for new ones though.

Got pay for men for half of February. Got in big bills again. Men got overtime tickets redeemed. Only 7 sick last few days and none serious!

Mabela issue but only 10K sugar.

Sunday February 20, 1944

Officer of the Day. Hot bath. Interpreter expecting more letters.

Rumour: we landed in Marshalls 21 days ago—getting closer to Japan!

Monday February 21, 1944

14 degree frost.

Yanks got parcel but it had been pilfered before it got here. Interpreter issued it and was then told off in front of our men for doing so without referring to Sgt. Then Sgt. "confiscated" (because of this) candy etc. from box! The Interpreter is certainly looked down on by other Nips in the camp.

2 cooks bawled out for clowning. Sgt. says that's for Yasume days—(not supposed to be happy other days). Admin had cooks make doughnuts etc. for them (using our bread flour) while Punk was away!

My weight 81 K.

Tuesday February 22, 1944

Bread—we only got 2 and one-half tins of baking powder (usually 6) of the 50 supplied. Bread good and toasted it.

Sgt. starting to raise a little Hell. Had chap out at tenko and made him apologize for complaining about work.

Wednesday February 23, 1944

Yank put in esso for cutting tin.

Getting news daily now. Attacking Truk Island.

Sgt. took 90 sens from Alf as presento.

Saturday February 26, 1944

Warm in the middle of the day now when sun out and sun riding high.

Better today.

Those who lost weight were called to administration and told they will be given special food! What a change.

Some evacuees appeared here lately and rumour Tokyo and Yokohama women and children have been evacuated.

Officers and work Hanchos had to write report on Eden's speech that many POWs had died due to ill treatment and also Nips are not doing their share in interchange of Red Cross comforts and mail. We had to write if we thought we had been maltreated here. Naturally every-one said yes.

Because Mr. Chater was an officer, he helped run the camp. The next entry illustrates just one of the almost daily meetings the officers held with the Camp Commander. Everything that was said would need to be translated by the Interpreter. For this reason the Interpreter was very important in the camp.

Sunday February 27, 1944

Warmish. Had tin of spam.

CO called me to administration and asked if I thought we had really been brutally treated. I said yes and he said if we thought that brutal, he would show us some real brutality. He said—wasn't most of it due to misunderstandings and the fact that this is a new camp whereupon I gave instances: (kicked because slow for funeral) (boys sent out without soles on shoes) saying they were not misunderstandings. When he said he would show real bru-tality I said they could only shoot me so go ahead and he grinned.

Then he said it's nothing like the brutality of the Yanks who bombed hospital ships and machine-gunned boats and ran over people with steam rollers. I said if this is true, it's prob-ably a mistake and he said no. I blamed misunderstandings on the old Interpreter and said I had no complaints re present treatment but 50 deaths at first spoke for themselves although I recognized the difficulties camp operated under at first and lack of medicine, etc. beyond control of this CC. Asked if we expected perfect treatment immediately and I said we got it in Java. He said but that was the front line and I said all the more reason for misunder-standings then. He said we arrived here in appalling health due to boat trip and that was one of the reasons why the death rate was high. Then he told me to talk to the other officers and find out if they thought we had been brutally treated or was not the majority of cases mis-understandings. We wrote out our opinions saying treatment on arrival due to irresponsible subordinates, language and Interpreter refusing to take complaints to CC and that this harsh treatment was being softened by the now just treatment and continued treatment as at pres-ent would rectify those mistakes. We took this to Interpreter and he told us to go.

Sgt. still browsing round and told our lads who were working cleaning out latrines that they were not working hard enough. Also blamed boys for taking boards from the roof of No. 3 billet and he would put them in esso if it happened again.

At p.m. tenko Glass Eye asked that those who had taken boards from No. 3 to make tables, etc. to speak up. No one did so he made all turn in their tables, etc.—except officers.

No fires allowed—(start of brutal treatment?)

My watch stolen from table in our cubicle—not much hope of getting it back I'm afraid.

Cleaned flues of bath. Tenko p.m. now at 6—chow 4:30.

Monday February 28, 1944

Hewitt called up and put through the mill like I was. Gist of CO's speech was boys will have to change their ideas.

Rabbit had pups.

10 degrees frost.

Thursday March 2, 1944

Noticed blood in faeces and M.O. says piles—took medicine for them.

Officer of the Day.

Rumour: Russians reached Baltic through Estonia. We're attacking Marianas.

Sunday March 5, 1944

Sick again. Flu I think. Rhys still 104 temperature and have sent for Nip Doc. Cpl. Bullock doing very well without Doc though in bed all day.

Canteen order came in and curry and pepper allowed this time (when CC says show us what brutality is). Enough for one each per man and to be sold through canteen shop (because someone put in his letter that the Red Cross Representative was hoodwinked.)

Tuesday March 7, 1944

Sent watch with Parker (124) to village.

Better today but a little weak. Rumour: STC are going to be sent to Malaya in 3 days!

Finished *4 Million* by O. Henry. Also *Passage to India*, by Forester.

206 to work—a record. 3 in hospital and 1 cocho.

Rhys has pneumonia according to Nip doctor and advocates half an aspirin a day and mustard plasters!! And we have some trianon (which we used, of course.)

Tuesday March 14, 1944

Put up hammock in billet.

Nip CC has issued orders that POW are not to be beaten up according to Interpreter.

I am okay now again. Cutting down on chow.

Binto stolen on job today and a couple beaten up but not turned over to CC.

Pig killed today and we got the bones.

Read *And Now Tomorrow* by Rachel Field. Also Irvin Cobb.

Thursday March 16, 1944

Yasume. Bath.

Yank Red Cross Clothes turned over to us. Following: 30 overcoats, 110 blankets, 110 denim jackets and trousers, 110 hats (felt lined with flaps) 223 handkerchiefs, 220 pair socks, 110 sweaters, 107 towels, 110 pair gloves, 110 pair pyjamas, 110 shirts, underpants and vests (wool all very good material.)

Mabela issue and pears—1 per man sold. Tobacco half ration (1 pack 2 men—sold) half because of theft of Binto Box. Pears-50s.

Those getting "Ema Rusa" for last 2 weeks weighed and they have lost weight. Nips can't understand it although they only get a dipper a day.

Friday March 17, 1944

Tenko 6 a.m. worse luck.

Distribution of Yank Red Cross clothes discussed. They want to cut towels in half! Talked them into keeping overcoats, gloves, hats and socks till next winter—also sweaters, because during summer the men would trade them off and say they lost them.

Sunday March 19, 1944

Watch strap 1.95. Toothbrushes -.50s.

Went up and got 157 English and 22 Yank letters. None for me! 8 for Dunlop. 13 for dead man. This will probably affect letters we are now writing. Interpreter has sent for more stationery. He said yesterday he could not even mention others had received private parcels as that was like hinting you want one and cannot ask for food or clothes! Scared he might get in Dutch if he lets it through.

Milligan ill with pneumonia. Tried to get trianon in village with Interpreter in a.m. but none. Asked him to phone to Eda and put on train but wouldn't—and yet they are scared stiff men will die!! Asked Hancho on job if he would go to Eda (we would pay fare) and he said yes, he would go in the morning and be back by 2 p.m. However he produced a bottle this afternoon!! And administration here couldn't get it!

Nippon Times came in—16th–31st of Jan.

Issued handkerchiefs one per man and blankets to those without private ones.

Hair cut.

Monday March 20, 1944

Bath. Issued sweaters to Yanks because we were issued with them in Singapore. I got one as well because I have only one winter shirt.

Wednesday March 22, 1944

Issued shirts to those who didn't get sweaters. They issued some underwear and I got a set. 9 degrees frost last night and cold. Started gardening!

Thursday March 23, 1944

They issued pyjamas to those not getting underwear and issued socks. I got both.

Working on garden. 9 degrees frost.

Bread came in and some vegetables.

Saturday March 25, 1944

Issued shirts—I got another suit of underwear in lieu of my pyjamas. Started reading *Thinking in English*.

S. San (Medical Secretary) and Kitasawa San (Limpy) left. Latter slobbered all over us.

Weight 79.1 dropped 2K.

Sunday March 26, 1944

Yasume but a lot of gardening and s___ slinging.

Last mabela issue—30 boxes.

Still fires in billets. Paid 5.50. Cigarette issue 92 s. Tobacco to men.

Hot bath.

Sorry to see Limpy go as he did his best for us.

Rumour: Nips in India.

Wednesday March 29, 1944

Officer of the Day.

Our lads are running more and more things on the job. Big winches, cranes, drills. Nips calling up more and more men.

Withdrew old clothes from billets for patching. Still coolish but wearing pyjamas.

Have not eaten a.m. rice for week and cutting down on other meals. Bread and cheese at night. Our food is being pinched.

Rumour: fighting in Philippines.

Friday March 31, 1944

Bath. Boys not to wear new Red Cross clothes on job.

Rumour: Nips inside India.

Saturday April 1, 1944

Pep talk to officers re supervision to see camp cleaned properly.

Showery. Bar work every night.

Yanks can take up to $10,000 insurance through Red Cross. Names handed in.

Sunday April 2, 1944

Rain and boys wet. Keep grass raincoats in our billet and by time get to job boys wet. Buik got H___ from Sgt. for slapping boy and making him deaf in 1 ear.

Wednesday April 5, 1944

Doc back and our own Whitfield and what news. Truck, Guam, Rubul and maybe Wake all taken and attack on Philippines imminent. Also Nimitz says they're going to attack China coast at the same time. Stillwell says will meet Nimitz in China Sea. Chinese attacking Hangkow. Russians through Latvia and Estonia and 60 miles into Poland. Also into Rumania. Luftwaffe broken as regards attacks on Germany as must keep all to repel invasion. Rumania and Hungary sued for separate peace but refused. Faction in Germany also asked but were told to kick out Hitler first. Systematic bombing of industries in Germany. Seven Nips to one Allied shot down in China. 1 out of 2 Nip ships leaving Philippines sunk. 70 ships sunk at Truck—Nips surrendered (7,000) in New Guinea. Roosevelt says war with Germany over in 44 with Nips shortly after, most boys being home for Xmas. Bombing 6-20 miles inland of French coast. English coast evacuated to 5 miles. 13 nations including Germany protested to Nips re treatment of POW.
Weight 78.

Monday April 10, 1944

Bath—can't start stoking now till 12 and last stoke at 5. Told the Nips could not get men through the bath but no use.

Interpreter says this place is closing down this fall and we are moving to a cooler place but I don't think he knows this far ahead.

Wt. 77.6. Noon mixes very good last 2 months. Fried vegetables and beans every time. Soups good these days—carrots and sort of spinach but stems of latter are hard. No fish for a long time.

Drafting letter to Mu. The letters are to be in by May 1.

Tuesday April 11, 1944

Finished finger printing everyone in camp. One copy to Tokyo and one here for medical purposes.

Stove at last taken out of sick quarters but they don't need it now and it has done good service. One-quarter loaf of bread on the side at night which had been going bad and even then they didn't want to put it out! Also spinach and ground carrot. Daikon with soya sauce on side.

Thursday April 13, 1944

Went to hospital to try and fix X-Ray machine. Nearly electrocuted myself. Think tube burnt out.

Lots of carrots these days.

Feeling okay.

Saturday April 15, 1944

Yasume. Cooks told to make 200 loaves!

Bath.

Tenko 9 and divided into 3 groups—49 Yanks, 49 English, 2 STC Then these put into No.1 barracks and rest in No. 2. All sorts of rumours. Night shift—some moving, etc.

CC called officers at 12:00 and said he had telephone call from Tokyo at 3 p.m. yesterday and said 98 men and 2 officers were to go to new camp. Men in No. 1 barracks to move and

Hewitt and myself. Ready to move off at 5 a.m. tomorrow. Colder climate but thought to be a better camp—oh yeah!

CC said he hoped we two officers would come under him in a future date. He was proud because his camp had been picked to open new camp as we had reputation for good health and discipline. Hoped we would do better. We were to carry six blankets and all kit. We told him this was impossible but he said we must. Later ordered to carry three only and later only one. Others done up in 9 and we took 26 bundles with us. Others arrived day after us. All to turn in green jackets. Lads packed and kits checked in afternoon to see if they were only taking allowed clothes.

Boys paid.

Rest of bully divided and one tin issued to those going and one-half remaining Yank Red Cross boxes. We had celebration at night with five tins of bully beef, spaghetti and cocoa issue.

Sorry to leave I can tell you. Breaking up friendships. Couldn't possibly carry all I had accumulated but got lads to carry most for tobacco, etc. Two STC lads gave me cigs. Some of sick also to move (CC wants to get rid of them!) Rumour we are moving to North East of this island. B. Scout said goodbye to me a dozen times and gave me rice balls and cigs. To bed at 11:00—up 2:00 and fall in at 5 a.m.

KANOSE CAMP

Sunday April 16, 1944

Marched off at 5 and entrained at 6:15, all in one electric car, half standing and bundles blankets and kit all over but all pretty cheerful. Changed to another electric at 6:30. Changed at10:04 to steam and picked up army guards! Changed at 10:30 to another steam.

Three-star Nip private gave order to Hewitt who misunderstood and then Nip kept socking him in front of Nip officer who was in charge of us and seemed decent bloke having joked with lads and given out cigs. Nip thought he had been made fool of. Said even if we were officers he could kill us and he had been sent by headquarters as Interpreter to teach us discipline. Bright outlook for our new camp!!

In charge of army again, all spirits dropped. Later on in the train he sent for us and said he was partly at fault for not saying who he was but we must obey—think CO had a talk with him.

One Arm and big Glass Eye were with us and staying. Tarada 3:45. Changed at Howits (where Doc was at Aussie camp on west coast). 3 feet of snow from now on in spots and cold. Bright outlook! Mountainous. Change at Nagaoka at 6:00 and again at 8:00. Arrived at our destination at 9:00 and half mile walk. New home new warehouse—tin. Partitioned off 6 rooms with corridors. 44 mats to room. Given new numbers. Wood fires with rice and stew! Some kind of furnace plant. New Tokyo Colonel coming day after tomorrow. Place cold and bleak. Went to bed fully dressed and 3 blankets each.

Tuesday April 18, 1944

66 men to work—some loading ore, some stoking furnaces. Still don't know what kind of plant but some metal it appears. Work not hard but stoking very hot. Will get glasses and masks later, issued with work suits and mitts and will get letters. Stoke 5 mins, rest 10. Work 8 to 11:30—12:30 to 4:30.

Inspection by Colonel and speech—we will treat you according to law. Give recreation. You have done your duty to your country and surrendered to Nips and we will treat you as heroes. Do as you're told and keep health—different speech from first colonel who was going to destroy our countries! Said 100,000 letters and parcels arrived in Tokyo first of this month. Food skoshi but still white rice.

Hot bath again.

Wednesday April 19, 1944

Heavy rain. 46 to work.

Cigs came in and we are to get 5 per day.

Time passes slowly. Doing pay sheets.

Boys issued towels and face masks. Some stoking furnaces to make carbide and others loading trucks with ore. Those outside worked in rain! Say plenty of rest. Big plant half a mile long. Get hot bath every day! Grand.

Sgt. decent bloke. Divided into 3 billets with partition between. Thirty-three to billet, numerical order. Have new numbers. Mine is no. 2. Very hot work and boys to get glasses, rubber shoes. Also to get salt issue. Tough hanging round billet all day with nothing to read but a lot of paper work to do. Have pay sheets to do. Same pay as Camp 2D.

Thursday April 20, 1944

Started working 3 8-hr shifts. Boys divided into 4 groups—3 of 22 for 8-hr. shifts stoking—8:00 a.m. to 4:00 p.m., 4:00 to 12:00, 12:00 to 8:00 and one loading 8:00 to 5:30. We take dinner with them. Long period between supper and breakfast however—one group 1 a.m. to 3 p.m.!

Handed in canteen order—good start. Everything at plant done in military manner. Saluting between Hanchos and workmen—workers tenkoed etc. Hanchos seem quite reasonable.

Weather cold though. Rain all day and heavy—boys outside wet. Seven sick including one koshu. Only one medical orderly and so far no medicine—no Doc but not very sick and I think they will do their best to get medicine. Say good hospital here for works. Very young children working here. Bath after each shift. Firewood allowed 1 bundle per billet a.m. and p.m. and does nearly all day. Asked for clock and got it because there are no watches! Mentioned vitamin B and they immediately phoned up and asked if there was any and got names of 5 types. Different from usual method of "Chotamati".

Not chasing sick out and leaving us alone nearly all day. Good lavatories and wash stands. Say officers will get own quarter soon but will be in this building, partitioned off—not so good.

Friday April 21, 1944

Tobacco issue 3 packs per 5 men.

White rice every meal with smoked fish on the side usually or spinach. Soup twice a day— mostly seaweed or daikon tops and fish. Some pickled daikon on the side and ginger. Sometimes binto white rice—sometimes half. Meals seem all mixed up. I think we're getting not quite enough but quality good. Sgt. says hard to get fresh vegetables here—mostly dried—but plenty of rice. They say they will get mixes when our kitchen is ready—in about 4 days—a good kitchen. Rice short for working lads. Nips are sympathetic and say wait. We get our meals from the Nip kitchen which cooks for whole works. We are supposed to get 100 gms of rice per meal and 100 gms make up of barley, millet, etc. Haitis got 200 gms rice.

New CC will arrive tomorrow.

Rain again.

Saturday April 22, 1944

New CC arrived—Second Lieutenant and looks strict but I think he will be okay. He made speech saying glorious POW and we will treat you well and respect rules but you must obey orders or you will be punished.

No fire guards from now on.

Tobacco issue 1 pack per 5 men—total—60 sens.

Started partitioning off quarters each for Hewitt and myself. Tried to get one between us but they said no. Big rooms 18′x 7′.

Had to sign usual no escape.

Sunday April 23, 1944

Boys doing all stoking now on day shift. Hanchos say they had meeting objecting to 12 hours on and 12 off for POW. Boys standing work well but need glasses and tabbies.

Hospital being built and A-1 place.

CO held sick parade and detailed two light duty men for tea boys with pay, and told others to go back to bed. Also asked what medicines sick men needed. I made complaint re quantity of food for one shift and they sent more out. Also at night got full binto of white rice each. Squid and daikon, also one-third cup soup. Soups poor, mostly daikon tops. Really can't complain about food—white rice. CC certainly gets results on complaints and we can get to him immediately. Old CO said this camp expect, and I think expect with good treatment, to see results. Boiling water in our new kitchen. CO interested in starting yeast here but says sugar and flour scarce. Started to carry chow bucket but guard wouldn't let me as I "shoko" [officer]—and we had to carry faeces in other camp! Pay same rate as first camp—10s and 15s.

Still have fires all day.

Rain showers and chilly. Have 4 blankets and overcoat on top and pyjamas.

Tuesday April 25, 1944

Rain again. Outside lads get wet every day.

CC says those with sore eyes or heat blisters from furnaces to stay in Kosho!

Own kitchen started cooking with 2 cooks and 2 "ocha boys" [helpers]. Hand in ration sheet every night and dry rice measured for each detail but still bitching! Mixing "na" (pickled daikon tops) with rice and bloody awful stuff! Quite good deal on meat—whale blubber every day. CC says going to give us 78K rice for 100 men each day. Pretty good deal at.78K per man. Other camp only getting about. 6 per man at best and mostly barley. Gave CC list of vegetable seasoning, beans etc. we used to get and he is going to see if can get these. He says if they give us barley he will deduct it from rice so still 78K. So we said no barley please although plenty complaints re food because naturally you don't get the bulk you're used to since rice doesn't swell so much. But you can't tell them that! Also each shift says other shifts get more and better food!

Some scivvies came in but heavy, small, single strap and boys say no good to work in. Lot of bad feet. Issued 15 pairs tabbies to outside workers. Swimming pool here! Hope they let us use it!

Thursday April 27, 1944

Weight 78.6 K. Nearly everybody up so they can't kick about meals. Tooth brush and pencil issued to each man and half a pack of tooth powder. Nip Doc from works looked at sick. One man to get treatment for rash on feet—ultraviolet ray! Keep asking for soap but still no issue. They say they make it here too!

Hanchos say furnace production gone up since POWs working on them! Also say tobacco etc. free issue from Company [Kanose Carbon & Carbide Co.]. Guard says more POW (English and Yank) coming next month. Also we (officers) are to get thick mats. Small canteen order went in. Also got vita ray, pepper, mustard, tea, cocoa (poor stuff). Looks like good canteen.

Lights and fires out at 9 p.m.

Sunday April 30, 1944

Only 5 Yasume as 5 men sick and 3 kosho. Sick increasing. Not much medicine supplied. Still bath every day.

Got pay in change. I asked for and paid men last half of April!

Tuesday May 2, 1944

Happy Birthday to yours truly! Let's hope it is the last as POW. Thanks to everyone who I know is wishing me well!

Quite hot today. Could lay out in sun stripped. Billet is going to be very hot if today is any indication. Opened tin of bully and smoked Yank cigs to celebrate birthday.

Sick increases. Medical inspection of all men by Nip Doc yesterday. He kept in 2 more men (CO says if men get bad feet through company not supplying proper things to wear that's their fault and men stay in). Had talk with him directly this a.m. He calls me in and doesn't bother with Interpreter and between his pidgin English and my ditto Japanese we get on okay! Sgt. says when CC goes away in a couple of days he will take me for walk. Also says from info from Tokyo doesn't think we will be here next winter but will be moved near Tokyo as many men would die here! Tapped him about sending Perry to Hospital in Tokyo! Still no medicines.

Wednesday May 3 to 17, 1944

CO got a lot of medicine.

Two men caved in on job. Most sickness due to bad feet from scivvies and shoes (no tabbies). Diarrhoea due to change of heat—furnace to cold—and drinking too much water. Also boils (probably rich diet and no soap.).

Poor old diary. I haven't had time for any entries. Today's the 17th, Mike's birthday—6 years old. Wonder if I will see him before his next birthday. Many happy returns.

Food—the all important thing to a POW. Still getting white rice, no barley, etc. Thank goodness! 78K a day—15K beans and 15 carrots alternate days about 8K. Whale meat every day—good ration. Soup sukoshi. Plenty pickled daikons. Some fish. Think everybody satisfied so must be good!

Red Cross supplies came in on 12th. 40 Yank individual parcels 2 between 5, same as 2D. 60 each of razors, tooth powder, shaving soap, sewing kits, toothbrushes, pencils, combs, laces, shoe polish packets, 10 razor blades. Toilet soap, 120 washing soap, 6 razor blade sharpeners, 2 scissors, 6 pipes, 11 cigs per man and either 10 cigs or 1 per 2 packets of tobacco. All put out within 1.20 minutes of arrival in camp. Pretty decent of CO to whom we gave 200 cigs and shaving soap! He paid 5.00y (wouldn't take as gift).

About 300 letters have come in. In all, half Yank, but none for me. Over half put out to date. Also some Red Cross medicine came in and CC has produced Nip medicine. Biscuit issue 10 per man (bean paste). Soap issue 1 per 2 washing soap, 1 toilet soap per man. Pen issue. Also toilet paper from Red Cross—the old roll!

Shifts have changed twice and plenty of work for me. First put on 2 12-hour shifts with 3 groups—12 hours on and 24 hours off. After 3 days CO asked lads if they liked 12-hours or 8-hour shifts with no Yasume and they all said latter. So he told me to arrange to change back again immediately. 12 hours was too long for lads. Anyway we are getting Yasumes again.

Pay not so much. Officers getting average 15 cigs a day which some issue! They treat us well here. The canteen has about 200y worth of stuff in it. They get us anything we ask for if procurable. Tea, cocoa, soya, pepper, seaweed, mustard, curry, fish powder, vitamins. Officers bought 2 stainless steel kettles at 18 y each.

I forgot bread. CO got us bread because we asked for it—1200 loaves and lashed it out in 4 days. Two per meal and big loaves!

Red Cross parcels just in time. Also a lot of rhubarb in. CC is a young chap and a going concern. Very decent. Can talk to him any time. Gives lads Physical Training himself and keeps them hopping.

Gardening started and we will have extensive ones. Planted beans on 16th and 17th. Yasume men do gardening. Going to build us canteen—library. Had air drill on the 16th and kept lads from work for 6 hours. Sickness gone up slightly. Thirteen now sick. Mostly septic blisters, diarrhoea and bad feet.

On the 16th, we got paid for May—45.50—no questions asked.

On the 18th good workers presented with prizes. Best one 2 packets tobacco, 20 cigs and 1.50 y. Better than tooth brush from last camp.

Civvy guards and office Hanchos very decent here.

Weather better now. More sun and taking sun baths. Have not worn socks since first week. Still paid 95.00y for April on 9th of May!

Note from Dunlop. 700 letters for us there including three for me. (On the 10th) Rumour: leaving here in July.

Rumour: fighting in Sumatra, France. Tojo, Churchill and Roosevelt agree to exchange POWs.

Friday May 19 and 20, 1944

Fire alarm at 7p.m. Seemed to catch Nips on hop. Went round blacking out lights (poor) and hung sacking round furnaces but didn't stop work. I wonder if this is the real thing?

Asked CO for high bar and he said are 3 enough? They got sketch out immediately and sent to shops.

Asked Interpreter if I could get photo made from negative of Mike and he said yes.

Hair clipped.

Monday May 22, 1944

Card from Mu! Her letters were returned! May go home! Hope not. Dated 11-10-43 after her letter. Both well, thank God.

Cook House Hancho took negative to get pictures made! Interpreter read us letter from CO Mitsushima thanking us for services rendered there so it doesn't look as though we're going back!

Thursday May 25, 1944

Sgt. and Interpreter in bad mood. Lads caught H___ for gambling. Ocha boy told me Sgt. wanted to see no. 44 so I told no. 44. Then I was called up to Sgt. by 44 and he told me to stand at attention outside with 44, giving me ugly look. I knew no use asking why so stood at attention nearly 4 hours in just pants and khaki shirt 5 to 9 p.m. Boy, did it get cold! Never so cold in my life.

Then he called me in and told me to ask CC tomorrow what was wrong and I said I certainly would. Then he told me himself that 44 had come to him and said "The officer wants to see you." Obviously he had misinterpreted what 44 said and I spoke to 44 later who said he told Interpreter that "The officer said report to you." Told Sgt. I never said that and after a while he apologized but that doesn't do my prestige with troops much good. And I was condemned without a hearing—is that the way Nips are going to run greater East Asia? In course of his talk with me he said, "Even if war finishes this summer you will be here till next winter!"

Also according to International law as officers we should not be with men.

Friday May 26, 1944

Rumour: exchanging POWs. Rate 50 Allies to 100 Nips. If true probably disabled men but should mean more Red Cross and letters. Also we have captured Burma taking 7,000 or 70,000 POW!

Monday May 29, 1944

Letter from Mu written 13-7-42! Second one she wrote by number—addressed to Batavia. My Batavia POW number on it—9733! Very newsy. Goode and gang got to Australia okay. All people that got out seem to have got jobs, damn it! She has had letters from my home. Four pages! Gosh it's good to hear from her but what lousy feeling after.

That finishes this bunch of letters, about 400 in all. Some got 20–30, others none. Think Mu must have written plenty but this only one that got through!

Now have fish pond and quite big garden planted here. Life same. Bit of sun today but still chilly.

Rumour: Churchill and Roosevelt proposed peace but Tojo says no. Another version Japan has asked for peace but Tojo says no! Russia declared war on Japan. Still rumour about exchange of POWs. Also half of us are leaving for another camp in 30 days.

Tuesday May 30, 1944

Interpreter had long talk with officers saying CC etc. had conference yesterday to discuss ways of improving camp. Said if there's anything we want put it in the suggestion book and he will translate for CC. Trying to get baseball equipment, high bar, fruit in season, cookies, 25 rabbits. (Yesterday fish pond stocked with 10 buckets small carp which will be big in fall and eat). Also eat rabbits in fall. CC wishes we could swim in river! Also Interpreter, when he goes back to headquarters (in a few days), is going to see about sending books, games, letters and card paper, etc. Gave us some sort of gelatine seaweed with sauce and said going to supply 32 a day for sale in canteen at 7s. Also going to get musical instruments. Said CO not an army officer and this is not an army camp so harder to get things but camp depends on energy heads for welfare of POWs and head here is trying to do all he can for us which is true. I think we get sugar and cookie ration like Nip workers. We also have had 2 goats for 2 weeks now and 5 small pigs for a week. He says all garden stuff is for us.

Wednesday May 31, 1944

Sunny and getting quite a tan.

Interpreter has asked officers to write report of our impressions of this camp. Total letters put out—450.

Had 2 pills each to prevent typhoid.

3000 fish—more fresh fish came in.

Paid troops.

Friday June 2, 1944

2 boys in esso for trading clothing to Nips on job. Nips turned them in after CO talked to them. CO gave speech saying if POWs wanted to trade things with Nips or wanted to give or receive presents, must be done through administration.

Nips had bird tied to tree with string round leg and also brought in bird nest and 6 eggs with mother bird they had caught on nest and these are grown men and want to rule East Asia!

Asked for ping pong table and wrote it in suggestions book in a.m. and it was here in the afternoon. They got it from their own recreation room.

Walt and I wrote report on our impressions of this camp. Administration got glasses fixed for boy who had his broken.

Given shots for typhoid.

Saturday June 3, 1944

Fever during night but I don't think due to shot as nobody else sick. Think due to too much bar work. In bed all day and very weak.

Sunday June 4, 1944

Still slightly sick but got up. Colonel from Tokyo coming in two days. Also Nips say 100 more POW coming soon.

Monday June 5, 1944

One apple sold per man at 11 cents.

Nips say we now have Rome but no fighting anywhere else it seems.

Now have 18 young rabbits.

Getting ready for inspection but not as much panic as other camp.

Tuesday June 6, 1944

Did one upstart on bar and felt very sick and muscles ached after so fever must have been due to bar. Works put up another high bar.

Fire drill. Whole place getting dug up for gardens — should have quite a crop of vegetables.

June 6, 1944, known as D-Day, Operation Overload, was the date of the invasion of Northwest Europe by Americans, British and Canadians.

Wednesday June 7, 1944

Inspection by army Colonel from Tokyo and Major Hamada. Only asked us one question "Do you like this or last camp better ?" And we said this. CC so pleased with inspection that he gave boys 3 apples each for working hard for it.

Thursday June 8, 1944

Still breaking more ground for gardens. Last few days sun bathing.

6 big boxes from Yank Red Cross of shoe repairing material.

Had shot for cholera.

Sent note to Dunlop via Big Glass Eye.

Rumour: landing in France. Paratroops, and boats and map in paper of channel and France, stressing Normandy.

Sunday June 11, 1944

Landing in 3 places in France and evidently still pushing inland. Looks like they are trying to cut off Cherbourg Peninsula so they can land there at will. Big landing at base on Paris side. Landing but up one side and looks like parachute landing on the other side. Anyway we have good foothold in France so it shouldn't be long.

Rumour: fighting between Nips and Yanks stopped and envoy has left Japan to talk!

Monday June 12, 1944

English Doc and 2 M.O. arrived from Shinagawa Hospital Camp. He's about 49, named Lane. Captured in merchant service in Indian ocean by German raider — turned over to Nips after about 4 months on a prison ship. Says Huns treated them fairly well. He was on a ship carrying refugees from Australia to India, plus landing barges, 3 million rounds of ammunition, etc. Ship was not even scuttled! Gave news — we have captured all Normandy and Burgundy in France which I don't believe. Says no fighting in Pacific for a couple of months. News about Russian Front about what we had at 2D with rumour Russians have all Rumania but last doubtful. Strikes me as credulous sort of bloke and I take everything he says with grain of salt. Says all camps excited about French news and I think we will be free by Xmas! He was captured in May 42.

One of M.O.s is Yank and came from Philippines in March of 1944 in convoy of 35 ships and none lost. Rather squashes Doc's news that only a quarter are getting through! Also, the other M.O. is English from Hong Kong and they had 5 ships and no escort and no alarms! CO looking over barracks for housing 100 POWs coming on 15/7. Doc says food here three times that of Shinagawa!

Rumour: another landing at Bordeaux. Also original landing force was 100,000 of which 80,000 got through.

After D-Day it became apparent that it was only a matter of time before the Germans would be defeated. That would mean the Allied Forces would then be free to concentrate on defeating Japan. Guessing that the outcome might not be to their favour, the Japanese CC and the guards became agitated and nervous and made an attempt to be more strict in the camp. The POWs had gotten along quite well at this second camp—in Kanose. The rumour persisted, (and no doubt the Japanese CC and guards had discussed it, too,) that all prisoners would be shot if the Allied Forces landed in Japan. Therefore, an attempt was made by the Japanese to distance themselves from the prisoners, to become more strict, and to tighten discipline.

Thursday June 14, 1944

No pay because Factory hancho on Yasume.

Doc to get 60 s per day.

Rumour: we are in Paris. Big raid in Mariannas, Carolines and Pelew areas. They claim 124 planes and 1 big ship. Sirens blew at 6 p.m. as result of this. Blackout at night.

Two more to dentist but report he is no good.

Think we are working our way to Cherbourg by landing in France by the way things are spreading. In meantime consolidating bridge head.

Friday June 16, 1944

Pay. Interpreter and Sgt. starting on rampage. Catching people for not washing hands coming out of lats and making them sign book.

Saturday June 17, 1944

Boy, the war is on. Interpreter on rampage with help from Sgt. I had to sign book for dismissing before Wakare given. Hewitt told to smack man for sitting on bed end. Did twice then refused to any more. Interpreter started on Hewitt and had him standing in rain 3 hours lecturing him and slapping him. Said we are responsible men and yet not obeying orders. Interpreter said Hewitt is not man but animal. Hewitt replied he was man and so on.

CC went to Sick Quarters and none of 3 M.O.s there so had them up and lectured them. Said they were afraid of infection. That's why they're neglecting their duties. They now must have one man on duty at all times which is okay actually because no. 48 has pneumonia. Seems our "happy" camp has come to an end!

Rumour: south end of Japan has been bombed and this may be reason for sudden change. Definitely something doing in Pacific last few days. Taiwan is supposed to have been bombed too. Still blackout and lights out at 9:00. Interpreter said officers must also go to bed at 9:00.

Sunday June 18, 1944

Interpreter still on rampage. Round this a.m. and slapping for wearing hats inside and not bowing properly. Has Hewitt standing at attention again. CC stepped in when Hewitt and I were standing attention outside administration and gave us a long lecture. Said we would be treated in Japanese army style which included slapping. We officers would be held responsible for breaking of rules and may also be slapped. Think CC sincere in doing all he can for us and taking breaking orders as slight.

Interpreter asked us do we despise Japanese? He says whole trouble between POW and Japanese is lack of sincerity on part of former. When they do wrong they lie, try to get out by excuses, quibble, etc. and that is what Japanese will not stand as they take it they are trying to be superior and put one over. Interpreter says Japanese noted the world over for treatment of POW!

We decided to give every section a talk and also got saluting and smoking rules cleared up. If the men break rules we are going to punish too as we don't want to be blamed for everything. They have certainly become slack lately under the good treatment.

Monday June 19, 1944

Bit quieter round camp today. Interpreter round but found no mistakes thank goodness. CC has my film which he took from Jap who was going to get it developed. The Interpreter had not told him he had given me permission to have this done. I asked him to say if I could still get it done and he said "Skoti Mati" [shortly].

One chap got big beating for having poem about Tojo in his possession.

Rumour: Moji bombed at 3:00 p.m. Tip that it was on this island and of course a lot of women and kids killed. Maybe that is why the change in attitude!

Tuesday June 20, 1944

F. Brancatisano, no. 48, died today of pneumonia and complications. First death for nearly a year and No. 1 in this camp. New Doc doesn't seem much use at all although hasn't proper pneumonia medicine to work with. Doc says CC wrote for sulpha drugs when he told him there was lots at POW Hospital in Tokyo. Cremated Brancatisano in afternoon having to take him and wood to next village, 8 km. away and what a long haul. Country is beautiful though, following river all the way.

Cut in food today. Cook House secretary says orders from Tokyo that if we have 15K beans, that much will be deducted from rice and same with vegetables. Bit of a blow—about 20% decrease.

Wednesday June 21, 1944

Presentation day for good workers up to 1.00 y. CO made speech saying boys working well and decided to raise pay from the 16th. 20 cents now for privates and 25 cents for NCOs. Also he gave the men about the same speech he gave us the other day re not talking about international law, admitting when we do wrong and not try to get out it, not make fun of Nipponese, etc. Also said 100 more POWs coming soon and we must educate. Rumour they coming from Sumatra etc.

Have learned Kata kana and very useful.

Friday June 23, 1944

Sgt. says another 100 POW coming on the 30th or 1st.

Lots of sun these days and quite tanned.

Rumour: another landing in France. Think we are making headway in France slowly but surely.

Saturday June 24, 1944

Preparation for more POWs underway. They are to occupy other 3 end bays huts. Middle bays for officers (4 more rooms being made). For Doc—recreation rooms and hospital.

All light duty men in camp now being paid.

Sickness runs about 6-8 per day plus 4-6 light duty. Mostly rheumatism, pleurisy, boils, diarrhoea.

Thursday June 29, 1944

103 new men came in. 1 officer, a Captain Janis Rasc and very decent chap. Speaks good Japanese. They are all English! Which surprises me. Came from Burma—Singapore to Hong Kong to Manila—Taiwan to Moji. A month trip—lost none on trip and all arrived on their feet! First impression bad but when they had bath this changed and I think they are going to be good bunch of chaps. Have about 24 beri-beri cases. They have had tough time in Siam and Burma for one and a half years and a lot of deaths from cholera, malaria, etc. Estimated 6,000 out of 16,000 Aussies have died building a railway from Bangkok to Moulmein! Enforced Tamil labour from Malay had even worse death rate. They are to have 10 days rest and they need it. Start at10 and 15s. They had first hot bath in two and a half years on arrival and washed clothes they wore so to keep lice down. Rest of kit left outside. We gave them 3 blankets each pending arrival of more from Tokyo.

They have had 1 Yank Red Cross box between 7 men and no clothes issue. They were under Korean guards—enough said! Food has been good and bad.

They had a couple of attacks on their convoy. One leaving Singapore and another 3 miles off the coast of Japan. I think they lost two destroyers and two other ships containing POWs. Worse luck. As to news—report Russians started big push. Also we have also started one in Italy. They didn't know we had landed in France. Yanks produced more aircraft than the rest of the world put together.

Friday June 30, 1944

Perry left for Tokyo Hospital to see if could get paralysed arm fixed. Interpreter went with him and is not coming back!

Men paid at new rate for 7th of June.

New men mixing well and getting settled in. This is paradise for them. It did my heart good to see them enjoy their bath. Reminds me of my first hot bath in Japan and that after 2 months and they, after two and a half years.

CC spoke to officers re observance of orders and asked if there was anything we wanted. We asked for clotheslines, eating utensils, etc. Latter came in an hour!

Saturday July 1, 1944

CC called officers to administration and said men had not obeyed orders and had talked to Nips re war. Said no necessity to talk about the war. He was doing all he could to make our life pleasant here and we persisted in disobeying his orders. Then he lined all men and us up and slapped everybody!

New men going to be good. They march in step and obey orders of NCOs with no grousing. We are supposed to set example for them but think shoe will be on other foot!

Had concert by Royal Command!

Sunday July 2, 1944

More slapping and one man struck with club behind ear by Sgt. for not getting out quick enough when called for fatigue.

Monday July 3, 1944

CC went to Tokyo. Asked him to see re calculus book. Asked for 10 of the new men to work to give some of mine a rest. He said okay but Janis asked if more could work as they wanted to. So sending out 2 details on carbide 4 hours in a.m., 4 in p.m. and 9 on rock pile. Issued work suits and tabbies in afternoon.

Thursday July 6, 1944

Rain. Not much doing. Sick 38 easy duty and 12 light duty.

Air raid alarm yesterday evidently for raid on Bonin and volcano isles. Janis bawled out for sending too many men to work.

Saturday July 8, 1944

CC back from Tokyo. Brought 2 different calculus books I asked for. That's what I call a real CC. 100 books coming for library and also medicine. He says officers in other camps only getting 390 gms per day unless they work! So many working rather than starve! Looks like they are going to force officers to work by this method. He says they are carrying things to the station.

Monday July 10, 1944

Inspection by CC.

Books to be turned in again for censor. Rain.

Cook House Hancho says he's going home shortly as "senso wari." Also says CC wants to send us back to Mitsushima as too many sick here! Says anyway we are going back in October.

Bread yesterday, today and tomorrow! Trying to get one meal per day bread. Rumour on the job is Germans are asking for peace and anyway they can't last more than 30 days.

Tuesday July 11, 1944

Another change. English and Yanks to be separated. Orders from Tokyo as fighting in other camps. All Yanks to go on No. 3 shift tomorrow and English on No. 2 with 7 on No. 1. New men all on No. 1 outside and still 4-hour shifts. They can't be put on night work for 2 months! Very busy day!

Saturday July 15, 1944

Pay day! Don't get any time off now and about 6 hours sleep! 10 cig issue free to all men! Seem to be pushing out here. Building and repairing air shelters on works and started one in camp.

Food not too bad these days. 105 gms beans per day per man, 600 gms rice and 80 kilos vegetables per day and side dishes.

Sickness of new group going down. 10 sick today and 11 light duty.

They are still only working 4-hour shifts. Asking for carpenters, welders, crane operators etc. so it looks as though we going to run these works.

Position France about the same with slight gain. Huns seem to have pushed Russians back a little on northern front.

Sunday July 16, 1944

Still no sun. Only 18K vegetables left for tomorrow!

Lot coming in sick off 2/3 shifts these days—passing out with heat.

Rumour 50 men leaving for another camp near here—same kind of work (segregating Yanks?)

Monday July 17, 1944

Rain again. Sick mounting! But not in new chaps.

Quiet round camp these days—no slapping. CC holding ping pong tournament. Lads came in early at noon. I think CC ordered this because one boy beaten by Nip Hancho on job and orders they are not to do that! Keeping that man in charge now.

Wednesday July 19, 1944

Think they are still fighting in Saipan.

Ping pong tourney finished. First prize 4 packs cigs and 3 prizes as well. Canteen kept well stocked. Always tobacco for men and cigs for officers. Lots of fish powder etc.

CC held sick parade and told lot of chaps to try to work in a.m. We have fights with Doc re sending chaps out to work we know wouldn't report sick unless sick! Not very good impression for Nips, to keep quarrelling like that. Lot of talk re "senso wari" in office.

$1/2$ rice and 1 loaf at supper.

Thursday July 20, 1944

Rain! Presentation day and Officer of the Day.

More bread came in and 2 loaves for supper.

Sgt. interviewing all men for medical history, civil occupation, special ability. Asked one of the men last thing he thought of before going to sleep—he said "tomorrow morning's breakfast." Which won him a loaf of bread.

Extensive air raid shelter construction these days. Even in camp for ourselves and also blackout for furnaces.

Friday July 21, 1944

I was talking to Sgt. and he confirmed men brought in early the other day because one man hit by civilian Hancho. Says civilians have orders not to hit POWs from Tokyo!

All men working 8 hours. New men 4 hours on furnace and 4 on rock pile. CC asked them when they came back how many felt sick and they all said they felt okay. Then he asked how many thought they could work 8 hours on carbide and all said no—said they were hungry and he laughed.

Heavy rain again all day. Water filthy and as consequence furnaces closed down for periods.

Saturday July 22, 1944

Argument with Hewitt again re Officer of the Day. He says I only did two days but he is doing today when I proved otherwise.

Heavy rain again.

CC setting no. 2 and 3 shift working parties in a.m. after sick parade. Sort of ties up my ration figures.

Sunday July 23, 1944

No rain but cloudy.

Works shut down for hours at a time because water supply silted up due to rain. Also furnaces exploding and bursting out sides and on some they can't burn out outlet.

Light duty men pounding iron and wire for pay. One of new granted men told one of our lads (so he says) Germany had quit!

Wednesday July 26, 1944

Swim at last. Party still digging at intake—CC took group of us over to swim. Unfortunately Janis got in difficulties and had tough time pulling him out but didn't seem to make much impression on an old man who laughed.

Friday July 28, 1944

Not much sleep these days. Never seem to get sleep in afternoon. Trouble with Jones again but settled his own hash.

Funny incident. Guard called me to send two men up to Guard Room (old trouble makers) and come myself. Lined them up at "kotski" then told me to stand with them. I thought we were in for it. Then he looked at us—said okay and let us go. Evidently had been having argument at Guard Room as to who was the tallest!

Thursday August 3, 1944

Two new groups went out of 10 men each—one day, one night shift on carbide crusher and pulverisers, with one rest man, all from new bunch. Bit more sick today. 35 on second shift to work and 30 on no. 3 shift and only 4 furnaces working. Rest men cut to 4 and 2.

Saturday August 5, 1944

CC bought mandolin.

Air raid still on. Our air raid shelters—5 big ones nearing completion.

Keep chopping and changing work parties and keeping me busy.

Hot.

Thursday August 10, 1944

Lot of new orders from CC—sensible ones to prevent disease.

Spud mix today.

Sirens blowing off and on all day practising.

Tuesday August 15, 1944

Pay day. Nothing else. Everything quiet on camp.

Lots of explosions from works last night. They shook our quarters. Seems as though they couldn't tap one furnace all day and at night it broke out of side and when liquid carbide hits water it goes off with terrific report. Often get these when water jackets burst. Machinery is in bad condition and someone is going to get hurt one day.

Wednesday August 16, 1944

Taking particulars of wife, kids, people, education, hobbies, religion, etc. Once more— about 50th time! CC now says don't change shifts till end of month and he insisted on 15 days when I suggested a month!

Thursday August 17, 1944

Hot. But cooler at night now. Wearing pyjamas and sheet.

Fleas very bad in billets this summer.

Sickness remains about the same but nothing serious except one pneumonia case. Medicine "skoshi" but keeps coming.

Wednesday August 23, 1944

Fall passes. How I'd like to be home. Hot.

Lots of paper work. CC talked to us re sick men. We say reason so much infection is lack of resistance but he blames it mostly on not washing. Going to provide 1 bar soap per 15 men for when they come off their shift.

Thursday August 24, 1944

Many happy returns Mu. Next birthday I will be kissing you! Roll on Happy Days.

Hot. Busy sweating plenty these days. Even the very air is thick with it.

On August 25 1944, Paris was liberated by American and French troops. At the camp, the prisoners made and operated a one-tube shortwave radio receiver for the first time on this date. They heard KFI Los Angeles broadcast the news that Paris had been retaken. This was not mentioned in the diaries for fear of retaliation if the diaries were discovered.

Saturday, August 26, 1944

CC held sick parade. Concerned re large number of men sick with boils and septic carbide burns. 500 gms of rice and 250 of beans these days as no rice at headquarters.

Paid for August—50y.

Sunday, August 27, 1944

Concert postponed because one man has pneumonia.

CC left for Mitsushima and Nowitts.

Lots of rumours. Nips insist war nearly finished

Weather still hot.

No more rice in yet so plenty of beans.

Sick has shot up lately.

Thursday, August 31, 1944

Feeling better these days. Nights cooler all of a sudden so I put blanket on.

CC returned.

Lots of sick because of bean feed. 400 gms rice and 350 beans today. Not eating all my food.

Nips running all over today—Germany fallen ?

CO says starting 4th of September men must get 4 days rest a month. Although working parties may be short.

We are to give command performance concert in village!

Saturday, September 2, 1944

Very good concert at night. Kanose follies. Originality and ingenuity unbelievable. Mossy nets for fairy dresses. Silver paper from tea packets for wands. Stage very well rigged with lighting effects. Coloured lights, etc. taken with these.

Bashings during night coincided with bombings again!

Sunday, September 3, 1944

5 years since European war started! And the last one, I hope.

Not much doing these days. Getting cooler. Shift change started on the 7th by 3 shifts working 10.40 hours each. Also men arranged into new groups and stay in those groups. Men to get $3^{1}/_{2}$–4 rest days per month regardless of how many are sick even if there are only 4 available for work, which is a good deal. This effective from 9th.

Pear issue of 9th—1 per man.

Sick gone down from 57 on the 1st (mostly due to beans, I think,) to 25 on the 9th.

Light duty now marked M.and D. and supposed to go to work on river and rest and sun bathe but so far haven't gone.

Sunday, September 10, 1944

Whitley fixing radio in my room last night under light of window in view of guard room. Nips saw W/T on my table in a.m. and "Nanda" and tore up to office, although Whitley had been fixing W/Ts for guards and office personnel for months! Later Sgt. said I shouldn't

The "Kanose Follies," one of several excellent shows produced by the POWs to boost morale. In the "orchestra pit"—three POW musicians.

repair this in my room and officer told Whitley must have all his stuff to Cook House and work there. Also hand in his phones.

River party went out today—light duty men.

Concert: "Gold Rush Review," starring "Head tucked underneath her arm"!

Women spreading manure again.

Down to last bag of rice in a.m. but a little came in later. Hardly any vegetables these days. Still 266 gms rice,133 gms barley and 350 gms beans per day per man. Things are looking tough. Rice comes in by ship to Niigata and Nips say lots of ships are going down.

Monday September 11, 1944

2 pigs killed today at local slaughter house by one of our men and brought to our Cook House to cut up. We get head and skin and village get rest. Factory men were watching cutting up and their mouths were watering. 2 pigs between 2-3-4,000 people won't go far!

About 100 letters came in but don't think I hit. Ear sore these days.

Tuesday September 12, 1944

Bone detail! When they kill a horse in the next village we go and get bones but must return same after use. This time we got some meat.

Detail picking weeds for food! It has come to that! No vegetables in and no sign of any although this the vegetable season. Still quantity of food okay.

Wednesday September 13, 1944

Colder now but still only one blanket and sheet and quite warm. Boys go to river and collect wood every day now. Don't know what we will do for heat this winter.

Thursday September 14, 1944

Letters put out—about 150 but none for me.

Things quiet for weeks now.

Rumour: new P.M. gone to Hawaii to make peace! If it's only true but we get plenty of those rumours.

Friday September 15, 1944

Cloudy but weather nice temperature.

New granted man arrived in camp.

Saturday September 16, 1944

Rumour more letters arrived. 80 more put out but still none for me although Hewitt got one from Yukon! All letters now seem to be limited to 25 words. Some lads got pictures. Latest date March 12, 44 which is pretty good.

In the final two years of the war food was very scarce, not only for the prisoners, but for the civilians too.

Monday September 18, 1944

Cooler. Went to bone headquarters in village 3 miles away for horse bones. Lovely country. People come to get their meat. 370 gms per family of 6 people. 185 gms per family of 5 and God knows how often they get it.

Sickness quite low now.

Friday September 22, 1944

Nips say going to put stoves in no. 1, no. 5, hospital and entertainment room and one for officers. Also nobbies from works will be run in on rails and set in halls so it shouldn't be too bad. Still no vegetables.

Inspection now to be on the 29th.

Saturday September 23, 1944

Grand concert at night "Whoopee" by Kanose Follies. Direction by Frank Smith is superb. The boys put in a lot of time practising and this concert was really appreciated. Lighting effects ingenious with spotlight of two magnifying glasses and slides.

Sgt. came back from Tokyo bringing about 10 old books.

About 150 letters came in but mostly Yanks.

Sunday September 24, 1944

Straight rice these days as no barley. Very little vegetables and rice polished so not so good.

CC says we must not accept any presents from Nips, even cigs!

Wednesday September 27, 1944

Nothing doing. Things slowing up in other part of world?

One of the new men given five days in Guard Room for pushing Nip.

Friday September 29, 1944

Inspection by clothing officer from Tokyo claimed my ration sheets wrong as he couldn't see how there could be more than 612 meals a day. Eventually got it across to Cook House Hancho. Things are tough. No rice available for a.m. so they gave us 3 bags of flour, (barley) and cooks had to stay up all night cooking bread. Things must be tough. Living from hand to mouth. What do we eat at noon? 6 bags of rice came in 2 days ago for whole district.

Sunday October 8, 1944

Chinook and quite warm.

F/Sgt. Perry came back from Tokyo Hospital but not cured.

Pear issue four per man.

Going up on wood detail but it rained.

Not much news from Perry who says all POW going to be moved to isle near Moji. Also cleaning out Shinagawa Hospital. They get bread three times a day. He says this camp is only one getting rice. Others get straight millet mostly now so we are doing not too bad. Lads from Mitsushima have gone to copper mine. Lads working docks say lot of ships coming in damaged.

Monday October 9, 1944

Out on wood detail up in the mountains. Tough work but grand outing. If I only had had sandwiches and beer instead of rice I could have imagined I was home on a picnic. It was good to get out and the country is glorious. We brought back chestnuts officially and persimmons, unofficially.

Cigs unprocurable these days.

All weighed again. 78.3 K—Rice 1.3K

Tuesday October 10, 1944

Very stiff after mountain climbing but went to river to dig out water supply intake. Wonder if digging out ceremony occurs after each heavy rain instead of fixing pipe?

CC talked to us at night. Brought up war himself and asked how long we thought it would last. He says Japan will fight to the last man if the Emperor orders and if English and Yanks will not give decent peace terms. Says we do not understand Nippon ideal of fighting to the last. Kids and women will be killed and men will fight or commit Hara Kari. Bright outlook for us! But if Emperor says no fight—okay. Also expecting letter paper tomorrow! And there is Red Cross in Tokyo but being sorted! We asked him if we could buy a pig for Xmas and he says we can have our own. ???

Friday October 13, 1944

Nips started killing cats and eating them—we will be next!

We can send 6 radiograms—3 Yank and 3 English—150–200 words. Obviously peace epistles because CC advises us to complain re existing governments. Ask for peaceful settlement—say we are tired of war. Say Nips will fight to last if forced. Say treated in Geneva Conference style, etc. otherwise may not get through. Doc, self, Janis, Hewitt, Dunn and F. Wilson wrote.

Had hair clipped as I have dandruff.

Seems things lagging all over re war.

Sunday October 15, 1944

Man put in Guard Room for one day for stealing vegetables out of containers near furnaces which has been going on for some time. However CC let him out after a day and allowed eats and blankets.

Tuesday October 17, 1944

Sgt. says big sea battle indicating near Mindanao in which we lost 11 aircraft carriers and 22 battleships and cruisers and still going on.

Wednesday October 18, 1944

Nips still talking big sea victory yet all seem preoccupied. Sgt. talking to Janis and seemed concerned that some of POWs would try and get him after war. He knows then who is going to win!

Saturday October 21, 1944

Nips not talking much about big naval battle now!

CC sick.

One Arm says we will be home soon now.

Very good concert—Cinderella etc. with picture slides. Some cabbage came in.

Tuesday October 24, 1944

Lots of men have worms now—big ones like earth worms but not too harmful. Treatment quite effective. Sickness not too bad these days.

Yeast now every day made with flour and Wakamoto!

Wednesday October 25, 1944

A lot of over-ripe persimmons came in, and sorted to put out in a.m. Beans will run out tomorrow and C.H. Hancho says we only get 600 gms cereal until more in. This blow but I managed to bump it up to 700 gms per day.

Out lumber-jacking and fishing. Lots of fish but no bites! Enjoyed it.

Above: Muriel Chater, Les's wife, in Singapore, 1941, after the evacuation from Hong Kong. Muriel and their son Mike escaped to safety, but did not hear news of Les until September 23 1943—18 months after his capture. Chater asked Muriel to send him this photo in the radiogram below.

Right: Records of radiograms, telegrams and postcards sent to Muriel Chater, written according to Japaneses requirements, praising life in Japan and pressing for an end to the war.

Text of radiogram to Mu handed in on October 10, 1944:

Darling Muriel and Michael,

The Nipponese authorities have kindly permitted me to send this message. Darling I love you more each day & I hope to be able to prove it to you in the near future. I am in perfect health so do not worry. We have reading, musical, exercising & swimming facilities so the time passes quickly. I have received 3 letters from you & a cable from home. We have had Red + food & clothing issues. Send pictures of yourself taken on yacht. I find the Nipponese amiable and fair and they bear no resentment against P.O.W. My present camp is a tribute to the ceaseless efforts of the C.O. and staff to make our life pleasant & healthy. Our treatment here is on a par with that of Nipponese civilians. We all realize how futile war is & hope for an early peaceful settlement. There is plenty of room for everyone in this world with a reasonable distribution. We all long to be home with those we love so peace propaganda is the order of the day. Tell everybody I am O.K. All my love, Les.

On a side notation F/L Chater records that the following postcard was handed in on January 14, 1945 and still had not been sent on April 7, 1945:

Dearest — Got 10 more letters from you, sisters & folks. Thrilled to get snap Mike. Showing him off to gang here. Sisters' kids look grand. Had jolly Xmas. Lots Red+ food, carols & pantomime. Health and Spirits better than ever. Darlin you'll know what real happiness is soon. All my love, Les.

This postcard was handed in on April 12, 1945 and still not sent on August 7, 1945:

Darlin. Getting letters often from everybody. Good to know all well. Keeping wonderfully fit & staying away from other women. Will soon be putting on summer tan. Hello Mike. You must be a good swimmer now. Send more snaps. Darlin I'm going to keep you busy when I get back. Can you take it? Heaps love, kisses, Les.

Thursday, October 26, 1944

One fire allowed in each billet consisting of carbon from elements which difficult to light but when well going throw off good heat and lasts a long time. 500 more loaves in.

Persimmon Hash ran 1.8 K per man.

Saturday, October 28, 1944

Lumber-jacking. Out of beans still.

Hewitt up in front of CC etc. and asked opinion about war. Said Nips started it, etc. I was to go in after but they must have had enough. Sgt. says we lost 150 warships and 700 planes in a big sea battle. They lost one battleship and a couple of other ships and 120 planes! Boy how they feed news to these people. Actual rumour is they lost 28 Front Line ships including 3 aircraft carriers, 10 battleships and 15 cruisers.

1 towel, 1 soap, 1 jock strap and toilet paper issued to each man.

Wednesday, November 1, 1944

Air alarm in afternoon and everybody had to go into shelters. Found out after southern part of this island had been raided! I was cutting wood and had to come back to camp.

Bread for supper.

Sunday, November 5, 1944

Stopped hour work details. Asked CC and he said okay. Evidently company is supposed to bring in wood etc. at their expense anyway and since boys work eight hours and then had to do one–two hours after CC says company will have to find other method of bringing in wood.

Not many bean days so rice 700 gms per man per day but no barley either. However beri-beri is raising its ugly head again so we have asked for beans.

Monday, November 6, 1944

10 bags flour handed to us and rice not cut. Janis talked to quartermaster re low rations and I think it had some effect. Curry, ginger, tea and powdered apple came in.

Two Yanks having fight over 3.00 y debt when CC caught them. Paid one their 3.00 and said if they want money don't fight but borrow it from him!!

Some difference between army personnel and factory representatives these days and talk is that latter, including guards, moving out—I hope not!

Carbon fired in every billet and very good. Last about 21 hours! No smoke.

Friday, November 10, 1944

Nips seemed brassed off during Presentation day and Sgt. slapped Compton's gang for coming out in overcoats. Tea presented to those with best working records for last 3 months.

Saturday, November 11, 1944

Armistice day but not for this war. Inspection by military police. Fifteen minutes from time into gate till out but should have seen the boys rush.

Monday, November 13, 1944

Overcoats (English issue probably—captured in Singapore) and tunics issued to new men. Just in time too.

Started fixing billets. Put 3 ply around top of billets and completely walled in hospital.

Tuesday, November 14, 1944

Rumour more POW coming—150 English! Supposed to be coming from nearby camp. May be true because inspecting Cook House and sleeping quarters.

Wednesday November 15, 1944

Man slapped and stood outside all day because he didn't admit he was wrong and tried to hedge. CC explained this is a bad thing in Nippon and they should always admit when wrong and no excuses. Our chaps have been warned repeatedly re this but still do. The man passed out twice and first time Sgt. just threw water on him and made him stand again. CC sent meal in to him after.

CC says all men on holiday Xmas day.

Friday November 17, 1944

Nobbies warm place up beautifully. Also good carbon fires. Change nobbies twice a day—8:00 a.m. and 3:00 p.m.

Handed suggestion for Xmas menu to CC with things required. Asked for 2 pigs! He will do his best for us, I know. Sgt. says we may have to eat dog in lieu of pig and asked if we have any dog catchers!

First frost.

Saturday November 19, 1944

A.R.P. drill. All lads came in from work! Inspection postponed.

Gravy every second day.

Soft soap issue to clean things for inspection. Cook House Hancho now has our menu with Nip translation and I went over with him. Looks good. I asked if we could get eggs and he said maybe in black market. Said could get other things also and we said officers would put up money.

Rumour last night and also today that Germany packed it in on the 15th. Don't put much stock in it but Nips certainly eating up papers and wireless these days. Gosh, if only true.

Sunday, November 20 to Saturday, December 3, 1944

Long time no diary entries—lots of work at the Cook House and nobby changing etc. so here goes.

On 21st—big day—got letters. 156 came in on the 20th and I got 10—on 21st. At last! What a feeling! Three photographs—one of Mike, one of Pat and one of Gwenneth. Four letters from Irene. Two from Mu. Two from Mother and two from Nora. Everyone okay. They say they can write once a month but can't send parcels.

Preparing for inspection up to 26th but not a lot of running round. More or less left to us to get camp into shape so lads got stuck into it. Inspection by Colonel. He growled a lot but gave good inspection. Spotted Hewitt's brew and I told him yeast! Didn't go for things set out for him but probed into other stuff. One of officers said maybe 2 Red Cross parcels per man coming soon. In whole inspection success.

Got pay on 27th and CO said could draw full amount for Xmas.

3 Red Cross American food boxes per man arrived and handed to us intact. We can dish out one now (27th) and one at Xmas and one at New Year. Later CO said to hold last one till colder weather.

Sickness increasing especially among new men. Five pneumonia cases. Three men going to Shinagawa with CC supposedly on 11th.

What excitement with parcels and usual trading and gambling. Cheese, sugar, 4 packs cigs, meat 3, and chocolate 3, butter 2, etc.

Lots of "quaning" going on now. Grand for new lads.

CC held all milk for sick patients.

Compton's gang put on half ration for three days on 29th for breaking up sign for fire wood but CC relaxed after a day.

On 30th CC had talk with officers re pneumonia and asked us to make a report giving reasons for increased pneumonia and recommendations for prevention.

Lots of daikons, onions, cabbages, etc. came in and busy time getting tops cut off and storing etc. A lot of flour came in and making bread without baking powder or I should say steamed dough balls. First time failure but last twice not too bad. Get 300 gms flour per man and make gravy as well. Cook Hancho now charging us with 10 bags of flour he presented"—to ration 700 gms per man till 20th of next month.

First snow on December 3rd and wet. Lads all got feet wet going and coming from work. Have asked for Red Cross boots to be issued but new lads have none !

CC going to Tokyo soon. Sgt. says more men coming here in New Year and lots of officers! No. 8 furnace being built to produce aluminum! CC says all but two furnaces closing down soon.

Air raid alarm on 29th night and rumour 5 planes over Tokyo.

Sunday December 4, to Monday December 18, 1944

Fixing line for nobbies. Tried baking bread under nobbies and okay. Another lazy or busy spell. It is now the 18th. Snow and rain nearly every day and now about 2 ft. of snow. Not very cold yet however. I sleep in our mess hall now and try to keep fire on all night.

All boots issued to owners on 17th after much pleading but most of the new lads have none and they are giving them old tabbies.

CC says no rest day on 16th, not giving reason. Next day he says three rest days a month. Sickness quite a lot now and working details low. This may be reason.

Inspection by Pay Corps on 14th but just walked through billet.

Still lots of trading for Red Cross food mostly on Christmas parcel. I have lots to come. Went to bone h.q. on the 13th and 15th and last time kept men in from work to help. They say that the factory is supposed to bring this in and therefore we shouldn't use rest days but pay men for it. Also at logger heads with fact re bringing wood in. Won't let our lads do and hence wood situation bad and living day to day.

Weight 79.5 on 17th.

Lots of spuds and carrots came in.

Talked with CC on 16th re Xmas dinner and going to get nearly all we asked for! Pigs, bread, oil, etc. all okay but no baking powder. However CC certainly doing his best to get stuff. Sgt. left on the 17th till after Xmas. Lots of air raids these days. As high as three a day. Give em ell!" Air raid shelters have fallen in again!

Billets quite comfortable. Have installed stove in each billet but haven't used them yet!

Spirits of men okay.

Red Cross medicines came in including sulpha drugs.

Christmas 1944 was destined to be the prisoners' last Christmas in captivity. The CC, who alternated between being very strict and quite pleasant, chose this time to be strict again.

Tuesday December 19, 1944

CC called officers up and said what he had done for us in past. Then he said we "doubt" him! Think he meant we don't trust him. Said from now on we are going to rule by Tokyo Book Orders. No Yasume on Xmas day! No rest days! Sick men and officers to go on 390 gms a day (others getting 705!) He wouldn't let us get a word in. Hewitt thinks it is because he watched all Red Cross medicines being unpacked. Later One Arm said CC put out about

American POWs at Christmas dinner, Kanose, 1944.

lack of discipline. Also says we couldn't have any more carbon for fires in billets! As not supposed to have fires.

Wednesday December 20, 1944

Wasn't sure if he meant half rations so made out sheet as usual but he was up in a.m. and weighed all rice cutting sick and officers to less than half. He also weighed at noon but got tired of it and I did it at night. However he sent man around to check. Cutting rice issue down also to make up saving of 11 K day. Boy it's tough on that ration!

Thursday December 21, 1944

CC went to Niigata to get Christmas decorations but they are pretty slim.

No developments on half ration.

CC says we will be allowed one card or one letter a month now and one telegram from group per month. First will be card.

Saturday December 23, 1944

CC cut Xmas menu to ribbons. Will be little better than ordinary day now. Still in bad mood. Don't think lads getting holiday! Killed one pig and would run 150 gms per man and Cook House Hancho thinking about killing goat as well but CC stepped in and says only 100 gms per man.

Sgt. Rose took Compton's place.

Sunday December 24, 1944

Got three small Christmas trees. CC's sternness not dampening boys spirits much except half ration men. They are making Christmas decorations. CC called us to office. Asked him if men could go on full rations Xmas Day and he eventually said all men on full rations from now on so we gain by small starvation because even sick now on full rations.

Up all night working on Xmas menu. In middle of the night word came no headquarter bread coming so we had to bake it. No lights out and most men up all night. No holiday tomorrow. Everyone feeling good.

Monday December 25, 1944

Menu—Rice, fried beans and pig fat. Thick bone soup. Noon—bread, potato, carrot, oil mix. Night, bread, pork 21K, spud, onion mix. Thick onion gravy. 2 oranges, 1 pear, 15 bis-

Top: Christmas Day, 1944. British POWs at Christmas dinner at Kanose camp.

Bottom: Christmas Day, 1944, at Kanose camp. Left to right: Friendly guard, Captain Janis (British Army), Les Chater (RAF), Japanese Camp Commander Lieutenant Azuma, Captain Walter Hewitt (US Army), camp doctor (British merchant marines), another friendly guard.

cuits, 1 turnover. Latter made by Chinless who spent 9 hours doing and very good. Tables laid out in billets and pictures taken. Also pictures of CC and us officers, of pantomime troupe and stage. CC very pleased and had coffee and cake with us at night. Carol singing, pantomime "Babes in Wood" and "Alladin" and both good. Stage very good. Xmas draw success, 1000 tickets at 10s each. In all everyone had a good day. Parcels were issued on the 24th. A good Xmas — I got no sleep for 43 hours but things ran very smoothly.

25 men from village and factory watched play.

Tuesday December 26, 1944

Pay. Drew 50 y. Lots of trading.

Thursday January 18, 1945

Another long stretch to entries. Now January 18, 1945. <u>Postcards written and handed in on 14th</u>. Wrote to Mu.

Ran out of carbon in billets on 14th and they say no more carbon fires. Got 6 nobbies on 17th which helps. We have been allowed carbon for our fire to date, the CC sanctioning inspection by Tokyo Major on the 17th and carbon fires allowed that day. Still not as cold in actual temperature as Mitsushima in my opinion. Snow nearly every day. Must have 6-7ft. on level now. Makes it tough changing nobbie. Changed track to run inside godowns for long stretch which helps.

12 wood detail for snow clearing and 6 oxygen party kept in from factory work to work.

In charge since 14th.

<u>Weight 18th January 77.75</u>.

Christmas dinner, 1944, at Kanose; Les Chater (wearing the tie) with his "boys," mostly British, RAF troops.

Yanks sent 13 cablegrams on 16th.

Two furnaces only, running since three weeks.

Getting 705 gms per man daily for the last three weeks. Lot of spuds and sweet spuds. Usually two meals of rice and one of spuds at 600 gms. Thirty sacks rice in store.

Hair clipped on 13th.

30 letters received on 10th—mostly Yanks.

Nips leaving us alone. Sgt. not bothering with us at all and says not having anything to do with us. Quite decent to us and drunk nearly every night.

Rumour: landing in Luzon on 14th. One army, 1500 tanks.

Friday January 19, 1945 to Sunday January 28, 1945

Old Doc left on 25th with Overend (136) for Shinagawa. New Doc (Yank) Robinson arrived 28th. Young and I think okay. Says Tokyo being bombed regularly by up to 80 planes. Not so much Tokyo as Yokohama, Osaka, etc. All military targets. Says order went out recently that treatment of POWs must improve (from Nip Headquarters). Good omen I think. Food quantity same as other camps but more barley. Nips hardly shooting down any B-29s. Nip shipping practically nil. 50% POWs captured in Philippines dead. Bombing H___ out of Formosa and Hong Kong. Doing well in Luzon. Russians have started new drive, nothing doing on western front.

Pay on 25th—drew 45.50 for January.

On 26th Sgt. found two men cooking raw rice on nobbies. Put in Guard Room and on 28th Nips descended on us and there was a surprise search. They found things men had made in factory and lots of raw rice. Says white race pigs and dogs and he treats us well then we steal. All promised not to steal any more and let off!!

Only 1 and 2 furnaces running now and carbide crews cut to twelve men on Sgt.'s orders who seems to delight in cutting down number of men who work in factory. Others using in camp for wood hauling, snow clearing etc. Snow now two metres deep but weather not as cold as Mitsushima. CO says now coldest period.

Granted men have not left yet and CC says not going to send some because we mentioned war!

Monday January 29, 1945

Medical Orderly in our billet and today talking mostly with new Doc re sick. Ordered complete clean up of all billets and good thing. Then asked lads what they thought of it.

Sunday February 4, 1945

Rumour: we have two-thirds Sumatra and all of Timor. Also fighting in Thailand!!
Rumour: 7,000 to 70,000 POWs in Philippines.

Ration yesterday very small at noon so saw Ohari (head Hancho). Says he will speak to Cook House Hancho and have ration increased.

Saturday February 17 to Wednesday February 28, 1945

Wt. 79.3 on 27th. Average weight in camp 61.9, an increase of 1.9 since June. Sickness down.

Eight packets Yank Red Cross clothing came in including three of overcoats. Rest enough for twenty-five men. There are going to be arguments re distribution between old and new POW.

Card from Mu's folks and letter from Nora on the 22nd. Over 100 letters in all. Third Red Cross parcel not issued yet.

Three men in Guard Room for 10 days for stealing from Cook House. Days now warming up but still have carbon fire.

Read *Henry Esmond* by Thackeray.

Yanks getting telegrams to send home regularly.

Surprise search again but only little rice and soap found on Jones.

Rumours landing Volcanoes 60K from Berlin. Nips now don't talk Ten Years war but more skoshi. All Nips on job sick of war and will be as glad as we are when it's over.

On February 19, 1945 the Fifth Fleet, under direction of Admiral Spruance landed on Iwo Jima. On February 23, after three days of heavy fighting, and suffering great losses, Marines hoisted the Stars and Stripes and Joe Rosenthal of Associated Press took one of the war's most famous pictures. Victory at Iwo Jima took twenty-six days and 20,965 American casualties, including 6,821 dead.

Monday March 5, 1945

Officers called up to administration and Sgt. says we are eating four meals a day. Tried to explain we saved some of our breakfast and cooked it up at 10—11 p.m. But he wouldn't listen and socked Hewitt and Janis but not me??? Says we are liars and stole other POWs chow. Fuming but couldn't do anything. Said no more carbon for officers now and must go to bed at 9:00 unless we have work to do. From now on he says he will slap officers even though it is shameful.

Tuesday March 6, 1945

Janis punched again when Nip toban lied! They all seem brassed off with something. No cigs which we were promised two days ago.

Colder today and windy.

Wednesday March 7, 1945

Weight 77.1. Drop of 2 K and I'm supposed to be eating 4 meals per day.

Nip officer went away. Incidentally CC came in during beating up on 5th and asked what it was about but didn't do anything.

Friday March 9, 1945

Serious accident at works. Bottom fell out of nobby and three RAF men badly burned. Jack Foster (89), Jack Buchan (68) and Jack Crowdell (70). Doc doesn't give them much of a chance. Lads started all work on furnaces but they were doing job they always do. Rogers (62) slightly burned. Three moved to Nip hospital. Nurses very good but Nip Doc poor. The Nips were laughing about it. Sgt. had just left the place.

Saturday March 10, 1945

Boys seemed rational enough but looked bad. No 189 (Dick Bush) got hand caught in crusher and lost first joint of two fingers, right hand, and second finger broken. No guards on machinery here and nobbies in terrible condition. Lucky we haven't had more accidents really.

Sunday March 11, 1945

Jack Foster (89) and Jack Buchan (68) died of burns. 2 grand lads of old English who have been with me since Makasura.

Lots of news out of newspaper.

Monday March 12, 1945

Crowdell better today and supposed to be worst of three. Lets hope he gets better.

Rumour: B29 over today!

Rumour: 150 more POWs coming here. They will stoke and our boys do soldering on furnaces.

Tuesday March 13, 1945

John Foster and John Buchan buried or cremated in next village. Nips put on quite a show at service and factory big shots were there.

Rations lower with vegetables cut.

Doc's skin graft case coming on wonderfully.

In mid March of 1945 the most destructive single bombing mission ever recorded took place. Using 334 B-29s, General Curtis LeMay directed the use of fire bombs on Tokyo which did more damage than even the atomic bombs which landed on Hiroshima and Nagasaki.

Friday March 16, 1945

Parcels issued out of clear sky and great rejoicing as rations skoshi these days with spud "Dos". Fifteen men's parcels held back—9 Yank, 1 of the old POW and 5 of the new because of thefts and caught with incriminating goods the last couple of months. I lost a heck of a lot on these people on future trade. Sgt. says some of them, if good workers, may get some later.

Sunday March 18, 1945

Jones (22) called up to office by Sgt. and given his parcel. He is one of worst if not the worst character in the camp and just finished fifteen days in the Guard House for stealing from Cook House including one sack of rice. None of the others got theirs although one man caught with only three grains of rice in bottom of tin!! And he traded for that! Something funny somewhere. Sgt. told Jones if CC asked him if he got parcel to say no!!

Tuesday March 20, 1945

CC says another furnace starting in a few days and he wants twelve more men per shift. Also water to be shut off for one day on 22nd. Sgt. says when busy time starts and five furnaces are running, men may have to work 12-hour shifts!!

Other parcels still not put out.

Wednesday March 21, 1945

Cook House Hancho says 150 more men coming on the 25th of next month!! Doesn't know what nationality!

Things quiet. Making puddings etc.

Wednesday March 28, 1945

Crowdell No. 70 died this a.m. at 9. He has put up a wonderful fight and it's too bad he has to go but maybe it's just as well as I don't think he would have been much use in after life. A big hand to Doc and M.O.s for their efforts!

Cigs issued to everyone. Four packs to carbide workers, two to others.

Thursday March 29, 1945

Crowdell buried.

Cook House Hancho said no "horrid Maisie" tomorrow as out of rice. I appealed to Sgt. who says use the little rice that is in store and he went on to rave about Cook House Hancho and factory. No. 1, as always, being drunk now. Using factory money to buy liquor etc. Says if Cook House Hancho says anything tell him to see me! Also if no rice comes in no work!

Friday March 30, 1945

Rice came in when factory told that if there is nothing to eat, there will be no work, which would have almost meant closing down factory!! Sgt. went to main office factory and gave them H___. No rice in Kobe! Things must be getting tough.

Caught Jones and Martindale stealing from Cook House again! They haven't been long out of Guard Room.

Weather good now but fleas waking up.

Saturday March 31, 1945

CC seemed to let #22 and 18 off when we reported it but may be more developments.

Have diarrhoea rather badly and going on luga [medication] tomorrow.

Sgt. told me he was finished! When I asked him if he was going away he said no but in a few days he was going to commit Hari Kari!!

Flash: Rumour from job—Peace talks between Germany, Japan, Roosevelt and Churchill. Former have asked for Peace terms but latter said unconditional surrender. Well that's all they offered us! Certainly something afoot. CC is supposed to have assembled Nips at factory at 3 a.m. and talked to them. They gave 3 cheers ??? CC also brought his wireless today and has been listening in.

On April 1, 1945 the Americans landed on the island of Okinawa, an island strategically located only 350 miles from Japan. Fierce fighting began on April 6 and 7 by a Japanese force of 700 aircraft. Six American ships were downed, attacked by 135 Kamikaze pilots. The *Yamato*, one of the largest of Japanese battleships also went out to meet the enemy, with fuel limited to only enough for a one-way trip. It was sunk in less than two hours along with its convoy of four destroyers and a light cruiser. In the ensuing battles to take over the island that followed, the death toll mounted to 110,071 Japanese, 12,230 Americans. On June 22, at their headquarters, Japanese Commander of Okinawa, Lieutenant General Mitsuru Ushijima along with his comrade-in-arms Lieutenant General Cho knelt in formal dress uniform and committed suicide by cutting out their own stomachs. American Lieutenant General Simon Buckner, Commander of the American forces, was killed on Okinawa as well.

Sunday, April 1, 1945

Stationery issued for letters but only one sheet. Postcards we wrote quite a long time ago have not yet gone!!

Rumour: we landed on isle half way between Formosa and Japan!

Monday, April 2, 1945

About 4th group of men start twelve hours on and twelve off. Ration cut today—550 rice and no beans. Saw CC about it as think he does not know and he called Cook House Hancho over later. Also saw Sgt. and he says if cut for tomorrow only send half men to work! Says factory representative and Cook House Hancho always drunk now and thinks they are trading rice off for drink as they don't get much money. He was peeved about it. I brought up question of Red Cross parcels which were held back for certain men and said some are good workers. He asked for their numbers and I gave him five. Then he sent for them and issued the parcels!!

Have swollen legs and still diarrhoea.

Tuesday, April 3, 1945

Last bundle of letters issued. I got postcard from Mu's folks.

Rations back to normal.

Wednesday, April 4, 1945

Sgt. called me up and said if Cook House Hancho and factory representative slap us in billets again to slap back and tie up and bring to him!! He will tie them to the tree outside!! He said that is your chance to slap Japanese.

Rumour: landing in this isle of April 2, O.K.

Thursday, April 5, 1945

Sgt. leaving in 2-3 days!! He says another Sgt. will take his place.

Thirty Red Cross books, some food and parcels coming.

Rumour: yesterday Russia had declared war on Turkey! I hope that's not true!!

Saturday, April 7, 1945

Wt. 76.3 Drop 2 and a half K. Diarrhoea still bad as ever and still on luga.

Rumour: Nips bombed Vladivostok!! Because Russians let Allied ship through and not Nip. Inspection by CC. Sgt. left. Also medical secretary left on one day's notice. They are calling plenty up now.

Monday, April 9, 1945

Spy says if Cook House and factory representative slap POW slap back! CC has got traps and coronet!!

Wednesday, April 11, 1945

Sgt. came. Looks okay and quiet.

150 more letters arrived and CC took home to censor! <u>Handed in letter to Mu.</u>

Saw CC re 700 gms rice per day we are now getting instead of 705 and he said he would look into it. Found rice stolen from Cook House on 10th and CC not very pleased.

Shift change tomorrow.

Killed pig in Cook House and they say we get 40 K on anniversary day.

On April 12, 1945, American President Franklin Delano Roosevelt died of a cerebral haemorrhage.

Friday April 13, 1945

Sirens went at 10:30 and about 3 minutes later a B-29 flew directly overhead going east. What a sight. Well over 30,000 ft. and 4 trails smoke extending behind it. It looked just like a comet. Talk about a sight for sore eyes!! No Nip planes anywhere near and no anti-aircraft. They seem to fly over this country at will now.

Rumour: fighting in Rangoon!! Strong rumour passed out by all Nips that Roosevelt has died!

Cleaned out my summer quarters!

Rumour: all new cabinet are civvies. This, if true, is best news yet.

Saturday April 14, 1945

Rumour Roosevelt dead from all Nips.

Vaccinated for smallpox 4 days ago. Weather grand during day.

Sunday April 15, 1945

20K pork in gravy night. Concert and very good.

Doc examined my stool and says I have a bug and may be amoebic dysentery!! No dysentery bugs visible yet. Boy, no wonder I feel rotten these days. Back on luga tomorrow.

Roosevelt definitely dead according to Nip rags. Rumour: 150 men coming to Tokyo area and seems true because they are speeding up on construction of new administration. They say they are evacuating all POW from Tokyo areas.

Have tricomonos bug.

Tuesday April 17, 1945

Speeding work up on new administration.

Put in fire tubs. Digging new zig-zag shelter trenches.

Thursday April 19, 1945 to Saturday April 21, 1945

Rumour: we are in the streets of Berlin! and I think this is correct. Have come long distance in the last 2 weeks. Looks like complete fold up of Huns.

Diarrhoea no better.

Sunday April 22, 1945

CC went to Tokyo to see about new POWs??

Another B-29 flew over about 20 miles away!! Panic when siren sounded.

Last day on attabrine and still squitting.

Adolf Hitler and Eva Braun committed suicide in Hitler's underground bunker in Berlin some time after their marriage on April 29, 1945.

Sunday April 29, 1945

Chinless says 100 more men coming in 2 days.

Officers' working party?? C C asked by Janis if we supervise and he said no. We work same as men and also all parade at 3:15. I can tell you we all felt low expecting speech to be something like "You have bombed our country and therefore we will not adhere to international law" which, in other words, we weren't worth anything. However he opened up by saying we may be bombed any day and what would we do? Well, the only sensible thing I heard was it would be up to the CC. He went on to say that Nips were very quick tempered and may attack us and warned us that the worst thing we could do would be to taunt Nips or laugh at them. He said, "If Japan should be defeated, what would you do?" We were astounded but couldn't see what he was driving at until later. It transpired that what he inferred was that if at that time we taunted the Nips, etc., we may be wiped out.

Later he called officers in and explained more fully. He said he was worried what might happen to us in event of bombing. He said he would protect us as best he could but attitude we adopted from now on would have biggest effect on Nips. That was main reason officers were going to work. The other was that if we didn't he would have to put us on 390 gms which he had ignored to date. We said if bombed we would help put out fires and do rescue work if Nips would allow it. If we were attacked at work, we would defend ourselves and try to come to billets. We also said the action of some of the Nips on the job created bad feeling.

The main point was, however, that he was warning us to get men to avoid incidents by working as told, etc. as thereby our chances of surviving were improved. All this I think was the result of the Tokyo conference. He said he had bought 3,000 y medicine for us and was going to start two more gardens outside camp keeping men in to work on them as vegetables would be short and perhaps if heavy bombing we would be without food. We thanked him.

We talked to boys at night telling them our position and warning them against incidents, pointing out that if they occurred the chances of any of us returning were slim. Janis and Hewitt went to work but Hanchos wouldn't let them do much and were very good to them.

Wednesday May 2, 1945

Another birthday. 35! What an old man. However last as POW and what a birthday present. Strong rumour which I think is true. Germans have surrendered. Also Nips are holding a big conference in Tokyo re peace.

Had cake for birthday!!

Janis and Hewitt going out with shift but not working. Wander round and talk with No. 1 Boss most of the time. Lads won't let them work and treating them like officers, saluting, etc. Nips are impressed.

Thursday May 3, 1945

Camp searched and razors, knives and all tools, in fact anything which could be used as weapon collected. We can get razors during day for shaving.

Red Cross parcels came in!! 103 but only 100 given to us—not to be issued yet. Also 2 comfort boxes, haversacks, British tennis shoes, tabbies, 24 pairs Yank service shoes, putties, and lots of clothes bundles. Also 2 volleyballs, cards, and a couple of books, dominoes. Why haversacks!!

General attitude of Nips queer. Very cheerful and friendly, not attitude of people going to fight the world. Certainly indications are they can see the end is very near and they are glad!!

Rumour: Hitler dead, also Mussolini.

Saturday May 5, 1945

Hitler dead okay and Germans surrendered on first. Well, we'll know soon what our fate will be. Days will drag from now on.

General inspected but cursory. Spoke perfect English and shook hands with Sgt. Roy.

Germany surrendered formally on May 7, 1945 in Rheims, France.

Monday May 7, 1945

Parcels—100 issued. Dragged 1 package cigs from each parcel to give some to men who didn't get any last time. While issuing Hewitt talked to Kaniyama about administration stealing 9 parcels etc. Soon as CC out of camp Hewitt was hauled up to administration and beat up. Sgt. says at other camps administration get good chunk of parcels that come in and don't steal. Said officers would now be held responsible for everything in camp and dealt with if things go wrong. Also he said to bring those parcels not yet issued to administration and put in CC's office.

Came back and held council of war and since all parcels had been issued decided it would be wise if we gave our 2 parcels in to keep peace. Went to Sgt. and told him all handed out but willing to give in our 2. We said the reason we had not given any was CC would not take the gift we offered the first time without a lot of persuasion. Also he had ordered us not to give Red Cross stuff to Nips. Sgt. says that only because of his fair nature and we should still make offer. He said it wouldn't be fair to take just from officers and every man should contribute. We decided to trade 24 milk and get back equivalent of 4 parcels to hand to CC which was done. About the third time Hewitt got us into trouble by indiscretions!! Certainly looked ugly for officers for awhile.

On May 8, 1945 the war in Europe was declared officially over.

Wednesday May 9, 1945

Made gift to CC of Red Cross food. He was loathe to take saying we don't get much as it is. Also intimated we had forced men to donate. We assured him all men had gladly contributed and we took only a little from each. Finally he took the food. He said he had asked school children to gather fresh grasses for us daily as vegetables would be short for while.

Thursday May 10, 1945

All men to hand in boots tomorrow! Also all men except carbon shifts to go on carbide. 37 men on shift and we will run furnaces, there being only 1 Nip per furnace.

Started new treatment for diarrhoea.

Friday May 11, 1945

Started new carbide shifts. Cold these days! Rumours scarce. Seems like we are left out here till the West is cleared up.

Rumour 100 new men coming in seven days persists. Getting on with administration.

Saturday May 12, 1945

Warning at 12:15 and then 3 lots of planes came over. All lights out and pretty good blackout. Bit of panic on job. Misty here and anyway I'm convinced they're not after this place. Hewitt is on easy duty because slapping by Kaniyama gave him ruptured ear drum.

Tuesday May 15, 1945

New civilian Interpreter came. One room in administration being used by stenos from factory. No POW allowed in administration.

Wednesday May 16, 1945

Cable from Mu. Living on farm and going home soon. Both okay. Hope I follow them soon.

Thursday May 17, 1945

New granted men. Soldiers building something in middle works. Also report they are in next town. Happy Birthday Mike—7 years old! Gee you must be getting big now. Definitely see you before next birthday.

Sunday May 20, 1945 to Wednesday May 23, 1945

Working on garden all but last day. Tough work but grand. Lots of sun and feeling better though still diarrhoea.

New Sgt. going concern. Busy all day but keeps lads working too. Keeps other Nips under control though. Put man in Guard House for giving gum to a woman and they let man off who perpetually steals from Cook House and gave him his Red Cross parcel!!

Nips up and about early these days. Keeping all out of administration! Something up!

Rumour: 30 day Armistice.

Thursday May 24, 1945

Rain. Warning at 12:30 a.m. Some planes went over.

Friday May 25, 1945

Pay for May. Another B-29 came over as reconnaissance.

Fresh fish have started to roll in and rolling in for last three days. Boxcar full at station. Lovely fish and getting lots. Best meals for ages.

Thursday May 31, 1945

Installing big transformer and heating unit in bath. CC around all the camp with civvy, still building administration. Wonder why all this construction at the last minute? Surely not for us!

Two B-29s went over going N.N.W. at about 20,000 feet and no sirens. Very large looking.

Friday June 1, 1945

CC told Janis to prepare billets for another 100 men. So they are coming at last. Beginning to think we were going.

CC has ordered concert for 3rd.

Saturday June 2, 1945

Lots of Rumours. We have big dope. New men only coming for 3 days. Seven Nip Big Shots in prison!

Diarrhoea a bit worse again.

Sunday June 3, 1945

Pay sheets for new men given so looks as though they will stay.

Tuesday June 5, 1945

90 Dutch (white are few) and Javanese including 1 officer—Lieut. Haber arrived. What a mixture now. Came from Kawasaki camp! Last camp a good one and could get lots of stuff from outside. They are in pretty good condition. F/Lt Catt was in their camp until recently. News from Dutch:—B-29s, P-51s and Curtis dive bombers, also B-24s raiding regularly. Mostly incendiary bombs. Area between Tokyo and Yokohama burned out—25 miles! Also large areas of Tokyo, Yokohama, Osaka, Kobe, Niigata, Moji, etc. flat. Last raid 500 B-29s on Yokohama and only 1 shot down. They say 95% Nip civvies worse off than us!

Russia has refused to renew friendship pact next April. New government is a military one and new strong party advocates fighting to last man. Rumour we have given them to June 7th to come to our terms. If not, we will bomb severely till July 7th and then they must surrender unconditionally! If not then Americans will land and wipe them out! Don't put much stock in this rumour however. They saw very few Nip planes and no warships. Very few ships at all. They were unloading coal boats but now none come in. Their barracks were hit in 50 places one day by incendiary bombs but fires put out. Nips laugh at homes being destroyed and cities burned!

Work seems to have stopped on new administration again!

Interpreter and Sgt. came back with new POWs.

Wednesday June 6, 1945

Of new men, 15 to work in camp! 15 on garden, 1 tailor, 1 cobbler, 1 M.O., 3 cooks, 1 watchmaker! Doesn't leave much for furnaces.

Thursday June 7, 1945

New men collecting weeds for soup and getting clothing steamed to kill lice. Some very good instrumentalists with them. All their watches collected and rings. Clothing inspection and if any Nip stuff damaged they will be taking Red Cross stuff away from them! Weight—75. OK.

Monday June 18, to Saturday June 23, 1945

Alarm 1 a.m. on the 19th and plane over. Men sent to shelters. Warbling note which means raiding planes in vicinity. Two men went back to billets and missed tenko when raid was over and got badly beaten up. Two days out and two days in now for officers. Two day alarms on 21st and 23rd. No planes. Things quiet.

Doc found worms in my stool so had worm treatment on 21st. Also on sulpha quanadine again because diarrhoea still bad. Lot better on 23rd. Doc says stool like a dysentery one but no bugs.

Interpreter went to Tokyo four days ago. Nip says biggest raid yet on Tokyo on the 18th.

Saturday June 23, to Friday June 29, 1945

Warning on 28th at 12:30 a.m.—every time I'm Officer of the Day. Interpreter made a lot of changes. By the time fire parties etc. fall out there's hardly any left for shelters.

Weight on the 27th 74 K. Gain of one and a half.

Diarrhoea still the same as ever—about 4 times a day.

Now have to hand in daily eating figures for next day and get menu figures of things to use for every meal. M.O. taking interest in feeding now. Light duty and easy duty on cut rations again—590 gms per day. Other food is good. Beans have run out but fresh vegetables and fish every day—also salted cherries.

Strong rumour from Nips—3 point landing on Kyushu on 29th!! Has it come at last? Nips admitted loss "big" a couple of days ago.

Rumour: Russia's allied with Japan and fighting Yanks and English—Ha Ha.

Lot of air activity by Nips during the last 2 days. A lot (50) of old decrepit bi-planes went over. Also rumour big Allied convoy coming from North. Nips around here don't betray by their actions anything unusual happening.

Camp being fixed up. Fly screens on Cook House and lats, etc.

Saturday June 30, 1945

Rumour again re Kyushu landing. Alarm at 11:15 p.m. but no planes. Most men went back to sleep this time and were not bothered.

Sunday July 1, 1945

Warning at 11:30 p.m. again. Chinless called up. Sorry to lose him as best Nip of all. Cook Hancho also going soon. Sgt. returned from Tokyo!!

Sweet spuds planted.

Monday July 2, 1945

Rumour from Nips we have 1/3 Kyushu but I don't believe it. Alarm at midnight again although heavy rain.

Nips found some of the spuds in our camp garden had been stolen and went off the deep end. Had officers and room Hanchos at attention for 3 hours and said would keep us there for days if necessary until guilty party came forward!! Started to rain at 7:30 and Sgt. let us off. Supper not allowed until 8:30 and tomorrow's rations cut to 600 gms. Sgt. says will give us till 12 tomorrow to get man who stole spuds. Questioned our groups but nothing happened. Little man, what now??

All medicines put in special raid shelters.

Tuesday July 3, 1945

Rumour parachute landing on north isle!! Also we are doing well in Kyushu!!

We couldn't find spud thief by 12 noon so we turned in a letter saying the men were willing to report stealing in future and wanted to see guilty persons punished. Also we believed guilty person pretty mean thief. Rather than come forward he is willing to see whole camp suffer and suffer with them.

Two men in headquarters caught with bamboos but just stood at attention for two hours!!

Order that all clothing except certain items to be turned in. We cannot keep pyjamas, winter undershirts, however!!

Rice cut to 699 gms a day. Reason given is because of spud theft.

Air raid at midnight but no plane.

Wednesday July 4, 1945

Two raids in early a.m. but only one plane. Don't get much sleep because must get up every time and wrap up beds and clothing!!

Rumour Sgt. leaving in 4 days, to join army.

Rain. Rice 600 gms.

On July 5, 1945, General MacArthur announced that American troops had annihilated 450,000 Japanese troops in the Philippines.

Thursday July 5, 1945

Sgt. left!! Rice still 600. Started inoculations against typhoid and dysentery.

Friday July 6, 1945

Rain and cool. Had my inoculation. Cook House say rice 600 gms a day until man who stole handful of spuds out of garden comes forward!!

About 84 letters came in. Latest dated February this year.

Saturday July 7, 1945

CC away for day. 600 gms rice.

Weight 71.5K. Another drop.

Kyushu landing myth. Spy had all standing outside for an hour because someone laughed too soon after tenko!!

Sunday July 8, 1945

Two alarms early in a.m. One actually 11:30 p.m. last night. Spy had Doc hold 2 cans of water because he said Doc had said Nip medicines no good. Actually Doc had asked for Red Cross medicines for certain treatment and when Spy offered substitution of Nip medicine, Doc said it was not suitable. Spy also had Yanks stand outside for half hour in a.m. but nobody knows why. CC called all officers and said shifts rearranged tomorrow. 10 men to furnace but we had this increased to 11. Three shifts with Dutch make up to 45. Five best men. Crusher shifts re-starting then.

CC said rations back to 705 tomorrow but if any more stealing will be cut again. Sgt. back.

Monday July 9, 1945

Trouble with garden party. Nip in charge has been riding them for a long time and finally POW 28 went for him. He took off and brought them back to camp. O.M. slapped 15 and 28 but then made 28 Hancho after he heard story!!

Blood taken for tests.

Tuesday July 10, 1945

As usual raid when I'm Officer of the Day. 12:30 a.m. about 6 planes came over. First one minute after siren so didn't get all furnaces really blacked out!! Could hear bombs (anti-aircraft) and see flashes. Figured by the time planes got here they must have been about 25 miles away and Niigata is 28 miles!!!

Blood test taken and I am "O" class.

Interpreter hit man across face with skivvy for being late for fatigue. Later had him up in office and apologized. Gave him food and smoke!

Have gramophone and records in billet every night.

Friday July 13, 1945

No. 5 put in Guard Room without food.

Presentation Day—having been here one and a half years. Ginger and tea given. CC says most have worked well and he has tried to put men in jobs suited to them. New Sgt. hardly ever leaves administration. No trouble to us at all. Seems just big self-conscious kid. Even had his own batman with him for 2 days!

Rice 630 gms a day. Asked CC why and he said would issue order later.

Spit and stool tests must be in by 7 a.m. tomorrow but paper given not correct and don't think will be much good.

Sunday July 15, 1945

No. 5 let out of Guard room and CC talked to officers. He says cut to 630 gms only to build up reserve food supply against emergency. 75 gms per day per man being put aside. He said transportation system may break down (obviously he meant in the event of a landing) and since our food came in by train we may not have any for a few days. He expects 22,000 kg spuds from our garden.

Dangerous time from now till fall he says. Also stressed danger of stealing from Nip gardens. Said Nips in village get same as we do and sometimes not as much and that at times may nark them. Consequently they supplement with their gardens and if POWs steal from there, there is liable to be trouble. He says we are still under control of Nip army and he will look after us as best he can. Also stressed how useless it would be to try and escape since the hills are full of Nip soldiers and villagers driven from cities who would probably kill POW if they caught him.

Then he said, "do you know what happened in Tokyo?" He was referring to chaos after bombing when transportation system, etc. broke down and that only with bombing. Personally I can see what it is going to be like with all rolling stock confiscated by services and it looks as though we will go hungry for stretches.

Play bridge every night now. Second inoculation for all.

Monday July 16, 1945

Tobacco came in at last—long time since last issue!!

Still rain. Two alarms in early a.m. Two planes over. Nips don't even bother to get us out now—I knew they would soon tire of it.

Almost impossible to get light bulbs now. Used to get as many as we wanted but now we just don't seem to have any.

They also hold more tenkos now than ever!! They even tenko the animals now! With a special tenko form for the animal men to fill in!!

Tuesday July 17, 1945

Panic. Alarm and warble at 10:30 a.m. and chased everybody out. CC jumping up and down and waving sword round. Sgt. splitting himself as I suppose he has seen lots of bombing. Heard some dull explosions and CC told Nips it was Kansai Ki in hills of Niigata. This means carrier planes!! Suppose they thought invasion had really come. They were certainly running round in circles and all the air raid shelters are full of water as we expected. Even with example of last year's water-logged and collapsing shelters in front of them they still build in low ground and still cover even though we tried to talk them out of it. Anyway we don't need shelters because nearly everyone is on detail: hose, demolition, buckets, food salvage, clothing salvage, clothing store, Cook House, etc. etc.

Troop trains going though all the time and Nips say that's why food is scarce as using all trains for troops—and that was before the invasion!! Nip confirmed carrier planes over Niigata—said CC told him. Also told him if it is an invasion we would be taken to Tokyo and shot!! Former may be true but it would be to prevent us being shot!

Another food cut. Now to get 570 gms a day and sick men 500 gms!! Cook House says it was to give us the same rations as Nip workmen. So far they have not put any of last saving away?? Get 100 rice and 90 beans per meal. I am still on luga however.

Vegetables small again too. Only seaweed in soup. Gave us some of Nip Dai Ichi food today "Flowering Fern" and boy I'd hate to have their Dai Ju. I certainly believe the man now who claims he can live on grass. Our greens are tougher than that. All turnip tops, sweet spud tops and all other tops go into our soups and tomorrow we are going to have a nice clover soup. Soon they will be putting us out to graze like the goats!!

Weight 72.3K.

Friday July 20, 1945

Big raid on Niigata at 12:30 a.m., Could see flashes and flares and hear bombs. Nip say 150 B-29s and 2 shot down!! Certainly sounded big. All nobby irons, etc. again collected so CC scared we are going to cut up. Another alarm at 7:30 a.m. this time by carrier planes, say Nips.

Saturday July 21, 1945

Kaniyama easy to get along with in Cook House and certainly does his best to get stuff in. Another forage party for clover. He puts out stuff that old Cook House Hancho had been hoarding.

Sunday July 22, 1945

Interpreter back and tonight is his first meal since yesterday noon he says. He certainly doesn't look too happy so he must have experienced things in Tokyo!!

Stock taking in Cook House.

New books started.

CC has ordered doors on air raid shelters. To keep out rain—best yet!

Monday July 23, 1945

Rumour Nips asking for peace and their papers saying they want peace. Nip on job says in 3 months we will be going home on "Queen Lizzy." But how often have we heard that!! Naber says Turkey came into war about last Xmas!! Also Rumour 78,000 British marines in Kyushu but think balls.

Tuesday July 24, 1945

No rain today!!

Mitchell, no. 25, back from Tokyo Hospital. Not a lot of news. Having raids all the time in Tokyo but he says they build houses again out of tin left over when burnt out. About one third of the factories are running and are fixed up when bombed. Kawasaki steelworks was bombed where there were POW and 20 Dutch and 7 Yanks and English killed. One raid consisted of 800 planes. Also airfield in South Tokyo has been shelled from sea! Never saw Nip planes. Nips say the war will be over in October but he doesn't know why they think so.

Food fair at hospital and good at Amori—Headquarters camp. Says not many planes shot down. Yanks are supposed to have landed 100 miles North of Shanghai and are driving to join the British coming from Burma. More news later. Lieut. Naber (Dutch officer) and 3 of his men have been told they are moving tomorrow!! They are oil workers!! They say they are going to new Headquarters camp on North East coast—"Senai"—new big camp for over 2,000.

5 men ate wild berries and were violently sick. Poisoned and one man is very bad.

300 letters and some telegrams in.

Wednesday July 25, 1945

Naber and 3 Dutch, 213, 214, 292 left. Going to No. 5 camp first at Niigata—then Senai. No raid last 2 nights and full moon!!

CC asked Doc why so many are sick and Doc told him cannot do the work on present ration. Only getting about 2,000 calories a day and doing one hour's work beside factory work. Today did 2 hours work—one at factory and one in camp. Carbide shifts working at river as intake plugged like last year. Interpreter mucking up work details. More and more forms to fill out.

I have one letter with picture of Mike at administration. Some of telegrams dated 5/5. All old English.

Sickness mounting.

Raid at 10:15 p.m. but no planes.

Thursday July 26, 1945

REMEMBER THIS DAY!!!

Quietly having bath at factory after first alarm had gone (wailing note had not sounded). Long blast is caution alarm and wailing means planes in vicinity in Japan. All clear long blast but only blows after wailer!!

Anyway, heard plane coming and thought it was Nip but all of a sudden it sounded like it was diving. I submerged and heard what I thought was three bombs drop. He circled and came back but nothing happened. Finally I got out of the bath, dressed and went outside. Windows of bath house broken and stretcher case passed us. Clouds of dust around but couldn't tell where bombs had hit. Took off for barracks. Found men just coming out of shelters. About half the windows and frames in billet broken and my room a mess. Things knocked off shelf. Heaps of theories, places where bombs had dropped, number and kind of planes, etc. Most authentic seemed to be one bomb had fallen about N.N.E. of barracks, 500 metres away on other side of the hill. Blast must have been big although it didn't sound like a big bomb. I think they were after railroad bridge E.N.E. of camp about 100 metres. Nips say three bombs and a couple near bridge. Bits of bomb fragments all over the camp and one chunk of rock came through the roof. Lot of people claimed they saw a big four engine bomber come over, about 25,000 feet, then bank, come back and make off. Others saw a twin engine machine with tapered wings come over much lower. I don't know but it certainly sounded low and as if diving to me but may have been the sound of plane revving after unloading. Think next time they will dive-bomb bridge. Nips fairly calm and not serious at all.

Nip CO called officers after and asked us POW reaction. We told him POW in same boat as Nips and didn't like being bombed. We thought they would be here again soon. Suggested that during the day men make for shelters on first alarm as may not be second one. Night okay to stay in billets. Finally, CO said that on the first alarm nobody does anything. On the second all up, bundle up things and gather by groups. On signal or when they hear planes they should make their way to shelters. Doesn't sound so hot to me but we'll see. However they have this bridge and maybe the factory was spotted and they will be back.

Not so hot being bombed by our own planes!! Still it was bound to come and if due for it will get it!! Evidently a few people were hurt in the area but I don't think anyone was killed!

Friday July 27, 1945

Warning again at 8:15 a.m. Planes heard but none passed over. Everyone jumpy. All got into shelters but as usual they are all flooded, and always will be because in low ground! Also very small and men like sardines, so had rest men bailing most of the day and fixing the shelters up. Nips call for so many men all day long and don't stop to wonder where they are coming from with people either at work, or sleeping after work.

Food thin these days. Rice weight per man low. Hardly any vegetables for soup. Also all gummy rice came in last time and doesn't make much of meal.

More and more men are getting sick. Six men on morning's carbide shift sick.

Three alarms at night. First two about 30—35 miles away and still heard bombs and saw flashes. Judge city south west of here. Last raid on Niigata. First raid all into shelters when planes heard. No warble as usual now!!! On two subsequent raids everyone stayed in bed. Nips soon got tired of lining everyone up when siren blew and tenkoing them. Full moon.

Saturday July 28, 1945

Alarm at 9:15 but no planes. Rumour: Russia declared war on Japan!! Another that Russian planes were over yesterday. Also that we are using Russian bases but Russia is not in war! Three warnings in the p.m. Two between 10:00 -11:00 and one later. Last raid plane circling overhead but misty and couldn't see anything.

Rumour: Churchill out and Attlee new Prime Minister and seems true as in rags.

Sunday July 29, 1945

Alarms, shouting, gonging and whistle blowing all morning but no planes. Rest men had to work on shelters for four hours. Perfect night but no raids. Men kept working frantically on shelters all day. Men did four hours. Carbide shifts do three hours on top of eight hours' work. Men working at river as water intake silted. Bomb crater about 5' diameter only—in hard ground. How come so much blast?? Can't understand it.

Officer coming from Tokyo at the end of the month so all activity. We don't bother to get up now at nights when raids.

CC checking Cook House books and making all the same as mine!

Nip plane over but everyone very jumpy and most men out of billets. They say Nips on job took off for hills.

Monday July 30, 1945

Alarm in a.m. twice but no planes.

Sgt. came up to me at 2 p.m. and asked me if I liked fishing. When I said yes, he told me to get worms and be ready at 2:30—only me!! Had grand afternoon out—went above dam and fished in reservoir. Didn't catch anything but had good swim. Also cigs. Tobacco scarce these days—about 4 packets a month. Sgt. didn't say much but didn't treat me like a POW. Quite a likable chap. Suppose he chose me because I wasn't in bed the other a.m. when he slapped Doc.

[F/Lt Chater remembers that he and the Sgt. walked a good distance up the river. Finally the Sgt. said, "I guess we're far enough away." Away from the danger of being bombed. He then lay down and went to sleep, leaving Chater to fish and swim.]

Tuesday July 31, 1945

Alarm at 9 p.m. but no planes. Raids seem to be easing off now.

Letter from Mu dated 16/11/44 with grand picture of Mike. She is in Durban now sharing a house with a friend. About 300 letters issued—at the latest—March 45!

Living from meal to meal now with rice. In fact we had to use over 2 reserve sacks today. Also vegetables practically nil. Still 190 gms per meal. Nips say landed in Kyushu 10 days ago but only announced today! Still don't believe this.

Electric heating unit fixed in camp bath at last. I am in charge of that too. Wish they would put some of the other officers in charge of these things as my hands are full in Cook House these days.

Wednesday August 1, 1945

Big raid at 9:30 p.m. on Nagoka. Could see big fire 35 miles away. Everyone in shelters. Nips party after at 12:30 a.m.

3 carbon shifts started today.

600 planes raided this country on 1st and 2nd. Rumour: Yanks say they are going to bomb this factory in 4 days! Also rumours say if Nips leave POW working on military targets and any get killed, God help them.

On August 6, 1945 the first atomic bomb was dropped on Hiroshima, a city with a population over 100,000, almost completely destroying it. Still, it took a second atomic bomb, dropped three days later on Nagasaki, to force the Japanese to admit defeat. On August 14, 1945 the Allied forces accepted the unconditional surrender of Japan. The Second World War was over. But in the camps, the POWs knew nothing. Only by observing the changes around them did they suspect that, at last, the end had come. Wonderful as this was, it also brought with it a time of great danger for the POWs. Frequently, through the years, they had been warned of the likelihood of their mass execution at the end of the war, if the Japanese did not win.

Monday August 6, 1945

New granted man. Alarm in a.m.

Swimming in afternoon and very good. Sandy beach and no current. Sgt. took us. Very hot. Still no sign of landing. Rumour Canadians landed in China.

Tuesday August 7, 1945

Bass came back from Tokyo Hospital. We asked him if 300 B-29s had gone over 2 nights ago and he said yes—also 400 P-51s!! B-29s came over at noon but didn't drop anything. Thank goodness because the take cover warning was too late (9 gong beatings).

People in Tokyo say the war will be over in October—even Nips say this. Three raids a day in Tokyo.

Two POW camps in Kawasaki hit and some POWs killed. Officers in hospital camp work in gardens all day or half rations. US airmen shot down are put on 350 gms a day!!

Rumour: paratroops landed in Niigata!! Baloney.

Very hot. Started carbasone treatment at night (1 capsule a night, 1 in a.m.) for about 10 days for my diarrhoea.

Wednesday August 8, 1945

Raid warning 2 p.m. but hardly noticed it. Sgt. called me to the office and asked if we wished to go swimming today. Grand.

Bass says camp prepared at Saipan for all POWs to be collected after the war before going home so it looks as though they expect to get us out soon.

Thursday August 9, 1945

Alarm at 7 a.m. and Nips say there were 40 fighters bombing and machine gunning near Niigata. Four shot down!

Woke up and had to hold tenko at 12:00 midnight. Found out one man—167—had been caught at town food depot!! CO and all Nips in camp. Also CO said we would be held responsible for anyone leaving camp till the a.m. so officers had to take one hour shifts.

Saturday August 11, 1945

No raid until 11:30 p.m.

Only one furnace running these days and that not all time. CC called officers to administration and says why we are not working. We explained we did plenty of administration work and he said, "Like hell"!! Then he calmed down and said billets dirty, etc. etc. Then he said we must start three men on fire watch at night on 2 hour shifts!! Says 167 going to be court marshalled.

Also robbery by two POWs—one tall, one short, 5-6 days ago. CC says we must stop men from stealing. We repeated it is impossible, that men will always steal if hungry. Also we had reported men who stole in past and they were not punished and in some cases the whole camp punished while men who stole enjoyed fruits of their theft. Also we said men could get out of camp anywhere. CC said shortly we would get a small increase in food, same as Nip army but if stealing continues we would get no food. Said Nip civvies only getting half the amount of food.

Sunday August 12, 1945

No alarms. Big stir up in Cook House again. Cook Hancho given boot and Kaniyama in again. Old business re drawing rations for next day again and are they small!! Military police here questioning etc.167. They couldn't speak very good English and hence didn't get his story straight so CC said confess to them and not to him.

CC narked about something. Ordered no more nobbies and track to be taken up—and we have practically no more wood in Cook House.

Rumour persists fighting in Sahklin. Looks as though these people are going to fight it out??

Wednesday August 15, 1945

How can I describe this day! One I will never forget. The first indication we had that something was up was when some lads said all the people in the village were listening to the wireless with rapt attention and as quiet as mice. Then about 10 a.m. the CC rushed out of camp with sword and revolver on. Followed by Egawa and Ishinogi. Then first crusher shifts and then carbide etc. sent back from work. Whole camp paraded and I think CC was going to make a speech but couldn't face us. We were dismissed. Then rumours or facts that Nips had said Nipponese had surrendered and war over. Next air raid post on hill was shut up and flags, etc. brought down. That decided me.

Then I think the CC, after thinking it over, decided he had been hasty. So he had carbide shift parade and gave them work in camp. Blankets were taken from store and put in raid shelters—that looked queer!! Garden weeded, etc. Then carbide shifts were told they were going to work just before chow. Previously they had been told no more work today. So all rations had to be changed. Just as they changed CO says they're not going to work. There would be two days Yasume. So all changed again. Then again told they were going to work and again changed, the last time falling out for an hour's work. I think the CC was a bit rattled but also wanted to keep boys on move.

Finally all settled down after supper. Tobacco issued. Nip source told us Emperor himself had flown to Okinawa to settle peace and Yanks would be in Tokyo tomorrow!! No blackouts tonight so I think we can take it as conclusive. So it's come and like a bolt from the blue.

I was so tired at night I went right to sleep—can you imagine that? The day I have been waiting for for three and a half years and it doesn't even keep me awake. Gosh what is Muriel thinking! And my people at home. A thousand questions. How long do you think we will be here Mr. Chater? etc. First reaction of lads seemed to be one of awe. They appeared stunned but at night went to town singing, etc.

Thursday August 16, 1945

Now 7:30 and nothing has happened! No raids today. CC told us to put all windows back in. No work. Woke up to Dutch singing in a.m. Lads more boisterous but not as much as I expected. Nips left us alone.

CO called all officers and asked us if we knew why we were being kept in camp and we told him yes. In other words, do you know the war is over? He said he had had no instructions from Tokyo re us and in meantime we would carry on as usual as he was responsible for us. Said if anyone was found outside camp he would be shot. Only instruction he had was we were not to work. There was to be no singing or shouting and lights out at usual time! We were responsible for law and order in camp. Anyway, conclusive evidence war over. Queer feeling, free and not free. Time will drag now! Yanks supposed to land in Tokyo today.

Friday August 17, 1945

Nothing doing in a.m. at all. Boys busy sorting out clothes, cleaning kit, etc. Lot of junk being discarded. In afternoon Sgt. took five of us diving and spearing salmon but didn't quite get any. We saw plenty jumping. Quite an experience though with water glasses on and swimming under rocks looking for salmon. Beautiful hot weather.

Asked CC if he would give shoes back to men and he said he was awaiting orders from Tokyo. He would issue all clothing, medicine, etc. he held of ours when he got orders. He still had heard nothing from Tokyo re us. Incidentally all phone connections with Tokyo were supposed to have ceased a week ago.

CC called all officers again and I arrived first. He drew his sword and said, I will kill. I assumed he was joking and I hoped so. He swung and brought sword down beside him. I just looked him in the eye and smiled. Then he told me to sit down. (In front of office, on the ground, in view of all the men). I just stood and grinned at him. He repeated order three times, getting sterner every time. I still just stood and smiled at him. He hesitated and then turned away—so his effort at humiliation didn't work! Then he told all officers he had not given orders for any old clothing, etc., to be thrown away so why were men doing it! He said we may not need the clothing but the Japanese haven't much and will need it. Quite peeved about it. He said we could have a concert tomorrow. Looked like Little Napoleon with revolver and sword on and arms akimbo.

We had a real meal at night. Bully, milk, strawberry jam and butter! We issued all milk left to men entitled to it. Suggested to men they give nine tins to administration and a few to Dutch but this idea was cried down. Men wanted it all to themselves—no Xmas spirit.

Last day of carbasone (10 days) and I'm a lot better now. Hope cured. I go once—three times a day now.

Saturday August 18, 1945

Rumour: 10,000 Yanks at Niigata and later they are spreading through the country! CC packed up in hurry and left for Tokyo about 3 p.m. There is supposed to be a meeting of all POW camp heads with Yank representatives there too. So it looks like a few more days here.

Big clean up in camp. Sgt. took us swimming in afternoon.

<u>Weight 72.2K.</u>

Concert night and very good. Dutch hula hula dancer and sketch "The Picture" especially good. Everyone in good mood. Main question is however, "When do you think we will be out of here Mr. Chater?"

Sunday August 19, 1945

Wimpy says Yanks not on island yet. Certainly no sign of them. Have seen a couple of planes but they are Nip.

Different look on Nips' faces these days. The strained look has disappeared and they are more cheerful. They certainly are relieved and glad war is over. Life will continue for them in same old rut, I suppose, though but they will be happier and the food shortage will soon be alleviated.

We don't bother kotsking for Nips now and they don't say anything. Administration Nips are a little more friendly but not much more. Time drags for us and we anxious to be on the move. Rumour: CC will be back tomorrow. What will he bring???

Monday August 20, 1945

CC came back in a.m. bringing new Interpreter with him. Alarmed everyone by bawling out a lot men laying on verandah for not kotsking. Later left camp again.

Nips ordered 50 wood and 50 garden party every day!! What now? Officers got together and decided to take the plunge and ask for understanding. Since the CC was not in, we talked to the new Interpreter. He speaks perfect English and was obviously educated in US. He was surprised position had not been explained to us. We told him we anticipated trouble if men were made to work. We asked him and he said "War is not over!!" That rather shook us. He said we were still under orders of Nip army. Said men in other camps are still doing original work quite happily. Said we would not be going home tomorrow or next day—in other words would be here a while yet. <u>But</u> he certainly gave the impression that if war was not over they expect it anytime—more or less stating they are just waiting to sign the terms of armistice.

Went back and told our men the dope but they wouldn't believe war was not over! They said—why are Yank troops on island (they have heard rumours of that but personally I don't think there are any). Why no planes? Why shut up air raid station? Why stop us working in the factory? Why pay officers full pay on the 20th? And why tell them we will receive full deposits? etc. etc. I told them we're sure they don't intend to fight again but until agreement was signed the war is not over! Lot grumbling about "They won't get me to work on this chow!" etc. But I bet those men will be working tomorrow!

Suppose things will settle down again. We stressed that harsh attitude by Nips in charge of details might cause trouble, especially the garden Hancho. He said he would put all these things to CC. I especially mentioned the food situation saying men saw their health disappearing when working on this food. Looks like guards moving in tonight!! Our escort??

Working on administration and put blankets and mossy nets in. CC called officers in evening and talked to us for one hour. We had to repeat what we had said to the Interpreter in the afternoon. He said war not over but peace negotiations still going on!! Still some fighting in parts of Japan although we saw no planes here. We are still under his orders and he had given order for details tomorrow. If we decided not to follow those orders he knew his mind or in other words he would take steps to make us. He was following convention re treatment of POWs laid down in Geneva in 1929. He said it would probably be 3-4 months after armistice was signed before we would be allowed to go home. As a parting shot however he said negotiations progressing satisfactorily and we could <u>desire</u> to go home in the near future. I brought up question of food and he said reason he had given orders for work on garden was because possibility that hostilities may break out again at a moment's notice and also that we may be here 3-4 months. Also food situation has not improved and may become worse. That's about all.

We told troops and they seemed satisfied saying they now knew where they stood but didn't believe armistice not signed and also poohed the idea we may be here more than 3 months. However men seemed satisfied to go to work.

CO promised to give a speech at 9 a.m. tomorrow.

Tuesday August 21, 1945

Nip guard of one officer and 30 men arrived for our protection, according to CC. He gave his speech at 10 a.m. and it was just reiteration of what he told us last night. Officers paid all deposits (mine <u>1771.50</u> yen)—are we leaving before men, to agree with segregation clause?? No work today. Very hot! Camouflage taken off engines now!! and they say nothing <u>signed</u>.

Funny remark when were lined up to hear CC's speech and a table and box were brought out. The CC stepped on the box and began his speech, just as the first CC did the day we arrived at the first camp in Japan. One man pipes up "This is where I came in!!"

Wednesday August 22, 1945

Evidently to be no more work details at all. Couldn't even get them to go out and get wood for the Cook House!!

CC ordered blackout shutters to be taken off Cook House. Sgt. left for Tokyo with nominal rolls. 167 was let out of Guard Room!

Swimming and very good.

My stomach upset again today however—oh when will it be functioning okay!!

Order no music till after 5 p.m. and good idea—the 8 records we have are driving me nuts. Vegetables etc. very short. Living from meal to meal.

Thursday August 23, 1945

CC ordered 150 men to go and bring back clothing removed to next village two weeks ago for safety. That looks as though move imminent! Making out more lists, date of capture, place of capture, place, etc.

Two soldiers arrived from Tokyo and we painted P.W. on roof—a fine time to do that. What does that indicate??

Seemed as though they came especially from Tokyo for this. Rest of Red Cross clothes were issued and what word battles. Especially between Janis and Hewitt. Absolutely childish over clothes they will only wear a few days. Such selfishness. What kind world are we going back to? Oh well, will soon be able to pick my own company.

CO told us he couldn't issue leather boots because they were evacuated here and belonged to Tokyo. He said we would be issued with them when we got to Tokyo and then as an afterthought—if we went there!! All issued with British tennis shoes.

Rations being issued day by day and short for tomorrow—513 gms per man!!

Looks as though we'll be leaving any day now.

Friday August 24, 1945

Mu's birthday and not home for it. However different state of affairs from last one and know I'll be home for next one!! Many happy returns darling!!

Rumour planes coming over tomorrow dropping food!! Not much doing. Water and lights off all day. CC away all day. Nips bringing clothes in at night. Enough rice in for usual issue tomorrow. Nips don't bother us any more. P.W. painted on roof!! A fine time to do that. Will our troops come into this country tomorrow?? 10 days since war stopped.

Saturday August 25, 1945

Boots (new Nip and very good). Nip jackets, trousers, underpants, socks, puttees (Eng.), shirts issued to those that <u>want</u> them.

Enough rice in for 3 more days.

Egawa gave officers a cup half full of saki at night. He said he wanted to bring it at other times but CC said no. Also said this CC best of 4 camps he has been in. Said dropping food and about 5 men for distributing food over Japan but thinks this place is too difficult to land. Some planes sighted today but long way away and couldn't see what kind.

Nip back from Tokyo says Yanks there and I think he is right as he described them quite accurately. Seems to think we are leaving in 3 days but it's just a guess.

No lights or water again today. Tired of hanging round. Yanks moaned like H___ because 12 pair of captured Yank boots were divided proportionally. They forget they were all given Red Cross English shoes when they really needed them. Also they were all given captured British clothes when they had no clothes in the middle of winter. What is the US going to be like after this war!!

Sunday August 26, 1945

Sgt. back from Tokyo and must have brought enlightening news and orders. CC called all officers and covered following points. He now revises his original statement that we would be allowed to go home in 4-5 months and he says it is almost certain we will be allowed to return to our countries within <u>a</u> month. He still maintains the pact for armistice has not been signed and he says when we go home we will know he is speaking the truth and it was not signed by Aug. 26. Says from now on we officers will be in charge of our own troops. He wanted one of us to act as Senior Officer but we pointed out that since we had different nationalities in the camp it would be better for us to carry on as before with each officer in charge of his own group. However the D.O. would act as liaison officer with Nip CC.

We have permission to use the Guard Room for delinquents. We assured him we could handle all men. He said in event of any trouble with civilians we were all to congregate in shelters. Said we were free to go anywhere with an escort. Anything we wanted we were to ask for. We brought up increase in rations and he said he was doing all he could. If we were being supplied by army he could get more but it would take a long time to arrange that. Nip civvies are only getting about 330 gms per day, less 10%. However he would do his best.

Xmas photos had been sent home. He would get the negatives, which we could take home but he asked for them to be sent back when we finished. Gave us a few copies.

We hold our own roll calls and the D.O. reports to CC or Sgt. Also got roll call times of 7:30 and 5 p.m. Later orders given that Nips get exactly the same food as we do!! That will shake them. I asked CC for lights for wash stand and he quietly got up and unscrewed light from his office and gave it to me!!

No lights out. Bell night.

Monday August 27, 1945

CC asked us to give any numbers of persons who wanted to stay in Japan. This order was from Tokyo. He said of course conditions would be different from before war. Now we could travel at will with every consideration whereas before the war we had to have special permission and were not welcome. I think it would be a good thing for a freelancer because Nip civvies are decent and hospitable lot of people and Allied currency would go a long way. However I think all want to get home!

Incidentally first question CC asked yesterday was—anyone that couldn't walk. We thought right away—this is it! Rather disappointing but anyway looks like it will be very soon. Six fighters flew over but didn't see our sign. For one reason—it's too small.

Nip CC called all officers at 9 p.m. and we thought this must be our marching orders. He started off (after seating us round a table) by asking if we knew present war situation. We, of course, said no. Then he said Japan had surrendered to Allies on Aug. 15th!

The Emperor had commanded the Japanese to lay down their arms and since he is a divine being to them and his word is absolute they obeyed even though they were prepared to fight to the end! However the pact for armistice was not yet signed but was expected to be signed very early in September and he thought we would be going home within two weeks of the signature. So more time to hang on!

He went on to say that he was treating us now under orders from Tokyo and even though we were still POW the treatment was now governed by the eventuality of the pact being signed and the complete handing over to us at that time!! He reiterated a dozen times that any mal-treatment we thought we had suffered while in this camp was his responsibility solely. He was responsible for the actions of all his staff and he asked us to mention no name but his if we reported those incidents or if we intended to take any retaliatory measures. He had always acted the best for the POW in his opinion but stressed he was not trying to excuse himself. He said the Sgt. was going to Niigata tomorrow to try and get canteen supplies. The old Interpreter had gone to Tokyo to find out why nothing had been dropped at this camp. He had gone as far as the Niigata Prefectural Offices endeavouring to get an increase of food and he has nearly succeeded. He is keeping the pig and the goat for the last day.

Then the fun started. Sgt. brought in a big bottle of saki, then one third bottle of saki. Then straight alcohol. We all got gloriously lubricated. What a feeling! Bed wouldn't stay still. Sgt. very amusing chap, graduate of university "who jumped into army." Some of the grant-ed men had women in the other room and one called me but get thee behind me Satan—I took no notice!

Tuesday August 28, 1945

CC in speech to lads said pact will be signed on Sept. 2. We should leave here then by 5 days after. Thinks he will take us. Also read us today's paper—150 men landing today (Yank reps) first in Japan. Two large planes flew over, one over camp and quite low but gave no indication of seeing our sign. Everybody jumping up and down but he sailed serenely on.

Wednesday August 29 1945

Nips say 4 B-29s flew over Niigata camps yesterday and dropped eight canisters the size of 44 gal. drums. We collected sheets today and made two large P.W. signs and are now sit-ting back waiting for the avalanche. Nip CC gave resume news out of paper to all men. At 5:00 tonight he told officers Headquarters camp persists in asking if any too sick to walk and he therefore thinks we may be leaving in 7-10 days and sick may be flown home.

CC handed all things in clothing store over to us. In fact he made it clear that everything here is now at our disposal!! He said at other camps they had taken what they required and turned the rest over to Nip Red Cross and we said that's okay with us. He also turned Cook

House over to me but I have been more or less running it now for months so it will make no difference. Said he would like to meet us when the armistice signed, on a friendly basis. He is certainly turning. I didn't expect this of him.

400 packets of tea brought in.

Sgt. goes to Tokyo tomorrow to try and contact Yank officer there to have stuff dropped at this camp. Hewitt giving him letter.

Diarrhoea still about same—good for couple days then off again. Swimming every day.

Thursday August 30, 1945

Ration increased back to 705 gms a day starting at night. Four-engine plane flew directly overhead at 10:00 but slightly cloudy and gave no indication of having sighted us. Still waiting patiently for "Manna from Heaven."

Swimming and two men in trouble but got them out. Had to swim across river to one of them.

M.O. said we should do as we see fit re saluting!!

Friday August 31, 1945

Queen Wilhemina's birthday and Dutch putting on a show.

Rain so no planes. Quiet day. I stopped our lad from waiting on Nips saying they would have to collect and serve their own food and wash their own dishes.

Concert at night and very good.

Saturday September 1, 1945

CC and some granted men left for Niigata to try and get Red Cross food etc. Heaps more Nip clothing issued to men out of store to which we now have key. Sgt. came back from Tokyo. Had contacted Commodore Maher (Yank) at Amori camp who had just landed from flagship *San Juan*. In reply to Hewitt's letter asking for Red Cross food he said dropping of food being done by army (in letter) but he would see his commodore tonight who would probably contact army. He said they were locating the camps and to be patient for a <u>few</u> days and we would be sent to ships so looks as though we go directly to boats.

Sgt. says Amori and Shinagawa camps already evacuated by warships. Lucky Devils.

Sgt. is going back tonight. He sent us 1500 packs "Kinchis". Boy were we glad to see theM. Sgt. humped them in!

Hewitt got phone call from Maj. Powell, Niigata POW Camp Commander. He says he is sending us enough type C ration for one and a half days—all he can spare since he has 1,700 POW to take care of!! Says he's going to try and get to Tokyo tonight and he will keep us posted.

Cloudy so no planes over today. We went on wood party for hike. We have stopped saluting all Nips now—even the CC and I think he felt it last night when he appeared in the middle of the concert and nobody got up or saluted.

Rather wild night. CC came back from Niigata and said a shipment of dropped goods were arriving at 8 a.m. Also he had succeeded in having our ration raised to 1K a day!! Too much I think but let them eat for a change. So orchestras played, people sang, gramophones played, etc. and they vowed nobody would sleep. I went to bed but had to get up again and I wandered over to Cook House. However when I came back at 11:30 nearly everyone was in bed!

CC also said Major Powell of Niigata camp has been sent to Tokyo as Representative of POW, in this area. Also he had contacted Nagoka camps and arranged for more dropped food to be sent here!

Sunday September 2, 1945

Guns etc. of administration staff turned over to us. CC produced radio-gramophone for our use. McArthur to speak today but we didn't hear him. Armistice signed in a.m. on Battleship *Missouri*.

Promised dropped food arrived plus <u>19 bags rice</u>. CC said I am now in charge of the Cook House and could use all food as I saw fit. Everyone was happy and well fed.

We built outside boiler. Dry type rations and wet, cigs galore, gum, fruit juices, soups etc. At night we had supper and saki with administration staff but went easy this time. Some men left camp A.W.O.L. and CC was much worried but they all returned. Hewitt was on the phone to Nagoka camp and they are sending more dropped food.

Still no inkling of when we are going home.

Monday September 3, 1945

Conducted tour of power station 50,000 KW. 66' head reaction turbines.

Plane dropped more food at camp 15 in Niigata. They phoned to say they were sending some here. Also Nagoka sending truck so we should be well off.

Men allowed out of camp on pass.

Major Powell back from Tokyo and phoned at night—at last some news of leaving. Hewitt may leave for Niigata tonight. They say Yank troops at Niigata and we probably will go direct by ship from there.

Later—Hewitt left by special train.

Got old short wave radio working again.

Tuesday September 4, 1945

Hewitt back in the morning. We are all to be evacuated through Yokohama as trains become available. More food in with Hewitt—dry and wet ration for dinner. All are going through hospital ships to transports and then to Manila. Radio news later says our camp is leaving on the 5th or 6th.

Later news phoned from Niigata that their camp is leaving tonight.

Row with Hewitt as usual about putting food out at noon. Hewitt left again tonight for Niigata. CC says to kill pig but we put it off till a.m.

Wednesday September 5, 1945

Hewitt back bringing a lot more food dropped yesterday. Says their billets are filthy. Very dangerous dropping stuff and one woman killed. 300 left there last night and more are leaving tonight. We leave probably tomorrow morning. Lots of lads are going out of camp with permission and bringing back souvenirs.

Read *Fortune* and *Time* and makes you wonder what kind of world we are going back to. Everything is organized for leaving at 7 a.m. tomorrow. 25 Nips are going with us. This village will feel like it has lost an arm when we leave. Civvies have been very good to lads last few days inviting them to their houses and giving them souvenirs and on whole lads have behaved very well. Last day in old billets!!

Pretty wild night—people coming in drunk all night hence no sleep. Sgt. Whitley stopped by guard going out so "kotskied" them, then took off!!

Thursday September 6, 1945

Up at 5 a.m. and everything went off okay. Marched to station at 7:30 and each section had large flags made out of sheets and parachutes at head of section. Once out of camp it felt like weights lifted from you. Started 8:15 on train. Journey uneventful just sleeping and eating. Some towns nearly completely knocked out by bombing. Terrific cheer when we saw Yank soldier in station near Yokohama. Finally we arrived in Yoko and lo and behold beautiful American women there at station giving us cigs, chocolates, etc. Gosh it was good to see them. Just before they left they asked us: "Now, is there anything else we can give you?" There were loud guffaws!

Taken to docks by lorry and then disinfectors, medicals, G2 [health examination] etc. I passed as fit to go out by air. That was a surprise to us. Going to fly us out to Manila and maybe all the way home!! Some of the lads even left tonight!! Boy these Yanks don't lose any time!! I was taken to a cruiser to spend the night and met Don Rice and lot of lads from Mitsushima. I got about two hours' sleep. Plenty of good food all the time but I'm afraid I had too much on the train and my stomach is bad again. I met a Canadian girl from Lethbridge at one questioning table. Gee, she was nice to me. In fact all the staff were grand. They worked all hours and had the patience of the world.

Friday September 7, 1945

White bread and butter!! First bunch moved to airport at 7 a.m. I had a couple of hours of sleep in a.m. and afternoon and then we hurried with supper and lined up. Took off for airport about 7:30. They had pushed about 500 through since 7:00 p.m. when we got to the airport. Just as we, the next group (80), got up to leave, planes stopped coming in and I am still at Atzugi Airport at 3 a.m.

Saturday September 8, 1945

Very little sleep but moved out at 10 a.m. at last. Beautiful C-54 transport plane and a dozen others behind us. Certainly got to hand it to these Yanks for equipment and action. Had grand trip of 5 hours to Okinawa. Gosh, that's some place. Every conceivable kind of machinery and the amount of work going on is terrific. Roads like main roads in busy city with traffic. Place is honeycombed with roads, stores etc. Bay is full of ships.

Arrived about 5 p.m. and got tent and blanket about 9 but nothing to eat. Saw P/O Dunlop who had brought some letters from Mitsushima for me in case he saw me—darn decent of him. And picture of Mu!! Lord hold me back—looks better than ever. Also Mike looks a lot fatter. To think those letters have been in Matsu a long time and those b___ wouldn't send them on. Also saw S/L Grant and gosh good to see him again!! Have not come across any of A.M.W.D. crowd though. Rumour all British NCOs and officers up one rank!! Lots of rumours how we are going home. Fly all the way via US—fly through Burma, etc. Seems first hop will be to Manila and some have taken off tonight.

Sunday September 9, 1945

1,500 left early this a.m., using B-29 and all available planes. Missed breakfast as run out but had 2 dinners!! Still no sign of me moving. Saw Doc Whitfield.

Monday September 10, 1945

Loaded in lorry and taken to Air Force at 10 a.m. but came back as flying conditions too bad. Met STC lads from Mitsushima. Not eating well and stomach still bad.

Tuesday September 11, 1945

In camp all day and only a few left for Manila as flying bad.

Wednesday September 12, 1945

Left camp at 5:30 and flew to Manila on B-24. Arrived 11:15 and a band greeted us. We were taken to Camp 10 M. S. Manila and segregated into British, Dutch, and US. Also officers were segregated and I am now in an officer's camp. Only a few have left here so far. Officer's mess, show, etc. Good tent camp.

Interrogated at night.

Left: Les Chater visiting his eldest sister Eva, October, 1945.

Right: Les Chater visiting relatives in Saskatoon, November 10, 1945.

Thursday September 13, 1945

Still get up early. Order all POW to leave Manila in 6 days. Still F/Lt. Got number and 32 pds pay advance. Saw picture at night and it was good. Sent Cable to Mu.

Saturday September 15, 1945

Met F/Lt Evans of the A.M.W.D. — first released A.M.W.D. I've seen. Lot of old acquaintances turning up. From talk, officers who have just come out from England say things there are tough in clothes, food line. I have asked to go back through Canada with stopover. Got letters from Nora, Irene and Eva. Gosh, good to get them and know they all thinking of me and glad I'm okay. This captivity has made me realize more than anything what a grand bunch of sisters I have. Group of officers who have signed up to go anyhow, and any class, told they could go on *Empress*. I'm still hanging on for Canada. Drew more clothing. Beer issued free 3 times a day. Also cigs and candy, cigars and tobacco. Show every night.

CANADIAN PACIFIC
TELEGRAPHS
World Wide Communications

W.D.NEIL, General Manager of Communications

SASKATOON, SASK.

MRS M J EDWARDS
508 7TH STREET
SASKATOON SASK.

THE ENCLOSED TELEGRAM FROM YOUR RELATIVE NOW LIBERATED FROM THE

JAPANESE HAS BEEN TRANSMITTED FREE OF CHARGE BY IMPERIAL CABLES

CANADIAN MARCONI COMPANY WITH THE COOPERATION OF CANADIAN PACIFIC TELEGRAPHS

WHO WILL BE PLEASED TO FORWARD WITHOUT COST TO YOU A REPLY CONTAINING NOT

MORE THAN TWELVE WORDS IN THE BODY THEREOF ON PRESENTATION OF THE ATTACHED

ORIGINAL MESSAGE FOR PURPOSES OF IDENTIFICATIONS

CANADIAN PACIFIC TELEGRAPHS
PHONE 3171.

A telegram to Les's sister Nora on his release from Kanose POW camp.

Monday September 17, 1945

Quite pleasant at camp but dying to be on the move. I am detailed with 39 others to be ready to embark tomorrow. Rumour: going to Vancouver!

Tuesday September 18, 1945

Moved 1 p.m. to dock. Loaded on Yank trooper for San Francisco. 14 day trip. Thank goodness we're moving at last. Grand accommodation. Eighteen in big cabin.

Wednesday September 19, 1945

Sailed at 7:30 a.m. but we were not stopped to take on oil until 1 p.m. So off at 1 p.m. Show at night. Food good and if not full can have more — ice cream at night.
Library.
About 150 Canadians aboard going to Frisco then Vancouver. Hope I can go with them.

Saturday September 22, to Friday September 28, 1945

Daily routine breakfast 7:30. On deck and read usually till dinner 12:30. Then sun bath, exercise on boat deck till 4:00. Read till supper at 6:30 then hang around till show at 8 p.m. What a life. Eat, sleep, read — no women, no drink.
On 27th I had first tooth out.
Finished reading *This Above All* by Eric Knight.
Wrote Mu on 27th.

Friday September 28 to Wednesday October 3, 1945

Just on board. Posted letters to Mu and folks on 2nd. We are to land today. Very excited. Boat with band on it met us in the harbour—full of women and hot jazz. Makes one's eyes water. Docked at noon and then we were taken to Ft. McDowell, an isle in the bay. We can't leave there, worse luck, except on conducted tours.

Thursday October 4, and Friday October 5, 1945

Cabled Mu. Trying to get permission to go to Saskatoon and think okay. Food good, flicks, beer, pool and bowling. Still want to get on with it though. On 5th I took a conducted tour of Frisco. Rest of party, except 8, left for N.Y.

Saturday October 6, 1945

Left for Vancouver on special train with 3 other officers and returning Hong Kong Canadian POWs. Whenever we stopped at a town many of them would get out and rush to the nearest bar and invariably one or two missed the train. We left a trail of missing POWs behind!

Les Chater, happy to be back home in Canada.

Les Chater visiting his middle sister Nora, October, 1945.

Monday October 8, 1945

Arrived Vancouver 2:30 p.m. Red Cross representative helped me, arranged berth and took me to supper—Thanksgiving Day. Met Fred and Emily, Cecil, Audrey etc. at station when we went back. Didn't know they were in Vancouver. Heard Mu in South Africa.

Although the ordeal of POW camp was over, Les Chater's health was still at risk. Canadian doctors had little experience with his condition and none of their medications appeared to be effective. Les suggested they try what the prison camp doctors had used to cure him—carbasone. They did, and it worked, but only temporarily. Two more trips to hospital were necessary before his physical condition improved. Unfortunately, like many POWs, he was plagued with nightmares about his experience in prison camp for the rest of his life. Now, another challenge lay ahead— adjusting to a life of freedom in post-war Canada.

Les and Muriel Chater with son Michael, Hamilton, 1947.

Afterword

MURIEL CHATER'S ARRIVAL IN CANADA in January of 1946 with their son, Michael, was the beginning of the Chaters' family life in Canada.

Les and Muriel Chater went on to great success. After working for Ontario Hydro, Les accepted an engineering position with the Steel Company of Canada and rose to become General Manager of Engineering. In 1958 Stelco sent him to Harvard Business School where he took the Advanced Management Program. He also worked voluntarily as the chairman of the Building Committee which was responsible for the great concert hall known as Hamilton Place, as a member of the Citizen's Advisory Committee for Via Rail, and on the committee that brought about the renewal of Hamilton's downtown area, and the building of Jackson Square. He was one of the inaugural commissioners on the change to the metric system. He was also the inaugural chairman of the Hamilton branch of the APEO (Association of Professional Engineers of Ontario).

Mr. Chater was invited to travel to Tokyo, Japan, to act as a witness at the trial of many of the personnel of both Mitsushima and Kanose. Like many others, he refused. He had just begun to establish himself with his new life and work and felt uncomfortable with returning to Japan. At the request of Major Walter Hewitt, he sent his diaries along instead. When the Camp Commander of Kanose POW camp was sentenced to 7 years' hard labour, Mr. Chater wrote on his behalf, suggesting leniency.

Les has always kept active with the YMCA, and believes that the leadership training he himself took as a youngster there greatly contributed to his survival as a POW. Most winter mornings still find him at the downtown Y getting in his morning swim. In the summer, he swims in his own backyard pool. He's an ardent golfer and has spent many holidays scuba diving in the Caribbean Islands.

Appendices

THE FOURTH DIARY

The fourth diary is a book of lists. Similar in size to the other diaries, $9^1/_2$ cm. x $15^1/_2$ cm. x $^1/_2$ cm., it is a black booklet. For the sake of those interested in tracing family history we have listed all information found in this booklet on these individuals. Time takes its toll on our memories, and, although Mr. Chater's memory is remarkable, the fifty-eight years' span of time does present its challenges.

BRITISH PRISONERS OF WAR

Each name of the British POWs begins with two camp numbers, the first one being the POW number from the first camp, Mitsushima. The second number was designated when Mr. Chater led fifty of his fellow prisoners to their second camp at Kanose, along with his friend Captain Hewitt who led fifty of his American comrades.

The letter following, either a K, S, T-M, gives us some history of the prisoner. Because we know the first number was the Mitsushima POW identification number, no M, which would signify Mitsushima, is used. But the K indicates which POWs went to Kanose. The S, we assume, might possibly stand for Semplak, the first POW camp in Java. The T.M., by the same process, we conclude, stands for Tasik Malaya. However since there are no Ms listed, for Mitsushima, one cannot be certain that all this is correct. Again, this represents another mystery that time has hidden from us.

Rank is listed before the POW's name, followed by two numbers, the first thought to be the regimental number, the next, again, beyond remembrance. The unit, of which we are certain, is then listed.

Early in the list, the name of next of kin is listed, generally up to POW 104. After this, only an address, no doubt where next of kin can be reached, is listed.

Notes usually offer specific explanation on the POW. They explain, for instance, in case of death, the cause and any known particulars pertaining to that death.

The order of names on the list appears just as it was in the booklet, by POW number. No doubt this would have been the quickest and most convenient way for Mr. Chater to refer to the list. For our own purposes, alphabetical listing might have been preferred. For this omission, I apologize to those of you tracking down family history.

51   1127   K
L.A.C. Findlay, William J.   619   605
Unit: 100 B Squadron
No next of kin listed.

52   1130   K
Cpl. Frank L. Smith   1004   854
Unit: RAF H.Q. Seletar
Mrs. Edward Smith, 8 East Orchard Lane, Liverpool

53   1131   K
F/ Sgt. Richard H. Whitley   611   628
Unit: 100 B Squadron
Mrs. H. Whitley, 52 Colchester Terrace, Sunderland.

54   1138   T.M.
A.C.2 Gerald A. Quays   786   215
Unit: Special Technical Corps
Eurasian—enlisted Singapore RAF
Mrs. J. S. Quays, 2 Barrack Rd., Penang

55   1140   S
Sgt. William C. Rose   917   922
Unit: A.H.Q. Briltaire, Bandoeng
Mrs. William C. Rose,
Heather Cottage, Robin Hood Lane, Walderslade, Kent.

56   1141   T.M
Cpl. Arthur M. Head   785   729
Unit: Special Technical Corps
Eurasian—enlisted Singapore RAF
Mrs. Effie Head, 10 College Square, Penang.

57   1142   K
A.C.1 Eric T.E. Collins   1614   715
Unit: 36 T.B. Squadron
Mrs. L.M. Collins, Morea, 8 Chairborough Rd., High Wycombe, Bucks.

58   1143   S
Cpl. Osmond H. Simmonds   572   465
Unit: 242 F Squadron
Henry Simmonds, Danycraig Terrace, Trebanog, Porth, Rhonda, Glam.

59   1144   S
Cpl. Leslie B. Preston   1032   821
Unit: Air H.Q., RAF
Mrs. W. A. Preston, 1 Linden St., Leicester, England.

60   1145   S
Cpl. Harold McDonald   950   260
Unit: 242 F. Squadron
Mrs. Harold McDonald, 70 Church St., Old Catton, Norwich

61   1146   S
Cpl. William H. Eaton   801   561
Unit: A.H.Q. Briltaire, Bandoeng
Mrs. W. Eaton, 10 Walsham Rd., New Cross, London, S.E. 14

62   1147   S
Cpl. Harold G. Rogers   979   453
Unit: RAF
Mrs. H. G. Rogers, 67 Brassey St., Birkenhead Ches.

63   1148   S
L.A.C. James Duffy   965   952
Unit: H.Q. RAF
6 Peasefield Rd., Dovecot, Lancs.

64   1151   K
A.C.1 James Chalmers   1550   415
Unit: 41st Air Stores Parts, RAF
Mrs. M. Chalmers, 1 Dudley Drive, Hyndland, Glasgow.

65   1152   K
A.C.1 Thomas Reynolds   1475   670
Unit: 41st Air Stores Parts, RAF
Mrs. D. Reynolds, 8 Averton Square, Wollaton Park, Notts.

66   1153   K
A.C.1 Alexander Milligan   1551   247
Unit: 41st Air Stores Parts, RAF
Mr. Alex Milligan, 72 Wallace St., Ayr, Ayrshire

67   1154
Gnr. John Mills   1653   895
Unit: 21st Regt. 79th Bty. RA
Mr. W.H. Mills, 46 Cambridge Rd., Anerley, London S.E. 20.

68   1155
Gnr. John Buchan   1653   996
Unit: 21st Regt. 79th Bty RA
Mrs. W.I. Buchan, 69 Albany Rd., Brentford.
Note: Burnt 9/3/45 at Carbide, died 11/3/45, cremated 13/3/45

69   1157
Gnr. Gerald Murray   1826   666
Unit: 21st Regt. 79th Bty RA
Mrs. S. Murray, 57 Colne Rd., Brierfield, Lancs.

70   1158
Gnr. Oliver Crowdell   1511   317
Unit: 21st. Regt. 79th Bty RA
Mrs. A. Crowdell, Main St., Smeeton Nr. Kibworth
Note: Burnt 9/3/45 at Carbide, died 28/3/45, cremated 29/3/45

71   1187   K
L.A.C. Desmond Foskett   741   514
Unit: 36 T.B. Squadron
Mr. R.T.B. Foskett, Sunny Croft Rd., Hounslow Middx.

72   1188
L/Bdr. Ronald B.H. Baker Leic.   161   4694
Unit: 21st Regt. 79th Bty RA
Mrs. R. B.H. Baker, 6 Cambridge Gardens, Croydon Rd., Wallington Sy.

73   1189   S
Cpl. John J.A. Botting   930   078
Unit: A.H.Q. Briltaire, Bandoeng
Mrs. R. Botting, 30 Appleton Rd., Wellhall Eltham, S.E. 9

74   1190   S
Cpl. Hugh Flyn   1350   348
Unit: 242 F. Squadron
Mrs. G. Auld, 26 Hillkirk St., Springburn, Glasgow.

75   1192   T.M.
A.C.1 Herbert Train   1137   533
Unit: 81st. Repair & Salvage Unit: RAF
Mrs. H. Train, 781 Albion Terrace, Shawforth, Rochdale Lancs.

76   1195
L/Sgt. Edward G.J. Sawyer   1550   565
Unit: 21st Regt. 79th Bty. RA
Mrs. E. Sawyer, 17 Castle Rd. Isle Worth Mddx.

77   1198   K
Cpl. Idris G. Llewellyn   543   546
Unit: 60th B Squadron RAF
Mrs. S. Llewellyn, 1 Stanley Terrace, Llawbradach, Glam.

78   1199   S
Cpl. Frederick Hill   915   071
Unit: A.H.Q. RAF
Mr. F. Hill, 660 Woolich Rd., Charlton, London.

79   1200   S
Cpl. William L. Gilbert   611   399
Unit: Transport Pool RAF
Mrs. A. Beale, 46 Laburnum St., Trunton, Som.

80   1201   K
F/Sgt. Richard Perry   528   723
Unit: 100 B Squadron RAF
Mrs. L.M. Perry, 105 Musgrave Rd., Bolton, Lanc.
Note: POW Hosp. Tokyo 29/6/44
Left 16D for Shinagawa, returned 8/10/44

81   1204   S
A.C.1 James Barry   1436   234
Unit: A.H.Q. RAF Bandoeng
Mrs. James Barry, The Grange, Bradford, Abbas, Dorset.

82   1205
Bdr. Arthur F. Compton   1552   186
Unit: 21st Reg. 79th Bty. RA
Mrs. A.F. Compton, 188 King's Rd., Kingston-on-Thames, Sy.

83   1206
L/Bdr. Edwin E. Collins   1614   715
Unit: 21st Regt. 79th Bty RA
Mrs. T. Collins, 49 Belmont Rd., Surrey.

84   1207
L/Bdr. William J.H. Quennell   1453   708
Unit: 21st Regt. 79th Bty RA
Mrs. W. Quennell 156 Empire Rd., Greenford, Madx.

85   1208   S
Cpl. James Archie   1155   772
Unit: A.H.Q. RAF
Mrs. A. James, Stockholme, Watchetts Lane, Holmer Green, High Wycombe

86   1213
Gnr. Charles McLachlan   1826   689
Unit: 21st Regt. 79th Bty RA
Mrs. C. McLachlan, 184 Randolph Drive, Clarkston, Renfrewshire.

87   1215
Gnr. Edward J. Pedder   1549   187
Unit: 21st Regt. 79th Bty. RA
Mrs. R.M. Dolan, 16 Tintern St., Clapham, S.W. 4

88   1216
Gnr. William H. Brown   1530   926
Unit: 21st Regt. 79th Bty RA
Mrs. W.H. Brown, 3 Railway Cottages, Warwick Rd., Coventry

89   1223
Gnr. John Foster   1826   569
Unit: 21st Regt 79th Bty RA
Note: Burnt 9/3/45, died 11/3/45, buried13/3/45

90   1226
Gnr. John Telford   1826   640
Unit: 21st Regt. 79th Bty RA
Mrs. J. Telford, 8 Creighton Ave., Rapples, Carlisle, Cumberland.

91   1227
Gnr. Bert E. Cowell   1614   631
Unit: 21st Regt. 79th Bty RA
Mrs. Winifred Cowell, 8 Harvist Rd., Holloway, London N.4

92   1228
Gnr. Harry Brenchley   1614   706
Unit: 21st Regt. 79th Bty RA
Mrs. Jessie E. Brenchley, Tower Bridge Rd., Bermondsey S.E.1

93   1229
Gnr. Walter Connell   6584   373
Unit: 21st Regt 79th Bty RA
Mrs. Sarah Connell, 154 Snakes Lane, Woodford Green, Essex.

94   1230
Gnr. Victor Brown   6401   643
Unit: 21st Regt. 79th Bty RA
Mrs. Lillian Brown, 29 Park Crescent Rd., Brighton

95   1232
Gnr. Michael Doolan   1779th   694
Unit: 21st Regt. 79th Bty RA
Mrs. J. Doolan, 41 Anderton Park Rd., Moseley, Birm.

96   1233
Gnr. Harry Cooper   1825   963
Unit: 21st Regt 79th Bty RA
Alice Cooper, 14 Tonge St., Haywood, Manchester, Lanc.

97   1234
Gnr. George Desert   1745   485
Unit: 21st Regt. 79th Bty RA
Mrs. Queenie E.E. Desert, 17 Highcroft Ave., Wembley Mddx.

98   1236
Gnr. Albert M. Reed   1653   948
Unit: 21st Regt 79th Bty RA
Mrs. A. H. Reed, 66 Montagu Cresc. Edmonton N. 18

99   1237
Gnr. Eric Flindall   1807   018
Unit: 21st Regt. 79th Bty RA
19 Dudley Drive, South Ruislip, Ruislip, Mddx.

100   1238
Gnr. Harry Stokoe   1453   209
Unit: 21st Regt. 79th Bty RA
Mrs. H. Stokoe, Tudhoe Village, Spennymoor, Co. Durham

101   2779th
Laing John Joseph (Civilian Ship's Surgeon)
M.K. Laing, 1 Hensley Hall, Park Rd., Bellevue Hill, N.S.W. Australia.
Note: Arrived Kanose 12/6/44 from Shinagawa.

103   4681
Pvt. Henry Wilkinson   7517   807
Unit: RAMC
W.H. Wilkinson, 152 Lodge Lane, Newton, Hyde, Ches.

104   4790
Capt. Janis Morris   184   749
Unit: 55th Inf Brgde Group Co. RASC
29 St. Margaret's Rd., Edgware, Middlesex, England.
Note: Arrived Kanose 29/6/44 with (103 incl) from Thailand.

105   4791
Colour Sgt. Stanley Jack Hodds   5775   287
Unit: 6th Bn. R. Norfolk Inf. Regt.
Mill Lane, Acle, Norwich

106   4792
Sgt. Thomas Charles Ramsey   T-161   249
Unit: 53rd Inf. Brgde RASC
37 Cromwell Rd., Southend on Sea.

107   4793
Sgt. Alexander Dow Grant   803
Unit: Jahore Vol. Eng.
10 Pitkenro Rd., Dundee, Scotland.

108   4794
Sgt. Arthur William Davis   5776   581
Unit: 6th Bn. R. Norfolk Inf. Regt.
22 Fitzroy St., Leicester

109   4795
Sgt. Edward William Taylor   5773   308
Unit: 6th Bn. R. Norfolk Inf. Regt.
14 Gresham Rd., Norwich.

110   4796
Sgt. Harry Russel Ingle   5830   920
Unit: 5th Bn. Suffolk Inf. Regt.
East Cot, Bassenally Rd., Whatlesey, Peterboro.

111   4797
Sgt. John James Whale   5830   701
Unit: 5th Bn. Suffolk Inf. Regt.
Silverdale, Blackacre Rd., Dudley, Worc.

112   4798
Sgt. Edward Frederick Bacon   5828   356
Unit: Army Catering Corps
22 Lynwood Rd., Hawick, Scotland.

113   4799
Cpl. Walter Cyril Wooll   5825   494
4th Bn. Suffolk Inf. Reg.
113 Alderton Rd., Hollesley, Woodbridge.

114   4800
Cpl. Walter William Miller   1888   732
Unit: Royal Engineers.
25 Goda St., London S.W. 11

115   4801
Cpl. Reginald Hemmings   1892   127
Unit: 560 Field Co. Engineers
5 Fairview Cotts.
Virginia Water, Surrey.

116   4802
Cpl. Harry Hart
Unit: 560 Field Co. Engineers
124 St. Helens Rd., Prescot, Lanc.

117   4803
Cpl. Richard B. Howe   5828   572
Unit: 5th Bn. Suffolk Inf. Regt.
5 Bolton St., Lavenham, Suffolk.

118   4804
Cpl. Francis Howard Byford   6013   922
Unit: 4th Bn. Suffolk Inf. Regt.
1 Church Lane, Wennington, Rainham, Sx.

119   4805
Cpl. Arthur Robert Jarvis   5828   346
Unit: 5th Bn. Suffolk Regt.
11 Duke St., Hadleigh, Suffolk.

120   4806
Cpl. James Lawrence Lane   5775   461
Unit: 5th Bn. Norfolk Inf. Regt.
12 High St., Gt. Budworth, Nr. Northwich, Chesire.

121   4807
Cpl. George Ralph Parker   489
Unit: Jahore Vol. Engs.
c/o Union Bank of Australia, Perth, West Australia.

122   4808
L/Bdr. William Peter Speller   948   979th
Unit: 135 Field Arty. Regt.
40 Eighth Row, Ashington, Northumberland.

123   4809
L/Cpl. William Robert Martin   5775   218
Unit: 4th Bn Norfolk Inf. Regt.
67 Burgh Rd., Gorleston On Sea

124   4810
L/Cpl Wilfred Harry Kidd   5832   406
Unit: 5th Bn. Suffolk Inf. Regt.
27 Queens Walk, New Flatten, Peterborough

125   4811
L/Cpl Philip Dixon   4858   355
Unit: 1st Leicester Inf. Regt.
Post Office Halwell, Melton Mowbray, Leics.

126   4812
L/Cpl. Raymond Charles Cranston   6147   741
Unit: 2nd Bn. East Surrey Inf. Regt.
c/o Midland Bank, Newington Green Branch, London, N 6.

127   4813
L/Bdr. Reginald Francis Waterman   912   423
Unit:148 Royal Arty Regt.
78 Leeside Cres., Golders Green.

128   4814
L/Cpl. Albert Facey   5947   460
5th Bn. Suffolk Inf. Regt.
67 Mours Hill, Olney, Bucks.

129   4815
L/Cpl. Sidney James Sadler   5830   683
Unit: 5th Bn. Suffolk Inf. Regt.
38 King St., Smethwick Staffs.

130   4816
L/Cpl Harold Sidney Turner   5827   672
Unit: 5th Bn. Suffolk Inf. Regt.
50 Poplar Hill, Stowmarket.

131   4817
L/Cpl. Charles Edward Postle   5829   853
Unit: 5th Bn. Suffolk Inf. Regt.
14 Vicarage Terrace Cambridge.

132   4818
L/Cpl. Charles Harry Phillips   5830   927
Unit: 5th Bn. Suffolk Inf. Regt.
Council Cotts., Foxton, Cambridge.

133   4819
L/Cpl. Sidney Henry Parker   5829   664
Unit: 5th Bn Suffolk Inf. Regt.
10 Bassett St., Kentish Town, N.W.

134   4820
P. Herbert Southerington   5776   580
Unit: 6th Bn. Norfolk Inf. Regt.
93 Leicester Rd., Syston, Leics.

135   4821
P. Arthur James Askew   6020   797
Unit: 6th Bn. Norfolk Inf. Regt.
16 Boxley House, Pembury Rd., Hockney, E. 8.

136   4822
P. Albert Overend   5777   032
Unit: 4th Bn. Norfolk Inf. Regt.
73 City Rd., Bradford, Yorks.

137   4823
P. Leonard George Stanton   5950   414
Unit: 5th Bn. Suffolk Inf. Regt.
35 Bletsoe, Bedford.

138   4824
P. Leslie Frank Wallace   5830   628
Unit: 5th Bn. Suffolk Inf. Regt.
Windswept, Lanshall Bury St. Eds., Suffolk.

139   4825
P. Basil Lloyd Friend   5828   371
Unit: 5th Bn. Suffolk Inf. Regt.
Felsham, Bury St. Eds., Suffolk.

140   4826
P. Arthur Leslie Knight   5832   682
Unit: 5th Bn. Suffolk Inf. Regt.
112 Monklands, Letchworth, Herts.

141   4827
P. Victor Lewis   5776   216
Unit: 6th Bn Norfolk Inf. Regt.
8 Primrose Cres., Thorpe St. Andrews, Norwich.

142   4828
P. Ronald Sidney Spatchett   5776   259
Unit: 6th Bn. Norfolk Inf. Regt.
8 Shipfield Sprowston Rd., Norwich.

143   4829
Dvr. Stanley Bertram Hale   T-170   519
Unit: 53 Inf. Brig.
58 Plashet Rd., Upton Manor E. 13

144   4830
P. Edward Herbert Wake   5340   396
Unit: 18th Div. RAOC
62 Montcrief St., Peckham, S.E. 15

145   4831
P. Arthur William Rolfe   5828   270
Unit: 5th Bn. Suffolk Inf. Regt.
141 Angel St., Hadleigh, Suffolk.

146   4832
P. Alfred Metcalf   6147   436
Unit: 2nd Bn. East Surrey Inf. Regt.
35 Burton Rd., Earlsfield, Wandsworth, S.E.

147   4833
P. Vernon Watson   6141   930
Unit: 2nd Bn. East Surrey Inf. Regt.
110 A, Highbury, New Park, N.5.

148   4834
Dvr. Ernest Brand   2115   073
Unit: 560 Field Co. Royal Eng.
Wyanton Lyes, Nr. Monmouth.

149   4835
P. Norman Franklin   5950   379th
Unit: 5th Bn. Suffolk Inf. Regt.
143 Wendover Drive, Bedford.

150   4836
P. Jonas Walter Driver   5829   674
Unit: 5th Bn. Suffolk Inf. Regt.
37 Elizabeth Terrace, Wisbech, Cambs.

151   4837
P. Albert Edward Flower   5832   987
Unit: 5th Bn. Suffolk Inf. Regt.
12 Foxhall Rd., Ipswich.

152   4838
P. Percy Raymond Hirst   4805   373
Unit: 5th Bn. Suffolk Inf. Regt.
1 Central St., Chesterfield, Derbyshire.

153   4839
P. Walter Sidney Boon   5832   486
Unit: 5th Bn. Suffolk Inf. Regt.
Gt. Glemham, Saxmundham, Suffolk.

154   4840
P. Albert Henry Hicks   5345   882
Unit: 6th Bn. Norfolk Inf. Regt.
32 Haig Rd., Hillingdon Middlx.

155   4841
SPR. Harold Aitken Quack   1   262
Unit: Jahore Vol. Engs.
27 Twyford Ave., London N. 2.

156   4842
P. Harold Freeman Ruoff   6147   763
Unit: 2nd Bn. East Surrey Inf. Regt.
75 Crossbrook St., Waltham Cross, Herts.

157   4843
P. Harry Roger Peter Neithercott   6147   447
Unit: 2nd Bn. East Surrey Inf. Regt.
5 Peerdale Rd., Herne Hill, S.E.24.

158   4844
P. Ronald Derick Wilson   2037   921
Unit: 2nd Bn. East Surrey Inf. Regt.
Green Pastures, Leatherhead Rd., Chessington, Surrey.

159   4845
P. Frederick Davis   6142   285
Unit: 2nd. Bn. East Surrey Inf. Regt.
53 Prospect Cres., Whitton, Twickenham.

160   4846
P. Patrick Murphy   6148   517
Unit: 2nd Bn. East Surrey Inf. Regt.
36 Low John St., Wexford, Eire.

161   4847
P. Ronald Fell   5828   934
Unit: 5th Bn. Suffolk Inf. Regt.
7 Linden Close, Histon Rd., Cambridge.

162   4848
P. Charles Sawyer   5950   618
Unit: 5th Bn. Suffolk Inf. Regt.
1 Belmont Rd., Luton, Beds.

163   4849
P. Edward Joseph Thurlow   5828   385
Unit: 5th Bn. Suffolk Inf. Regt.
21 Victoria Hill, Eye, Suffolk.

164   4850
P. Alec Cecil Merry   5830   577
Unit: 5th Bn. Suffolk Inf. Regt.
178 Church End, Cherry Hinton, Cambs.

165   4851
P. Harold Peet   5950   583
Unit: 5th Bn. Suffolk Inf. Regt.
19 Holden St., Mansfield, Notts.

166   4852
P. Frederick Chambers   5774   726
Unit: 6th Bn. Norfolk Inf. Regt.
Heath Rd., Hockering, Nr. East Derenam, Norfolk.

167   4853
P. Albert Ramshaw   5776   244
Unit: 6th Bn. Norfolk Inf. Regt.
15 Rishwerth St., Dewsbury, Yorks.

168   4854
P. Fred Towns Cason   5776   165
Unit: 6th Bn. Norfolk Inf. Regt.
17 Kenneth Ave., Stanforth, Doncaster, Yorks.

169   4855
P. Arthur Frank Pardon   5774   750
Unit: 6th Bn. Norfolk Inf. Regt.
Pond Cottage, Paston, Nr. Norwich.

170   4856
P. Ernest (Cliff) Kitchener   4857   738
Unit: 1st Leicester Inf. Regt.
22 Sherwin Rd., New Lenton, Notts.

171   4857
P. Samuel Richard Giobens   5828   940
Unit: 5th Bn. Suffolk Inf. Regt.
14 Russell St., Cambridge.

172   4858
P. Albert Victor Thacker   5775   622
Unit: 4th Bn. Norfolk Inf. Regt.
1 Row 97 Gt. Yarmouth.

173   4859
P. George Harold Bedder   5773   748
Unit: 4th Bn Norfolk Inf. Regt.
7 Drayton Rd., Norwich.

174   4860
P. Walter Ernest Warner   5775   531
Unit: 4th Bn. Norfolk Inf. Regt.
361 St. John's St., Clerkennell, E.C.1

175   4861
P. Derek John Furgnal Falby   5774   517
Unit: 4th Bn Norfolk Inf. Regt.
Bow St., Gt. Ellingham, Attleborough, Norwich.

176   4862
P. Charles James Dickerson   5825   389
Unit: 5th Bn. Suffolk Inf. Regt.
Thatched Cottage, Beaumont, Clacton on Sea.

177   4863
P. Charles Wellesley Kerridge   5828   254
Unit: 5th Bn. Suffolk Inf. Regt.
21 Church Walk, Stowmarket.

178   4864
P. Arthur Reginald Rainer   5826   866
Unit: 4th Bn. Suffolk Inf. Regt.
4 Bosmere Terrace, Bramford Rd., Ipswich, Suffolk.

179th   4865
P. Robert Frank Hill   6020   146
Unit: 4th Bn. Suffolk Inf. Regt.
13 Hill View, Doo__ Down, Bath, Somerset.

180   4866
P. Charles Skeet   5835   722
Unit: 5th Bn. Suffolk Inf. Regt.
13 Carmichael Rd., S. Norwood S.E. 25.

181   4867
P. John Savage   5950   475
Unit: 5th Bn. Suffolk Inf. Regt.
33 St. George's Rd., Watford, Herts.

182   4868
P. Stewart Dulling   5630   578
Unit: 5th Bn. Suffolk Inf. Regt.
15 Hone Park Ave., Plymouth.

183   4869
P. James Gordon Baker   5778   178
Unit: 6th Bn. Norfolk Inf. Regt.
Rose & Thistle, Melbourne St., Kings Lynn, Norfolk.

184   4870
P. Douglas Hand   5888   134
Unit: 6th Bn. Norfolk Inf. Regt.
107 Bagnall Rd., Basford Notts.

185   4871
Spr. Frank Brocklehurst   2149   806
288 Field Co. Engs.
Cowlow Lane, Dove Holes Via Stockport

186   4872
Sgm. Herbert Balmforth   2356   645
Unit: Royal Corps Sigs. South Area
106 Woodland Rd., Malton, Leeds.

187   4873
P. Walter John Passey   6020   753
Unit: 5th Bn. Suffolk Inf. Regt.
High Rd., Fobbing Pitsea, Essex.

188   4874
P. Penn Stanley Freer   5830   820
Unit: 4th Bn. Suffolk Inf. Regt.
49 Robin Hood Rd., Quarry Bank, Brierley Hill Staffs.

189	4875		
P. Charles James Bush		6020	738
Unit: 4th Bn. Suffolk Inf. Regt.			
16 Ivy Lodge, Elm Tree Rd., Pitsea, Sx.			

198	4884		
P. Jack Sylvester Bennington		5778	193
Unit: 6th Bn. Norfolk Inf. Regt.			
3 West Parade, Wisbech.			

190	4876		
P. Arthur Sidney James Waller		5774	408
Unit: 6th Bn. Norfolk Inf. Regt.			
Japonica House, Stokesby, C.T. Yarmouth.			

199	4885		
P. Kenneth Arthur Barnard		5775	647
Unit: 6th Bn. Norfolk Inf. Regt.			
34 Leopold Rd., Norwich.			

191	4877		
P. Robert Ernest Longman		5775	606
Unit: 6th Bn. Norfolk Inf. Regt.			
24 Gertrude Rd., Norwich.			

200	4886		
Spr. Ronald Charles Simms		1902	772
Unit: 288 Field Co. Royal Engs.			
22 Godolphin Rd., Shepherds Bush, W. 12.			

192	4878		
P. Arthur Turner		5774	443
Unit: 4th Bn. Norfolk Inf. Regt.			
1 Hardy Rd., Thorpe, Norwich.			

201	4887		
P. Henry Dedman		5779	558
Unit: 6th Bn. Norfolk Inf. Regt.			
36 Sutton Rd., Southend on Sea.			

193	4879th		
P. Jack Walter Wallace		5775	015
Unit: 6th Bn. Norfolk Inf. Regt.			
45 Colbert St., Norwich.			

202	4888		
P. Alfred Hindle		5774	396
Unit: 6th Bn. Norfolk Inf. Regt.			
14 Cyril Rd., Thunder Lane, Thorpe, Norwich.			

194	4880		
P. Frank Baker		5775	684
Unit: 4th Bn. Norfolk Inf. Regt.			
35 Dereham Rd., Norwich.			

203	4889		
P. Ronald Alec Beament		5777	671
Unit: 6th Bn. Norfolk Inf. Regt.			
Colley Cottage, Homefield Rd., Chorley Wood, Rickmansworth.			

195	4881		
P. Frederick Collison		5775	356
Unit: 5th Bn. Norfolk Inf. Regt.			
138 Saunders Rd., Thorpe Hamley, Norwich.			

204	4890		
P. William Allen		5782	063
Unit: 4th Bn. Norfolk Inf. Regt.			
Church Lane, Wicklewood, Wymondham, Suffolk.			

196	4882		
P. Alfred Robbins		5779	458
Unit: 6th Bn. Norfolk Inf. Regt.			
Hilly-Wood Lane, Dagenham, Essex.			

205	4891		
P. John William Powell		7147	201
Unit: Reconnaisance Corp.			
16 Fearnhead Lane, Fearnhead, Warrington Lancs.			

197	4883		
P. Bert Wainwright		6021	086
Unit: 6th Bn. Norfolk Inf. Regt.			
34 Liverpool Rd., Whitchurch, Shropshire.			

206	4892		
P. Stanley Alexander Wilby		5768	723
Unit: 6th Bn. Norfolk Inf. Regt.			
Top Farm, Gt. Moulton, Aslacton, Norfolk.			

The following is a list stating time and place of capture of various British troops, including Mr. Chater's own group.

Timor: Troops—date captured—23/2/42
1st camp: Osapa Besar on 25/2/42

Kaijati: Troops—date captured—8/3/42
1st camp: Kalijati on 27/3/42

Tasik Malaja—date captured—8/3/42
1st camp: Tasik Malaja on 8/3/42 (where Mr. Chater was first captured and detained.)

Semplak: Troops—date captured—8/3/42
1st camp: Semplak on 25/3/42 (the more permanent camp in Java for Mr. Chater)

Wilkinson:—date captured—25/12/41 (one of Hong Kong force.)
1st camp: Camp A, B.M.H., Hong Kong. 2/1/42

AMERICAN PRISONERS OF WAR

Mr. Chater also recorded the American POWs in his camp. There were a great many deaths among the American prisoners, mainly from diarrhoea. Often these men were not allocated camp numbers, or at least Mr. Chater did not record them. As well, next of kin were usually not listed in these cases.

The following heading begins the list of American names:

16D. Following 82 Americans left Cabanatuan POW camp, Phillipines 29/10/42 & arrived at No. 3 (Now 2D) Camp Mitsushima on 26/11/42. Those with 16D numbers opposite their names left Mitsushima 16/4/44 & arrived at Kanose the same date.

44   1075
P. James T. Aiken   15045   534
Unit: 17th Ord. Co.
c/o Nola Aiken, West Point, Ky.

45   1076
P. Beverly F. Atnip   18052   228
Unit: 59th C.A.
c/o Sersarah Atnip, Box 279, Boswell Okl.

12   1027
Cpl. John R. Atwell   37042   049
Unit: 194th Tank Bn.
1859 8th Ave. N., Ft. Dodge, IA.

13   1028
Cpl. William E. Bandish   6971   025
Unit: 27th Bomb Gp.
c/o Mrs. May A. Bandish, 107 E. Bellevue Place, Chicago.

7   1019
S/Sgt. James O. Bass   6227   209
Unit: 3rd Pursuit Sqn.
c/o Mrs. J.O. Bass, c/o A.J. Crain, Humboldt Oil Refinery Co., S.O.
San Antonio, Texas.

46   1077
P. Cullen W. Berry   6250   483
Unit: 27th Bomb Gp.
Mrs. Lottie Berry, Lufkin, Tex.

No POW number
P. James E. Bitner   13022   538
Unit: Air Warn.
c/o Shuemanstown, P.O.Box 242, Harrisburg PA.

47   1079th
P. Bedford F. Bolin   34049   133
Unit: 803rd Engineers
Mrs. J.W. Bolin Snr., Dabney Ave., Vicksburg, Miss.

48   1080
P. Frank Brancaticano   6893   549
Unit: 31st. Inf.
No next of kin listed.
Note: Died pneumonia 20/6/44, Kanose.

49   1081
P. Matthew B. Braun   32045   386
Unit: 192nd Tank Bn.
Mrs. Andrew Braun, 206 Madison St., Rome, N.Y.

31   1056
Sgt. Glenn D. Brokaw   20900   657
Unit:194th Tank Bn.
Mrs. Glenn D. Brokaw, Salina, Calif.

No POW number
T/Sgt. Alfred J. Burke   6718   582
Unit: 93rd Bomb Sqn.
No next of kin listed
Note: Died Mitsushima 14/12/42, diarrhoea

No POW number
Cpl. Kenneth C. Campbell   13001   451
Unit: 21st Pursuit Sqn.
114 Oak St., Cumberland, MD.

32   1057
Sgt. Mike N. Chavez   20842   496
Unit: 200th C.A.(A.A.)
Mr. Mike N. Chavez 400 No. Zinc St., Demming N.M.

No POW number
P. Raymond Chavez   20843   361
Unit: 200th C.A. (A.A.)
No next of kin listed
Note: Died Mitsushima 16/2/43, pneumonia

No POW number
Maj. Allen M. Cory   0-317   610
Unit: 51st. Inf. Bn. (P.A.)
No next of kin listed.
Note: Left Mitsushima for Zentsuji 28/7/43

15   1032
P.F.C. Burlin C. Cupp   35001   552
Unit: 192nd Tank Bn.
c/o Mrs. Irene S. Cupp, RFD 4 Carey, Ohio.

16   1033
P.F.C. David A. Dement   14014   561
Unit: 27th Bomb Gp.
c/o Mrs. G.E. Dement, Elm Grove, LA.

No POW number
P.F.C. Roger G. Derr   35030   891
Unit: 803rd Eng.
No next of kin listed
Note: Died Mitsushima 6/2/43, diarrhoea

34   1059
Sgt. Joseph J. Duncan   20843   956
Unit: 200th C.A.(A.A.)
Mrs. Maggie Hunter, Silver City N.M.

14   1030
Cpl. Eugene C. Dunn   6472   998
Unit: 16th Bomb Sqn.
c/o Mrs. A.O. Dunn, Box 412, Newport Tenn.

No POW number
P. Elmer E. Engle   35121   426
Unit: 192nd Tank Bn.
No next of kin listed
Note: Died Mitsushima 29/6/43 (Cause unknown)

20   1044
P. Earl E. Ennis   19052   177
Unit: 803rd Engs.
Mrs. Emilie Ennis, 23 E. Alder St., Stockton, California

No POW number
Capt. Ace E. Faulkner   0-308   907
Unit: 14th Engs.
No next of kin listed
Note: Left Mitsushima for Zentsuji 28/7/43

21 1045
P. Bernard A. Fields 7040 173
Unit: 17th Ord.
Mr. Joseph Fields, St. John, Ky.

No POW number
Sgt. Francis B. Sherwood 19052 825
Unit: 60th C.A.
No next of kin listed.
Note: Died Mitsushima 11/2/43, diarrhoea

17 1035
P.F.C. Charles B. Gavord 20842 474
Unit: 515th C.A.
c/o Mrs. Florence R. Gavord, 600 So. Silver St., Deming N.M.

No POW number
P.F.C. Garth Ginther 6274 804
Unit: 27th Materiel Sqn.
No next of kin listed
Note: Died Mitsushima 5/3/43, malaria.

3 1015
1st/Sgt. Marshall W. Goff 6253 514
Unit: 409th Sig. Aviation
c/o Louise McFarland, Rt. 1 Globe, Arizona.

No POW number
Sgt. Albert R. Gordon 12007 158
Unit: M.P. (Phil. Div.)
No next of kin listed.

No POW number
P.F.C. Leo T. Grabowski 6878 147
Unit: 808 M.P.
Rural Free Delivery No. 3 Medina N.Y.

19 1039
P.F.C. Paul A. Grassick 35001 515
Unit: 192nd Tank Bn.
c/o Mrs. A. Grassick, 331 E. 4th St., Mansfield, Ohio.

No POW number
P.F.C. James T. Groves 35100 656
Unit: 17th Ord Co.
91/2 So. Main St., Henderson Ky.

No POW number
P.F.C. Winfred O. Hayes 6931 832
Unit: 31st Inf.
No next of kin listed
Died Mitsushima 11/4/43 (Cause unknown)

No POW number
P.F.C. Clarence Hendrickson 37028 042
Unit: 803rd Eng.
No next of kin listed.
Died Mitsushima 27/2/43, kidney trouble.

No POW number
P.F.C. Pete B. Holland 14014 943
Unit: 48th Material Sqn.
Wiltin Park, Greenville, Miss.

35 1061
Sgt. Jay Holstein 20500 721
Unit: 149th Tank Bn.
Mrs. Arthur J. Holstein, Box 1812, Miami, Ariz.

1
Cpt. Walter J. Hewitt 0-338 977
Unit: 12th Sig. Co. (P.S.)
No next of kin listed.

No POW number
Sgt. Kenneth G. Hunter 18038 791
Unit: 60th C.A.
No next of kin listed
Note: Died Mitsushima 14/2/43, diarrhoea

37 1066
P.F.C. Revis C. Hyde 6396 050
Unit: 803rd Eng.
Mrs. Neva Hyde, Benjamin Franklin, 549 Sta. Washington D.C.

8 1020
Sgt. John B. Ivy 6265 784
Unit: A.C.
c/o Mrs. J. H. Walker, Huntington, Tex.

No POW number
Sgt. Asa. A. Jackson 6248 651
Unit: Ordnance
No next of kin
Note: Died Mitsushima 15/4/43, kidney trouble

24 1049
S/Sgt. Leo L. Johnson 6980 422
Unit: H.Q. 5th Bomb Command
Mrs. Leo L. Johnson, New Berlin, N.Y.

33 1058
Cpl. Eugene Jones 6292 899
Unit: 31st Inf.
Mrs. Eugene Jones, 1817 Orleans Ave., Dallas, Tex.

22 1046
P. Verble L. Jones 19015 688
Unit: Q.M.
Mr. E.L. Jones, Star Rt. No. 2, Selma, Alabama.

102 3646
P.F.C. Harold Kingen 19052 225
Unit: Medical Corps.
Mrs. Emma Kingen, 5238 E. Washington St., Stockton, CA.
Note: Arrived Kanose 12/6/44 Shinagawa

No POW number
P. Raymond S. Kirch 14014 390
Unit: 27th Bomb Gp.
Lake of the Hills, Lake Wales, Fla.

4 1016
T/Sgt. Ray J. Klassen 6565 295
Unit: H.Q. + H.Q. Bty Hdm. + S.B.

23 1048
P. Fred L. Kolilis 20956 487
Unit: 194th Tank Bn.
Mrs. Charles R. Edrington, 3103 No. 27th St., Tacoma, Wash.

No POW number
T/Sgt. Gusta R. Krause 20720 302
Unit: 194th Tank Bn.
No next of kin listed.
Note: Died Mitsushima 28/1/43, diarrhoea

38   1067
P.F.C. Donald C. Lilly   15061   732
Unit:31st Inf.
John R. Lilly, c/o Mrs. William Jones, 234 Walcott St.,
Indianapolis, IN.

No POW number
Cpl. John A. Lobe   19051   950
Unit: 3rd Pursuit Sqn.
c/o Mrs. Christine Dummitt, 5578 Ivanhoe St., Detroit.

36   1062
Cpl. Erret L. Lujan   20843   147
Unit: 515 C.A.
Mrs. Jessie Lujan, Navajo+ Taos St. R.R.2 Santa Fe N.M.

No POW number
P. William H. Mann   33043   704
Unit: 803rd Eng.
307 Frankford Ave., Baltimore, MD.

9   1022
Sgt. Vernon B. Marble   6977   685
Unit: Ord. Det. Hdm + SB.
c/o Mr. Claude E. Marble, 5 Liberty St., Oneonta, N.Y.

18
P. Don A. Martindale   19050   911
Unit: 7th Materiel Sqn.
Mrs. Ester Martindale, 224 G St. Salt Lake City.

50   1036
P. Ray H. McGill   38022   993
Unit:17th Ord.
Joe McGill, Chickasha, Okl.

25   1050
S/Sgt. Arthur J. Mitchell   6864   512
Unit: 31st. Inf.
Charles C. Mitchell, 840 Upham St., Klamath Falls Ore.

No POW number.
Cpl. George J. Peil   14042   451
Unit: 31st. Inf.
1727 Marigny St., New Orleans, LA.

26   1051
S/Sgt. Dorris R. Pratt   6960   136
Unit: 5th Interceptor Cmd.
Mrs. Ethel Pratt, Sherman, Tex.

39   1068
P.F.C. William R. Richards   18049   853
Unit: 31st. Inf.
Mrs. E.M. Whittiker, Cartersville, Okl.

No POW number
P.F.C. William B. Richardson   38012   566
Unit: 200th C.A. (A. A.)
No next of kin listed.
Note: Died Mitsushima 7/1/43, diarrhoea

No POW number
P.F.C. Albert H. Roberts   6334   878
Unit: 19th Bomb Gp.
Note: Died Mitsushima 1/3/43, diarrhoea

10   1023
Sgt. Joel L. Rogers   38011   946
Unit: 200th C.A. (A.A.)
c/o Mr. Lee M. Rogers, Bayard, N.M.

27   1052
S/Sgt. Samuel J. Rouse   6842   414
Unit: Chem. Warfare Service
Mrs. Eliza Rouse, 604 No Church St., Rocky Mount N. Carol.

40   1069
T/Sgt. John C. Roy   6896   934
Unit: Far East Air Force
901-17th Ave., S., Nashville, Tenn.

5   1017
P.F.C. Alvin Silver   12026   748
Unit: Air Warn.
c/o Mrs. F. Strauss, 250 E. 94th St., Brooklyn.

No POW number
Cpl. Guerald M. Simpson   6384   738
Unit: Signal Corps.
No next of kin listed.
Note: Died Mitsushima 28/3/43, diarrhoea

No POW number
P.F.C. Alfred G. Smith   20938   926
Unit: 31st. Inf.
No next of kin listed
Note: Died Mitsushima 4/3/43, diarrhoea

No POW number
1st Sgt. J.M. Smith   20843   476
Unit: 200 C.A. (A.A.)
No next of kin listed
Note: Died Mitsushima, 21/12/42

6   1018
1st Sgt. Clifton O. Snodgrass   6824   973
Unit: 803rd Eng.
c/o Mrs. Alma Taylor, 428 W. 6th St., Junction City, Kansas.

41   1070
P.F.C. Paul R. Spencer   18050   440
Unit: 31st Inf.
Mrs. Hazel Spencer, 2224 S.W. 30th St., Oklahoma City Ok.

28   1053
S/Sgt. Kenneth D. Stanford   6265   574
Unit:A.C.
Mrs. R.L. Stanford, Hoxbar Rt. Ardmore Okla.

No POW number
Cpl. Arvile L. Steele   6861   252
Unit: 3rd Pursuit Sqn.
1420 Nalthenins, Texarkana

29   1054
S/Sgt. James E. Sutterfield   14002   078
Unit: 48th Materiel Sqn.
Mrs. Eva Sutterfield, Collinston, LA.

No POW number
P.F.C. Robert G. Teas   6915   655
Note: 19th Bomb Gp.
No next of kin listed
Note: Died Mitsushima 5/3/43, diarrhoea

No POW number
Sgt. Thomas P. Tison   6973   420
Unit: 27th Bomb Gp.
821 So. Main St., Maultrie, GA.

| 42 | 1072 | | | 30 | 1055 | | |

P.F.C. Simone N. Vallerga 19052 525
Unit: 809th M.P
Giovanni Vallerga, 1139 Broadway St., Alameda Cal.

No POW number
Sgt. James A. Jr. Vitelli 14047 690
Unit: H.Q. Phil. Dept.
No next of kin listed
Note: Died Mitsushima, 9/3/43, diarrhoea

No POW number
P.F.C. Wayne N. Wasson 38012 123
Unit: 200th C.A. (A.A.)
Regina N.M.

S/Sgt. Frank E. Wilson 38017 385
Unit: 515th C.A.
Mrs. Margaret Wilson, Box 534 Santa Fe N. M.

43 1074
P.F.C. Russel A. Williams 6270 737
Unit: 48th Materiel Sqn.
Mrs. Annie Williams, Detroit, Tex. Bx. 107

11 1026
Sgt. Jack D. Wilson 6286 742
Unit: 27th Bomb Gp.
c/o Mrs. J.D. Wilson, 2724 Portland Ave., Shreveport Louis.

SINGAPORE TECHNICAL CORPS PRISONERS

These men, primarily Chinese, were all from the Singapore Technical Corps.

A.C.2 Thng Bok Seng S.T.C.
1566 Tokong Lane, Butterworth, P.W.

A.C.2 Quah Kok Leong S.T.C.
9 Gopeng Rd., Penang.

A.C.2 Sak Fook Piew S.T.C
c/o Miss Daisy Sak, Maternity Hospital,
Nurses Qts. Penang.

A.C.2 Kooi Kean Hong S.T.C.
5 Jalan Daloh, Kuala Kangsar Perak.

A.C.2 Loong Yoke Wahstc
c/o Mr. Tan Soo Tee (Sunnyap)
3 3/4 N. Been Tong Rd., Kuala Lumpur

A.C.2 Khoo Cim Swee S.T.C.
122 Lorong Slamat Penang.

A.C.2 Chew Moon Khong S.T.C.
27 Jalan Datuh, Ipoh.

A.C.2 Lim Beng Choon S.T.C.
14 Presgrave Rd., Penang.

A.C.2 Lim Heng Keng S.T.C.
17 Rope Walk, Penang
Note: Med. Ord.

A.C.2 Chan Kong Chin S.T.C.
182 Chamberlain Rd., Ipoh.
Note: Cook.

A.C.2 Chow Swee Soon S.T.C.
174 or 282 Chulia St., Penang.

Sgt. Chang Chang Kwang S.T.C.
83 Sophia Rd., Singapore.

A.C.2 Goh Kim Huat S.T.C.
41C McAlister Rd., Penang.

A.C.2 Chee Haie Deong S.T.C.
38 Balik Pulau, Penang.

A.C.2 Goh Au Yeok S.T.C.
21 Chan Koon Cheng Rd., Malacca.

A.C.2 Francis Tan Kee Fah S.T.C.
1 Cameron St., Seremban.

A.C.2 Chew Chin Peng S.T.C.
18 Kajang Rd., Penang.

A.C. 2 Yeoh Swee Chuan S.T.C.
14 Presgrave Rd., Penang.

A.C.2 Wong Kam Ying S.T.C.
c/o 50 Dato Kramat, Penang.

A.C.2 Poh, Soo Ewe S.T.C.
46 Cecil St., Penang.

A.C.2 Tang Gool Yew S.T.C.
67 Argyll Rd., Penang.
Note: Weight lifter.

A.C.2 Lim Teong Sin S.T.C.
144C Burma Rd., Penang
Note: "Little Lim"

A.C.2 Tan Keat Hoon S.T.C.
88 Irving Rd., Penang.

A.C.2 Low Wah Lean S.T.C.
Federal Dispensary,
IA Hale Rd. Kuala Lumpur

A.C. 2 Wong Yong Tet S.T.C.
79th Jalan Hospital, K. Kangsar
c/o Wong Heng Kooi, State Treasury,
Ipoh.

A.C.2 Tan Au Too S.T.C.
50 Dato Kramat Rd., Penang.

A.C.2 Lee Peng Kong S.T.C.

A.C.2 Khoo Soo Seng S.T.C.
42D Jahudi Rd., Penang.

A.C.2 Wong Moon Twee
c/o M.T.Dong, 8 Petaling St., Kuala
Lumpur

A.C.2 Thong Min Sin S.T.C.
7 Changkat Rd., Batu Yajah, Perak

A.C.2 Liew Foot Soon S.T.C.
17 Chung Thye Peng Rd., Ipoh.

A.C.2 Lim Kheng Guan S.T.C.
40A Batu Lan Chang Rd., Penang.

A.C.2 Yeap See Wee S.T.C.
14 Presgrave Rd., Penang.

A.C.2 Lee Siang Heng S.T.C.
136 Western Rd., or 66 Half-Way Rd.,
Penang.

Cpl. Ho Cheng Wan S.T.C.
101A McAlister Rd., Penang

A.C.2 Lee Ah Ngow S.T.C.
c/o Hock Chuan Ciev, Rice Mill, 125
Permatang, Pauh, Butterworth.

A.C.2 Ooi Leong Teik S.T.C.
135 Ayer Itam Rd., Penang.

A.C.2 D'Silva, Daniel Theodore S.T.C.
New Supreme Court, High St., Singapore.

A.C.2 Cheah Hong Wan S.T.C.
No. 11 Peng Nguan St., Singapore

A.C.2 Goh Hoe Boh S.T.C.
293M. West Jelutong, Penang.

A.C.2 Teh Seng Keat S.T.C.
586R Penaga Rd., Penang.

A.C.2 Tan Keng Liat. S.T.C.
16 Oxley Rd., Singapore.

A.C.2 Lim Chung Bee S.T.C.
325 Marks Rd., Taiping.

A.C.2 Boey Kam Fook S.T.C.
25 Cinema St., Taiping.
Note: Masseur

A.C.2 Loh Anthony Joseph S.T.C.

A.C.2 Diaz, Joseph Anthony S.T.C.
25 Bengoolen St., Singapore.

A.C.2 Baba Toolseram S.T.C.
77G Tanjong, Tokong, Penang.

A.C.2 Ingram, Lefroy Solomon S.T.C.
58 Chaw Thye Rd., Penang.

A.C.2 Fernandez Cecil Ricardo S.T.C.
c/o Mrs. Fernando, Gout English School,
Tronoh, Perak.

A.C.2 Khoo Khey Huat S.T.C.

A.C.2 Chua Teng Hwee S.T.C.
5 Jalan Kemaman off Balestier Rd.,
Singapore.

A.C.2 Tan Kay Choon S.T.C.(Amos)
c/o Tan Kay Chua, Sabak Bernam, Via
Telok Anson.

A.C.2 Chong Kam Poh S.T.C.
c/o 1586 5th Ave., Ipoh.

A.C.2 Goh Hong Huat S.T.C.
325 Marks Rd., Taiping.

A.C.2 Ng Pow Onn S.T.C.
K56 Jalan Benda Hara, Ipoh.

A.C.2 Tan Tack Seng S.T.C.
39-8 Jalan Senang Off Changi Rd.,
Singapore.

A.C.2 Ng Kim Choon S.T.C.
51 A Bukit Bintang K.L

A.C.2 Leong Kwai Weng S.T.C.
45 Tupai Rd., Taiping.

A.C.2 Yap Boon En S.T.C.
74 Anderson Rd., Ipoh.

A.C.2 Ingram, Lionel Samuel S.T.C.

A.C.2 M. Veeramuthu S.T.C.
13 Perak Flats, Travers Rd., Kuala Lumpur.

A.C.2 S.N. Raja Durah S.T.C.
Ainsdale Estate, Seremban.

A.C.2 Nganoo, Anthony S.T.C.
c/o V.C. Nganoo, Pahang Consolidated Tin
Mines, Sungei, Lembing, Pahang.

A.C.2 Gill, Rajindra Singh S.T.C.
15 Hospital Rd., Kuala Pilah.c/o Dr. Sanb
Singh, c/o H.H. Maharaja of Farid Koab,
Punjab, India.

A.C.2 Soorier Pillai S.T.C.
Vellavathai, Colombo.

A.C.2 Chong Teik Kooi S.T.C.
428 Chulta St., Penang.

A.C.2 Choo Peck Boh S.T.C.

Cpl. Alfred Scott Keasberry S.T.C.
23 Rosyth Rd., off Yio Chu Kang Rd.,
Singapore.

Sgt. Kamala Rai, M.V.A.F.

A.C.2 Liaw Hee Seng S.T.C.
3105 Sungei Nyor R.J. Butterworth.

A.C.2 Chua Teong Swee S.T.C.
K 71 Jalan Tokong, Ipoh.

A.C.2 Chin Yin Sin S.T.C.

A.C.2 Koh Heng Choy S.T.C.
29 F Henderson Rd., Singapore.

A.C.2 Lim Teck Guan S.T.C.
48 Hale Rd., Kuala Lumpur.

A.C.2 James Cecil D'Olivero S.T.C.
23 Jalan Abdul Jahl, Greenstown, Ipoh.

A.C.2 Cheah Wat Kian S.T.C.

A.C.2 Stanley Rufus D'Rosario S.T.C.
42 Waterloo St., Singapore.

A.C.2 Francis Aloysius D'Cruz S.T.C.
197 Joo Caiat Place, Singapore.

A.C.2 Robert Addie Campbell S.T.C.
20A Ben Coolen St., Singapore.

A.C.2 Oscar Felix Gregory S.T.C.

A.C.2 Gerald Jalleh S.T.C.
c/o M.C. Jalleh, 68D Kuala Kangsa, Ipoh.

A.C.2 Teg Jeu, Cyril Raymond S.T.C.
198 Birch Village, Taiping.

A.C.2 Roland Oliveiro F. S.T.C.
148 Race Course Rd., Singapore.

A.C.2 Dominic Sebastian S.T.C.
Bukit Nanas, Seremban.

A.C.2 Fernando V.R. S.T.C.
786103 New Area Rd., Sentul, K.L.

A.C.2 V. Kathirsu S.T.C.
32 King's St., Chulikeram, Ceylon.

Surg/Lt. R.G.S. Whitfield, Royal Navy
Volunteer Reserves.
7 Cadogan St., London, S.W.3
Note: Arrived Mitsushima, 9/9/43 from
Shinagawa

H.C.R. Fuford Williams, Colonial Rep.
Gilbert Isles, (Makin) At Doddon Hill,
Northam, Devon.
Arrived Mitsushima 17/12/43 from H.Q.
Camp Zensuji

Dr. Donald W. Robinson, US Medical
Corps.
Garrison, North Dakota
Arrived Kanose 28/1/45

E.I. Turner
479th Portage Ave.,
Winnipeg.

OTHER NAMES

Below is a list of various names, perhaps of those who were closer to Mr. Chater and with
whom he considered corresponding after returning home.

Donald Rice
160 1st Ave., Verdun, Montreal

Sgt. Gibson Harrison Brown
21st Regt., 79th Bty. RA

F/Lt. Rhys, Griffith RAF
A.D.F.E. stores, Seletar.

P/O John Ralph Renton Dunlop
RAF Engineering Officer,
Aircraft Depot F.E., Seletar
Next of kin: Eversley Rectory, Basingstoke, Hants.

Cpl. Reginald Bullock
RAF Medical Orderly, Seletar.
Next of kin: R. Bullock, 32 Woodlands Grove, Harrowgate, Yorks.

Sgt. Aubrey Jones
21st Regt. 79th Bty RA
Next of kin: A. Jones, Gonville," 1 Franklin Rd., Walton-on-
Thames, Surrey.

Sgt. Leslie Edmond Fullock RAF
Next of kin: 5 Washington St., Chichester, Susex.

Cpl. Henry Evans RAF
Next of kin: Pontbrenmydr, Ciliav Aeron, Lam Peter, Cardiganshire.

Gnr. Kenneth Arthur Bridger
21st Regt., 79th Bty. RA
Next of Kin: 2 Fairfield Rd., Kingston-on-Thames

Gnr. James Webster
21st Regt. 79th Bty. RA
22 Fife St., Fife-Kieth, Keith Barffshire, Scot.

Sgt. James R. Hepburn
21st Regt. 79th Bty. RA

AIR MINISTRY WORKS DIRECTORATE PERSONNEL

W.O. Cullin (Eurasian?) came to Singapore from Java and taken away at the docks with severe stomach pains. F/L/ J.H. Esmond Dorney in Maksura Camp Batavia when I left on Oct 17, 42. W.O. Albert Loveday

The following last seen by me at Porbollingo Transit Camp near Powerkerto, 4th March 1942 but later reports say they were on train shot up by Japanese en route to Garoet. Lobo reported killed.

S/L Harrison, Surveyor	F/L Harrison A.C.E.	Martin
W.O. Angus, Clerk	Jackson, Station Engineer	R.K. Pillai
F/L Acton, Assistant Surveyor	Lamb	Nazareth
P.O. Bird, Draughtsman	Parsons, Surveyor's Clerk	P.S.Nair
F/L Brown, Assistant Mechanical/Electrical Engineer	Rudgard, Foreman of Works	Hari Haran
	Temple	J.S. Nair
F/L Boardman, Assistant Surveyor	POWhitby, Draughtsman	Anthony
Fitzgibbon	F/O Wilson, Pay Clerk	Lobo
Field	P/O Heggie	Acheton
Fostekew	Lewis	N.O. Pillai

Following last seen at Tasik Malaya Aerodrome when I left there about 15th March 1942. They had arrived there from shot up train on 12th March.

Cameron, Foreman of works	W.O. Kennieson, Foreman Works	Whitehorn
P.O.Anderson, C. of works.	P/O Mason, C of Wks.	P/O Linge, C. of Wks.
Geach	P/O Morgan, C of Wks.	Fraser
F/L Hawkins, A.C.E.	F/L Willmot	
W.O. Hisgrove, Clerk	F/L Attenborough	

Appendix

TOKYO WAR CRIMES TRIALS:
LETTERS AND PRESS RELEASES

FOLLOWING ARE A NUMBER OF LETTERS pertaining to the War Trials held in Tokyo in 1947.

The Americans, after the war, were determined to bring to justice those in the camps who had caused death and sickness to prisoners in their care. Mr. Chater was invited to testify at these trials, but declined. He did, however, submit his diaries as evidence and therefore was entitled to information regarding the trials. Whether or not the diaries were carefully read by the Commission is questionable. The microscript would certainly discourage anyone who was working under a time constraint. At least one discrepancy can be seen. On March 5, 1943 Mr. Chater records that Robert Teas died of diarrhoea. This is also confirmed in one of the lists in the fourth diary. Yet at the trial of Sukeo Nakajima, a Camp Commander of Mitsushima, sentenced to death by hanging, it is recorded that Teas was beaten to death." If, indeed, it is true that Mr. Nakajima was not guilty of Mr. Teas's death, one cannot ignore the great number of other deaths that he may have prevented if he had allowed the POWs to have adequate heat, clothing and food.

Major Walter Hewitt, the Commanding Officer of the American POWs, had suffered a number of beatings at the hands of the guards. He attended the war trials and testified as to the true conditions of the camps. He also wrote Mr. Chater a number of personal letters regarding the trials.

26 August 1947

Mr. Leslie Chater
c/o Mrs. J.E. Chater
821 Fifth Avenue North
Saskatoon, Saskatchewan
Canada

Dear Mr. Chater:

From Major Hewitt, former prisoner of war officer in Kanose PW Camp, I have obtained your address. Major Hewitt has alternate addresses for you and not knowing which is correct, I am sending a copy of this letter to each of the two addresses.

My purpose in writing is to inform you that Azuma, Kaneyama, Fukijima, Ichiyanagi and Ishibe, along with two company employees named Saito and Minagawa, were tried as war criminals before the Yokohama War Crimes Commission. Major Hewitt and Sergeant Roy testified for the prosecution and more than seventy affidavits were admitted into evidence against these accused.

The sentences were: Azuma 7 years, Kaneyama 14 years, Fukijima 7 years, Ichiyanagi 5 years, Ishibe 2 years, Saito 5 years, Minagawa 1½ years,

We should like very much to know your reaction to these sentences and particularly to know if you think that any of them might, with justice, have been lighter.

Although we would appreciate any comments you have to make on these accused, we are particularly interested in your reaction to the sentences of Azuma and Ishibe. Insofar as Azuma is concerned, it may seem that his excellent record in general as a camp commander and in particular with regard to the furnishing of heat in the barracks, adequate medicines, recreational facilities, and above all, in the fact that there was only one death due to illness, that the

Letter from War Crimes Defence Division asking for F/L Chater's help in obtaining a lighter sentence for a number of Kanose guards and Camp Commander Azuma. Chater replied suggesting the 7-year sentence given Azuma be lessened, stating he felt the camp commander was only doing his duty and didn't deserve to be imprisoned at all.

5 March 47
Legal Section GHQ SCAP
APO 500 C/O P.M.
San Francisco.

Dear Chate!

Herewith a little souvenir for your scrap book. Am glad to
hear you are free wheeling along so well on Civvy St. Keep up
the good work and best of luck to you.

I have been quite busy over here but have found time to get
in some play along the way. Have visited most of the scenic
spots in this country and must say that the country itself is
beautiful. We of course were never aware of it all while living
here before. Just returned from a week vacation in the Jap
Alps" at beautiful pre-war resort on Mt. Nujoka-Akakura Hotel
known as the Sun Valley of Japan. The terrain and snow were
reminiscent of Kanose. Did a lot of skiing and had the time of
my life. The hotel has a ski tow on the slope to pull you the
half mile back up the hill so all the work is taken out of the
business.

Am now working on the Kanose case. There will be two trials.
One of the "boys" in the factory, re working conditions, death
and injuries. The other will be on the camp personnel, from
Azuma on down, now in Sugamo prison. (Tokyo Sing Sing)

You mentioned your personal diary. If it wouldn't be too much
work you might pick a few reminders out of it for me—though I
have a good memory (as evidenced by the Mitsushima results old
chappey")—or if it doesn't contain info which you consider too
personal, I'd appreciate it if you would mail it (registered
air mail) to me and I'll guarantee its return to you by myself
personally.

Personally I am not interested in hanging that gang but I do
think a few of them should swing a good old Allied pick and
shovel for several years. How do you feel about it? What about
Azuma, for example. I'm somewhat prejudiced in favor of him.
Kuyama got his and Orchida is being tried on a murder rap so
the bad boys still left are Kaneyama, Spy, Fukishima (the second to last Interpreter who required shoe removals pre office
entering—he was picked up today incidentally), Bulldog and a
couple others. Am going out to Sugamo this afternoon to identi-
fy some of the guys..... Coorah!!!

Will close for now fellow hoping to hear from you by return
mail.

Incidentally I picked up a lot of pictures around Kanose—the
camp still stands. If you would like I'll send you copies.

So long—
Hewitt.

General Headquarters
Supreme Commander for the Allied Powers
Legal Section
APO 500

21 Feb. 47.
File No. 014.13
Public Relations Informational Summary No. 506.

Subject: Result of Trial of Sukeo Nakajima and six others. (By Sgt. Wm. D. Cox.)

The four man EIGHTH Army Military Commission having heard the prosecution's case against these seven accused today returned a verdict of guilty on all seven accused. The accused were sentenced as follows:

Sukeo Nakajima — Death by hanging.
Sadaharu Miramatsu — Death by hanging.
Kumio Yoshizawa — Death by hanging.
Tamotsu Kihura — Death by hanging.
Harumi Kawate — Death by hanging.
Takeo Kirishita — Life imprisonment at hard labor
Rikio Shiotri — Life imprisonment at hard labor.

Following one of the longest trials on record at the Yokohama District War Crimes Trial Court House, Yokohama, Japan, the Sukeo NAKAJIMA Commission reconvened 21 February 1947 for its final session. Following a week's deliberation, in closed session, the four man EIGHTH Army Commission, headed by Colonel Clair F. Schumacher, of St. Peter, Minnesota, punishments for these seven accused war criminals were meted out subject to rulings by the Commanding General, United States EIGHTH Army.

With over three months in trial, scores of witnesses were produced by both the prosecution and defense panels. Four former Prisoner of War survivors of the Mitsushima Camp, Nagano, Japan, number of Japanese witnesses, both civilian and former camp personnel. The principle charge against these seven accused was included in two specifications involving the death of scores of American and Allied Prisoners of War. These Japanese engaged in daily acts of brutality against all the internees, charged prosecution, and through their brutal treatment, the withholding of foods, medicines and other supplies, they brought death to these prisoners.

From among the innumerable affidavits introduced by prosecution, are the following excerpts: "We were addressed by the commandant and threatened with death and dire penalities for any attempt to escape or for other breaches of regulations"... "On this day, November 29, 1942, all personnel, including the seriously ill, were ordered outside, naked, for measurement and weighing"... "there was a sharp frost and thick ice on the

ground"... "One dead officer was kicked by the Japanese because
he did not rise to attend the weighing"... "those who could not
adapt themselves to the diet of half-cooked barley, died of
diarrhea and starvation"... "He (NAKAJIMA) weeded out the sick
according to his own ideas, ignoring the doctor, and sent most
out to work. Many returned to sick quarters shortly afterwards
to die"... "All men in the hospital were made to go outside in
freezing weather and stand at attention all night, three men
died"... "All camp personnel looted Red Cross supplies"...
"Teas was beaten to death."

The prosecution representative for Legal Section, General
Headquarters, Supreme Commander for the Allied Powers, were Mr.
Max Schiffman, New York Attorney, of 2155 East 24th Street,
Brooklyn, New York, and Mr. Alexander Pendleton, of 89 Valley
Circle, Mill Valley, California. In his closing argument, Mr.
Schiffman stated before the commission that prosecution had
proven its case beyond a reasonable doubt, and requested the
penalty of death for each defendant.

General Headquarters
Supreme Commander for the Allied Powers
Legal Section
APO 500
Tokyo, Japan

31 July 1947.
File No. 014.13
Legal Section Informational Summary No. 25.

Subject: Result of the Trial of Kiroshi Azuma, et al.

The common trial of seven more Japanese accused of perpetrat-
ing war crimes ended today when the Eighth Army Military
Commission hearing the case returned a verdict of guilty and
sentenced the seven men to terms of imprisonment at hard labor.

Hiroshi AZUMA, Lieutenant in the Japanese Army, was Camp
Commander of Prisoner of War Camp 16-D, Kanose, Niigata, Japan,
from April 1944 until August 1945. He was charged with command
responsibility for numerous severe beatings and abuses that
were administered to prisoners by non-commissioned officers and
civilian factory guards under his control. AZUMA also personally beat and mistreated American and Allied prisoners held at
this camp. He was sentence to seven years' imprisonment at hard
labor.

Hisao KANEYAMA, former guard at the Kanose Carbon and Carbide
Company where the prisoners were compelled to work, was known
as one of the worst guards at camp. He was charged with beating and torturing prisoners, sometimes striking, kicking and

stomping the victims into a semi-conscious state. One one occasion he beat Major Walter J. Hewitt, Ulen, Minnesota, who appeared at this trial as the prosecution's chief witness, with such severity that it broke Hewitt's right ear drum. KANEYAMA was found guilty of clubbing Fred L. Kolilis, 409 South L Street, Tacoma, Washington, and Don A. Martindale, 405 East 5th Street, Salt Lake City, Utah, after they had been discovered playing cards in the barracks. He then forced the two men to stand at attention holding large cakes of ice in their bare hands until the ice melted. This happened on one of the coldest nights in February and the men were forced to stand this way all night. KANEYAMA was sentenced by the commission to fourteen years at hard labor.

Noburo ICHIYANAGI was employed by the Japanese Army as a medical orderly and guard at Camp 16-D. His nickname among the prisoners was "The Spy". He was sentenced to 5 years imprisonment after being found guilty of severely beating and abusing American and Allied prisoners.

Tokio MINAGAWA and Kiyoji ISHIBE, civilian guards, were each found guilty of beating and mistreating a British prisoner. MINAGAWA was sentenced to 1 year 6 months, and ISHIBE to 2 years' imprisonment.

Hiromitzu SAITO, known as the "Bulldog," was sentenced to 5 years' imprisonment after he was found guilty of consistently beating numerous prisoners.

Keitaro FUKIJIMA served as Interpreter at Camp 16-D. He was charged with brutally beating American prisoners with wooden shoes, clubs, and other instruments. He was sentenced to 7 years' imprisonment.

The Legal Section prosecutors for this case were Mr. Max Schiffman, 2155 East 24th Street, Brooklyn 29, New York, and Mr. Robert T. Brunckhorst of Platteville, Wisconsin.

General Headquarters
Supreme Commander for the Allied Powers
Legal Section
Tokyo, Japan,
APO 500

28 August 1947.
File No. 014.13
Legal Section Informational Summary No. 54.

Subject: Result of the Trial of Shichinobu Shichino et al

This morning an Eighth Army Military Commission at Yokohama wrote the final chapter of atrocities in the Mitsushima Prisoner of War Camp, in Nagano Prefecture, Tokyo Area, Honshu,

Japan, when it returned a verdict and sentenced the accused as follows:

Shichinobu SHICHINO was found guilty of willfully and unlawfully mistreating and abusing numerous American and Allied Prisoners of War thereby contributing to their deaths; by neglecting his duties as a medical sergeant, by failing to control and restrain SHIORI, the medical orderly under his command, permitting him to commit cruel and brutal acts, atrocities and other offenses against American and Allied Prisoners of War. SHIORI was previously sentenced to life imprisonment. SCHICHINO was sentenced to twenty-five years imprisonment at hard labor.

Masanobu MICHISHITA, the Camp Executive Officer, was found guilty of willfully and unlawfully mistreating and abusing numerous American and Allied Prisoners of War by beating them, by inflicting cruel and inhuman collective punishments on them for alleged offenses by a few, by forcing and compelling sick prisoners to perform arduous labor, by withholding necessary and available medicines and medical supplies from sick prisoners, thereby contributing to their deaths. He also ordered and caused camp guards under his supervision to mistreat and abuse them, thereby failing to discharge his duties as Sergeant Major of said Camp. MICHISHITA was sentences to death by hanging.

Mineo Nojima, the Number One cook who was responsible for forcing the men to eat raw barley and rotten fish, was found guilty of willfully and unlawfully mistreating and abusing numerous American and Allied Prisoners of War by beating them, by failing to properly prepare their food, and by inflicting cruel and inhuman collective punishments on them for alleged offenses by a few, thereby contributing to their deaths. NOJIMA was sentenced to life imprisonment at hard labor.

Previously the Camp Commandant and four of his guards received sentences of death, and three others received life imprisonment at hard labor.

Legal Section's Prosecutor for this case was Mr. Alexander C. Pendleton of Gary, Indiana.

Headquarters Eighth Army
War Crimes Defense Division
Judge Advocate Section
APO 343

26th August 1947.

Mr. Leslie Chater
c/o Mrs. J.E. Chater
821 Fifth Avenue North,
Saskatoon, Saskatchewan
Canada.

Dear Mr. Chater:

From Major Hewitt, former prisoner of war officer in Kanose
PW Camp, I have obtained your address. Major Hewitt has alternate addresses for you and not knowing which is correct, I am
sending a copy of this letter to each of the two addresses.

My purpose in writing is to inform you that Azuma, Kaneyama,
Fukijima, Ichiyanagi and Ishibe, along with two company employees named Saito and Minagawa, were tried as war crimnals before
the Yokohama War Crimes Commission. Major Hewitt and Sergeant
Roy testified for the prosecution and more than seventy
affidafits were admitted into evidence against these accused.

The sentences were: Azuma 7 years, Kaneyama 14 years,
Fukijima 7 years, Ichiyanagi 5 years, Ishibe 2 years, Saito 5
years, Minagawa $1^1/2$ years.

We should like very much to know your reaction to these sentences and particularly to know if you think that any of them
might, with justice, have been lighter.

Although we would appreciate any comments you have to make on
these accused, we are particularly interested in your reaction
to the sentences of Azuma and Ishibe. Insofar as Azuma is concerned, it may seem that his excellent record in general as a
camp commander and in particular with regard to the furnishing
of heat in the barracks, adequate medicines, recreational
facilities, and above all, in the fact that there was only one
death due to illness, that the sentence might, with justice,
have been lighter. Certainly many American boys are alive today
because they were in his prison camp rather than some other
prison camp.

As to Ishibe, charged with beating and kicking Rogers and
Willoughby, Sergeant Roy testified that neither on the occasion
nor at any other time did Ishibe kick an American, and that his
activity in that particular incident was limited to a light
slap on Willoughby with the open palm, and that since this did
not please Kaneyama he took over and completed the job. Major
Hewitt was too far away to see Ishibe's actions at this time,
and could not testify on it. Through the medium of affidavit
testimony, not subject to cross examination, it is sometimes
difficult to arrive at the exact extent of participation of an

accused in a certain incident. We would very much appreciate
your opinion as to whether this sentence may reflect some of
the difficulties experienced by everyone connected with War
Crimes in arriving at truth and justice.

Certainly the sentences of these two men will be appealed and
perhaps others, and in appealing we will make a plea for
clemency. If you see fit to send us a letter, stating your reasons, for desiring to join in a plea for clemency, we would be
most grateful to you and further, it might serve to advance
somewhat the cause of the democracy we are attempting to teach
to the Japanese. We would appreciate your contacting any other
former prisoners at Kanose Prisoner of War Camp to see if they
would join in a petition for clemency.

As above stated if you feel that any of these sentences might
be lighter we would appreciate your comments, but we are especially interested in Azuma and Ishibe. Thanking you very much,
I am,

Very truly yours,

BURTON K. PHILIPS
CC: Mr. Leslie Chater,
HEPC of Ontario
Room 1016
620 University Avenue
Toronto, Ontario
Canada.

General Headquarters
Supreme Commander for the Allied Powers
Legal Section
Tokyo, Japan
APO 500

5 Sept. 47
File No. 014.13
Legal Section Informational Summary No. 63

Subject: Trial of Kanemasu UCHIDA

Already sentenced to five years' imprisonment at hard labor for
his part in the bayoneting of an American Prisoner of War,
Kanemasu UCHIDA again faces an Eighth Army Military Commission
at Yokohama today, 5 September 1947, charged with the brutal
beating and abuse of numerous other Allied Prisoners of War.

Charges and specifications, signed by Alva C. Carpenter,
Chief of the Legal Section, Supreme Commander for the Allied
Powers, are concerned with events taking place between 1943 and

1945 at Tokyo No. 3-D POW Camp, Yokohama, Honshu, Japan; Tokyo POW Branch Camp No. 5-B Niigta, Honshu, Japan, and Tokyo POW Branch Camp No.16, Kanose, Niigata, Honshu, Japan. American, British and Canadian Prisoners of War were interned at these camps.

The accused, former Japanese sergeant major, had the reputation for being among the most vicious of the Japanese personnel at all four camps. Variously nicknamed by the prisoners as "Foxy Pete," "Cyclone Pete," "Pete the Tramp" and "The Wop," UCHIDA is said to have always carried a bamboo sword which he used freely on the prisoners. On some occasions it is alleged that he beat prisoners with a bull whip, in spite of the protests of the prisoners that this weapon had been outlawed in England under penalty of a heavy fine and ten years' imprisonment. UCHIDA is also charged with misappropriation of Red Cross supplies.

Numerous instances of brutal treatment of prisoners by UCHIDA are alleged in affidavits on file at Legal Section. Although he spoke English well, Uchida is said to have always given drill commands in Japanese and then beaten prisoners severely when they could not understand the orders and failed to comply. One one occasion he forced twelve Allied Prisoners of War to stand for several hours on one leg, each with his arms and other leg extended, imitating B-29s. When the prisoners attempted to change position, they were beaten. UCHIDA abused other prisoners of war by causing their heads to be shaved on one side only. The death rate of Canadian Prisoners at Camp No. 5-B at Niigata was nearly thirty percent.

Most vicious of the alleged beatings was inflicted upon a British Prisoner of War, William B. Shaw of 59 Bath Road, Bambury Oxfordshire, England. Shaw was beaten so brutally with a bamboo sword that one of his eyes was knocked from its socket. An American Prisoner of War, Cpl. James T. Aikins of West Point, Kentucky, was said to have been beaten and then tied to a tree in the snow for a period of approximately three hours.

UCHIDA was tried formerly in May of 1947 in a joint trial with four other Japanese for his part in the murder of Frank Spears, (c/o Mrs. Louise Pruet, 1537 Wabash St., Kansas City, Missouri) an American Prisoner of War interned at Camp No. 58 Niigata. Escaping from the camp, Spears was pursued by the five Japanese, who carried a coffin which had been built for the occasion. When Spears was caught one of the five held him down while the other four successively bayoneted him.

Prosecuting the present case for Legal Section is Mr. Charles J. Smith, of 222 Vermont Avenue, Irvington, New Jersey.

General Headquarters
Supreme Commander for the Allied Powers
Legal Section
Tokyo, Japan
APO 500

10 OCTOBER 1947.
PRESS RELEASE

SUBJECT: MAJOR HEWITT IN THEATER 13 MONTHS "BALANCING THE BOOKS"
FOR WAR CRIMES.

Major Walter J. Hewitt of 722 Eustis Street, St. Paul 4,
Minnesota, arrived in Japan on 28 August 1946 with a retentive
memory and a desire to go to work in the cause of justice.
Thirteen months later his very important part in the work was
completed and he remarked, "Well, the books are balanced. This
past year has been the happiest year of my life." On 27
September 1947 he departed for the United States by air.

* * * * * *

Back in prison camp days Major Hewitt and other prisoners were
suffering a great deal and dying off quickly and they used to
talk about the time when the war would end. Probably, they
thought, everything would be forgiven and forgotten and Japanese
criminals, who were then causing death to so many of their campmates and injuring others for life, would never be brought to
justice. This group of prisoners thought, among themselves, that
after being repatriated they would find it either impossible, or
inconvenient, ever to take individual steps towards bringing
some of these criminals before the proper courts of law. It was
a pleasant surprise to them to find out when the war ended that
a special section in SCAP Headquarters had been set up to ferret
out these war criminals and to see that they received their just
dues.

The program started the very day they got out of prison. At
that time, large groups of specialists and legally trained
investigators were assigned to the freed prisoners for the purpose of soliciting all information they could obtain regarding
these war criminals, camp guards and administrative personnel.
However, at that time, after three and one-half years of being
prisoners and being in a weak, run-down, and worn-out condition,
the majority of the men had just one objective in mind. And that
was a goal towards which they had been looking for many years—
and the years were very, very long in prison camps—FOOD. They
wanted to get back to the United States as soon as possible and
"cram" as much food down them as they possibly could. Until that
time, they were not in a mood to mentally relive the horrors of
the past years, by recalling their unpleasant wartime experiences as prisoners of the Japanese.

A PRISONER-OF-WAR CAMP IN "NAME" ONLY.

"A Japanese camp," Major Hewitt emphatically says, was not a prisoner-of-war camp in any sense of the word. They were CONCENTRATION CAMPS." One must visualize the rigorous conditions— so severe that 75% of the prisoners captured in the Philippines died between the time they were captured and the end of the war. When the Japanese Army selected prisoners for transfer to Japan they picked out the relatively physically fit, and 25% of that group died in Japan between the fall of 1942 and the spring of 1943.

Major Hewitt's group was the first labor camp unit transferred from the Philippines to the Island of Honshu. They arrived in Japan in November 1942 where they were received by the Japanese Army—and what a reception! The Japanese had no concern whatsoever for their well being. It was months before the Japanese permitted the prisoners to take a bath, although there was plenty of lumber and coal, and even bathtubs were available. The prisoners' clothing was inadequate, for they had been in the tropics for a number of months. It was wintertime and suffering was extensive due to having insufficient clothing although there were plenty of clothes available but the Japanese military authorities would not let the prisoners wear them. In fact, there were a pair of shoes and a Japanese Army overcoat in nearby warehouses for every man held as a prisoner in the camp in December of 1942 but such items were not issued until the summer of 1943. Supplies and food were kept from the prisoners, despite their accessibility, making it appear as though the Japanese military was set upon a deliberate plan to kill as many prisoners as possible during the winter of 1942-1943. These deaths were brought about by the Japanese prison personnel intentionally and maliciously, Major Hewitt asserts.

The Japanese drove sick and dying prisoners to work, constantly beating them with clubs, and continually forced the prisoners to stand at attention as group punishments through the cold winter nights for periods often in excess of 12 hours. The weather was bitterly cold and the men were not adequately clothed. No heat was permitted in their barracks. There was seldom a night passed when some Japanese guard did not enter their barracks and awaken the entire prison personnel just for pure devilment or "orneriness." When a prisoner died the Japanese had his personal belongings within 30 seconds, says Major Hewitt. They could "smell" a man dying. Food, clothing and medicines were available for the prisoners of war in the same quantity and quality that were available for soldiers of the Japanese Army. During the winter of 1942-1943 some 600 prisoners of war met an untimely death in the Tokyo Area prisoner of war camp. In contrast, out of more than 1,500,000 Japanese troops stationed in the same area at that time, not one man died from unnatural causes.

BARE EXISTENCE "A LIVING HELL" AT MITSUSHIMA

Major Hewitt has given much valuable testimony at the Yokohama trials concerning conditions at Mitsushima. His descriptions of life at the camp have coincided with those given by other live witnesses brought to Japan to aid in the prosecution of those responsible for the horrors of the camp.

Lieutenant Colonel Alan M. Corey and Master Sergeant John C. Roy of the American Army testified in person as to conditions existing at this infamous so-called camp and excerpts of the testimony of Squadron Leader William T. Blanchard of the Royal Air Force compared conditions at Mitsushima unfavourably with the "Hell Holes of Calcutta." Corporal Harold C. Rogers of the British Forces also testified in person as to conditions existing at Mitsushima. Beatings were the order of the day. The prisoners themselves doubted gravely whether any of them would survive that first severe and trying winter.

"The truth is," Major Hewitt states, "that the prisoners themselves do not like to have to recall and report upon the unpleasant incidents of their camp life while prisoners because of the mental suffering entailed. After the former prisoners have properly rested and regained their physical health, SCAP's Legal Section Investigation Division, under the able administration of Lieutenant Colonel Rudisill, seeks these suspected war criminals out who have caused so much suffering and extracts the necessary information needed to apprehend and bring to justice these offenders."

The very scum of the Japanese Army underworld ran Mitsushima, the majority of them being veterans of the campaigns of carnage in China in the early years of the China Incident." On one occasion when Major Hewitt complained to the camp commander about the cruel treatment they were receiving he just laughed sardonically and said, "You don't know what real cruelty is." Evidently he was speaking of his own experiences in China. The camp commander possessed a chestful of ribbons and the first sergeant at Mitsushima would beat his own personnel with his fists, kick them with his feet, and sometimes use the flat of a sword against some of the Japanese in administering punishment.

During the months Major Hewitt was in Japan, "balancing the books," he testified in five cases against 25 accused from various camps at which he was interned. Some of these cases lasted more than two months. According to the major, Mitsushima was by far the worst camp which he encountered during his internment. Here is the unexpurgated index to Major Hewitt's completed book, arranged by cases.

Sukeo Hakajima—Death
Sadaharu Hiramatsu—Death
Harumi Kawate—Death
Tamotsu Kimura—Death
Kunio Yoshizawa—Death
Rikio Shioiri— Life in Prison
Shinobu Shiochino—25 years
Masanobu Michishita—Death

Mineo Nojim—Life in Prison

Hiroshi Azuma—7 years

Noburo Ichiyanagi—5 years.
Tokio Minagawa—1 year 6 months
Hiromitzu Saito—5 years
Kiyoji Ishibe—2 years
Hisao Haneyama—14 years
Keitaro Fukishima—7 years

Kanemasu Uchida—20 years

Yoshio Taguchi—Life in Prison
Yuzu Aoki—Death
Kengo Hatayama—20 years
Hiroaki Kono—Life in Prison
Michio Kuriyama—Life in Prison
Narumi Oota—Life in Prison
Tadao Shibano—Death.

FORMER PRISONERS OF WAR IN UNITED STATES BEHIND THE WORK

Major Hewitt stated, "Camp mates in the United States have made it clear to me that although they are busy now trying to reestablish themselves and catching up on the years they lost they are behind the efforts and work performed by the Legal Section of SCAP one hundred percent. "Such work is unpleasant," the Major continues, but it is a job that has to be done to protect the interest of that large body of prisoners who died at the hands of the Japanese and are not able to present their own cases before the proper tribunals of law. Somebody has to look out for them, and somebody has to teach the Japanese that the first requirement of democracy is to protect the rights and interests of every man, dead or alive. SCAP's Legal Section is doing this."

INTRODUCING THE CHIEF OF LEGAL SECTION TO THE EX-PRISONERS OF WAR

Alva C. Carpenter is the Chief of the Legal Section. He was formerly a colonel in the Judge Advocate General's Department and has been in charge of the section since its inception in Manila in July 1945. During September of that year the section was divided into two branches and he moved to the Tokyo Branch. After that he made personal trips to Manila by air, keeping contact with the branch office there.

Major Hewitt stated, "Alva C. Carpenter's personal initiative and drive is the spark plug that keeps the complex piece of legal machinery, known as SCAP's Legal Section, going. He is well acquainted—from his knowledge of the facts concerning life in these so-called Japanese prison camps—with the absolute

necessity of ferreting out and removing from society those anti-
social prison camp administrators and guards who are responsible
for atrocities so cruel that we prisoners at the time, years
ago, in camp, used to say among ourselves, "The world will never
believe our stories as they are beyond the grasp of minds cul-
tured in a humane civilization such as our own."

MR. BLACKSTOCK, CHIEF OF THE PROSECUTION DIVISION

Continuing, Major Hewitt said, "Mr. Blackstock, by his close
supervision of the numerous and ramified details of cases in the
process of preparation, is responsible for the successful prosecution of the war criminals who have been brought to trial.
Hundreds of cases have received sentences which were appropriate.
To me it is an indication that the Prosecution Infantry is 'The
Queen of Battle' and all other components of the service have
one primary function and that is 'to put the Infantryman in the
front line and keep him there well supplied with plenty of ammunition so he can fight—hard and clean.' Likewise, the Prosecution
Division is 'The Queen of Battle' in the Legal Section and the
other Divisions of the Legal Section, focussing all their facts
into the hands of the fighters—the prosecutors themselves—organize the legal battle field, then stand by and quietly share in
the victory of truth and justice. Truly, this is one war where
the pen is mightier than the sword." Concerning the individual
prosecutors Major Hewitt remarked, "I was highly impressed by the
painstaking preparatory work engaged in by the Prosecution
Division in general as well as the individual initiative, force,
interest, and legal skill of the prosecutors in particular."

Major Hewitt asserts that he appeared before excellent commissions. The major's own words are, "The commissions were the most
fair-minded, unbiased and humane group of men I ever spoke to."

Concluding this specific phase Major Hewitt said, speaking
slowly and deliberately, "It has been a great source of satisfaction to me in realizing the continuing accomplishment of a
very necessary job well done by the Legal Section whereby every
single Japanese who caused suffering, hardship and death to my
campmates at Mitsushima and other camps has been apprehended,
tried and punished with a sentence commensurate with his
offense."

THE MAJOR'S ADVICE TO FUTURE WITNESSES

Commenting on the business of being a witness and the duties
and responsibilities involved, Major Hewitt has this advice for
future witnesses in war crimes trials:

"Sit down with a camp roster, check off the names of each man
you know who died, then spend 15 minutes silently recalling
everything you knew about that poor unfortunate fellow in prison
camp, down to and including his appearance, his statements just
before dying and then review the thought that you experienced as
you helped to bury or cremate him. This will equip you with sufficient facts to neutralize nature's softening reaction against

hardships by forgetfulness. It is understandable that a man can't spend all of his spare time brooding over the horrible years he spent in prison camps as this can cause him serious mental illness, so nature has this little mechanism of forgetfulness which is designed to purge his mind and body of unpleasantness in order to facilitate a normal and healthy life. Nevertheless, it is a solemn duty and responsibility of every prisoner of war who is alive today to remember those friends of his who suffered and died at the hands of certain Japanese prison guards and to protect that dead friend's interests in justice by mentally going back over that cold and rocky path recalling every detail that brought about his friend's death and do his talking for him.

"One last word to a witness: Always tell the truth, and only the truth, but be sure you tell the whole truth and don't even leave out any small part of it. Always remember your oath as American citizens to uphold the Constitution of the United States and don't forget its main purpose is to look after the rights and interests of the individual man, whether he is alive or dead. This will be your responsibility and duty as a witness."

16 Feb. 48
AOC 14 Signal School
Ft. Monmouth, N.J.

Dear Les:

Received your Xmas card and was glad to know thereby that you were still kicking around. Your diary was introduced at the trials and I later sent it back to you. Trust you eventually received it.

I am now back here at Ft. Monmouth, New Jersey, going to school for a year and learning how to be a 1948 style Signals Officer—this new army of ours is quite an improvement over the latter.

Got back last October and met my new son (now 10 months) visited a while in Minnesota and then proceeded on out here. Wasn't able to take my family along however because of the housing shortage in this area and so miss them a lot and hope to get them out here this summer. The East coast is pleasant about that time and I'm only 10 minutes away from the beaches so was quite happy about this assignment. Busy and back in the groove again. I'll raise the next mug of beer to your memory, fellow.

Yours,
Walt.